P9-AGM-827

JOSEP PLA

SALT WATER

Translated from the Catalan by Peter Bush

archipelago books

Library of Congress Cataloging-in-Publication Data available upon request.

Archipelago Books
232 3rd Street #AI11
Brooklyn, NY 11215
www.archipelagobooks.org

Distributed by Penguin Random House
www.penguinrandomhouse.com

Cover art: The Miriam and Ira D. Wallach Division of Art, Prints and Photographs: Photography Collection, The New York Public Library. Lee, Russell. "Unloading boxes of salmon from fishing boat at docks of Columbia River Packing Association, Astoria, Oregon" The New York Public Library Digital Collections. 1941.

This work was made possible by the New York State Council on the Arts with the support of Governor Andrew M. Cuomo and the New York State Legislature.

Funding for this book was provided by a grant from the Carl Lesnor Family Foundation.

Archipelago gratefully acknowledge the generous support from the Institut Ramon Llull, Lannan Foundation, the National Endowment for the Arts, and the New York City Department of Cultural Affairs.

CONTENTS

SALT WATER

PREFACE

It would have given me the greatest pleasure to be able to devote myself systematically to narrative literature. I cultivated the field with a degree of vitality up to the age of twenty-five. After that, the necessities of life embroiled me in the world of journalism and an implacable dispersal of energy. I wouldn't want to portray myself as a man of "frustrated potential." I have put all the good will I have into tasks I had no option but to take on. However, if it may be true that heady journalistic endeavors are a good schooling in one's literary infancy, if subsequently one can't free oneself from them, they become an annoying burden. I have yet to free myself, which means that I think, nostalgically, of the writing in *Salt Water* as evidence of my potential, of what I might have achieved.

The pieces that make up this book are what I wrote as a young man. Most were unpublished; others, a few, had been published years ago and have now been included after a revision that aimed to eliminate all that was too opaque that they inevitably contained. This impels me to assert yet again that the early versions of these pieces should be seen as mere drafts that lack any authenticity. The use in any form whatsoever of the early versions of these texts cannot be signed off with my name or presented as my work.

Moreover, I must repeat that these pieces – and generally speaking, everything I have put on the page – bear witness to successive moments and situations in my life and form part of vast memoirs, of a succession of reflections of my insignificant but actual existence. In that sense, when Carles Soldevila wrote, in one of his articles, that my project was to provide an *imago mundi*, an image of the world that I have experienced, he hit the nail on the head. That image will be more or less vast, depending on the years remaining to me. It cannot be placed under the rubric of triumphal, rhetorical, pompous literature. Rather, it is something day to day, writing that is insignificant.

A FRUSTRATED VOYAGE

When the news began to circulate in Palafrugell that Hermós had forsaken the life one normally leads in this world and gone to live by himself in the remote spot of Aigua-Xelida, a large number of people thought it was entirely reasonable.

The truth is that at that time in my birthplace, and along that whole coastline, many were attracted by the lure of the free life. In their youth, they had been more or less able to keep this attraction at bay. However, when they reached a certain age, the dream of the free life returned irresistibly. It wasn't an outlandish illusion. It was the hope of a life without clocks, timetables, bells, conventions, clichés, factory hooters or obligations, which are always onerous. The saddest day in the history of Palafrugell was the day when the first blast from one such hooter wailed. That was a fateful day.

"Now we're all trapped on the same. . ." was the cry from melancholy locals, whose arms dangled limply by their sides.

The physical embodiment of that free life was the beach in Tamariu. They had yet to build the new roadway. You reached it along the old track, via Vila-seca and the En Cruanyes spring, a track that had wonderfully sheltered corners in winter. And when you got there, the empty, secluded cove was like a nutshell protecting you from fierce weather: concealed, peaceful and delightfully remote. All of us who dreamed one day or another of going to live there trod the sand vaguely recalling how secure life was in the womb.

Hermós didn't go to live in Tamariu: he went even farther away; he reckoned there were too many people and too much bustle in Tamariu. He settled down in Aigua-Xelida.

In this way, and in this roundabout fashion, I think Hermós captured the essence of my country, the marrow in the bone of Palafrugell. Because I think – and I say this after prolonged reflection – that the true spirit of Palafrugell can be found in its Tarongeta neighborhood; the longed-for essence of Tarongeta is in Tamariu, and the ultimate manifestation of Tamariu is Aigua-Xelida. . . However, if you want to penetrate these mysteries you must, perhaps, have been born in this country of fried fish.

When I was a child I caught a glimpse of bygone times on that coast. The Ampurdan temperament was expressed in all its rawness: rebellious, individualistic, unfettered, unreal, contemplative, messy, dreaming, boastful and often amazingly discreet. The local character was formidable and the place was awash with anecdotes.

As the years go by, and the expectations of progress grow, many of Palafrugell's ancient charms have been lost and its people have become much diluted – we have become pernickety and picky, and at the rate we are going, we will all end up barbers or dinner-jacketed, like so many café waiters.

Joking aside, it's not that I don't like all these changes, especially if they are accompanied by something material that make life less chaotic and more efficient. At some stage this country will have to sort itself out. After days spent in the hot sun, your skin flaking and sore, your eyes bloodshot from its bright rays, your body suffused by the strong midday scents of herbs – rosemary, fennel and lavender – your brain in a haze and your stomach queasy, it is immeasurably pleasant to see two roses in the shade, a dull light glinting in a watery mirror, and the moon glimmering on the burnished wood of a lovely, long-lived, patient piece of furniture. These are delicate, refined sensations.

Even though life has brought me to this conclusion, it doesn't mean I haven't constantly been haunted by the idea of the free life. Sporadically, at the odd moment, I have enjoyed contact with spontaneous, untrammeled individuals, the immediate pleasures of their cooking, the delights of speaking when words have a flavor in your mouth. . . I have been a pilgrim to Aigua-Xelida.

Getting there wasn't easy. They'd not maintained the paths and, although it was barely half an hour from Tamariu, access was difficult. Nevertheless, it was worth making the effort to reach that small, pale-crimson cove blessed with shade from the branches of pine trees. Hermós lived there and kept a small fishing boat and four fishing lines. He was absolutely alone.

Reflecting on my memories of contact with this man, I decided that the essence of his personality – even though he was illiterate – was the rock-solid culture he possessed. His name was Sebastià Puig and he belonged to one of Palafrugell's oldest lineages: he was from Can Cuca in Vila-seca. Physically he resembled an anthropoid: he was bald and his skull was an extraordinary sight; his jaw was fiercely set, his skin, hard and hairy; his eyes sparkled under bushy eyebrows;

his sternum protruded and his arms were over long. He wore a battered sou'wester, velvet breeches, clogs and a skipper's black silk cap. Facially, he bore a strong resemblance to the famous doctor Samuel Johnson, Esq., the renowned author of *Lives of the Poets*. Generally, his entire body seemed like an unruly version of Benjamin Disraeli – that is, the very same Disraeli who Queen Victoria elevated to Lord Beaconsfield. To underline that similarity, I once tried to dress him in a frock coat, with an orchid in his lapel, but failed miserably.

"I'm not one for frock coats. . . !" he announced with an amused rasp.

And when I mentioned his resemblance to the great English politician, he'd say: "You're always talking to me about people I've never met. . . Why do you do that?"

He was a fine man, in the sense that he knew how to do lots of things and did them well. He was extremely useful and very good company. He was a fisherman, sailor, hunter, cook and cartman, knew how to shop in the market and was an excellent servant who waited wonderfully on table. At the same time, he was a good conversationalist, sang reasonably well, could play a good hand of *tresillo*, wasn't a clock watcher and was ever ready to get up and go, which made him irreplaceable. He could be rather stiff and arrogant toward people he didn't care for and restrained with those he loved. One day I was shocked to find him wearing dark spectacles, like the ones holidaymakers wear.

"So why do you wear those spectacles?" I asked.

"They are what we who don't see from either eye must wear, they're exactly right for my kind of eyesight. . ." came his quick, pithy response.

Hermós and I went on many coastal and inland excursions. Everyone, everywhere, knew and appreciated him.

One day when we were anchored by the beach in L'Escala, opposite the tavern of Maurici, a good friend of ours, we spoke at length about the Greek settlement in Empúries a subject about which he felt passionately. He would defend the theory that L'Escala's present-day inhabitants directly descended from the ancient Greeks – "Supposing, of course," he'd add sententiously, "that those Greeks brought women and children along, which I doubt, because women on board ship are more bothersome than servants." At that point, a renowned archaeologist came over to his skiff for a coffee and Hermós rehearsed his theories for his benefit. The archaeologist guffawed loudly.

This distinguished scholar, like all of their stripe, believed that the Greeks were simply objects in a glass case in a museum and that their movements and way of being could only be explained with the help of archaeologists' nebulous, fantastical theories. In his view, the Greeks lived and behaved exactly as archaeologists had prescribed two and a half thousand years later. You probably think I'm exaggerating. Not at all. That's what often happens in archaeology.

"You reckon," said Hermós, "that these people in L'Escala aren't the descendants of those Greeks. . . but where, then, can those Greeks have gone to? Besides, where would they ever have gone to improve on what they had here? The anchovies and sardines here are the tastiest. . . Do you see? People are never as simple as they seem at first sight. Those Greeks were no fools. They chose to come and live in the best of places. . ."

The archaeologist promised to show us some German books in his specialist field, but the years went by and we saw no more of him.

Hermós was a contented, happy fellow. He accepted his poverty-stricken state without protest. He felt life was splendid. After a more or less decent supper, he'd add, as he lit up a small cheroot: "If I were a rich man, I'd not sup better. . ."

At the same time he was very demanding in respect of certain things and would never compromise. Once some young lads from Barcelona came to see him in Aigua-Xelida, I think, on my recommendation. They were carrying on their shoulders a giant homebred rabbit that was as huge as a well-to-do doll. When Hermós saw it, he wrinkled his nose. It was very late. Those youngsters had lost their way in the mountains and were famished. They asked him if he would cook them rice with rabbit; they'd pay him handsomely. He roundly refused.

"If you want, I'll cook you," he continued, "wild rabbit, partridge, hare, quail, thrush, woodcock, crested lark, any kind of little warbler. . . You only have to give me the go-ahead. But I will not cook you a pet rabbit, out of self-respect. Who do you think I am?"

Those poor youngsters reached Tamariu as dusk was falling, on their last legs, realizing they had met a quite singular man, the kind you rarely meet in life.

And it was a fact that Hermós's culture was so solid and well defined he tended to be dogmatic and querulous. His ideas about domestically reared rabbits were entirely in keeping with tradition.

On another day we were sitting on the fine sand of Aiguablava beach, enjoying the benign shade with Doctor Arruga and Don Joan Ventosa. All of a sudden, in a dead-pan tone, Hermós announced that the moon on the previous night had appeared at least two minutes late according to the forecast. He added that several other fishermen had also noticed.

"My dear Hermós," replied Don Joan in his usual serene, gravelly voice, "that's quite a claim. . . The moon is a serious business. . ."

And he explained in a simple, clear and animated manner the combined movements of the sun, moon and earth.

Hermós listened in silence. He realized he was losing the argument and scowled darkly. Then he lost his temper, thumped the sand and said: "Don Joan, you know that Senyor Pla and I love and respect you. What's more I am your gamekeeper, and very honored to be so. . . But if you go on like this, I'll give you back my cartridge belt, ammunition, badge and hunting gun. . ."

Like Anaximander, Parmenides and so many others, he was of the belief that the earth is flat and motionless, that it hangs from a hook in the sky. . . and that if the train from Flaçà to Palamós often arrives late, then the moon could also be occasionally late and with much more justification. . .

I promised him that if he died before me, I would put a stone in Aigua-Xelida to remind people of his sojourn in that solitary place, between the trails of foam tracking across the sea and the lovely scent from the pines. This stone will carry the inscription that his affectionate warmth and wild nature deserve. The slab will be made of granite and the letters will have an uncouth, rustic charm.

BETWEEN 1917 AND. . .
THERE LIVED IN THIS SOLITARY PLACE,
FAR FROM OTHER MEN AND WOMEN,
SEBASTIÀ PUIG, KNOWN AS HERMÓS,
ILLITERATE, A HAPPY, HOSPITABLE MAN,
FISHERMAN, SAILOR, HUNTER,

GREAT COOK.

PASSERBY, YOU SHOULD KNOW

THAT IF HE HASN'T RETURNED IT IS BECAUSE HE COULDN'T.

OR BECAUSE THEY TRICKED HIM LIKE A CHINAMAN

This epitaph doesn't display the composure of Roman words carved in stone, and I don't believe it will ever be a renowned inscription. It is the fruit of my humble gratitude and the feelings inspired by a friend and companion on so many adventures. It will simply be a small tribute to the memory of the pitch-black and moonlit nights we spent together in these coastal waters and the four or five thousand fresh grilled sardines we ate... Not forgetting the bread and wine.

These are realities that are noteworthy, because one could say, and not at all flippantly, that all else is madness, smoke and ashes.

The First World War was declared in 1914. While the war lasted, Hermós couldn't go to the Roussillon, where his parents lived, or to the Roussillon coast, where he had so many friends. That really upset him, and it was a pain he felt deeply.

In the summer of 1918, he made every effort to go to France. He persisted repeatedly that fall. It was foolish of him: he didn't have a suitable boat or proper documentation. The war, which had officially ended in November of that year, was still being fought. However, in the end, as a result perhaps of my insouciance and bonhomie, we did eventually set sail from Calella.

The reader will find in the following pages a detailed chronicle of our voyage and everything that befell us.

26 *September.* At eleven a.m., not waiting on ceremony, Hermós strides into my bedroom and opens the shutters wide, and a stream

of light hits my eyes. Then he walks over, pulls back the turn of the sheet and bawls like a man possessed: "This can't go on. . . We must go to France right now. . . You've overslept too long! And don't start cursing me. . ."

I have always hated being woken up like that. It makes me bad tempered, a mood that can last for hours. Yet I can't feel angry toward this man. I've always been quite at a loss when faced by the boisterousness you find in these parts. They are traits I loathe but find fascinating. . . I am twenty, Hermós is fifty, but he's much younger than me. Life exhilarates him, and at times exhausts me.

After clenching my fists over my sore eyes for a while, as I adapted them to the usual glare of the local light, I see Hermós at the side of my bed, a cheeky grin on his simian face, his long arms dangling down, his skipper's black silk cap tilting over an ear and exposing a strip of baldness his cap renders white and pink.

"What's the weather like?" I ask.

"A southwesterly breeze, just what we need for our trip. Up you get! And hurry up! Don't make me suffer anymore. . ."

Our local braggarts are always on edge, plagued by the discomfort others cause.

"So where is it you want to go?"

"We should go to France along the coast, in the Prim boys' sailing dinghy. I've organized everything, and the dinghy's all ready to launch off from El Canadell beach. Isn't that what we agreed the last time we spoke?"

"You do realize the war isn't over yet?" I ask, looking serious.

"Forget about wars. Who is going to worry about us? Do no evil, hear no evil. Besides, we've got to teach people a lesson, we've got to create a stir."

People spend their lives trying to create stirs.

"What lesson are we poor souls supposed to teach? Don't you start trying to teach people a thing or two. . ."

"We have to! We have to show them you can sail and row to France. Now everybody uses motorboats, they're all cocky daredevils. When they pass Aigua-Xelida at night, their revving disturbs me. They ruin my shut-eye. . . We have to show them what's what. The Prim boys' dinghy is small, it's twenty-one hands, but it's a good sailer. I've fitted out the boom, hoisted the sail, and nothing will hold us back."

"And what's the weather forecast?"

"I've got the calendar in my bag. I just bought it in the market."

"What earthly use is the forecast in a calendar?"

"But if you don't believe the calendar, what can we believe?"

"And we've got the right papers?"

"I've got my skipper's. . ."

"Yes, but that is a very limited permit."

"As limited as they come. Just for line fishing opposite where I live."

"So you're intending to go to France without any papers, just because you feel like it. . ."

"That's right, as we always have. . ."

"It's really tempting to sail like that, without any papers. . ." I reply, as if I'm talking to myself. "It's worth a try."

"I knew you'd back me. . ." he says gruffly, in a deeply serious tone of voice.

By the seaside Hermós uses the informal "tu" with everyone – except for Donya Rosa Barris, whom he has waited upon all these years. A mile or so inland, he uses the formal "vostè" all the time. I note that though we're in the latter situation, he uses "tu" with me, a sign of his trust in me.

After lunch, we hire a cart to take my things to El Canadell: a mattress, blankets, a bag with the necessary clothing and toiletries. Hermós and I walk slowly behind the cart, as if we're off for a spot of sunbathing. It is a gentle, sunny, delightful afternoon. The earth's contours seem to vibrate in the warm air.

The moment we reach the beach, we load everything on board: we carry on mattresses, blankets, a stove, a sack of coal, potatoes, demijohns of wine and oil, a crate with plates, pots and pans, cutlery and a grill. We also embark four paternoster lines and the basket with the cast net. In winter Hermós never forgets this net, which is the color of vine stalks. We also load on a sack containing two live chickens. Because they can't keep still, there's a danger the sack might fall into the water, Hermós loses patience. He stuns them with quick blows from the tiller. The sack goes quiet and the chickens are still.

"You've probably killed them. . ." I say, taken aback.

"I only gave them a clout. . ." he says, carrying on working. "They'll taste even better. Don't start crying over all the dead chickens you've eaten. . ."

We push the boat out, and by the time we go to lock in our oars, El Canadell is completely deserted. The place is enjoying an autumnal slumber. The September sun splashes streaks of orange over the windows of its empty houses. The boat is heavily laden and floating too low in the water. As we leave the bay, old Palet's cart crosses El Canadell. Old Palet is a fierce-looking, bearded countryman, with a vicious temper. We can see him standing over his cart: one hand scratching his beard, the other gripping his horse's reins.

"I wish I'd not seen him at this time of day. . ." says Hermós, turning away.

"Are you superstitious?"

"Don't you start with them strange words. . . I've never liked men with beards. . ."

"Lots of gentlemen sport beards. . ."

"Lots of gentlemen aren't worth a cent!"

A few oar strokes and we reach Torre Point outside Calella. A miserable, moribund southeasterly is blowing. We hoist our sail and light our small lamp so as to have better visibility. Hermós mans the helm. We sail windward as much as we can and pass Llafranc Bay. When we glimpse the place our friend Mata owns on the beach there, we inevitably acknowledge that the first views on our voyage should have been from his hospitable, much-respected tavern. But that's out of the question. Days are shortening and afternoons are simply flying by.

Our dinghy sails perfectly round Cape Sant Sebastià, and the moment Frayre Point looms before us, Hermós grins and issues an order: "Ease the front. . ."

I loosen the front cleat, Hermós loosens the sheet and we move to the stern. There's only a light wind, but that's helpful. The vessel sails ahead. In the stern, even the marrows are rolling around. And it cuts straight on. We leave behind the coastline of Sant Sebastià, Els Frares, Pedrosa Cove and La Musclera. It's a spectacular sight. I've observed it dozens of times and am familiar with its stony indifference, but its magnetic pull remains as strong as it was the first time. That's childhood images for you – they are uniquely irreplaceable; they stay with you throughout life. Against the light, the Pedrosa Cove cliffs are a wealth of warm, muted colors, of shimmering shadows. On La Musclera we can see Lord Islington's house in the course of construction.

"He is a gentleman who suffers a lot from sore throats. . ." says Hermós, with the air of a man who knows about these things. "Which is hard to believe, as there's nothing like pine trees to cure a sore throat!"

And now he tells me the story of Lord Islington he's picked up in the taverns. It's wild fantasy, but to make it seem more realistic, he starts giving an English twist to what he's explaining. His English consists in giving the four French sentences he learned in Africa a lunatic nasal drawl.

"You'll soon get how those people speak," he says, as if about to give me a repeat lesson. But he suddenly shuts up and straightens his back.

"We need to do an inventory right now. . ." he declares gloomily. He drops the tiller, jumps and starts rummaging among the marrows we've loaded. Then he shouts out, as if someone had just stamped on his toes: "Just what I thought! We forgot the onions. . ."

"So what. . ." I reply blankly.

And then he begins on another long story: the reason why he forgot the onions. Early that morning he'd ordered onions from Marieta Batlle, as Marieta is the person in Calella who has the best onions money can buy. Moreover, Marieta is very kind; when Hermós was a young lad and went on board Big Boy's boat to go hake fishing in far-off waters and returned home starving and shivering, she fed him. In other words, no onions can better those sold by Marieta Batlle. However, when he ordered them, Marieta was grilling a sea bream for her son-in-law's breakfast, because it is his favorite breakfast and

Marieta thinks it's absolutely fine for her son-in-law to eat one or two grilled sea bream for breakfast. Hermós couldn't tear her away from the embers smoldering on the grill. . . In the meantime, he went to the kiosk to buy a packet of fifteen-cèntim cheroots which he had to select one by one, thus relegating his obsession with onions to the back of his head. The fact is that what with the grilled sea bream, Marieta's way of keeping her son-in-law happy, the cheroots and the huge amount of things you must have on your mind on such a day, the onions remained on land.

"I reckon we can get by without onions. . ."

"Oh, no we can't!" retorts Hermós, in that imperious tone he uses on board. "We cannot proceed without onions. . . What on earth are you thinking?"

We are opposite Tamariu and he steers the prow toward Aigua-Xelida. From the sea, Tamariu has the simplicity of a Japanese print. The soft, hazy contours of the expanse of land behind the beach possess a melancholy charm, a grave beat. We anchor in Aigua-Xelida. Hermós jumps onto land and heads toward his hut to fetch onions. I watch him from the boat. He can't find his key. He nervously searches his pockets. He spends ages impatiently looking for it everywhere. He finally finds it in a pants pocket, even though it's a large key. I hear his blood-curdling curse, which vanishes among the solitary pines. He eventually returns with half a string of onions. We've wasted three quarters of an hour. A few strokes of our oars and we're out of the bay and hoisting the sail again. The wind weakens and is about to die. It takes us as far as Gavina. When we're level with that rock, the sail flaps and we feel the first gust of the northwesterly on our faces. I tighten the cleat, Hermós the sheet, then we secure the sail and begin to sail out to sea. The aim is to reach Fornells by tacking to the wind.

We sail in silence, as evening falls. Against the light a bright patch of green silken sky hovers over the pink cliffs of the Cabres cove. The wind rises, the waves surge, the sail ropes tighten, the canvas stiffens. From time to time our boat crashes against the sea, throwing up a curtain of water into our faces: it is cold, hard and fast. Nothing is harder than salt water: it is as hard as steel. Our boat is well ballasted and flies over the water, now with a tail wind. It slips along miraculously gently, but it's a rather uncomfortable miracle: streams of water soak our clothes and give us goose bumps.

We must keep the baggage we carry on board dry. Above all, our blankets, mattresses, clothes and sack of coal mustn't get sopping wet. Hermós searches everywhere for a tarpaulin cover, with that nervous impatience he always brings to urgent tasks. But he finds nothing: no trace of a cover, not even a miserable scrap of canvas. He breaks two bowls while he's about it. It's all rather chaotic.

"I wasn't expecting such a violent wind. . ." he says almost shamefaced, bent double, turning his back on the streams of water flying at him from the stern.

"It's not your fault!"

"They were soup bowls!"

"Don't worry, we'll eat solids."

"Have you got any money on you?" he asks all of a sudden, changing the subject.

"Two hundred pessetes in notes."

"That's a lot of money. It could come in handy: enough to get us to Collioure and back via Figueres. We must keep our heads and, above all, make sure those notes don't get wet! Seawater discolors them, and when they're discolored, nobody will touch them. In any case, it would be a pity to turn back at this time of day, when there are cafés and taverns around and we have money in our pockets. . ."

Darkness was falling. Sant Sebastià was right in front. We watched iridescent sheaves of light spread from the lighthouse over the cliffs and sea. To the north we could see the motionless light from the Medes Islands and farther north, like a wavering firefly, the light from Cape Creus. It was time to take down the sail, not an easy task in such a heavily laden boat. We began our return to land. From where we were, Fornells gave no signs of life: no lights, no embers, no smoke.

It was a magnificent night: the stars shone brightly against the darkest of blue skies. Not a single cloud in sight. A typical northern sky: burnished and shiny. The cold wind whistled through the halyards. Now and then water showered over the boat or poured off our backs. Everything glistened. Our attempts to light a cheroot proved futile.

"Where do you reckon we are?" I asked, after taking the sail down.

"By the light of day, I think we'd see the town of Torroella. . ."

"There's no sign of Fornells. . ."

"Don't you worry. Every man jack is inside under cover, and some will be trying to spawn the baby they produce every year when this weather comes around. . . Everything will be drenched, that's for sure."

"Everything *is* sopping wet."

"No need to worry. Nothing could be healthier in this weather than sleeping on a mattress soaked in seawater."

When things turned against him, Hermós put on a brave face and became larger than life. With one hand on the helm, wet as a barnacle, bloodshot eyes bulging, and full of energy, he'd have been ready to risk his life. At other times, when things eased up, he became inexplicably depressed. He was every inch a man from hereabouts.

We barely exchanged another word. The boat was too low in the water and we had to be ready for any sudden gusts. After an hour's sailing we reached the coast. As we slowly drew nearer, the wind blew more fiercely, but we easily rounded Mut Point. Small vessels, even the most seaworthy, are no use when it comes to sailing in a driving wind. They have no balance and the waves stop them in their tracks. When they sail, it's in a series of stops and starts. Once in the bay we pick up our oars, and with their help and favorable gusts of wind we find shelter in El Port de Ses Orats. We make for the huge pine tree that dominates the small cove. A wonderful silence reigns in that windless place. We had sailed three hours to progress half a mile. We were weighed down by drenched clothes, and salt water irritated our eyes and skin. While we were mooring on the small beach, a viscous, vertical line of light appeared at the window of Xicu Caló's house, which was nestled on the cliff.

"Xicu!" shouted Hermós, in a voice that echoed off the jagged rocks.

"What's wrong?"

The meager stream of light broadened out and his silhouette became visible.

"How are you fixed for fish?"

"We've got red mullet."

"Enough for two?"

"More than enough. . ."

"Where are they from?"

"From Illa Negra."

"They're the best! Put seven or eight on to grill, we're on our way."

We put bread, oil, vinegar and a bottle of cognac in a basket. I carried the demijohn of wine. Hermós took the basket in one hand and with his other grabbed one of the stunned chickens by the neck.

"When they see that we've brought a chicken," he whispered, "they'll pay us more respect. . ."

Lots of people were in the kitchen. A yellow, pinewood fire was crackling in the hearth. Four magnificent, garishly red mullet lay on the embers on the grill. A carbide lamp was burning on the table with a metal shade behind the wick. Consequently, one half of the kitchen was almost in darkness; the other was bathed in a wan white glow. As we were freezing and sopping wet, that fire was a blessing, and the smell of pine resin mingling with the mullet on the embers, a deliciously sublime fact of life.

When Hermós placed the wine, cognac and chicken on the table, it aroused the expectations of the crowd of adults gathered there, but not as much as he'd anticipated. Everyone had eaten dinner and the vague hubbub floating through the kitchen was as sweet as honey.

Half of Fornells was there. Small fishing communities tend to be split into two enemy clans. The tinier a village and the fewer people that live there, the less they can stand each other. The idea of fraternity and mutual help is an idea that belongs to big cities. In solitary places, where contact might seem indispensable and altogether natural, people tend to be more individualistic and live more separately. One of the Fornells clans was by the fireside. I was surprised to see so many children together. Hermós laughed and asked: "This is water from Fornells, right, Tereseta?"

"Water with a little extra. . ." replied a woman with a youthful, radiant face; she was blonde with sturdy legs, moist, white teeth and gleaming lips.

Every woman had a child sleeping on her lap; others were asleep on the boxwood chairs by the fireside or on the earthen floor, on beds of dry leaves. The sparking flames from the crackling pinewood brought a pink glow to their cheeks. When they saw us come in, some of the children half opened an eye or whimpered; most slept on.

Despite Hermós's fame in the locality, adult interest in our presence lasted a mere couple of seconds. Then somebody yawned and other yawns followed in a chain reaction. It was too late; it was almost two o'clock. When the carbide light began spluttering its last, Xicu hung it from a hook on the wall. That increased the chatter in the kitchen and the heaviness of eyelids. For a while various people slept stiffly in their chairs, in a state of precarious equilibrium. As we sat down at the table, people said goodbye. They lit up two or three oil lanterns and departed. We were left alone with Xicu and his family.

A thick haze hung over the kitchen and we didn't need to get close to the fire to dry our clothes. We dined feeling a priceless hunger we wouldn't have sold for any amount of money: we each dispatched half a dozen crisp, red mullet. The supply of rosé wine was endless. After that we ate biscuits. When Xicu put a small pan of water on the fire for coffee, we watched his wife's nonstop yawning. Hermós looked at me as if to say: "This party's over. . ."

Hermós prepared his favorite drink: *el roquill.* Coffee, cognac, sugar and a few drops of lemon juice. He filled the glasses to the top. That made us even more lethargic. We lit fifteen-cèntim cheroots and, after paying our bill, bid farewell. We tiptoed silently out. I wondered whether the noisy hum and lethargy in Fornells might not represent the quintessence of happiness in this world. However, I barely had to time to think on that: the night was so pitch black that, before we ever reached the boat, we came close to cracking our skulls a couple of times.

It was a dark, chilly, cloudless night, with a dazzling display of stars and the starkness the north wind gives to the shape of things. We transformed our sail into a tent over the dinghy. The wind blew across the sweep of the bay and whistled through the pine trees. You could hear the sea surging against the distant cliffs. In sheltered, coastal spots, the dull sound of the swell crashing against the rocks or beaches brought a pleasant feeling of safety, safety so secure it might have been won in open battle. We spread out our mattresses and blankets and I lay down under the prow. Everything was wet and freezing cold. Hermós set up on the thwart, under the stern. We left the oil lantern flickering on the side bench. It was all incredibly uncomfortable; however unlikely this might seem, the first thing you need if you want to sleep is to feel tired. By the light from the lantern I saw Hermós's first snore come with the extinguished cheroot still in his mouth; he was already deeply asleep. As he had removed his cap, the hazy light touched his bald pate, and he seemed engaged in an intimate act, dozing in the family bed, with his wife at his side, half obscured by the shadows.

27 *September*. I'm writing this at ten p.m., on Sa Riera Beach, by the light from the boat's lantern. We have just bid farewell to Florià Pi and his crowd.

We set sail from Fornells midmorning and rounded Cape Begur with a becalmed sea, a low, cobwebby sky, and a dingy, damp breeze. We had rowed and reached Sa Riera by hugging the coast. Hermós talked tirelessly almost the whole way. I felt I'd been given a comprehensive lecture on the coast and its place-names. The appearance of Pals Beach from the waters of Ses Negres – a sudden opening out of horizons – is an unforgettable sight. Hermós knows every inch of that terrain.

"Do you think I'm afraid of rain?"

"Not now we're close to port. . . In any case, I couldn't care less whether or not it rains. . ."

"There's nothing worse than rain when you're traveling like this. . . I'm afraid you'll get bored."

"No, I won't. If it rains, we can go up to Begur and play *canari*. Perhaps our most pressing need now is to get a bite of lunch. Morning coffee was. . ."

"What do you mean 'morning coffee'? It couldn't have tasted better in Maison Dorée. . ."

Hermós has a weakness for the French names of some establishments. He affectionately remembers a number.

Our friend Florià Pi was waiting for us on the beach. He is a large, imposing man with a Muslim air: a tall giant, with dark marble skin, gleaming white teeth and shiny black pupils in pools of yellow lymph. He welcomes us noisily and I find his affability overwhelming. He is a widower and always lives in the cove, surrounded by a large family that includes lots of women. They all work nonstop carrying out his orders. His is the household that eats the best in the area. He has all the necessary tackle, owns boats and buys fish; he is never short of a hunting gun or dog. He always has one dog or another – a good one – to give away. The first thing he did when we reached his house was to show us the telephone he'd just had installed.

Frankly, I'm not at all interested in his telephone. Luckily, he immediately offered us half a box of freshly caught sea bass and three wild rabbits that were hanging on the back of the kitchen door.

"How shall we cook the bass?" asks Florià.

"*A la marinera!*" Hermós replies emphatically.

"And the wild rabbit?"

"Roasted with aioli?"

Reparada, the patriarch's daughter-in-law, starts cooking the fish. We help her. Hermós peels the garlic. I finely chop onion and parsley, and prepare tomatoes for a hash. The boys go to the fountain with pitchers. The women prepare the rabbit.

Sensible, with foresight, Florià is in charge. The kitchen is soon filled with the smell from the strong sauces.

Lunch and the subsequent table talk lasted from three to well past nine o'clock. Everything was tasty and in abundance. The aioli was solid and consistent, quite remarkable: the handle of the pestle held itself erect. We ate grapes for dessert and spent the evening drinking *roquills*. Nothing makes you long for this liquid like the aftertaste aioli leaves in the mouth. There was a lot of lively singing: it wasn't a moment for self-restraint. We ran through the supplies of our cognac and the house's. People are inexhaustible and go into a spin: tell stories, eat, drink, smoke, sit down and leave the table, nonstop. In his element, Hermós enjoys moments of Dionysian energy.

"For how many centuries," I wonder, "have people around here been leading this kind of life? Can it last forever? Won't this primitive, decadent lunacy ever come to an end? Sometimes jollity in these parts scares me. It is so exuberant it must be fated to disappear."

It started raining at dusk, and as nobody around here does anything when it rains, the people from the cove headed to the kitchen.

Not everybody – because the word "everybody" doesn't exist here – only friends. It was drizzling gently, as it does, to borrow a phrase from Hermós, and that makes you thirsty. Through the grayness framed by the window, you could see rain falling on the becalmed sea, on the white, soporific water and the small, fish-eyed bubbles the spitting rain throws up on the surface. On that solitary, dreary evening, backwoods male cavortings seem completely futile, inexplicable and gratuitous. And, in the end, physical exhaustion brings everything to a conclusion.

The moment I go out, the cool air and small drops of rain revive me and clear my head. Our sailing dinghy is moored right on the beach. The sea is totally still: a deep, pearl-colored silence. I make it to my mattress under the prow; the dampness brings out the dank stink of the wool. I'm as restless as usual, the usual nerves. Rain beats down on the boards and awning, streams down the canvas. Now and then I vaguely hear a drop of rain falling on my bed, as if there's a leak somewhere. It's miserable to think my mattress will slowly become drenched.

28 September. I'm still writing, as I was yesterday, by the light of the boat's lantern, on Sa Riera Beach. We were unable to sail this morning. It rained all day – till four p.m. – a gray, meandering drizzle. When I glanced outside, I saw Hermós plucking a chicken under the canopy. A skinny, starving old black cat was sitting by his side – a local cat.

He'd made a brown stew and boiled up some meat and vegetables. The stove had been lit the whole day under the awning. It sometimes created a thick fug. The sound of rain on the wet sail, the monotonous pitter-patter of raindrops on the sea lulled you to sleep. I spent the whole day smoking and watching the rain. There was very little movement in Sa Riera. People must have been sleeping off their hangover from yesterday's binge.

It's been a delightful day with that frothy haze and marvelous silence. Now and then I stuck my head outside. Everything was gray and muted: if the sky ever cleared, everything seemed a rusty-tin blue. The sea seemed somnolent all day, as it was yesterday, becalmed in eternal indifference. Water streamed down the pines and the foliage was sometimes so green it seemed to dissolve into pure color, into pristine pictorial tints – like the pearl of the inlet's waters, like the opaline air. In the drowse, mineral veins swelled on the rocks and the beach fell into a crimson faint. The silence was intense, as if cotton wool had been plugged into our ears. The sound of clogs and distant wailing of an invisible child seemed like failed attempts to break it.

Hermós spoke more moderately now. He's afraid I will tire of this life. I've caught him scowling furiously at the low sky and sinister rain. He cannot imagine how I could like days like this. He is a man wedded to the sun and eternal pepper and tomato salads. I'm feebler. I wouldn't change today's rain-swept placidity for yesterday's vociferous hubbub.

"We'll set sail at daybreak tomorrow!" he shouts imperiously, grabbing his mattress.

By the dim light from the lantern, I observe him in his warrior's white, ghostly, buffoonish long johns.

29 September. We set off at seven a.m., with a breeze from inland as fresh as a rose. Out of the inlet, by Torre de Pals, we encounter the boat of Pepet, Florià's eldest son, who's been out doing some early morning fishing. He hands us a basket of magnificent plump sardines.

Hermós hands me the tiller and immediately lights up the stove. It is a delightful wind to close haul, with the sheet loosened; the lively sea ripples gracefully. When the embers glow, he lays out the sardines. The fumes from the fish fill the air with splendid sweet-scented expectations. The sun shines ever more fiercely and takes the bite out of the breeze. The land above Pals Beach glistens with yesterday's rain like a blessing from heaven. Our boat scythes through the water. The sky becomes astonishingly luminous, a luminosity that seems to make everything it touches light and weightless. I feel I too am about to levitate, but that's probably down to the pangs of hunger aroused by the smoke drifting from the grilling sardines.

Hermós slices the bread and places a huge plate of sardines on the starboard quarter. He generously sprinkles on oil and vinegar. As the gentle breeze is dying, we secure the tiller and start eating as if we were in a tavern. My traveling companion takes a fish head between the fingers of one hand and the fish tail in the other and eats his sardines as if he were playing the ocarina. He devours them in a sucking process. Their spines emerge clean and tidy from the operation. The spectacle of avid hunger becomes this antique sea. There are corners of this sea where you can smell the stench of Homeric hecatombs. Modesty aside, I eat them more primly: on bread, though with my fingers.

After we have each eaten our first twenty, washed down with the requisite wine, Hermós makes a pepper and tomato salad. The sun glints on the scales of the fish and the oil, glitters off the skin of the peppers and the bottle of wine. It is a glorious morning. The sun shines brightly. The dazzling blue sky is like a cushion of delights. The wind drops slowly.

"This accompaniment," says Hermós, "will help us do the deed. . ."

After eating half a dozen more, we look into each other's eyes. Enough is enough! Nothing in excess. The right amount. We have a smoke. I immediately feel my body reacting to the sardines: they produce a sense of debilitation, fraying at the edges and lethargy. We decide to boil up some coffee.

We are approaching L'Estartit. We can see the town's white walls, and cobs of maize hung up to dry in windows. The sunlight cascades down the mauve, turtle-colored rocks above the roofs and cavorts over the Medes Islands, which are reflected in the still, cobalt sea, in the most outrageous shapes rocks can assume.

"We should find out what the current is. . ." says Hermós. "Get close to the first inlet or boat you see. . ."

I sail slightly away from the wind and our boat slips toward a paternoster boat fishing by Cavall Bernat. Hermós shouts: "What's the current?"

"Southwesterly. . ." answer the fishermen.

That's the one for us.

The sea is becalmed. We hoist the sheet up the mast, and the boat is now rudderless. The current pulls us slowly across the Medes straits into Roses Bay at an almost imperceptible rate. Our sailing dinghy groans gently. Hermós lies down in the side of the boat and falls asleep. I still feel quite frayed. An iridescent nap. But I'm not that drowsy, and don't in fact fall asleep. Slouched in the stern, I smoke endlessly, looking sleepily at the sky. The Torroella coastline slowly fades; we sail into the gulf, a magnificent spectacle of expanding horizons. There's not a cloud in sight: the sky is a soft, gentle blue. Light pours over the low ground in a flood of bright gold. Rising above the plain, the jagged contours of the mountains shimmer. We spend two or three hours wandering freely. The limp sail flaps at the top of the mast. Our boat drifts.

"What's the time?" asks Hermós, suddenly sitting up, his eyes streaked red and yellow.

"How do you expect me to tell you, if we're not carrying a clock?"

"First it was onions, then the tarpaulin, and now the clock. . ." he says bad-temperedly. "You know, we're both a waste of time. . . We always mess up!"

Then he looks at the sun for a while, blinks several times and solemnly declares: "It's exactly twenty-five to three. And anyone who doesn't believe that is an idiot."

Then he stood up: "What's the weather like? Where are we?"

We had made little progress. We were opposite Ferriol Cove, opposite L'Escala floating on the water to the west. We discussed the weather. There was a very light, southeasterly breeze. We loosened the sheet, stood aft and pointed the boat toward L'Escala. The sky was still pure and clean, but all of a sudden, a thin, streaky expanse of dark-copper cloud appeared above the Portús col. Hermós scowled in its direction.

"That could be a north wind, you know?" he said, instinctively raising his oars.

Smoking, rowing hard, making the most of a backwind, we sailed on for quite a time. Hermós said very little. His eyes were locked on that distant bank of cloud, which grew and darkened as evening fell. What's more, those sardines were weighing him down. We reached L'Escala at dusk. He didn't want to anchor the boat, insisting on dragging it up the beach. I was surprised so few people were in the harbor, especially where we moored, opposite the carpentry work-shop of Senyor Tassis, who makes the best oars in the country and whose workshop is usually crowded out.

"People are frightened of a north wind. . . Can't you see that? They've hauled their boats up. . . You can be sure not even a rat will leave harbor tonight!"

We made up our canopy, and by the time we'd erected it and our beds were in place, it was pitch dark.

"We should go for a drink," said Hermós straight away.

We went into Maurici's tavern and drank a glass of beer. The café was empty. The street was deserted. You could see small yellow lights through the cracks in doors and windows.

"And what if we hit the hay. . . What do you reckon?" Hermós asked, almost pleading.

"That's an excellent idea."

We were both on our respective mattresses by eight p.m. Sardines can be tricky.

30 September. I'm writing at eleven p.m. in Arquímedes's tavern. It's been an extremely hectic day.

A mistral settled in mercilessly at five a.m. First, we heard the sea crashing on the sand, monotonous waves in a crescendo of noise; then the initial, wild gusts of the northwesterly. It was soon blowing violently, impetuously and without letting up. We immediately felt it was sweeping our canopy away. We got up and secured it with ropes on the four sides. The sky was full of stars that faded in the cool, green brightness of dawn. Blown from the Pyrenees, a bank of clouds had spread unchecked, towers billowing dark and menacing. Now and then an expanse of black cloud broke away and flew off in vertiginous disorder. By daybreak, the gulf had become visible, a mass of white foam and high murky waves under a livid light. We fixed the boat down with a couple more staves and went back to bed. But I couldn't sleep. The violent wind and sea battered my brain.

"When the wind is like this," I heard Hermós say, as he pulled his pants on, "it's best not to do anything stupid."

"What do you suggest?"

"We should settle down in the tavern. You can see what other people are doing. . . Here we'll get wiser rather than wealthier. . ."

"What are your thoughts on the weather? That mistral is blasting like a cannon."

"I'll tell you the evening after next."

It was almost impossible to hear one another talk. The wind blew our words away. A cloud of spray hovered over the beach.

We secured our things on the boat as best we could and headed to the tavern. First to Senyora Neus's tavern, also known as Can Gelada, though it wasn't icy, and then, we hardly need add, Arquímedes's tavern – the owner's surname is Ballester, though he had no crossbows – is down a street by the harbor. The wind gusts us there, almost without touching the ground, you could say. It's open – it's seven a.m. – and we go through the door and into the kitchen. The stoves are on and the people who live there are already sat around the table, forking up breakfast. It's a promising start.

Hermós is renowned in the area. He's given a cordial, boisterous welcome. I benefit from the overspill of hospitality. A few seconds after we arrive, at a loss to know how or why I've gotten into this position, I'm sitting at the table, surrounded by the family, facing a plate of food and an amazing array of wine. It's home-produced wine. In L'Escala they make a dry white from Macabeo grapes and a dry cherry pink from Carinyena grapes. Both are wonderfully easy and light to drink. Who could resist them?

Meanwhile, the tavern regulars start to arrive and I look at them as I eat and drink. They are real regulars, no doubt about it, fishermen who have been coming here for years and years; nevertheless, the privileged position I enjoy leads me to think that as a tavern customer, I am as stalwart as they are. Sitting and drinking at that table, I feel like an ancient, fabled, preeminent parishioner. One who would defend his rights tooth and nail against these other folk. . .

This kind of reflection, which isn't typical of me, leads me to think – once I've a cup of coffee in front of me – that it might be the effect of the copious amounts I have drunk. Nothing to worry about, naturally! These wines are so light! But perhaps it's premature to be acting with such arrogance. Outside, in the meantime, the mistral is still gusting ferociously. Through the tavern windows you can see very few people walking by, stooping, hands in pockets, furiously battered by the wind.

A wooden bench goes right round the wall of the saloon. The locals like to recline there: fishermen lolling back like Romans on a triclinium, as they say, without a care in the world. On the small table in the entrance stands a water jug with a curved spout and two demijohns of wine that look as if they'll never run dry. People go over to the table with a glass or their own little wine jar, open the tap and the wine flows remarkably quickly and surely. It's the ideal tavern for thirsty people.

Skipper Lill from Begur, who now captains a longboat in L'Escala, walks in: a tall, thin, fair-haired man with gray eyes and the neatest of pointy mustaches, one of those men who, the moment they drop their guard, look as if they're in their Sunday best. He's a good friend of

Hermós's, and in no time they start singing. Lill is a wonderful singer of tavern songs. They immediately get into the swing. . . Friends of Lill's soon arrive and the camaraderie is fired up. Someone sends for Grandad Xaixo; he walks in shortly, skin leathered by the wind, a guitar under his arm.

"I thought," he whispers tremulously, "it would blow me through the air. . ."

Xaixo is a small fellow, dressed in black, with very long white hair, a dandruff-dusted jacket and a well-preserved mustache. Famously he wears someone else's shoes. He is slightly humpbacked and seems plagued by poverty and hunger.

When they're all there, they set up in the back corner, Xaixo tunes his guitar and the program commences. *Al pie de un jardín florido – lloraba una colombiana . . .* The tavern rapidly fills up. Hermós is beaming.

"What a wonderful country. . ." he says to me from afar, glass of wine in hand.

When the door to the road opens, you can hear the wind whistle and blast, and clouds of tobacco smoke billow out.

When it's lunchtime, we grab a quick bite. Arquímedes serves us homegrown rabbit with peppers and tomatoes. Hermós complains about the homegrown nature of the rabbit. Everyone else finds it delicious. Clasping his guitar between his knees, old Xaixo scours the bones with his small, white, famished, bohemian hands. Then we each eat a dry fig, a raisin, two nuts and four roasted almonds. The singing leaves such a pleasant taste in the mouths of these folk that they can't resist striking up again between one dry fig and another raisin. Then it's time for coffee and rum. Now that they've eaten, the singing becomes more full throated and tuneful. By seven, their repertoire is going from strength to strength. Wine has lit up most faces. Some regulars are asleep, heads on arms folded on the marble-topped tables. I feel exhausted and have a headache that's not going away.

I finally make my escape. Arquímedes's Francisqueta takes pity on me and leads me to one of their bedrooms. The cool sheets, the silence and the feeling that I am totally alone work wonders. As my thumping heart won't let me sleep, I use the time to pen these lines. For a good long while I can hear their singing, as if from another world.

First of October. When I get up in the morning, I feel wearier than the previous day. My mouth is dry and my tongue even drier. The top of my head aches. My legs feel weak. The mistral continues to blast away furiously: it sometimes moans like a distant clap of thunder. Very fine sand from the gulf raps against the windows as if a cat's claws were scraping them. The sky is limpid and pure, a metallic blue. The strong, dry air has an enervating effect on my whole body – I'm peculiarly edgy. My vocal chords don't seem to be responding: I've almost lost my voice.

Hermós is eating breakfast at the table. He tells me he's slept on our boat and has had a very bad night, and that he didn't take his pants off, something he'd not done for many years, so he would be ready for any eventuality, and that at times he'd felt the wind was blowing him up and away.

I spend the day in Arquímedes's kitchen, by the fireside, not speaking or eating, lethargic and weary, drinking glasses of cold water, listening to the wind wail down the chimney. I see no sign of the people we were fraternizing with yesterday. Even Hermós seems to have vanished. Nothing strange about that: he doesn't want to see me and I'm in no hurry to talk to him. I ask Francisqueta how much wine was consumed. First she looks at me and laughs and then seems bewildered. If you think about it, quite frankly, it was a stupid question. Everything flees, is more or less eliminated, everything passes. . .

I sleep in the same bedroom where I slept yesterday. Now my head is clearer, I can see that the room is spick and span and contains a bed, a chair, a wardrobe and a washbowl. Such simplicity – it is a seventy-five-céntim bedroom – quickly and efficiently helps me to recover.

2 October. Hermós wakes me up midmorning and tells me he has bumped into Ramon Pins, a fisherman from Begur who skippers a longboat here, and that he has offered to tow us as far as Jònculs. Ramon wants to go to Jònculs tonight to see whether he can land forty or fifty boxes of mackerel. The combination enthuses Hermós. To be honest, he thinks the gulf is frightening rather than exhilarating. As he tells me all this, he praises Ramon to the skies.

"Just imagine, he is *even* an anarchist!" he whispers into my ear, rounding off the series of qualities he has praised in Ramon.

Hermós is like that. Everything is either heavenly or hellish.

"And doth the north wind still blow?" I ask.

"It's dropped a lot. And will drop even more. All will be calm come sunset. . ."

By the time we begin lunch, we are incredibly hungry. L'Escala wines are light and delicious. We prepare to embark in the afternoon. Ramon Pins comes over to our boat. He's thirtyish, tall, strong, fair haired, blue eyed, straight-backed and a man of very few words. He helps us to clear the sand the wind has deposited on our boat and tackle. We have to ditch some of our food supplies because they are full of sand. In the meantime, he gives us instructions on how to hitch up. He doesn't want to pull us behind the skiff with the light. Instead, he wants to carry the light on the portside, with our dinghy on the starboard. He speaks clearly and precisely, reminding me sometimes of a Norwegian sailor.

The sea is placid at sunset. After the whiplashes of the mistral, nature seems to be convalescing at dusk. Everything feels faint. The harbor livens up and is full of chatter. The mountains are haloed in a delicate, altarpiece light. The gulf's choppy waters are a hazy green and suffused by a wan, murky inner glow. We push our boat out and approach the large longboat. Standing in the stern, Ramon throws us the end of a rope and starts the engine. In the distance, the Roses lighthouse glimmers at water level. When a strong pull on the rope moves our boat off, a sudden rush of air hits me and makes me shiver with cold. Cap tilted over his ear, Hermós is at the helm smoking a cheroot, seemingly the happiest man in the world; he notices that I'm scowling.

"Take my word for it!" he shouts. "You won't feel any breeze under the prow. . ."

I don't hang around. When I crawl into my cot, I find it is lovely and warm. Now that I'm lying under a blanket, I'm gripped by an ineffable feeling of safety. I can hear the boat's engine chugging far off. Strong tugs on the towrope make the sides of our boat creak and speed it along as if it were in free fall, as if its prow were being dragged down into the sea. At first these sudden jerks make my heart miss a beat, but when I realize nothing is amiss, I sense I'm beyond harm.

In my cot, with my head on the pillow adjacent to the top of the stern, I can hear the water glugging against the timber behind my head. When there's a yank and the sea crashes against the stern, it feels as if the water is flooding me out; when it's an average tug, the water slips along the wood as smooth as silk, curling endlessly, as if wavy shapes were sliding between the nape of my neck and head. I have no time to smoke. Sleep takes over, irresistibly.

When Hermós taps me on the back, after an indeterminate period of time, I feel an unease I find difficult to conceal. Ideally, I'd have liked to be towed to the bottom of the Mediterranean in my sleep. I reluctantly abandon my warm berth and, once on deck, drowsily light up a foul-tasting cigarette. I dither, trying to find my bearings. I feel cold. The sea is calm. It is a pitch-black night, a blackness that seems embedded in the silent air. No hint of a breeze. The panorama is one of deepest solitude.

"Where are we?" I ask.

"Ramon towed us as far as Figuera Point."

"And where's his longboat?"

"Can you see that light near the coast?" asks Hermós, pointing to a patch of white light bobbling by the rocky coast. "He's sailed right over there."

"He looks very close to land. . ."

"That's where the mackerel are. . ."

"So is this what night fishing is like, Hermós? None of this holds any mystery for you. . . You're a past master. . ."

"Come on now. . ." he says, apparently indignant, but preening himself at the same time.

Then he revives the wick of the oil lamp, which only serves to intensify the surrounding darkness. It's like being inside a cavern floating over the water.

"What do you expect me to say?" he says after a while. "Set up the oars and let's take it slowly."

"How far is it to Cadaqués?"

"A good hour's row to Farmàcia."

We start rowing, quite mechanically. I soon feel perfectly in shape; I'm no longer cold, and my muscles are firm. We hug the coast. Rowing behind me, Hermós acts as if he knows where he is going. The Calanans lighthouse appears: a yellow, rather anemic glow. Seen from within that haze, our boat must look like a fly trapped in cobweb that's hanging in the air. We enter Cadaqués Bay.

"How did the crossing of the gulf go?" I ask, to pass the time.

"We crossed it as if it were Llafranc Bay. . ."

"Ramon is a terrific skipper. . ."

"A truly great skipper! Do you know what he told me when you were still under the prow. . . ? He said that when it's the mushroom season, which will soon be upon us, he wants to come to Sa Tuna to see his family, and if we meet up, he'll tow us. . ."

"Hermós, you're always wanting to be towed by someone or other. . . That betrays a servant's temperament. . ."

"So what? It makes no difference if you're master to a servant or servant to a master. Both positions are equally bothersome. But you can't do any different, just as you can't eat two dinners or smoke two cheroots at the same time. . ."

As I know one can't challenge Hermós's fixed ideas about society, I let it go.

"Do you know," I say, "I think the water here is blacker than ours?"

"Cadaqués is as black as a wolf's maw. You'll see. . ."

It's a pitch-black night. By the light of the stars the water is so blue and shiny it looks like dark syrup. When our oars hit the water, they scatter small spongy lights like fireflies and the wood gleams.

"It will soon be the Day of the Dead. . ." says Hermós, in a gruff, rather theatrical voice that pitches lower and lower.

"Why do you say that? What's the connection between a phosphorescent sea and the Day of the Dead?"

"That's what Big Boy used to say when we went paternostering and were starving. . ."

There is a lull.

"Don't raise your hopes," he continues. "We found it thus and will leave it ever thus."

At times this fierce, elemental fellow is unbearable and odious. He's like a geological sediment set unchangingly in granite.

As I'm rowing in the prow, I occasionally swing round to see where we are. But the darkness is impenetrable. All I can see is the shore silhouetted against the starry, luminous sky. After what seems a long, long time, white blotches appear out of the black: the houses in El Baluard. From where I'm sitting, I can see dismal, greasy lights appear, as if suspended in the air; they look like a vessel's signal lights.

"I've seen them. . ." says Hermós quickly. "They are three-masters or mizzen boats on their way to France. . ."

He speaks sententiously and confidently, as he does when speaking of marine matters.

With that my companion puts down his oars and takes out his cigarette case.

"Have we reached Farmàcia?"

"We're by El Poal, which is the same thing. Row for a while and then we'll cast out the grappling hook. We'll anchor with the prow to the wind and that will keep the flies at bay."

We each eat a slice of cold sausage with a hunk of bread and drink a half liter of wine, then we have a smoke and tidy our mattresses. Rowing is a delightful sport: it never exhausts you too much and leaves the body in just the right state to rest. We think bed is wonderful. Sleeping in a small boat is like returning to life in the womb for a few seconds. It's nice, though hardly easy to get used to.

3 October. When I wake up and poke my head out on deck, I feel agreeably secure: I am surrounded by houses. We are in the back of the egg that is Cadaqués Bay. When one is living out to sea, it can be comforting now and then *not* to see the horizon as just a thin line between the ocean and the sky. The infinite can be draining. It's easy not to see the horizon from Cadaqués. A telling detail.

I am struck by the silence over the town and intrigued by the contrast between the white of the houses, the bull's blood of the grand front doors and the mysterious dark green of olive trees against the gleaming black of slate and rock.

I yawn nonstop for almost a quarter of an hour. Then I spot a relaxed Hermós gesticulating on the quay while lecturing a venerable old gentleman. From time to time, this gentleman guffaws loudly.

I disembark and walk over, and Hermós introduces me to Don Víctor Rahola, who welcomes me in a way I shall never forget. Straight away we are invited to be his guests. While we walk at a leisurely pace toward his house, enjoying the sun and gulping on northwesterly gusts that shiver and shake us, Don Víctor tells us most amiably: "I'm so happy you're here. I've known Hermós my whole life: from when he came here for the first time with Joan Vergés and his friends, who were mine too. You'll keep me company. One needs company in Cadaqués. After lunch I like to play a game of *tresillo*. I have always relied on the cleric in town to vouchsafe my session. It never failed me. . . Now can you believe that the rector they've just appointed doesn't know how to play? Can you imagine anything more ridiculous or unthinkable? How on earth will we fill our afternoons in Cadaqués from now on? Try to grasp the importance of what I'm saying. If this rector is visited one day by his superiors in the hierarchy, if the bishop or the vicar-general appears, what will he do to relax them, so they can while away their time pleasantly at the rectory? Please tell me. Small-town life becomes unbearable if one can't enjoy a minimum of social life. A town priest who is ignorant of the rules of *tresillo* is an absurdity, an aberration, a huge error of judgment. I have asked the rector to come to my home tomorrow. I will teach him how the cards go. It is an urgent matter that cannot be deferred, especially when one thinks of his career in the church. I feel sorry for defenseless chaplains to an extent I am unable to conceal."

Don Víctor is a gentleman who has passed the fifty-year mark. He dresses like a rentier, with a South American touch; in the summer season: a peaked cap, blue-and-white-striped clothes, a white shirt with a perfectly ironed collar and sturdy, comfortable espadrilles. However, Don Víctor's rather anachronistic bourgeois features, his distinguished apparel, cannot camouflage his most marked trait: Don Víctor looks poor, absolutely, undeniably poor.

"I am sure," he himself says, "that the day I decide to sit on a stool in Carrer Petritxol with a hat on my knees, every passerby will give me a céntim or two."

His face is full of lumps and he sports a large salt-and-pepper beard. His lugubrious, bulging eyes carry a yellowish lymph where the pupils float amid a web of red veins, and his moist lips droop in a weary, unpleasant, sensual fashion. When these features take on a serious air, Don Víctor looks depressed. When they are animated, a mixture of irony, insight, subtlety and sensuousness lights up his face.

As I can see he has a slight limp, I ask him if he is in pain.

"I've been able to do next to nothing about my rheumatism this summer," he replies. "I've been very busy. I expect you are aware that I am a doctor. . ."

Hermós titters. Don Víctor says, "I see that Hermós doesn't have much faith in medicine. . . I have even less. . . Rheumatism is like so many other illnesses: we don't know the cause and there is no treatment. However, I use a remedy that really helps in my case. I have observed that sweat eases the pain. And now I have found a way to sweat at home. By dancing. . ."

"Dancing with a lady, naturally. . ."

"Forgive me, that might be taking it too far. . . I simply dance the polka with a chair for an hour every day. . ."

We drink espressos in the Casino and then visit the church. The old town of Cadaqués, with its narrow, sloping streets, vines spreading over house façades and fishing tackle everywhere, is stunningly picturesque. The main altar in the elevated church is flaming, baroque, full of movement.

"I know you have a very pretty altar in Palafrugell," he says. "I've seen it. . ."

"It's larger than the one here. . ."

"Yes, but this is subtler."

"That's quite possible."

Don Víctor stands and stares at me with an air of surprise. "I see that you have a tendency to accept someone else's. . . That's not very common."

"Thank you! No need to exaggerate. It's hard to throw off preferences, especially when they're homegrown."

As we leave the church, he suggests a visit to the Sant Baldiri hermitage, the cemetery and Port Lligat. I'm astonished by his generosity and tell him so.

"Oh, please! Can't you see I have nothing else to do?"

I don't think you could find a better guide in Cadaqués. The smallest detail becomes a pretext for him to speak vividly and at length, drawing on his prodigious memory, about this fascinating, remote place. His words flow with curiosity, emotion and love.

On the path to Port Lligat we meet a woman carrying a basket of fish who greets Don Víctor with a stream of strange, extravagant compliments. She is evidently a villager, but her attire hints at overblown ladylike pretensions: she wears an elaborate hairdo, a garish blouse covered in ribbons and bows, a skirt that went out of fashion five years ago and poor, sad-looking shoes with twisted heels. This getup makes her look a mixture of a bawd and a lady down on her luck.

Embarrassed by her extravagant circumlocutions – which remind me of the language used by gentlemen in my childhood – Don Víctor tries to sidestep her and slip away, as best he can, using us as his excuse.

"What a peculiar individual!" I exclaim.

"That's Lídia, daughter of Sabana, the last great witch we've had in Cadaqués. The poor woman thinks she is the *Ben Plantada*."

"Xènius's *La Ben Plantada*?"*

"Absolutely, Xènius's *La Ben Plantada*."

"That's curious. . . But does the female character in Xènius's novel have any connection to hereabouts?"

"That would be a tale long in the telling, you know, it's a very complicated business. In the first place, I should tell you that when people say that *La Ben Plantada* was constructed from elements of Barcelona, they don't really know what they're talking about. The *Ben Plantada* does have traits suggested by the poor woman I've just been speaking to, traits from Lídia and others related to a beautiful, majestic woman from Figueres. *La Ben Plantada* is a book that contains lots of elements from the Ampurdan and Cadaqués. Only minor details come from other places."

"Do you think the theory behind the book also stems from the Ampurdan?"

"I couldn't say. I'm hardly a man who deals in theories. . ."

Don Víctor understands why I'm curious and, as we walk slowly along, he recounts the following: "One day, when I was here, I received a letter from Doctor Ors, a colleague of mine working for the charity services in Barcelona. In this letter he told me that one

---

* A didactic novel written by Xénius, the pseudonym of Eugeni d'Ors (1881–1954), and published as a series of glosses in his column in the daily *La Veu de Catalunya*. The heroine stood for what d'Ors considered to be the eternal values of Catalonia. Pla tends to write ironically about a self-promoting, showy writer who went from defending Catalan values to the post of Franco's minister of culture. The novel has never been translated. The title suggests a beautiful woman who has strong roots and a resilient character.

of his sons, Eugeni, was planning to spend a few days in Cadaqués, because his health was rather delicate and he needed rest and a suitable diet. He added that his son would be bringing a friend. He then begged me to find an adequate private house that would treat them in the considerate, generous fashion the young man's poor health required.

"At the time, there was a very nice, well-mannered, good-looking fishwife by the name of Lídia who was the daughter of old Sabana, the town's last witch. She was married to a first-rate fisherman from Cape Creus and the couple had two small children. Lídia lived in La Riba in a house that was excellently situated, clean, well appointed, a house next to one owned by my cousin Tianet Rahola, the apothecary, who would later become harbor master. Lídia was a wonderful cook and managed a buoyant business to boot: the best fish taken from Cadaqués waters passed through her hands. I arranged terms: the two lads would stay in Lídia's house and pay four pessetes a day for full board.

"Subsequently, the mail coach deposited the two friends in Plaça de les Herbes: Eugeni Ors, who later converted to Eugeni d'Ors, and a young man by the name of Jacint Grau Delgado, also a writer, who spoke Spanish with a lisp. Grau Delgado has graced the Spanish stage with various works that have attracted a variety of comments. As for Eugeni d'Ors, one has only to mention his name these days: he is renowned, and controversial and has done very well for himself. As the two youths had come with my recommendation, I went to see them settle in at Lídia's house, and after a few days I felt duty bound to see how they were faring. I found they were fascinated, literally dazzled, and very happy with the house where they were lodged. It seemed they couldn't find sufficiently ecstatic words to describe their bliss.

"'Thiss, Sssenyor Rahola,' Grau Delgado told me, 'iss sso splendid. Good God, thiss lady cooksss us such fissh! She'sss such a wonderful cook! We're delighted! We couldn't be better looked after. . . '

"Indeed, both looked extremely well, had recovered their color and seemed in magnificent health. Eugeni Ors gave me a detailed and voluptuous description of the quality of the lobsters and crabs, black scorpionfish, Cape Creus mussels, groupers, sea bream and dentexes that Lídia habitually served. They couldn't credit what had come their way. I realized that the succulent local cuisine, prized for its quality, had led the two friends to see themselves as Renaissance men, according to the cliché in vogue about such individuals: a mixture of respected spiritual figure, man on the make and artist, which is usually the case when people feel they are at once Aretino, Boccaccio and Borgia. This rush of self-esteem usually happens when food is full of nitrogen and nitrates, and has the prodigious richness of victuals from these parts. What's more, there is excellent game near Cadaqués, so the fish was followed by partridges, rabbits and meaty woodcocks. . . In short: from my visit to their lodgings, I concluded that the euphoric well being of those young men of letters was both splendid and entirely visible."

Don Víctor pauses before continuing: "One of the undoubted reasons for good cooking is, as you know, the passion of love: good cooking can arise from love, in the hope that it will arouse an amorous response from the person loved. There are women who, when they fall passionately in love, tend to become patient, skillful, excellent cooks, all for the object of their love. Lídia had always been a good cook, but the degree of perfection and generosity she now brought to her culinary wisdom made me think she had fallen in love with the man who was later to be known as the Glosser. If it weren't for the intervention of a real, profound movement of the heart, that table would never have attained the level of distinction it did. Lídia's cooking brimmed over in a flood of tenderness transmuted into sauces, gravies, soups and broths. It was an apotheosis of palpable pleasures, exactly what is most appreciated by those who devote themselves to dry, philosophical word games.

"When I have sometimes reflected on these developments, I have concluded that Lídia's striking generosity and emotional abandon must have impressed Eugeni Ors to a degree that any normal person will understand. There was another decisive factor: the youth of this country is always at once turbulent and uptight. . . Youth is the only stage in life when a Catalan male isn't finicky, self-interested and ironic.

"Meanwhile, young Ors had begun his literary career through his surprising, controversial Glossary in La Veu de Catalunya. Perhaps the intuition of La Ben Plantada, the idea of La Ben Plantada, was previous to Ors's arrival in Cadaqués. I am in no doubt that in an attempt to repay Lídia's generosity, to thank her for the undeniable power of her culinary-emotional rapture, Ors did tell her at some stage that she was the Ben Plantada. It was a sincere compliment, though a rather measly recompense for the tasty feats of a passionate fishwife. The drama, the real drama, began when Lídia believed him. . . Perhaps you will ask: 'How could she have possibly believed him? Was she really as Ben Plantada as the compliment indicated?' Physically perhaps she was nothing out of the ordinary, but by any yardstick she was extremely curvaceous and lively; a veritable presence. I mean to say, she was as well set up as any woman in this land.

"Nothing untoward happened while the young literati stayed in Cadaqués. One day, however, they had to bring their sojourn to an end. They left on the mail coach, a bit plumper and weightier than when they arrived, to the sound of the things usually said in such situations: till next time. . . or till next summer. . . That departure was the beginning of that poor woman's ruination. For ages she sent the best fish she had to the Ors household in Barcelona. One day she even dared present herself, with her jaunty, common ways and a basket of fish, in the office of the Glosser himself. His family had no alternative but to invite her to lunch. They were embarrassed and quite at a loss as to how to handle the situation. Poor Lídia!

"That was when Ors began to publish *La Ben Plantada* in the Glosser's section in *La Veu de Catalunya*. Lídia found out and at once started telling people: 'You do realize I am the *Ben Plantada*, don't you? Yes, that's me, I am the *Ben Plantada*. . .'

"'Hey, here comes the *Ben Plantada*. . .' people started to say in Cadaqués.

"'You don't believe me? Ask the gentleman who lived in the house in Riba del Poal, ask Xènius. . .'

"And it was impossible to chase this obsession away. Lídia's obsession with Xènius and the compliment he'd paid her that one time became a delirious mania.

"Naturally, a book like *La Ben Plantada* contains highly amusing episodes. I am quite sure that specific details related to young Ors's stay in Cadaqués are in the book. Lídia is one of the many anecdotes held within its pages. However, nothing authorizes one to think that Lídia served as a model in the construction of *La Ben Plantada* as a category. But that's what the poor woman believed from the moment Xènius left Cadaqués, which happened to also be the point at which that good lady began to be a hazy memory, fading fast from the mind of that young man of letters.

"The person who really counted in the creation of the *Ben Plantada* as a category – to use Orsian terms – was the beautiful lady from Figueres I have already mentioned. Xènius's ideas about the elegance, grace and rootedness of ladies on this earth, the subtlest observations the book contains about life in this country, were driven by that woman. That lady was absolutely the *Ben Plantada*; she had perfect poise, was full of character. . . However, Lídia's obsession now verged on lunacy. And as the minute details of his stay here were relegated to the recesses of the writer's memory, the fishwife became more obsessed and broken by the vivid relief of her own memories.

"A series of tragic consequences followed. The family life of the wretched lunatic was destroyed. Lídia went into a limbo, immersed in her obsessive illusions, distanced from any practical matter or concern for hygiene. Her flourishing fish business was as neglected as the house in La Riba. Her husband, an excellent fisherman, went to live as a recluse in the rocky solitude of Culip and died in obscure circumstances. Her two children, who were twins, went mad and died on the very same day. As the years passed, the lunacy driven by her tragic obsession transformed Lídia into the spectacle you have just witnessed: the most depressing spectacle hereabouts.

"When Xènius, now at the peak of his renown, was the main judge in the Jocs Florals of Ampurdan held in Castelló d'Empúries, Lídia heard the news and went to the festivities. The whole time the Glosser stayed in the Ampurdan, Lídia didn't leave his side for a second. When he decided to go to Sant Pere de Roda, the poor madwoman didn't abandon him. The saddest of stories!

"The presence of that strange woman, dressed so eccentrically, her lunatic manner and insistent declarations that she and *only* she was the *Ben Plantada* intrigued society ladies in Figueres and Castelló and several visitors at the festival. Someone insinuated she might be Xènius's wet nurse. One lady dared ask him who she was.

"'Senyora,' replied Xènius, in an astonishingly solemn tone, with a hint of melancholy, 'Senyora, that woman is an atonement. . .'"

On our return from a most dismal Port Lligat, Don Víctor gives us lunch in his house. He offers us Cape Creus mussels, rice with grouper heads, bream stew, local cheese, coffee and French cognac. The lunch is indescribable.

After lunch, Hermós offers to play *tresillo*. Surprise all around.

"But Hermós, do you know how to play?" asks our friend gleefully. "Who do you play with?"

"Don't be so surprised. . ." says Hermós, glowing with local patriotism, "everybody in Palafrugell knows how to play *tresillo*. Even the ladies play it on the quiet. Donya Rosa Barris, whom you know and I serve, plays a fine hand."

"Good God!" laughs Don Víctor. And he instructs his maids to seek out two other players.

"Call in at the rectory," he says, "and tell the rector we shall start tomorrow. Today we'll have a school."

While we await the two gentlemen, Hermós, who is smoking a cigar and exhaling impressive clouds of smoke, tells us, enthused by the compliments he's been paid, that there once was a gentleman in Palafrugell, who is dead now, old Senyor P., who personally taught his children to play *tresillo*. When they were very young, their father took them for walks as soon as the good weather started. In the summer, Senyor P. sought out the shade of cork and pine trees, took a pack of cards from his pocket and gave his three children a lesson in *tresillo*.

"Did they turn out good players?"

"First class."

Hermós conveys to us that one of the best legacies Senyor P. left his children is their knowledge of *tresillo*. Don Víctor is amused. Our fellow players soon arrive: a doctor and an *americano* from the Cuban town of Camagüey. Very likable people.

The game lasts the entire afternoon. The room is filled with dense smoke and bliss: the players look to be having a wonderful time. If anyone is suffering, it is perhaps Hermós, because he has to concentrate too much and that inhibits him. No matter, he is happy. In this country, after lunch, *tresillo* players are a kind of incarnation of the highest form of happiness one can attain on this earth.

I spend the afternoon looking at the books in the library. Other people's libraries always hold pleasant surprises.

We say goodbye at supper time. In any case tomorrow morning Senyor Rahola wants to tow us behind his motorboat as far as Portaló. Hermós is beaming: he is a resolute supporter of this kind of sailing.

Back on board we have a bite to eat and get into our cots. Our vessel is anchored on the shore of El Poal. My final survey of the town gives me an overwhelming sense of remote solitude. Its small lights glint faintly on the mysterious, black harbor waters.

4 *October.* Don Víctor, in the stern of his vessel, sails swiftly toward ours before nine. It's a sparkling day: a northwesterly breeze, a limpid sky, a delightful sun, cool, fresh air. We secure the towrope, and embark by Don Víctor's side, intending to pull our boat without using the rudder.

"We'll go as far as we can. . ." says Don Víctor, as his sailor starts the engine.

"The weather looks good," I reply.

"We'll see by Cape Creus. . ."

We hug the coast as we follow the bay round, entranced by the silence of the olive trees on land. We sail around the island of S'Arenella, which belongs to our friend. Hermós admires Don Víctor hugely, but when he discovers that he owns an island, his enthusiasm grows in leaps and bounds. His eyes gleam when he glances his way; he is thrilled to be so close to him. I anticipate how often Hermós will boast that he knows a man who owns an island. . . Then we turn into Mar d'Avall and marvel at the rocky majesty of the landscape. Don Víctor, at the tiller, knows every single coastal contour and name.

When we sail by Port Lligat, I think of the tragic story of Lídia, which my shocked subconscious links to the previous day's splendid lunch. I can't resist the temptation to tell Don Víctor that one eats extremely well in Cadaqués. He listens and can hardly hide the pleasure my compliment gives him.

"Yes, senyor," he says. "One eats wonderfully well in Cadaqués. In my book, better than anywhere else. I don't know if you have ever traveled abroad." I shake my head. "I have a little. I've not found a cuisine like it in the whole of Europe. For my taste, cooking with butter is inferior to the cooking here, even the sophisticated, impressive French cuisine. Cooking with butter is characterless, dull, how can I put it? Cooking that seems touched by the light of the moon. . ."

"How curious!" I interject. "Garreta says exactly that about French music. . ."

"What does Maestro Garreta say about French music?"

"He says precisely that: it is music touched by the light of the moon, rather wan, lifeless, lacking sun, that full, radiant, strong, explosive energy. . . And I don't mean explosive in the manner of regimental music, but in the sense that it is full of vitality. . ."

"Exactly so. The cuisine of Cadaqués has three unique ingredients: the water, the quality of the fish and the oil from the olive trees you can see now. They offer a culinary base of unrivaled quality. It's an incomparable cuisine that gives an emphatically solar, beaming, tasty aspect to its raw materials. The fish taken from these waters, which are so pure and driven by such strong currents, cooked with this oil and the light sauces made here, infuse the blood of humans with exhilarating fullness and transcendent energy. In other places, the origin of many things may be spiritual; here the source of everything is almost always the substance of the raw material."

"I don't understand any of that," says Hermós, who feels the need to interject, "but I'm sure Senyor Rahola is right."

"Are you at all familiar with other kinds of cooking?" asks Don Víctor.

"Yes, senyor. I've gone to peel cork in the hills of Toledo, in Extremadura and Algeria. . ."

"If you've visited only those places, it's not surprising you appreciate what I say."

"Don Víctor, if you only knew how much I suffered away from this country when the time came to eat! May lightning strike them!"

The coast shelters us from the northwesterly and allows us to sail slowly and majestically. As we draw nearer to Cape Creus, the swell visibly increases. Beyond Massa d'Oros we see white horses thrown up by fresh gusts. As we round the cape we meet strong winds and a crashing sea. Neither Don Víctor nor his boatswain says a word: it's the usual local weather and they find it completely normal. They secure the towrope and, excellent at the tiller, Don Víctor makes the most of every sheltered spot on the coast to avoid the pounding waves and intermittent downpours.

We sail like that for a long time, painfully slowly. Our tug has a small engine and our progress is grievous. Even so, we round the bend into Portaló, find shelter there, and then embark in our boat, after bidding farewell to our generous, unforgettable friends.

"And our thanks to you. . ." says Don Víctor with a grin, beginning his return to Cadaqués. As we watch his vessel sail into the distance, we see him waving goodbye with the whitest of handkerchiefs.

Portaló is a narrow funnel of the shallowest water cut into the mineral cataclysm that is the plain of Tudela. As the wind and sea aren't at all favorable and we are hungry, we decide to head to the tiny beach and wait for better weather. We check our provisions and realize we are running short.

"You," says Hermós imperiously, "jump on land and make a fire, wherever you can, while I go and try my luck with the cast net. . ."

On the beach, I'm immediately struck by the solitude of that place, reinforced by the deserted communal hut, a deep silence floating on the wind and the distant echo of the sea crashing against the rocks. I reflect on the number of times I have proclaimed my love of solitude, yet how unappealing I find the idea of spending more time than is necessary in Portaló. Vanity and petulance make us spout so much nonsense! While I'm searching for firewood, I think I glimpse the eyes of a fox behind the corner of a rock. Of course, it's a figment of my imagination. But I suspect that if Hermós wants to stay in Portaló, I will use the eyes of this fox I've never seen to scare him off and make him change his mind.

There is little in the way of wood. I use all the rubbish the sea has deposited on this small solitary strand. I find a lady's shoe in a remarkable state of preservation. I add it to the sparse bundle of reeds, strips of cork bark, and scraps of wood I have collected. I create a space for the fire with three rocks and try to light it. Literally speaking, it isn't the first time I have tried to do this; in any case, lighting a fire is such an elemental activity! After using ten or twelve matches, I'm dismayed to see that the fire isn't taking. I start doubting my ability. I try again. But however often I do so, the result is the same. I can't light a fire. I can't light a fire! I have used up a whole box of matches and the fire isn't lit. Lighting a fire appears not to be as elemental and simple as I'd thought. I'm embarrassed and feel extremely ridiculous. All that buoyant exuberance in almost every aspect of my life, and now I had really fallen short: I'm unable to light a fire cradled by three rocks. I think: if only I had the strength of mind to cherish that episode! However, in a few hours' time I'll be once again holding forth frivolously and light-headedly on whatever topic crops up, and will have forgotten I couldn't light that fire. I feel irritated and uncomfortable with myself. Perhaps the most stupid thing in life is the way we are permanently inclined to forget our own futility, our own ineffable, intrinsic ineptitude.

Hermós arrives in the boat. He brings a magnificent tray of mackerel. However, he seems silent and down: it must be the void left by the departure of Don Víctor. When he notices I've not lit the fire, he reacts indignantly. He bawls at me. I respond: "Hermós, I have a confession to make..."

"What's the matter?"

"I must tell you that I was unable to light a fire..."

He goes over to the stones, looks at the firewood, touches it and says: "This fire can be lit. The wood is dry."

He slightly changes the position of one rock and applies a match, and the fire lights...

"Now you can tell everyone I couldn't light a fire. I'm hopeless, a total disaster."

He stares at me for a while and then grins and says: "But didn't you know that men like you are good for nothing? You never know which way the wind is blowing. . ."

We eat grilled mackerel with vinaigrette. They taste a touch bitter, and deliciously fresh. Then we drink coffee. We eat our lunch in silence. We eat the fish on slices of bread, glancing at the sky from time to time. Meanwhile, we see that the northwesterly is slowly abating. The long white horses disappear. Shortly, a gentle southeasterly breeze blows up.

"What are you planning to do now?" I ask Hermós when he's finished tidying things up.

"We'll raise the sail and off we go to Portbou. . ."

"Do you want to make it in one day? It's quite a long way."

"If we can. . ."

We hoist the canvas within the cove of Portaló. The light wind favors us.

"It is a light wind. And aren't they light. . . !" says Hermós, thinking of lobster catchers. Lobster catchers, when they haul their creels aboard, always say, "Aren't they're light?" And then after a short pause Hermós says, "Take the tiller. I must catch up on my sleep. If the wind strengthens, you handle it. If it stops, give me a shout! When you see Portbou, turn landward."

He stretches out on the boards, lights a cigar and is soon blissfully asleep. He dozes off staring at the open sky. Dozing off like that must be like turning the blue of the sky inside out. His cheroot dangles from his lip and over his cheek. It's a comical sight.

We make little headway. It is a limp southwesterly, but all the same, the coastline trundles by, imperceptibly, like life itself. "The patient use the sail," say sailors. After four or five hours sailing, late into the twilight, we arrive opposite Portbou. I wake up Hermós. I hear a train whistle. We anchor on the small quay. I register the precision of the place-name – "Port-oxen." The mountains within which Portbou is tucked have bovine shapes. The town seems animated. From the quay, one can see glowing cafés.

We spruce up a bit and jump on land. We order an aperitif on the terrace of one establishment. Suddenly, two tables over, we spot our dear friend Morató, universally known in the Lower Ampurdan and Palafrugell as Zorrilla. Boisterous cries of delight. Morató thinks we have come by train. He refuses to believe we have come by sea, from Calella, in such a small sailing dinghy. When he accepts that we have, after we've insisted time and again, he suggests we go and say hello to the mayor.

"We should. . ." says Hermós enthusiastically. "You have to keep in with the powers that be. . ."

I'm on the verge of throwing the saucer for the glass of absinthe at his head. I restrain myself.

Morató is a man who is always ready to join in whatever life has to offer. He works in Portbou with some members of his extended family. He departs for a moment and reappears shortly thereafter with bottles of magnificent French champagne. We're all set to go. I struggle to stop Hermós from singing "Vostè que s'en va a Nàpols" at the top of his voice in the middle of the café. Morató is a great fan of theatrics, and of singing, hunting, eating and drinking, declaiming, and generally of anything that helps kill time uproariously. He is a tall, thin, fairish man, with large earlobes and a dynamic, engaging character. He's the Ampurdan sort who is spontaneous, rather childish, playful, light as a feather and frivolous. We spend the night with him. Vast quantities of alcohol. Afterward I don't dare ask how our night in Portbou ended. I barely remember a thing.

5 October. At around nine thirty a.m., the sea is placid, the sky cloudless and there's no hint of a wind. The sun is bright but gets cooler by the hour. We row off after stocking up on supplies and drinking cups of black coffee. The previous night has left us feeling weary and moody.

We reach the post indicating the frontier, rowing mechanically, in silence. When the post is behind us, Hermós says: "We're now in French waters. What do you reckon?"

"That's obvious enough!"

"Aren't you pleased? Who'd have thought it?"

"I'm surprised it's so calm. What do you think the weather will do?"

"The day hasn't settled yet, but I'm sure it will be the mistral. In this neck of the woods when the wind's not sure what to do, it's always a northwesterly."

We make slow progress. Cape Béar, the color of brown stew, stands out clearly. The atmosphere is radiant, delicate, crystal clear: time for the mistral, naturally. Hermós is staring hard at the horizon on the French side. Suddenly, as we are about to turn around Cape Cerbère, he stands up straight and, pointing to a blotch on the sea, says:

"What can you see over there?"

"I see a buoy. It must be marking out some creels."

"Forget the buoy! Farther on, past that. . ."

"It looks like a ship. . ."

"Right. It's a war ship, a coastguard ship, or perhaps a gun boat. . ." he says excitedly, turning quite pale.

"Well, so what?" I say. "What do you mean?"

"What do I mean? For Christ's sake! I mean I don't like the look of that ship one bit. I don't want to be near that kind of vessel. They scare me. They are much worse than the little skiffs belonging to the customs police. . ."

"But that vessel is at least four miles away. It can't even see us."

"You won't convince me it can't see us. Those vessels miss nothing. They carry all sorts of telescopes. Compared to their telescopes, the one Senyor Joanola has in El Canadell is like a drinking glass."

We row for a stretch. The houses of Cerbère heave into sight, their rooftops a roast-beef red. What most surprises me when we pass the frontier is the way the color of roofs immediately change. However, Hermós is getting increasingly agitated. I'm intrigued to know what he'll decide to do.

Out of the corner of my eye I can see he's making an effort and building up some Dutch courage. He says imperiously: "Take my word for it! Let's turn our back on that vessel and get on our way this instant."

"Hermós, that isn't the deal?"

"What do you mean 'that isn't the deal'?" he asks, up in arms.

"Weren't we supposed to go to France? This is what people call a cop-out."

"Yes, right: it's exactly what they call a cop-out, but I give the orders here, don't I?"

And trying to impress me even further, he punches the floor of the boat so hard it almost makes the vessel tip. Then he restates his position: "Besides, you know I really don't like these wars. . ."

"Don't you worry yourself. We can argue about that back in Palafrugell. . ."

To dispel any sense that I think he's being ridiculous, I adopt the jauntiest look from my repertoire. We turn around, hoist the sail and a northerly tail wind slowly pushes us along. After that maneuver, he looks relieved, as if a huge burden has been lifted from his shoulders. However, he soon swings to the other extreme: he seems depressed.

We start preparing lunch with the food we bought in Portbou. He lights the fire and says we'll have a stew and a boil-up at two, weather permitting.

"Head for Cape Creus, and when lunch is ready," he says "we'll eat lunch. . ."

"Don't you want to stop in Port de la Selva?"

"There's a police control in Port de la Selva, and you know we're not carrying any papers. There's always the chance we'll get put in the slammer. . ."

No doubt about it: today is a fantastic day for acting the fool.

When the frontier post has completely disappeared from sight, Hermós starts singing a *havanera*. Then he strikes up with "Vostè que s'en va a Nàpols" at the top of his voice.

It continues to be a magnificent, clear, sunny, sparkling day. The northerly breeze hardly ripples the gleaming mirror of the bluest of seas. Our progress is slow but steady. It's delightful. By five p.m., we're opposite Culip. For a moment I anticipate that Hermós will want to spend the night there. I'm wrong. I hear him say: "It might be better if we slept the other side of Norfeu. . . There won't be so many mosquitoes there. In times of war, perhaps it *is* best to keep your head down. . ."

It's crisp and calm by Jugadora Cove. Darkness begins to fall. The Cape Creus lighthouse switches on. We lower our sail and row close to the shore. We cross Port Lligat Bay in the pitch black and leave through the northwesterly strait which is full of rocks and reefs, blindly finding our way. We strike submerged reefs and almost break an oar. Even so, despite the dark, dark night, Hermós finds his bearings. We row the full length of Cadaqués Bay, then row on for hours until we reach Jònculs, quite exhausted. It's a long way to row from Jugadora Cove to Jònculs. Hunger and fatigue at sea produce a state of physical sanctity, an impoverished form of Franciscan sentiment. We anchor on the beach, our prow to the wind, and in no mood to eat, we doze off in a mineral sleep triggered by empty stomachs and aching bones. It must be past one a.m.

6 *October*. We raise our sail midmorning with a fresh northeasterly breeze and point the prow to the bank of the River Fluvià. The wind hits our stern full on.

To the west, the luminous lands of the gulf are dazzling. Sea and sky are simply glorious. It is on days like this that I understand the captivation the sea and air generate in our sickly spirits. There are moments when the sea is so wonderful, so delightful, so fulfilling that however much one resists the flow, all else seems meager and puny. When I think about such moments – and I'm experiencing one now – I feel most envious of Hermós. He has sacrificed everything to enjoy these moments in their full. Beyond the sea, nothing interests him. I am so much younger than he is, and feel that youthfulness in my veins, but I'm but a feeble apprentice writer and ridiculous, recalcitrant barfly.

Hermós lights the stove. One or two hours before waking me up, he threw a multiple-hooked fishing line into the water and caught a tray of shimmering, iridescent combers and catfish. Now it's a matter of putting them in the pan and turning them into one of the finest meals on offer in these parts. I watch him. When boats sail with a back wind, they constantly dip and sway. This means that at any second the oil may spill, the pan fall, the stove roll onto the floor. To avoid that, Hermós is forced to hug the stove and the pan all the while. He's wonderfully skilled. Not a single drop of oil falls from the pan. He reacts perfectly to the swaying of the boat.

"Congratulations, Hermós!" I exclaim, when I see he has fried the fish.

"That's all right!" he replies, rather stiffly and seriously, with an undertone that reflects the previous day's deplorable events.

We breakfast while we head toward the bank of the Fluvià. The taste of the fish, bread, oil and wine is so intense and subtle, so close to the genuine, real taste of things, that it is rapturous. Eating good, fresh, delicately flavored food in the open air is immeasurably precious. The difficult bit is coping with the open air. Hermós lives there as if he is in his native element. I, less so.

It's ten days since I left home and I'm beginning to feel fatigued. It's been a long time since I had any contact with this life. While I eat and drink, I feel the fresh air on my skin, the voluptuous light, the divine warmth of the sun. It is pleasant, nay, magnificent. . . but I immediately feel a kind of nostalgia prompted by inner weariness. A nostalgia for an air that is still, a light that is weaker, a sun that is dimmer. I think about how this open-air life we're now leading, at once immediate and boundless, may be quite incompatible with the degree of foolishness an urban culture creates. In other words: the tragedy is that a moment comes in life when one can tolerate only bottled sun and the fresh air described in books. Culture is a sickly form of life.

There's a brisk wind and we make rapid progress. The town of Roses stretches out before us bathed in a light that seems freshly made and alive. Lime white, shadows the color of black bread, apricot roofs.

"Don't take us so close to Roses!" says Hermós, looking at me out of the corner of his eye, with the yellowy gaze of a rabid dog. "The harbor master will see us and stick us inside. Remember, we don't have papers. . ."

Outside the Fluvià quay we see a boat fishing. Of course, we know the silt in the river mouth means the underwater sandbanks are constantly changing position and height, and that makes entry dangerous. To find out the latest on entry conditions, we draw close to the boat. Two men are rowing hard and dragging a net to catch shellfish. Hermós bellows: "Where's the entrance to the river?"

The men keep rowing as if they've heard nothing.

The sea crashes against almost the entire quayside. Seagulls fly above the glinting crests of the waves, above the foam that the wind blows away. A group of herring gulls stands motionless on the crimson sand of the beach, like a line of penguins.

We lower the flat sail and lock in our oars. We keep clear of the breakwaters. We assume the men in the boat didn't hear us, and draw even closer. Hermós shouts out again: "Where's the entrance to the river?"

As yet again he gets no response, he hollers and gesticulates violently.

"Are you mad or what?" he shouts wildly, like a lunatic.

Finally alerted by his gestures, the fishermen wave their hands and shake their heads strangely, as if apologizing for their lack of reaction.

"Now I understand!" says Hermós, laughing raucously and showing his teeth. "These men are deaf-mutes like the people you sometimes see around Canaletes. What do you bet that's what they are? It's very odd to come across deaf-mutes at sea, for Christ's sake. It's like being served an empty bottle of wine. . ."

The deaf-mutes continue to make signs with their hands and pull all kinds of faces. Hermós contemplates them for a while and then waves his arms at them in a blood-curdling, obscene fashion. Suddenly he makes up his mind . . . He grabs the tiller with both hands, turns the stern toward the waves and lets the boat be driven by the force of the sea. Everything happens as quick as lightning. Our dinghy rises on the back of a wave and, as if driven by an invisible power, is speedily deposited in the placid, murky waters of the river mouth. We're slipped in there in a second. If we'd have brushed against a sandbank, it would have turned us over. The wave was eminently sensible and took us through the most feasible channel. . .

Now we're in the middle of the river, we hoist our sail, and Hermós looks at me seeking approval for his latest crazy feat. When I feel I've recovered from my panic, I compliment him. He replies, contentedly: "When you are in that kind of jam, you have to do something or other. . ."

The northeasterly pushes us further upstream, through reddish, muddy waters. The bank on the right is low and green. The one on the left is a three- or four-yard-high embankment, an expanse of rich loam that glistens in the sun. As we push on upstream, the river bends gently and the current drops. A countryman ploughing behind a plump, pompous mare comes slowly into sight. A cart squeaks along the river bank. We pass a barge, bloated like a frog, hanging over the water. The peaceful countryside and silent land are as restful as a feather pillow. When you've just left the sea, land seems so peaceful and safe! As we sail upstream, the current becomes almost imperceptible. The water becomes shallower. Reeds and bulrushes grow on the mud of the banks. We anchor under the bridge in Sant Pere Pescador. Past its arches women are beating washing on rocks. A Gypsy caravan stands under rusty, autumnal leaves.

"Are you thinking we might sleep in Sant Pere?" I ask Hermós.

"No. We'll wait until the wind from inland can carry us downstream. In the meantime, we should go to the barber's. . ."

Hermós is sporting a five- or six-day-old beard and looks like a bandit. I must be a tubercular shade of gray. We make for the village. The streets are full of fat, moribund flies that buzz between the patches of sun, awaiting the cold lash of death. It must be lunch time, because there's a cow mooing behind every front door. There is a great amount of dung and piss, or something of the sort, in the streets. We have swapped the distilled purity of sea air for that horrendous stench. People exude pungent vapors. The smell of the Latin race.

The barbershop – where small yellowish plates dangle over the door – is filthy. The wallpaper is covered in fly shit. A dense, dank fug floats in the air: a smell of poor families, cheap perfumes and the effluvia of domestic animals. The barber is the chatty, cheerful local sort, wearing a dingy, almost mourning-black apron that hangs down to his feet. He has an iron hand – and this epithet, usually reserved for presidents – must have its origins in barbershops. He scrapes stubble with a razor as if he were using his nails. We inevitably suffer for a while, but when we leave, at any rate, we must look quite different and probably much more presentable. The barber's hand has given Hermós the air of a thinker of the anarchist variety. My expertly clipped fringe makes me look clownish.

We wait for a decent wind to blow, and roam the elegant banks of the Fluvià. We stretch out in the sun for a while on the cool grass. We listen to the distant noise of the bells of cows who are slowly chewing their cud. As soon as dusk descends, the sad, muted song of crickets reaches us.

The wind doesn't seem to be in a hurry to blow up, so we embark in our boat and row downriver. The current helps us along. The belfry in Sant Pere, orange in the sunset, is silhouetted above the smoke. We hear the sound of carts wearily returning to the village from the surrounding fields, the clatter of a flock of tired mares and the weary monotone of crickets.

We reach the quayside as darkness falls and slip out without any difficulty. The becalmed sea is a great help. When we are past the sandbanks and in the open sea, we hoist our sail and a cold, light wind blows up. The wind from inland allows us to tack our way to L'Escala. It takes us three hours, as smooth as could be. In the course of the silent, uneventful crossing, I ask Hermós: "Why did you decide to go upriver to Sant Pere?"

"To give us something to talk about in the café. . ." he responds, after giving it a moment's thought, decisively, as if he were being totally sincere.

Despite the new moon, it is too dark to see his face when he makes that statement. I wouldn't want to bear false witness, but I reckon those words don't come at all easily.

7 October. We spent an unremarkable day in L'Escala. Autumn is advancing, like a slow-paced convalescent. Everything is turning more fragile. It's been a gray day: an opaque, pearl-white day, with the sea a wan blue, almost green, its surface tracked by huge, dead waves. Roses Bay, in gray and pearl, is an exquisitely gentle, ineffably beautiful sight. Horizons dissolve in a pale-blue haze where the contours of mountains are ever shifting, weightless, purple and mauve. Autumnal smoke floats languidly above the plains. White, wispy trails rise up from the town's chimneys, slowly and morosely fading in the pallid sky.

I walk a roundabout route, unhurriedly, along the streets to the Casa Gran, close to which Vadoret Sala, the ship carpenter, has his workshop. L'Escala is an earthen, brown-stew-colored town. It has few amenities and seems neglected. Its population is a mixture of fishermen and country folk. Next to a woman mending a net sits another hulling broad beans. It's all rather charmless, dreary, gray and dusty.

Vadoret has left two or three skiffs out in the street. There's a pulley between the skiffs. He wants to bend this pulley slightly. He lights a small fire next to the timber. It is resinous pinewood and fills the air with a delightful smell. It crackles and flames cheerfully. A couple of feet from the master carpenter, a young lad with a brush is applying hot tar to the old keel of a boat. The mixture of the smell of tar and the scent of pinewood is marvelous. The air is thick with that scent, which seems to impregnate everything. Herring gulls keep flying over the workshop yard.

Vadoret works in silence. He is a most laconic man, today more than ever. I'm grateful for the silence. This is a day for being distracted rather than talking. I can't concentrate: I feel aimless and at a loss. I've been exhausted by an excess of fresh air.

On the way back to the port, I bump into Donya Caterina Albert. I greet her respectfully. With her hair cut à *la garçonne*, her sparkling, velvety eyes, her pallor (which comes from working at night), her simple attire – a jewel on her chest – and petiteness, I find her more alert than ever. I don't attempt to speak about literary matters: whenever I've tried, I have had to desist because it is impossible to break through this lady's unassailable modesty. Víctor Català is the most modest writer there is. She brings a most pleasant femininity and volubility to the conversation, but I've often wondered whether her chatter wasn't a deliberate façade. I have always thought that façade hides an unusual tenacity and gentle firmness. She is a woman who cuts her own path in life, who is absolutely on her own, hermetic and inured to any kind of "uncontrolled" influences. She makes a most striking impression on me: human frailty that is constantly and consciously being overcome.

Laughing loudly, she tells me how some days ago a huge herring gull with a broken wing fell into her garden and that the big wild bird, rather than dying – as she and everybody initially thought it would – began adapting to a domesticated life, with few problems.

"What do you think?" she asks me. "Perhaps this magnificent bird could get used to living in my flat on Carrer València in Barcelona. . . Wouldn't that be a great pity!"

She says all this with a mixture of candor and irony that acts ineffably, mysteriously upon the listener. And when we are saying our goodbyes: "Come and take a look!" she says. "It's not a highly stimulating sight for a young writer, but it's not without interest. . ."

Hermós, whom I haven't seen since the start of the day, comes back in the evening and tells me that tomorrow morning, whatever the weather, Ramon Pins will tow us to Sa Tuna behind his boat.

"Whatever the weather?" I ask.

"Ramon has heard what people are saying. . ."

When I take to my boat bed that night, I feel yet again that the mattress is as uncomfortable and horrible as it was on that first day. It's absolutely hopeless: I can't adapt. I am a man corrupted by creature comforts, pleasing surfaces and the good life.

In the early morning – after an extremely sleepless night – I hear the wind whistling. Yet again the mistral has its sights on us.

8 October. By eight a.m., it's a brisk mistral, but Ramon says he's hoping it will drop when the sun warms up. He gives the order to set sail immediately. Ramon takes two or three men from his usual crew and suggests I join them in his longboat. Our sailing dinghy is carrying too much weight. That way Hermós will be on his own and can organize the rudder to ensure the best tow possible. Everything's agreed.

As we leave harbor, the wind and sea hit us in the stern, making us sway violently. Our boat leaps over the sea like a kid goat. At times, the boat leaps too high, it's speeding dangerously and Ramon orders them to reduce speed. And that's how we sail along the rugged Torroella coast. We turn with Cape Salines and the coast gives us fair shelter as far as L'Estartit, but when we sail past Pals Beach, the wind and sea turn rough once again.

After reaching this point, Ramon would have clearly preferred to head directly to Sa Tuna, but he discontinues this strategy due to the foul weather. He does so without flapping or moving a single muscle of his face. In effect, he decides to skirt the beach's sandbanks, an operation that only someone really familiar with the local sea could do. This allows him to sail – given the way the wind is blowing from the beach across his stern– along the strip of water that is being punished least by the gusts and is, as a result, considerably calmer. We cut close to the underwater sandbanks that are visible from the side of the ship, under turbulent but transparent water, and don't hit a single one.

Seated next to Ramon, I glance now and then at Hermós, who is controlling his boat's rudder, his gaze fixed on our stern. When we turn to sail along the beach, he seems edgy and apprehensive for a second and can't hide the fact, but then Ramon's confident, agile command of the tiller brings a smile back to his face.

Once we reach Torre de Pals, the boat moves away from the beach and Ramon points his prow toward Ses Negres. We have a tail wind as we did along the Torroella coast, perhaps blowing even more fiercely now. We make a glorious entry into Sa Tuna Bay.

"That's what you call sailing, Ramon!" says Hermós, greeting his approach to land with an enthusiasm he can barely repress. "You're a champion. . ."

"That was the only way to do it. . ." says Ramon shyly, but confidently. "If I'd gone too far out to sea, your dinghy could have been in trouble. . ."

Those were the only words I heard him utter on the whole trip. He then anchored his longboat, said goodbye and scampered up the path to Begur.

Hermós is welcomed enthusiastically by the inhabitants of Sa Tuna, three or four families and two single men. Everybody knows him. When he says we've come from France, people's eyes bulge out of their sockets. Pere d'En Lor, a fisherman, also known as Pere Pagell, offers us his kitchen range to make lunch. We go to his house.

The kitchen fills up with people. It's a bright, sunny, radiant day, but not one to be outside: the wind is blustery, cold and unsettling.

We buy a magnificent wreckfish from Pagell. Hermós suggests making a stew with a spoonful of aioli. Everyone offers to help. He likes that. He likes to order people about. According to him, the two most pleasant things in this world are knowing how to play the guitar and knowing how to get people to work. Meanwhile, we prepare a succulent repast.

As I'd heard a story years ago concerning Pere Pagell – to be precise, the story of a box of pound sterling – when we're on our coffees, I ask him if he can tell us about that incident, if in fact there ever was one.

"There's no question about there being an incident. . . !" says the fisherman, rather shamefaced.

Pagell is a middle-aged man of middling height, with a face covered in red freckles and a salt-and-pepper mustache and beard. He's slim and has a stoop. He looks every inch a tireless toiler and is very poor, very fatalistic, and extraordinarily good-natured.

"Just imagine," he says, "I was out with two other men from Begur, who have since died, fishing for lobster in the Llims' reefs, the most distant part of the Llims. One morning, when we were raising the creels, we saw a small box floating over the sea. We gathered it up, and once we'd finished work, we broke the lock. The box was very well made from fine wood, and although it had been in the water for many a day, it hadn't let in a single drop. There was a bundle of papers inside. We read them but couldn't understand a word. They were pieces of white paper with beautifully shaped letters. The three of us in the boat agreed they were worthless. We threw them into the sea as if they were newspaper cuttings. But we did like the little box. We reckoned it would soon fetch ten pessetes in Begur. We threw all the bits of paper away, except for two or three that happened to drop in the bilge.

"When we reached Sa Tuna, Senyor Nap came over to the boat to see what we had caught and buy the odd fish. As we were haggling, we showed him the little box and told him about the bits of paper. 'The papers were like this. . . ' I said, showing him one that was half-wet, which I rescued from under the stern seat.

"Nap gave the paper a long, hard look. He looked at it back and front and against the light. He was a man who knew about the commercial world. He did the books for the cooperative. He finally said: 'Were all the bits of paper you threw away like these?'

"We said we thought they were. In fact, they were exactly the same. Nap looked at us sadly and very oddly: I'd never seen him give a look like that before.

"'So what is that bit of paper, Senyor Nap?' I asked.

"'It's a sterling five-pound note. . .'"

Hermós, who listened to the story spellbound, cannot contain himself: "That's what I call playing the burro. . ."

"You might well say that, Hermós, yes, you might. . ." says Pagell's wife blankly, as if she were talking about the weather.

When he finishes telling his story, Pagell is as dumbstruck as he was on the day that Nap made that revelation. His face becomes angelic when he says, a moment later: "In any case we'll cock our toes up all the same. . . They gave us three duros for the box. . ."

"Three burros!" snaps Hermós furiously, his cap on the tilt.

A painful silence follows. Everyone looks at Pagell, who simply sits and stares into the bottom of his empty glass. To clear the air once and for all, I ask him: "So, Pere, what did you think of the incident? What do you think now?"

"What do you expect a poor wretch like me to think? That money. . . and there was a lot of it . . . wasn't ours. It came from a shipwrecked vessel or someone who'd lost it! God knows!"

"And that's all?"

"Sometimes I've also thought that frankly there's no merit to being poor. Anyone, however quiet he keeps it, can be. . ."

After spending the afternoon with those good people, we join them for supper. When it's time for bed, they offer us a spot by the fireside. Hermós declines.

"Pagell, there are too many rats in Sa Tuna, too many rats to be sleeping on the floor."

"Yes, there is the odd one, Hermós, there is the odd one. . ." says the fisherman's poor wife, resignedly, respectfully, routinely.

9 *October*. The wind blew briskly throughout the night, but by midday calm was restored and we set off. Ramon Pins has come down from Begur with a basket of mushrooms. He boards his longboat, starts the engine and sets out for L'Escala. We row out later. We meet a choppy sea round Cape Begur but survive. Fornells Bay gives us a light inland wind. We hoist our sail, and thus, with the help of that breeze and a placid sea, reach Port Bo in Calella by sunset. We have supper on board: a fry up of fresh fish.

After supper, Hermós goes to Can Batlle, the tavern. I imagine the warm welcomes he will receive. I try to shave by the ship's light, which is so weak it's a real struggle. Then I put on clean clothes and jump on land.

Through the half-open tavern door, I watch Hermós holding forth to twenty or twenty-five gawping fishermen. Marieta is looking at him – she is a tall, sturdy, stout woman, with a small mustache and a bovine stare – as if she were contemplating her own son. His speechifying must have begun some time ago, because I can see three or four empty wine glasses lined up in front of him. From the doorway – the street is deserted – I hear him recounting, in minute, childish detail our adventures in Banyuls, Port-Vendres and Collioure.

To avoid any unpleasant arguments over his version of events, I decide to go back to bed and sleep.

Early the next morning Hermós returns with a gutful of wine, clearly happy with himself and in a petulant mood. When he sees I am awake, he comes over and whispers in a hoarse, aphonic voice: "If they only knew! I really fooled them. . . You'd have enjoyed it!"

10 October. I get up thinking that our excursion must be at an end, but Hermós suggests we go to Palamós for the day in our sailing dinghy.

"So what do you want to do in Palamós?" I ask.

"I've so many friends there. We'll have a good time!"

He pauses and then, plucking up courage, though always a touch timidly, he says: "What's more, that rascal En Gilet told me there's a blonde around with a hairdo and fair skin to cause an earthquake. . ."

"You like fair skin?"

"If it's not fair, it's not worth a thing!"

"But Naval Command is there. . . How will we manage without papers?"

"No worries in Palamós. One gentleman there deals with all that, you know?"

"And who might that gentleman be?"

"Senyor Gaspar Matas, whom you've met already."

We unload part of our tackle and set off midmorning with a wind from inland. However, by the Formigues strait it's all calm and we have no choice but to pick up our oars. It's almost a winter's day, bright, chilly and biting.

It's a hellish row from the Formigues strait to the port of Palamós. To make matters worse, a southwesterly wind blows up opposite Els Canyers and doesn't go away. Fortunately, it too is light. When we reach the end of the breakwater, I feel exhausted. We make for Sa Catifa and when we're close we see a man smoking a cigarette in the stern of a large coal barge. He is middle aged and the whitest of mustaches stands out against his coffee-colored face. His eyes are bloodshot and his ears, big, fleshy and purple. He's wearing a black silk cap. He looks surprised the moment he spots Hermós.

"What's up?" he asks, in a gruff, vinous tone. "Where've you come from?"

"I saw you, I saw you right away. . ." says Hermós solemnly, but sounding pleased as Punch.

"So you managed to get past the mudbank?"

"Did we get past the mudbank, did you say? I'd like to inform you that we just got back from France, and if you'd like a drop of anything, come. . ."

A loud burst of laughter doesn't allow him to finish his sentence. Hermós is upset and embarrassed; for the moment, he's at a loss for words. Then he shrugs his shoulders bad-temperedly.

We anchor our boat by the stern of the barge. We will have to use it to reach land. That way we're a bit protected from any of the possible mishaps that could unfold in a port. We throw a rope to the man with the silk cap and he ties it to his prow. Our boat sits nicely there.

Hermós is in a rush. He obviously wants to go to the café to tell his friends about our recent trip. I see he's putting on his Sunday best – the clothes he wore to visit Mussiú Forgas, the mayor of Port-Vendres and a great friend of his – white espadrilles and a skipper's cap. Once he's all spruced up, we get ready to jump on land.

To do that we must first walk across the barge. A sharpish south-westerly is blowing. When I step from one vessel to the other, I take a wrong step and fall stupidly into the water.

Hermós shouts and waves his arms for a moment and the man on the barge throws me the end of a rope. However, I'm soon out. I grab the side of the boat, haul myself up and back into our boat, sopping wet and splashing water everywhere.

I soon feel freezing cold, and all the weariness from the last few days invades my numb body. It's as if my insides are falling apart. Hermós offers me his clothes and I struggle to remove my drenched garments. I must cut a curious figure in clothes that are too short and quite shabby. Although they're completely dry, I react slowly. I shiver with cold, my teeth chatter and my exhaustion worsens, as if I'm about to faint.

I decide to go back to the inn and get into bed. We jump on land, this time perfectly easily. Senyora Trias sorts everything out in a second. With Hermós's help I'm settled down and wrapped up in bed, in a cheerful room. I'm flanked by two magnificent hot-water bottles.

"Should we get a doctor?" asks Senyora Trias kindly.

"Bringing him a good supper tonight and that will do him more good. . ." says Hermós, with a smile.

I still react slowly, but finally I feel the cold ebbing along with the depressing limpness caused by fatigue. The effect of the bed is like being in paradise. I'd never have thought a bed could seem such an ideal place as it did that night. . .

11 October. When Hermós opens the shutters, the bedroom is flooded with the bright rays of the sun. I wake up. It's eleven a.m. I don't know how long I've been asleep: maybe fifteen or sixteen hours on the trot. I feel fresh and rejuvenated. As if to undermine my state, I notice that Hermós's face grows darker.

"What's wrong, Hermós?" I ask. "Have you had some bad news?"

"Not exactly bad news. . . but we're unlucky, you know! We always look ridiculous. . ."

"Ridiculous? Have we done something ridiculous?"

"I'd already decided they wouldn't believe me. . ." he says confidentially, putting one buttock on a chair.

"What did you decide they wouldn't believe?"

"That we'd been to France. . . But now they've seen you fall into the water, how on earth will they believe a thing? We've really buggered it, for Christ's sake! They're not impressed; they won't believe a thing. . ."

"What can I say, my dear Hermós? People are quite incredulous. . ."

"Are you having a go as well?" he says sadly, down in the dumps.

"Not at all! However, I must say that, if you were to make me recount everything we've done over the last few days, I'd think I was dreaming. . ."

"So you too think we didn't make it?"

"Do you remember Don Víctor, Hermós? Such a nice gentleman. . . And do you remember Lídia?"

"Right, Don Víctor. . ."

"Do you remember how I couldn't light a fire in Portaló? What a useless bum I am!"

"Damn me if I understand a word you. . ."

I ask him to hire a covered trap from Ros to take me to Palafrugell. We agree that he'll take the boat to Calella when there's a suitable moment. I give him all the money I have left: sixty pessetes. I put on my clothes. They're dry. When I hand him back his, he laughs contentedly. "I'd been so long in my best clothes," he says, "I was beginning to feel sick. . ."

The trap is waiting by the entrance to the inn, with a fat man inside, who's wearing a blue jacket and checked hat and smoking a coffin nail. Hermós has had the forethought to bring me the blanket from the boat that smells of the sea, in case I need a travel blanket. I bid farewell to Senyora Trias. Hermós's expression is suitably drawn and sad. He says: "The day you feel like eating mackerel, come to Aigua-Xelida."

"You bet I will. . ."

"Hey, what did we decide? Did or didn't we make it?"

"Of course, we made it, for Christ's sake!"

The pony trots cheerfully off. The man beneath the cap silently smokes his coffin nail. His cheeks gleam and his eyes sparkle behind the acrid white smoke.

I reach home in the early afternoon, evidently starving to death. My mother improvises an edible repast. Then I feel weary of fresh air again, a kind of horror before nature. Once again I feel tempted to go back to bed.

14 October. I have spent these last few hours in a state of twilit sloth, feeling, in contrast to the unease brought by memories of the sea and wind, all the pleasures of an enclosed, cosseted life. The fierce thrust of natural things leaves me enamored of all that's wan and indistinct. After the intensity of water and reefs, of salt and wind, of eyes full of sun, skin flaking, thoughts scattered – after all that, a bouquet of roses, the dull glint of light in the depths of a mirror, and the gleam of old wooden furniture are wonderfully relaxing.

Hermós has showed no signs of life. He must be a happy man. Sensible, ingenuous folk, living somewhere or other hereabouts, must be listening in rapture to his dramatic descriptions. May God grant them all a long life!

Personally, I have to say that the trip did me a lot of good. I'd never have thought that you could feel so comfortable at home, that it could be so easy and agreeable to renounce the open air. It's just a pity you have to travel so far to learn that!

ONE FROM BEGUR

Of the countless people who visited the Pla farmstead when I was an adolescent, I have distinct, very precise memories of two men.

In the summer a traveling musician used to drop by, a short, even-tempered old man with sad eyes, a long, drooping mustache and such pale white skin he looked as if he'd been boiled or at least would faint at any moment. He roamed the world with a violin he kept in a pillowcase as his only baggage. Although he was a tramp, a vintage tramp of the old school, he was a relatively dapper dresser, which was in a way a requirement of his profession; he went round farmsteads, hamlets and villages and was hired to play on official holidays or to entertain at marriages or baptisms, in celebrations held at home. He wore a straw hat with a broad black band, a celluloid collar, round cuffs and a green tie fixed on a piece of wire that hung from his top button. However, when he was on the road, he took off his tie, wrapped it in a piece of paper and tucked the small bundle in his pocket. Only his huge, dusty shoes betrayed a messy, tottering way of life.

His musical repertoire was limited; he played a mazurka – his signature tune – a languid little waltz and two or three ancient rural airs. At the time country folk had no pretensions and were happy with very little. Besides, the artist was a pleasant, likable fellow, and if his repertoire was restricted and hardly diverse, he was always ready to play his tunes for as long as his honorable customers wanted. He found it so quick and easy to roll them out that youngsters tired of shaking a leg before he wearied of scraping his bow over his violin's ravaged strings. He was highly respected by everyone and was invited to eat at their tables and even offered the odd spare coin; he rarely had to sleep in the barn, a boon not guaranteed to all tramps, particularly those who are the worse for wear. There was always a bed in the house for him, and come the morning, out of respect for his gray hair, nobody gave him a wakeup call. He could sleep in and get up when he felt like it. That fine fellow had another excellent quality: he left the places where he lodged without making a fuss, and tried to do so unnoticed, not saying a word. Nothing is more wearisome for sensitive souls than to be forced to contemplate the existence of so many people condemned to sleeping rough, to poverty and insecurity, and be unable to offer a helping hand. Feeling pity is tolerable, not to say pleasant, provided one doesn't have to feel too much. If people go too far, it can be counterproductive and have the opposite effect. It can lead to frosty responses. That wretched musician understood that his poverty-stricken life and destitute air shouldn't overtax other people's feelings, so when he'd eaten, slept and received the pittance they gave him, he tiptoed off – as they say – without so much as a by-your-leave. Thus, his presence never overly stirred anyone's conscience, and his subtle sense of tact was much appreciated.

In the winter a man from Begur by the name of Miner occasionally called in; he had one arm and seemed shy and distant. He engaged in long conversations with my father and always spoke in a deep, muted tone.

As a young man he preferred to fish with explosives, and one day, by the Fitor lighthouse, hoping to slaughter sea perch, he kept his hand on the charge for a tenth of a second too long and the device shattered his wrist as if it had been severed by an axe. He always gave me goose bumps when he talked in his gruff, monotonous voice about the pool of blood that spread over the sea and the rim of the boat after the accident. He had strength enough to reach Sa Tuna Beach by his own means; he wasn't the kind to ask others for help. He kept the accident quiet and not a single word got into print. What's more, he was lucky with his doctor and his arm turned out fine: he was fitted with a first-rate stump. Even so, he could never again call on his truncated arm; it was completely useless. He generally wore a jacket so he could put his dead-arm sleeve inside a pocket. After such a horrific accident, another man would have turned to begging, but Miner never came to the farmhouse for charity. He came – as he himself said – to relax and while away the time. Throughout the Begur winter he never scrounged, and I don't think he *ever* asked for anything. He learned to do countless things with his remaining arm and reckoned he did them better than before, because he had to concentrate more. He couldn't use much muscle, but resolved everything with guile, doing so perfectly, with a serenity the crippled often possess.

In fact, the main traits of his character blossomed after that unfortunate accident. His individualism became more marked. He'd never been fond of working for others; he now turned into a complete loner, a free agent disconnected from what people call everyday life. It became impossible to say, with any confidence, where you might find him. He had what one could describe as his official abode, a large half ruin of a house on Carrer de Vera in Begur, though he often went months without going there. He had the key to a hut on every beach. He gallivanted around the coves following no fixed timetable. Poacher, fisher of eels in the Ter marshes, smuggler, card player and money dealer, Miner cannily exploited every immediate and elemental resource the area could offer. Endless gossip circulated about his activities and a time came when the Guardia Civil decided to keep an eye on him. This tussle was completely wrongheaded. It could never have been a tussle over anything on paper, as Miner was mysteriously discreet. I mean it would have been hard to imagine they could ever have prosecuted him. Nevertheless, for that very reason, the tussle – a tussle over the tiniest things – became fierce in a restrained kind of way. One day, a perfectly aimed bullet drilled a hole through a civil guard's three-cornered helmet. Nobody could say exactly who had fired that bullet or where it came from. . .

"During the 1914 war. . ."

"Go on, Miner, go on. . ." said my father.

It was a winter's day and the north wind was blowing. When Miner called on a day like that, my father took him to an arbor of cypress trees behind the farmhouse. The temperature was ideal in the shelter those old trees gave. The sun blistered down. The wind blasted over the fields. The brightness in the air and sky was dazzling. In that shady spot, the roar of the wind seemed to deepen your sense of tranquility. I'd sit next to my father.

"As I was saying, then, two German gentlemen came to see me during the 1914 war. I'd known them for years because I'd had dealings with them in the cork trade and they were very congenial. They said: 'Miner, we should have a word. . . ' 'I don't know what there is to have a word about,' I replied, 'no doubt you will tell me.' 'Have you anything on this evening?' 'No, gentlemen, I don't.' 'It would be best if we had a quiet word where nobody can bother us.' 'This part of the country is ideal for a quiet chat,' I answered. 'There's not a soul about at night.' 'How about along the road with the traffic lights, past the third telegraph post, after the last houses?' 'All right, what time suits you? Ten o'clock?' 'No, one o'clock,' they replied, after conferring for a while. 'Agreed, one o'clock it is. I'll be there.'

"At midnight I took a roundabout route to that spot. I stretched out on a patch of dry graybeard away from the road and lit up a cheroot. It was a muggy, murky August night. There was a light, clammy breeze. The sky was overcast. Lightning flashed over distant Canigó. From time to time a hot gust blew. Everything pointed to the start of summer's stifling heat. It was a solitary place, without a sound, where everything seemed to hang in midair. From my vantage point I could see the distant walls of Begur in the yellow glow from electric bulbs. I smoked and thought about those German lads. What could they want from me? I started to think how well they spoke the language of our country. Talking to people who don't understand you can be dangerous and dull as ditchwater.

"At the time we'd agreed to meet, I heard footsteps along the road. Theirs were good-quality shoes. I went over and whispered: 'And a good night to you.' It was them. But my first surprise was that they were three and not two. I glanced at the newcomer. It was a pitch-black night. I didn't think I'd ever seen him before. He was young and fair like the others but taller and thinner. He smoked a pipe and I noticed how he kept looking me up and down. The others, who could see I was on edge, said he was a close friend of theirs and completely trustworthy. When the stranger realized we were talking about him, he offered me his hand, though he didn't say a word. We shook hands.

"'Fire away. . .' I said, to start the ball rolling.

"'If you like, we can take a walk. We have the time. You have no urgent business to see to?' they asked.

"'No, sir, I rarely have anything urgent. . .'

"'Good,' said the young man, who was clearly in charge, when we started on up the road, 'we've known you for a long time. We think you know the locality like the back of your hand. If we can reach an accord, you could be very useful to us. We don't think anyone knows this coast as you do. . .'

"'From Port-Vendres to Garraf, inch by inch. . .'

"'Precisely. I'd now like to ask you a question. How do you fancy earning a good weekly wage for doing next to nothing?'

"'What's your idea of a good weekly wage?'

"'A hundred pessetes a week.'

"'Can't argue with that: it's a good weekly whack. So what do I have to do for a hundred pessetes a week? Cook your meals?'

"I saw the two Germans I knew smile broadly. The stranger – though he didn't seem to understand a word – also smiled, no doubt following their lead.

"'You'd have to board. . . Listen carefully: you'd have to board a submarine. . .'

"'A submarine, what on earth. . . ?'

"'A German submarine. . .'

"'And where is this German submarine?'

"'You don't need to worry about that. That's completely secondary.'

"'And what could a poor fellow like me do on a submarine?'

"'You'd act as pilot. . .'

"'Piloting what. . . ?'

"'Piloting the submarine along the coast.'

"'Ah, now there's a thought!'

"'I mean. . .' said the young man, after hesitating for a moment, 'that while the submarine is sailing, you'll have nothing to do. You'll obviously be subject to ship's discipline. Now, when the submarine is close to shore, you must answer every question the captain asks and answer him clearly. If he orders you to take the helm, you must take on that responsibility.'

"'And that's all.'

"'That's all. What do you reckon?'

"'And what if something goes badly wrong? What do you think my skin is worth?'

"'You must nominate someone you trust completely,' the German replied in a strange, stiff voice, 'and there will be proper compensation. A man is worth three thousand pessetes.'

"'That's fine. But what if, for example. . . ?'

"'Don't worry. It's all taken care of. If you have to disembark, we'll give you a wonderful reward.'

"I thought it over for a moment and said nothing. I was rather weary of my dreary life in Begur, of walking up and down to and from its beaches. The tobacco trade had fallen away and the Majorcans seemed to have disappeared. It had been a poor summer and winter wasn't looking flush. I was a bag of nerves because of the Guardia Civil. I immediately agreed to their proposal – at least to myself. Naturally I was slightly put off by that German's bossy manner. It was quite different from when we were chatting on the beach! On the other hand, I've always been one for adventures. . . To hit the thing on its head I said I needed to sleep on it for a couple of nights.

"'Of course,' chorused the two Germans.

"'And supposing I accept, when do we start?'

"'Straight away! You'll be hearing from us.'

"A few drops of rain started falling and we walked back. The heat was oppressive. We sped up, in silence. The huge drops were few and far between and plashed on the dusty road. We stopped in the spot where we'd met half an hour earlier. The young man who had taken the lead so far – a tall, fair, blue-eyed, muscular fellow – suddenly gave me a strange look and said: 'The conversation we've just had is confidential. Do you know what confidential means?'

"'Yes, sir. . .'

"'At the start of our conversation, I said we held to you to be a friend we could trust one hundred percent. Do you know what a hundred percent trustworthy person is. . . ? Yes, of course you do. I must also tell you that if there is the slightest indiscretion, you should realize what might happen. . . You'd pay very dearly. . .'

"'Of course, of course. . .' I laughed quite spontaneously, though the German's chilly tone shocked me.

"In the meantime, the rain had gotten worse and the sky looked even more threatening. We said goodbye. I saw them continue rather stiffly along the road toward the village. I took the shortcut, put my jacket over my head and was back home in a flash."

"All that happened on a Tuesday. The following Sunday evening, past midnight, I was drinking a beer in the bar run by my old friend Judas Elias in L'Estartit. The café had emptied out come one o'clock. The owner said he wanted to close. 'If you'd like to wait for the sardine fishers, I can leave you these chairs in the street and a table.' I thanked him for his kindness, because I don't know where I'd have found a bed at that time of night. The acetylene lamps slowly went out and everything sank into a deep silence. You could barely hear the sea. It was a still, tranquil night.

"I don't know how much time went by. I fell asleep; all of a sudden I noticed a man standing next to me. I blinked as I woke up and caught a glimpse of a pale, hazy dawn light over the sea. I'd been asleep longer than I'd imagined, even though summer nights are short. I heard him say: 'Are you Miner from Begur?'

"It was a voice I'd heard before. It was the voice of the skipper of a small fishing smack from L'Estartit, an acquaintance of mine. I'd brought tobacco ashore with him on other occasions. He was known as Genoese. We had a long chat. He gave me my first weekly wage packet. He then added that as 'there was nothing in sight,' I simply had to wait. There was no knowing how long the wait might be. Meanwhile, to avoid arousing suspicion, we agreed I'd sign up on the boat he skippered and we'd go and try our luck with some lobster pots near the Medes Islands. I'd lodge with Genoese's son-in-law and that way everything would look above board. Nothing came up in our conversation that hadn't previously been agreed upon.

"My life in L'Estartit started to get pretty boring. Genoese's family was very friendly. Both the skipper and his son said very little. They were people who got on with their lives, honest, hardworking types. Every week they paid me the promised weekly wage. In the early morning if the weather was good we'd go and haul up the lobster pots. We'd return in the afternoon. These forays were a pretext to familiarize me with the sea beyond the Medes. That doesn't mean we caught nothing. There were lots of lobsters in our patch, although we lost a number of catches when the bad autumn weather began. At the equinox, with the storms from the east, we lost our markers.

Then we fished longline. In fact, the main point of our comings and goings was to watch out for the submarine on which I was to embark. Week after week went by like that. In the course of our many trips to the empty sea beyond the Medes Islands, Genoese spoke to me now and then, and quite offhandedly, about the work I was involved in. I didn't reckon he was very enthusiastic. He'd been a submarine pilot the year before. He'd refused to let his son-in-law take his place when, on the excuse that that way of life didn't suit him, he had managed to disentangle himself. 'I don't know if you'll like it,' he'd say, as if he were talking to himself, though making sure I heard. 'Frankly, I don't know if you'll like it,' he added in that gruff, deadpan voice of his. I didn't dare ask what was behind his views. The drowsiness of life in L'Estartit had stirred my spirit of adventure. I started to think I was capable of anything – of any escapade whatsoever. When that cautious old salt – who was perhaps past his prime – looked at me, and constantly worried about a northerly wind blowing up, I decided his views were shaped by considerations of age and that kind of work was for younger, bolder people. I tired of hearing him repeat his litany of 'I don't know if you'll like it' in such an impersonal, unpleasant tone, and one day I told him to stop worrying on my behalf. I was amazed how he reacted to my mild remarks, as if I'd issued some kind of challenge. He gave me a withering look, then chuckled under his gray mustache and didn't say a word. I don't know if he intended to show that he felt contempt for me. At any rate, that's how it seemed.

"It was a dull dead afternoon. The days had gotten shorter. We were in the middle of December. Daily life was beginning to pall. When it was fine, we went out fishing. Once we were done, we laid anchor for a couple of hours in case they turned up. If we couldn't take the boat out, we spent hours by the fireside or dealing cards.

On Sundays, a hurdy-gurdy played in an abandoned warehouse and people danced. I never managed to get off with anyone, married or single. An unfriendly lot.

"That afternoon we sailed into the dim light of dusk. The sky was gray and low. Covered in wisps of gray, matte mist, the horizon seemed to have moved nearer. The air was heavy and humid and a light, languid southwesterly blew over a sea, which was a dirty tin color. The breeze gave you a headache and puckered up tiny, choppy waves that splashed to their death on the beach. Countless hungry, shrieking seagulls circled above the sea. The day seemed ready-made for staying by the hearth in the lethargic round of winter life. In any case, it wasn't cold and there were no signs of gales or rain.

"When we passed Meda Gran Island, the horizon opened before us and we saw a boat rigged up as a schooner close to land. It looked like a small coastal trader. Its sails were furled and it seemed to be at anchor. Genoese gazed at the boat looking highly intrigued, though he said nothing. Then a hint of a smile came to his lips. The schooner was less than a mile away and, although its masts were a blur in the mist, it stood out clearly enough.

"'It looks like an Italian. . .' Genoese's son suddenly blurted out.

"'An Italian?' rasped his father. 'Why do you say that, you fool? Don't you recognize it?'

"Then he added in the same tone: 'We will drop anchor right here. We'll soon have work to do. . . Miner, your time is up. They've come for you.'

"We dropped anchor and in the meantime dusk fell. For a second the mist seemed to thicken, but it was just an effect of the vanishing light. As soon as the last long fishing line was pulled in we rowed silently toward the schooner. Meanwhile, Genoese lit a lamp he placed on the rim of the boat that flashed green. A couple of seconds later we received back a very faint signal in the same color. Then the beam from the Meda lighthouse began to swirl. The wind had dropped and the sea was lathery. It was extremely humid and the air was heavy. When we reached the beam of the schooner, we saw no signs of life: no people moving, no noise of any kind.

"'Good night,' shouted Genoese gruffly.

"The silhouette of what looked like a large stout man appeared over the ship's rail and replied: 'Aye, and a good night to you!'

"The Majorcan let down a rope. We moored our boat to it.

"'You got the goods?' asked the stout man.

"'He's right here. . . ' answered Genoese, pointing at me.

"'He can get on whenever he likes. . . We're in a hurry. We must set sail in the early hours. Have you got any fresh fish?'

"The skipper showed him a basket of hog- and scorpionfish.

"While he unraveled a rope ladder, I said goodbye to Genoese and his son. The Majorcan was quite surprised to see I had only one arm that was any use. We hoisted up the basket of fish. L'Estartit father and son sailed home. They appeared to leave unmoved, with no regrets.

"The Majorcan was talkative. He wasn't the skipper; he was the first mate. He said the crew was asleep because they'd just sailed from the northern coast of Majorca to the Medes Islands – against the current and into a driving wind – and were exhausted. The schooner was carrying a supply of fuel for the submarine. He asked after the fishermen who'd just left, whether they were to be trusted or not.

"'It's quite OK in these waters,' he added. 'The Meda rocks would shield us against the northwesterly, but there's too much traffic here, we can't hang around. We're also close to land. Once we've done the business, best scarper, right?'

"'Is that right. . . ?' I offered vaguely.

"He didn't respond but indicated I should follow him. When we reached the poop, I saw a cable extending into the water and, below, a long shape, like a giant fish. As my eyes adapted, I could make out the blur of a submarine turret in the early nighttime glow. Even though the darkness meant I saw things more with the eyes of my imagination than my real ones, I thought it was fascinating. It was obvious that was the submarine I'd been waiting for all those weeks. When I suddenly noticed the palest orange steam rising from the turret, all my doubts disappeared. The schooner was acting as a buoy for the submarine. I couldn't tell you how long I stood on the poop deck staring down. A good long time, I expect. I only recall there was a moment when I asked the Majorcan a question, as I thought he was next to me. But nobody replied. He'd tired of waiting and I expect he'd gone off to work without telling me, respecting my natural curiosity.

"I saw a small crack of greasy light in the galley and went over. I have to confess that we men who've always sailed in fishing boats without bridges are always thrilled to be on the deck of a vessel like that. Everything seems more spacious and well appointed and rather fantastic. It's like being a child again. 'In this ship,' you think, 'you could go down to Davy Jones's locker.' A lovely, succulent smell of fish stew wafted my way from that same crack. The cook, who heard me tramping around, invited me inside. While he stirred the potatoes with a big spoon, he told me he was from Ibiza via Oran. Then he put the rings of fish on top of the stack of potatoes, poured water over everything and stoked the fire. The small cabin was filled with an out-of-this-world aroma – from paradise. The pot had been boiling only for ten minutes when I heard footsteps on deck and immediately heard people's voices. I expect the smell from the scorpionfish gravy had woken up the crew. They opened the door looking dreamy eyed; their faces and eyes lit up after the first sniff. It was instantaneous.

"They carried the stew pot up to the poop deck and we sat in a circle and ate supper in complete silence. Five men and the skipper. I don't recall their faces, because an oil lamp next to the pot gave out very little light. However, the way they stayed so quiet made me realize that they were very practical people, because of the kind of work they did. Old smugglers, no doubt. The sea demands silence and calm. Everyone was ravenous. The night was an inky black. The sea was tranquil and seemed very mysterious. The only sound – and that barely – was the small scraping noise of the hemp anchor ropes against the ship's rail. The place was completely solitary. The Meda light burned like a firefly hanging in the air. Toward the end of supper, I thought the pale orange glow floating above the submarine turret had thickened and become more visible to the eye."

"After supper, they lowered the schooner's dinghies into the water and began the operation of transferring the fuel the vessel was carrying in a mass of drums to the tanks of the submarine. Any operation at sea is tricky, but I could see at a glance that these men were highly experienced. Though they were working in the pitch dark, they transferred the liquid via the skiffs completely calmly, making almost no noise, with amazing skill and orderliness. The night was on their side: the sea was still and empty and it was humid rather than cold.

"I didn't take part. Smoking my pipe, I leaned on the railing and watched them hard at it. It took several hours. It was past midnight when the first mate came over accompanied by a tall man who was wearing a sailor's cap and a leather raincoat. I didn't immediately recognize him, but after I'd shaken his hand and looked him in the face, I saw it was the same man who had accompanied the two Germans when I met them that night in Begur. I understood almost everything he said because he spoke a smattering of Spanish. The Majorcan introduced him as the submarine's commander. Although he seemed to be following the loading operations with a mixture of irritation and impatience, he struck me as being open and friendly. We watched them for ages from the poop, but whenever the beam from the Meda light dragged over the water and seemed to strike – or maybe that was an illusion – the submarine's sopping wet iron frame, the commander clenched his teeth. He'd have been much happier eighty miles from land. It was as if he felt we were boxed in.

"Finally, the transfer was completed. It was the middle of the night. A wind had blown up inland. I moved to the submarine in the last trip the dinghies made. I was traveling light – a bag with a change of clothes – and didn't make them waste a moment. The commander was in the turret. The submarine switched on its engines, which had been on standby. The men from the schooner released their moorings. You could hear the halyards squeal as they hoisted the mainsail. The moment we moved off, I felt the iron hulk judder, first almost imperceptibly, increasing until every hinge in the vessel vibrated. From the foot of the turret we saw the schooner switch on its sidelights. The commander glanced at me and laughed. With a back wind, the sail billowing, gearing up for a sirocco, the Majorcan made rapid headway. We turned our prow eastward. We soon lost sight of the schooner. We proceeded quickly. The Meda light faded. As we forged ahead, the commander seemed to calm down.

"When the engines were turned on, I felt as happy as a small child, as if I'd been released from the terrible boredom of the last few months. The vessel was flying at a clip and I felt I was in a really fast boat, much faster than any I'd sailed in over recent years. Hardly rippled by the wind, the sea was so still the submarine moved effortlessly forward. It was like sailing across a lake. However, after half an hour I started to feel the engine vibrating on the iron hull. It wasn't a great din; rather, the engines turned with a muffled hum. But the juddering was so violent it seemed to penetrate the bones in your legs and climb up your body until your teeth started to click together most unpleasantly. It felt as if someone was shaking the outside of your body. The vibrations reached into your guts. I felt forced to lock my jaws tightly together – the commander was by my side. It was exhausting. I felt anxious, increasingly so, as we continued to cut through the water. The cold took hold of me. A cold from within, as if my bone marrow had frozen. But now wasn't the time to give in. I kept up appearances until the commander decided it was time to retire. It was dawn. To the west land hovered like an uncertain shadow, veiled in grayish mist. We'd traveled more than twenty-five miles. The sea was white and blank. Damp drops dripped on my eyelids. They rested there like a slug and made me feel colder than ever; I shivered. A time came when I didn't know whether I was shivering from the cold or the vibrations of the submarine."

"We clambered down the metal-rung ladder. The lukewarm temperature immediately put me in better spirits. I thought there was less vibrating. Perhaps the submarine had slowed down. I followed the commander to a small bedroom. By the dazzling light of an electric bulb, I tried to imagine what I must look like: in poor shape, I expect. The commander filled two cups of cognac – two big aluminum cups – and silently pushed one my way. I gulped it down without flinching.

"He then signaled to me to accompany him and we left his bedroom. The hazy glare inside the submarine would sometimes turn to an oily glow when reflected off the surface of a machine. We walked down a long corridor. Inside, the submarine was just that, a long narrow corridor with a large number of things stowed on either side, admirably tidy in their rightful places. Rather than the things themselves – for if I started on them the inventory would be endless – what struck me was the neat way they were organized. For a man like me, used to arranging stuff any old how, it seemed somewhat manic. What's more, it was all iron and that made for an even eerier effect. As we proceeded down the corridor to the poop we walked past two or three crewmen – very young-looking lads in mechanics' overalls. They stood to attention and saluted the commander. I thought their skins were a bright yellow and that made them look tired out, but it may have been only the greenish-yellow light floating inside.

"We reached a spot with berths up against the ribs of the vessel. There were three to the ceiling on each side and nearly all were taken. I could hear one lad snoring evenly. The commander pointed me to one that was empty and left. I stripped off and climbed in. The bunk was narrow and gave little room for movement. But I was so tired I was soon sleeping the sleep of the just.

"When I woke up the next morning, I didn't feel at all well. My head felt heavy. My senses seemed to have sunk into some peculiarly thick morass. It was an effort to sit up. As if my whole body was surrendering to some invisible, spongy pressure that was both heavy and suffocating. I was surprised how long it took to get a clear grasp on my surroundings. I felt poisoned by a kind of air I'd never breathed before, one that had spread through my body tissue via my lungs. Yes, that was it: I was being poisoned by air that was stale, if not exactly polluted. I was used to the open-air life and have always been sensitive to everything that comes in via the nose. My sense of smell appeared to be compromised by a gas that had entered my innermost cells and sent me to sleep. The faint, hazy light floating in that iron cylinder was unreal. With a great effort, I dressed and walked toward the turret. As I drew nearer, the air became purer and the light brighter. The turret was open. The submarine was sailing above water. I climbed up the iron ladder and poked my head outside. Some sailors were on guard duty. It was a dull, gray day with a very low sky; the odd drop of rain fell. The horizon had closed in; there was no wind and the sea was still calm. I tried to figure out where we were, but with no sight of land that was impossible. With its engines turned down, the submarine was making slow progress. It was on patrol. Evidently expecting something to happen. Now and then I thought I must be on board a smugglers' boat waiting for the fateful hour to head to an exact spot along the coast to unload.

"Contact with fresh air cleared my head and the drowsy buzz in my head slowly faded. When I felt more in control, I went back down inside. That was when my pituitary gave me a real sense of the air floating there. It was not the fetid smell of decomposing matter. On the contrary, all was tidy and sterilized. But it *was* air I had never breathed before. It was air charged with the fumes from fuel oil, lubricants, mineral oils, human odors, greasy flock and the acrid stink from the engine room and all that iron plating. I'd never breathed an atmosphere like that and couldn't possibly describe the smell. Perhaps if life had led me to work in a place with machines, I might be able to give you an idea of that air, though I doubt it. I'd always been a woodcock that could tell wild pine from cultivated pine, and that stench was so new to me and so repellent I could never have got used to it. It was worse than fetid. It was air I couldn't adapt to.

"The commander reappeared and ushered me into his small cabin. A tiny table had been laid. He sat on his bunk and asked me to sit by the table. We spoke at length. He said we were patrolling twenty-five miles off the coast between Sant Sebastià and Cape Creus, and if nothing changed, we would stay in these waters for several days. He seemed much calmer than on the previous night. He gave the impression that he was absolutely confident in what he was doing and couldn't even imagine that danger was round the corner. He was a pleasant, really nice fellow. He laughed and said that way of life was soporific, but he was sure we could stay on the surface for several days, and that was always better than being under water. He asked me if I played chess, but as I play only draughts, he promised to challenge me to a few games of draughts. I told him the air in his vessel gave me headaches and that sometimes I felt strangely queasy. He laughed and replied that I should ignore it; it was nothing to worry about.

"Then a sailor served lunch. A mug of hot broth, boiled greens and a slice of salt fish that had been soaked, and stewed plums. Beer to drink. I wasn't hungry, but I'd not eaten for so long I knew I had to eat something. It was all well presented and cooked, but I couldn't say what it tasted of. Rather: it all tasted the same, a taste that was completely impregnated by the foul air floating inside that submarine. The commander said the bread was excellent. It was served in very thin slices, a somber toasted color, with a crust that was practically black. I tried it dry and then buttered. I didn't like it either way. To be frank, the butter seemed to consist of a substance that was the greasy essence of the whole lunch. I can't say I've ever eaten a lot of butter. But I'm sure that stuff had nothing in common, in terms of taste, with what they sell in this country. It tasted of axle grease. It was disgusting. The commander, who saw I was forcing a slice of bread down, told me I didn't have to. At the end of the meal, smiling as broadly as ever, he poured me a glass of cognac. It was the only thing that didn't seem impregnated. I left the table with quite an empty stomach. That was the least of it. I had an extremely unpleasant sense of physical discomfort – as if I'd eaten something so alien my body couldn't digest it. I felt that indigestibility above all in my sense of smell.

"After lunch we went up on deck and spent a long time in the open air. I immediately felt better and much perkier. The vessel was moving slowly. It was using as little fuel as possible. The weather was unchanged, perhaps everything was a little lighter and less closed in. We couldn't see land but the commander said we were off Cape Norfeu and sailing toward the edge of the Gulf of Lion. 'We'll carry on like this for another three hours,' he added, 'then we'll turn our back on the gulf and head south. All we have to do is keep a watch on this expanse of water...'

"Then he asked me lots of questions, particularly about the ships we'd see near the coast. I told him what I'd seen, the truth, I mean: lots of small coastal traffic with France. And that these vessels plied close to land. That there wasn't much in the way of big ships; it was rare to see a lone steamer sail by. 'On the other hand, from time to time,' I added, 'convoys of quite large vessels do come through.' The commander barely seemed to be listening, as if he knew all that.

"The natural feel of our conversation led me to ask if lack of visibility was an advantage or not. He said that right then it didn't matter either way, because they weren't expecting anything immediately. He added that he was expecting something big, but it wouldn't show up for several days. 'When the time comes,' he added quite matter-of-factly, 'we shall go closer inshore and see what happens. For the moment we can enjoy a few days of peace and quiet. It's all about being patient and waiting. I'm sure you won't be disappointed...'

"He didn't laugh when he said that. He said it – no doubt reluctantly – with a taut, nervous expression on his face."

"I don't know how many days went by. The monotony of life aboard made me lose all idea of time. The fact that I had nothing to do made me sluggish. Life in this place wasn't exactly great fun, but I could've put up with that. What I felt was disgusting from the very first was the air we breathed below deck and the dearth of tasty food. I made an effort to adapt. It was impossible. I visibly wilted. My clothes were too big on me. My body felt drowsy, then queasy. I spent as long as possible on deck, breathing in the fresh air. It was my only nourishment.

"I missed one other thing: conversation. I could make myself understood with the sailors only by way of signs, and they'd viewed me with suspicion from the beginning. Some knew the odd word of Spanish, but such words only helped to make their gestures more obscure rather than to shed any light on them. I sometimes spoke to the commander but he was very busy and I spent days on end without saying a word. I couldn't seek out the commander if he didn't summon me. It was very tiresome communicating with the others with gestures. When I felt like saying something, I'd start to whistle or hum, though never too loudly.

"Discipline on board was remarkable. Everybody knew what he had to do and jumped to it mechanically. I saw sad faces, resigned faces, dead faces. I never saw one that expressed violence or indignation. I don't think anyone on board was unaware of the dangers of that way of life. Perhaps I was the most unaware. Beneath that dull silence of interment and demeaning discipline, a hidden current of understanding ran between the crew and their commander. Life at sea creates a kind of tame resignation and tendency to daydream, both of which were much in evidence on that vessel. These qualities of reservation and dreaminess were also compatible with outbreaks of crazy violence. They composed a robotic, listless state; a nervous depression that hid simmering explosiveness; quiet, duly regulated expectations before the ever-imminent eruption of an incident that could decide one's life. When the sailors heard me whistling or humming on deck, they looked wide eyed in amazement at the way I expressed my feelings.

"We had fair weather that whole time. Though it was midwinter, every day was fine. Some were splendid. January usually sees bright days, gentle breezes, placid seas, clear skies and no rain. The benign January waters never fail: they always return. Of course, there are the usual blasts from a northwesterly that made us toss and turn a little, but they were short-lived and never vicious. If it hadn't been for the cold they brought – a cold that made me abandon deck and ask for extra overcoats – it would have been hardly noticeable. After this cold spell, I found the gray days, low skies and humid, light southwesterly much more unpleasant. There's nothing so irksome as being wet and icy when everything around you is also sopping and freezing cold.

"We stayed twenty to thirty miles from the coast over that time. The ships we saw as we kept watch were of no interest – the smallest kind of coastal traffic. Though we almost always sailed above water, I don't think we were visible from the coast. If we ever moved closer to land it was to take advantage of the dawn's or twilight's unsteady glow, or nighttime."

"It must have been around 20 January and early morning. The eight o'clock watch had been relieved. We were a long way from land, and as it was clear and bright, we could see the Sant Sebastià lighthouse across the water. All the signs were that we would swing round at any minute and once again make for the waters off Cape Creus. The commander, with his binoculars, was leaning on the turret and scrutinizing the sea to the southwest. At first sight, the sea by Cape Tossa seemed deserted. But the intent look on his face suggested that might change. As the sky was cloudless, I was surprised to see something like a slightly darker brushstroke on the sea near the spot where the commander was training his binoculars. Time passed and I registered that no order was being given to turn round as was usually the case; I decided that something had indeed changed. Another half an hour went by. Then the order was issued for the vessel to point its prow westward and to land. What had seemed an almost invisible brushstroke mere minutes ago now looked like smoke from a steamer's funnel or perhaps from a number of steamers. It was obvious: we could see the front of a large convoy coming from the southwest and probably heading toward Marseille. The commander didn't seem at all surprised by that sight. He was clearly expecting it. The discovery made him nervous, and though he kept his nerves under control, they were apparent enough.

"We cruised above water for almost an hour. Meanwhile, everyone took up his position and the silence seemed denser. Preparations were made to go down. The convoy was still a long way away, but the silhouettes of the first ships were clearly outlined against and beyond the Tossa promontory. We submerged without a snag. At first it didn't seem any different from sailing on the surface. However, as time passed, the air stewed and thickened, the temperature rocketed and the stench in the air seemed more unpleasant than ever. My shirt felt tight, and my clothes sticky and uncomfortable.

"Now the commander was rooted by the sights of the periscope, with an admiralty chart spread out next to him and his system of communicating with the services on board all at the ready. As we moved closer inshore he beckoned to me and pointed several times at a spot on the map that really seemed to be bothering him. They were the tiny, insignificant Formigues Islands. They were still many miles away, but as we know, when real sailors see a rock, they start to quake. We now began to get a proper perspective on the convoy, even though we were hugging the coast and could see a line of over twenty large ships. Most were camouflaged. Whenever I could, I looked at the sights out of the corner of an eye so I could interpret the commander's reactions. It was my impression – my first surprise – that the convoy was under heavy escort. The first twenty or twenty-five merchant ships were being patrolled by at least four large anti-torpedo boats on either side. That made the commander repeatedly moisten his lips. The second surprise came when I saw that the vessels, against usual custom, weren't sailing within or beside jurisdictional waters; they were quite far off from them and that gave them much greater freedom of movement. I also thought that if we attempted any kind of attack from a position close to land, we would be lethally trapped. We recognized the sense of security the presence of a heavy escort gave that long procession of vessels – more than thirty were now visible – as the distance between us closed. We were as near as we could be. Not a soul was to be seen on their decks, except for the watch on the bridge. Not a soul manned the cannon on prow or poop. We even noticed that some had been covered. It was now clear that those men believed themselves safe. They probably thought the danger was over, as far as they were concerned, that the worst patch was behind them and closeness to French seas justified their complete self-confidence.

"As the convoy drew nearer and became easier to see, the strength of their escort also became evident. We counted over eight anti-torpedo boats. The commander reluctantly issued the order for our submarine to slow down. The absolute inequality of firepower between that fleet and our small submarine was all too obvious. Was there anything we could do? The convoy, which was now level with us, proceeded slowly, but their escort vessels were frantic. These boats reconnoitered inshore and on the open sea, crazily speeding from the front to the center of the convoy. The submarine continued in parallel for a long time – three or four miles away with a firm eye on their gunboats. Meanwhile, I watched all the officers pay the commander's cabin a visit. I didn't understand a word of what was said. In effect there was no attack. The inequality of firepower clinched it. When the front of the convoy drew level with Cape Sant Sebastià it veered off toward Marseille. You couldn't ask for better proof of how safe those people felt they were.

"The peculiarly painted procession filed past: more than forty large cargo boats and eight to ten anti-torpedo boats. The officers watched them pass through their sights with rage on their faces. But could they do anything? I don't think so. The commander was simply acknowledging their immense superiority.

"So I thought that must be the end to our little adventure – it was past one p.m., with glorious weather and visibility, and the cloud of smoke from the convoy was disappearing over the eastern horizon, when a vessel suddenly came into view in the same manner as the fleet had done that morning. Orders went out to go full steam ahead. Within the hour we could see it perfectly. It was evidently a hostile ship – an American tramp of some eight thousand tons (said the commander) – and it belonged to the previous group but had gotten delayed for some reason or other. Perhaps it hadn't joined them at the agreed time. In any case, it was making extremely slow progress and seemed damaged. It was a magnificent four-master, the like of which we rarely see in these waters. When we were close enough for the commander to get a precise look, he burst out laughing. There didn't seem to be any watch; it was a ship without defenses, one hit and. . .

"From that moment on it all happened amazingly quickly. We maneuvered close and took up a position where we had perfect freedom of movement. We were ten or twelve miles off Sant Sebastià. They noticed nothing until they heard the crisp, simultaneous, shattering impact of two torpedoes on iron panels at the float line. The submarine surfaced almost at once. I had a perfect view of what happened from the bridge. The vessel lurched slightly twice on the side where it had been hit and very soon began to keel over. Meanwhile, hordes of people appeared on deck amid the predictable confusion and uproar. Nobody went near the cannons; everyone headed for the lifeboats. However, we hardly heard any of the human hue and cry because of a din from the bilge that made your hair stand on end. The frenzied neighing and whinnying of three, four or five hundred horses – I probably underestimate – inexorably trapped within the dying ship rose above the majestic sea. Their chilling neighs were followed by a dull, heavy, terrible clatter, as if the cargo of horses was trying to break through the iron plating with their legs, teeth and whole bodies. The horrific din, high-pitched shrieks rent with explosions of sound, made a deep impression on me. I started to cry like a child. And through a veil of tears, like a vision in a dream, I suddenly saw the great breaches in the hull packed with a frenzied succession of terrified horses hurling themselves into the sea. Our crew watched the tragic exodus as if they were at some sporting event. The animals churned up the water as they swam, heads and manes windswept, kicking up their front legs as if about to take flight at any moment. But the ship continued to keel over and water soon engulfed the gaping holes. The last horse to get out seemed to erupt from the depths of the sea. Then the ship went slowly down – not that the frenzy and neighing ceased for a moment. The vessel slipped down solemnly like a lead weight. Peace was restored. We could see the crew rowing strongly toward land. When we departed, the horses were still swimming tirelessly. The pinkish-yellow glow of a wintry twilight – cold, pure and stark – touched the foamy broiling water churned by the horses' legs. . ."

"A few hours later we were off the north coast of Majorca. Those hours of my life were haunted by what I'd been so unfortunate to see. I couldn't pluck up the courage to say a word. I'd not enjoyed that spectacle one bit. We met up in a place – which will remain nameless – with the schooner I had first seen by the Medes Islands.

"My state of health wouldn't allow me to sail any farther. I disembarked. A few months later, when I happened to be in Begur, I received a present: some wonderful binoculars I sold a few days after for three hundred pessetes. They were obviously worth much more. But some things are best forgotten, don't you agree?"

BREAD AND GRAPES

It wasn't so many years ago that a lot of small border towns had sizable military garrisons, depending on local requirements. Cadaqués had one too.

I still remember that Christmas night in Cadaqués, the furious mistral that blew up at twilight and howled for two days nonstop and the pure, pale-blue mineral expanse of sky dotted with fiery twinkling stars.

A group of three or four soldiers staggered out of a dance hall in high spirits because they were plastered or perhaps feeling liberated by that special day; shouting and swearing in the freezing air, they headed toward the Bar Marítim. There was a small boat on the beach opposite the bar. Those poor lads had the bright idea of dragging it into the water and taking a trip around the bay. When they saw what the soldiers had in mind, the people in the bar tried to warn them of the dangers of such an escapade. However, they were country boys and it was impossible to dissuade them from their drunken enterprise. The Cadaqués mistral is treacherous. Because the wind blows from the beach, the stretch of sea closest to land appears calm; it was a waste of time trying to tell those hapless youths that twenty-five yards beyond the breakwater the sea was roiling furiously. It was clear to the eye: the wind was raising a flurry of fine foam, like a mist of tiny glass particles, like luminous, ethereal white tulle. The exchanges became so violent it almost came to fisticuffs. Those lads pulled the boat into the water and jumped in.

I think I hardly need add that nothing more was ever heard of those unfortunate youngsters and no trace of their boat was ever found, and nothing *will* ever be heard of them, however many years go by.

That terrible episode brought on by human folly reminds me of a mysterious event years ago in which I was randomly and indirectly involved. My intention isn't to suggest that the events on that Christmas night might elucidate that past experience. Not at all. I simply mean that what happened that night allows me to suggest a hypothesis – one I believe to be quite plausible – as to what happened in El Jonquet Cove one November night in 1920. . .

I've been familiar with the coves of Cape Creus for many a year, and if anyone was so kind as to ask me which part of that striking landscape I prefer I'd say that El Jonquet – or Es Jonquet as locals say – has stolen my heart.

I've often thought of building a small, comfortable house there when I get to be a millionaire. Until that day arrives – which might even come to pass – my contact with the place is that of a loyal, infatuated passerby. Whenever I can, I go and spend an hour there – it is my favorite Cadaqués excursion, whether by land or sea. It is a longer haul from Cadaqués to El Jonquet by sea than by land. The distance by land is just what my body demands to satisfy its daily routine needs. In the course of my dark, twilit life, dominated by the strange phenomenon of unavoidable, intermittent forays leading me into the most unlikely places at the most extraordinary times, I consider El Jonquet to be a model haven.

I know there are more exciting, more precipitous, headier places on this unique peninsula. Some perhaps enjoy a purer, more virginal and profound silence, while others enshrine a more compelling, entrancing solitude. The teasing irregularity of some rock formations can have the same obsessive allure as the feverish calm of olives groves. It's not that I don't like all that – and other things besides. But if a landscape is to be at a human level, it needs a hint of sweetness. El Jonquet has that hint of sweetness, which is not to imply it doesn't share the area's general tonic: the taste of bitter olives.

If you happen to be in Cadaqués and feel like a walk there, you must leave Plaça de les Herbes and take the Sa Felipa side street and then the road to Port Lligat as far as the fork that leaves the cemetery on the right and continues on the road to the En Duran farmhouse. Keep on this path enclosed between two drystone walls for a while until you come to the path that goes down to the Bucs stream and En Morell stockyard. The Bucs stream is the one that shapes Port Lligat Beach and carries that name because in bygone times its banks, perfumed by the most delightful southern plants, were a home to bee-hives – beehives that in Cadaqués are called "*bucs*," as befits a town with such a huge and varied character.* Then walk past the En Morell stockyard and on your left the telephone posts to the Cape Creus lighthouse and take the track over the barren land by S'Alqueria,

---

* "Buc" can also mean a swarm of bees, the belly, or the hull of a ship.

and if you keep to this track, it will take you to the entrance to the El Jonquet olive grove. Walk through the grove, make a gentle descent across a series of terraces over the cove and you will reach your journey's end.

This path is one of the most satisfying in the Cadaqués area. It passes through hollows bound by walls of slate; the deep silence of the olive groves hangs over the path; ecstatic in the still air of that haven – slightly shadowy in winter, air turned a crisp green by the olive trees – and in the summer enjoys the sun's divine, intense heat and gilded pink haze. It also passes through high, barren, wind-blown places, a convulsed geology of stone belfries, thorn bushes, nettles, gorse and tamarind allowing glimpses of expanses of sea, the blackish-yellow bare terrain of the cape, and the olive-treed slopes and side of Puig Alt.

That olive grove in El Jonquet is the exact spot where I intend to build the small house I mentioned a moment ago (if when I'm a millionaire, they agree to sell it to me). That olive grove is a wonder, one of the most beautiful and best tended around Cadaqués. It is a kind of terraced garden wrapped in a transparent, pristine glow. Gardens of green-leaved trees are always full of gentle shade, liquid in some places, wrinkled in others. The only gardens that are bright, dry and brimming with life and grace are olive groves. The one in El Jonquet is amazingly elegant and well ordered. The height of its elevated terraces is perfect. The drywalls supporting them are hand built to perfection, quite sumptuous. The three small steps to go up and down the terraces are beautiful. The stones channeling the irrigation water seem voluptuously placed. The trees don't bear a single blemish. The sweet tension of such order amid the landscape's romantic wildness leaves an unforgettable impression.

Now if you look for El Jonquet on a maritime chart, you will find it in the southwesterly depths of the great Guillola Bay. The cove has the same geographical orientation as Cadaqués Bay and, thus, turns its back on the mistral. It is an incision made by a stream – the *riera* from Puig Alt – through two relatively high walls of slate. The eastern wall is home to an olive grove and a semiruined hut; the western wall, the olive grove I have described and a hut in a perfect state. At the foot of this wall there is is a very narrow strand of fine, lead-colored sand, which two or three Cadaqués fishermen use as the summer base for their boats. In winter it is a solitary place. That *torrent* from Puig Alt carries, I reckon, the most water after the Cadaqués and perhaps Els Jònculs *rieras* along this stretch of coast. This doesn't mean it always carries water but simply that it is always ready to do so. Jònculs and Jonquet are names that allude to a plant – *els joncs*, or reeds – that grows in damp, watery places. One curious aspect of El Jonquet is that the sea rushes in through the opening the stream has created between the two slate walls and penetrates a long way upstream, creating a small fjord that is a thing of pure joy. The mix of sea and stream is quite shallow, so that El Jonquet represents the strange phenomenon of a beach in the process of formation, a marsh that is solidifying. Now, I couldn't say whether this beach will remain in a perpetual state of attempting to become one or if, on the contrary, it will eventually attain the actual state of a small beach. That probably depends on a "significant" swelling of the stream or a "significant" stormy sea.

The reeds I mentioned grow in this confluence alongside aquatic plants flowering at water level, water that is lethargic, drowsy and idle.

Guillola Bay is so solitary, because fishermen sail from one end to the other, to and from Cape Creus or Mar d'Amunt, rarely stopping, but that solitude and silence seem to bestow on El Jonquet the special quality brought by the pure, impassive joy that sea and land seem to possess – all fine-tuned by bloodless, skeletal water.

If you have a temperament given to living on the edge of the madding crowd, you can spend many a blissful hour in that place. And I *have* spent many hours there, listening to the silken wind stirring the olive trees and gazing at the light transfiguring the placid, sleepy sea, watching the majestic progress of sea bass in the inlet's transparent waters, red mullet dozing on the glassy sand underwater or sand smelt jumping over the translucent surface of the watery mirror.

El Jonquet's location makes it quite exceptional. It is a natural haven when north winds blow. When the wind blows from inland – mistrals and southwesterlies and westerlies – it offers complete shelter (that is, for small vessels). Talladolins, a rock towering by the southern entrance to the cove, guarantees – we would suggest, providentially – the emptiness of the present beach, and elongates the horn hewn by its gentle sweep ensuring the stillness of its waters. As these winds dominate on summer days, these rocks shelter the waters. During wintertime, the situation is quite different. A vessel anchored there wouldn't survive storms from the east. Sudden southwesterly squalls hit El Jonquet with highly unpleasant surges of water. When a mistral wind blows from the small fjord created by the stream, a boat must be firmly moored if it is to stay put. However, maybe with two anchors cast like a cat's whiskers there might be an opportunity to begin a more or less hazardous escape. . .

With this information in mind (objective information, which can be confirmed by locals), anyone would find fully justified my surprise at seeing that unknown vessel anchored in El Jonquet in late November.

That afternoon I started my walk back to Cadaqués when darkness was falling. I'd been daydreaming too much. When you catch sight of something new, an unusual presence, a vessel you've never seen before in a normally empty expanse of sea, you are taken aback. The chitchat the sea can generate is remarkable. Anything out of the ordinary provokes curiosity. That's perhaps down to isolation: the more isolated and deserted your environment, the more striking any novelty. I think you could prove that the biggest gossip is the individual who's most isolated.

As I said, it was late November. It had been a protracted Indian summer and we'd had very fine weather for days: gentle winds and sunny seas. The sun warmed less and less but showed good will. People were starting to harvest the olives, and by day the groves were full of muted conversations.

However, the weather changed that afternoon. The sky was covered by a low, gray ceiling, a light but persistent, monotonous south wind set in like a throbbing migraine, and I think the odd drop of rain fell on my way back from El Jonquet. They weren't exactly separate drops of rain, more a damp viscosity in the air. The change in the weather imbued nature with a calm, quiet sense of expectation.

When I reached the En Morell stockyard I heard someone speak, close at hand, in a gruff voice: "Good evening!"

A greeting I returned mechanically with another "Good evening!" I stopped instinctively and took two or three steps back because I thought the person who had greeted me was behind me. Then I saw the silhouette of a man leaning on the corner made by the stockyard shed and wall. If someone had walked by on the path from the Cape

Creus lighthouse – the customs police, for example – they wouldn't have registered his presence, even though he was only a few feet away.

The individual I'm referring to stepped away from the wall and approached me. He struck me as small, stocky and ill shaven, and I saw the butt of an extinguished cigar on his lip. I didn't recognize his features at all and couldn't remember ever seeing him in Cadaqués.

"Excuse me. . ." he said rather shyly. "You are Senyor Pla, I believe. I'd like a couple of words with you."

"Fire away. . ."

"Come closer to the wall. . . and you won't get wet. You've come from El Jonquet, *fa*, right?"

I must confess that that "*fa?*" was reassuring. It was a word that could be used only by somebody from thereabouts, by someone with local roots.

"Yes, senyor, I've come from El Jonquet," I replied.

"Did you notice anything unusual?"

The question was formulated – the dim light of dusk enabled me to see this – with unrestrained curiosity. He was the kind of man who, when speaking about something close to his heart, dilates his pupils so his eyes appear to bulge.

"There's a boat anchored in El Jonquet that I think isn't from these parts," I replied matter-of-factly.

"What kind of vessel?"

"I think it's an old sloop, the kind of boat they don't build anymore."

"It's got a main jib and a forestaysail, *no fa?*"

"That's right."

"Did you see any movement on board?"

"I didn't see a living soul all the time I was in El Jonquet. I'll tell you one thing though: the boat is wonderfully anchored and in exactly the right place."

"Course it is! It's got a proper pilot! It could have been steered by a Cadaqués sailor."

"Oh, so you know the crew?"

"Only too well!"

"Hey. . . what if we resumed our walk? That sheepskin coat you're wearing is keeping you dry, but I'm getting soaked. . ."

"Fine by me. I'll keep you company for a while."

"So you're not going to Cadaqués?"

"Yes, I am, senyor, but I won't use the same path as you. I'll go along the track to my neighborhood. . ."

Before he starting walking, he looked all around; he did that instinctively, but it was very noticeable. Then he strode off quickly; once we'd crossed the Bucs stream he walked at my pace. Initially we walked in silence. Then I thought it would be more relaxing to exchange a few words, at least to break the sinister twilight atmosphere.

"Don't you think it's rather rash," I asked, "to anchor a vessel in El Jonquet at this time of year? If the wind blows from the east, they'll be in trouble. . ."

"Course they will. . . but those people are always lucky. Besides, it's a strong boat. It may be an old, shabby, unpainted boat, but it's a little sloop built in Marseille and they're strong swimmers. What's more, it's well treed and with the right sail it would last a good while – and gracefully – in the gulf."

"Where's it from?"

"From Ibiza. The master, who's on board, is from Ibiza."

"A smuggler?"

"No, senyor, if he were a smuggler, he wouldn't be so close in."

"So what's this man doing hereabouts in winter? Is he fishing, convalescing, contemplating the scenery?"

"Nosey-parking."

"What exactly do you mean by 'nosey-parking'?"

"It would take ages to tell you. If you like, we'll talk about that later."

"You said there's a pilot on board. Is the pilot from these parts?"

"Yes, senyor. He hails from the port of Llançà."

"An acquaintance of yours?"

"You know, he's an acquaintance of sorts, one of the few enemies I've got on these rocky shores. A bad character, I can tell you."

"The sloop is carrying a crew of two. . ."

"Yes. The master, Verdera by name, we call him Fatty Verdera because he is so stout. And the pilot is Tanau. When they were in Port de la Selva, another person was on board, a woman, but she's left by now."

"And who was she?"

"You can imagine! A skinny blonde from the French coast who drank like a trooper."

"And do these people lead their lives on board? Do they eat and drink on the sloop?"

"When Tanau is around, they do. When he's not, Fatty disembarks and eats in the inn. Tanau's not on board right now. He's gone back to Llançà to see his wife, who's doing poorly."

"Is this Fatty an old sea wolf?"

"You bet he is! He's skippered small merchant ships. He knows this coast really well. He'll have had many narrow escapes sailing to France."

"That's all very well, but I still don't understand why these people anchored in El Jonquet when they could have easily moored by Cadaqués and been without a worry in the world. How come they're being so rash?"

"I expect it's because they think that's the way to be nearer to the action. . ."

"And what action might that be?"

"Don't ask me! But they reckon something is going to. . . They're nosey-parking. . ."

"So we're back to nosey-parking? What exactly do you mean?"

"We'll talk about that in good time, perhaps sooner than you think, if you really want to, that is. . ."

We'd reached the fork by the En Duran farmhouse, and I felt he wanted to say goodbye. The lights of Cadaqués were flickering, and here and there I could see stretches of white wall. It was very dark. The viscosity in the air had heightened. You could feel an unpleasant muddiness underfoot. The tower of La Creu, the color of squid ink, stood out vaguely in the damp, clammy haze.

"Before we say goodbye," I told him, "I'd like to ask a favor of you."

"And I'd like to ask one of you too."

"That's fine, then we'll be quits. . . Please tell me who you are."

"I'm somebody they call Bread and Grapes."

"Are you from Cadaqués? I don't recall ever seeing you."

"No, senyor. I'm from Llançà."

"So you are *the* Bread and Grapes from Llançà? That's a lovely nickname! I've heard about you. I've heard it said that Bread and Grapes is more or less a full-time smugg. . ."

"No, senyor, you've been misinformed. . . ! That's not to say that, if something comes up, you don't make the most of it, if you get my drift?"

"Naturally! And now it's your turn. . . Get a move on, or we'll be soaked like a couple of geese."

"Yes, senyor. I just wanted to ask if we could meet up tonight. . ."

He formulated that question with the same intensity as the one he'd asked by the En Morell stockyard. His face set in a forced smile, his pupils swelled.

"Where do you want to meet? I'm staying at La Marina tavern. You can come any time after dinner."

"No, senyor, the tavern is out of the question. I realize this will be a bother but we should meet at home, or rather, the house where I'm staying. It's behind the church. . . The door will be ajar. . . no need to knock."

And he gave me details of the house's whereabouts.

"So when would you like me to come?"

"Is eleven all right?"

"That's perfect. . . And then you can tell me something. Why they call you Bread and Grapes."

"I'll tell you whatever you want. Don't you worry."

I begin to like living in Cadaqués when all the summer visitors have gone, when the town is imbued with the emptiness of so many shuttered houses, the gloomy presence of ruined buildings, when nobody strolls along the streets and the mistral lifts cats' tails, when behind those rather theatrically decorated façades you sense the pulse of a hard, persnickety, rather mysterious life, full of self-denying misery. It's then that I like the town, no matter the weather.

After dinner – the tavern's dining room was empty – I spent some time in the café – which was empty too – and at a quarter to eleven started to walk down El Portal on my way to the rendezvous we had agreed upon. When it rains and turns damp and overcast, Cadaqués – the geology of Cadaqués, its landscape – turns black and shiny, the dark slates become slick with a lead-tinted juice where the light seems to dwell and soften into a matte dark blue. That night, there was a faint, icy drizzle. Rainwater dripped monotonously off roofs. The slates were sticky and moist. The dearth of street lighting seemed deliberate, so you would slip and break your skull. Not a soul on the streets. An almost dramatic silence. The odd window let out a small crack of light: yellow light seemingly from a sickly person's bedroom. Sometimes you thought you heard the vaguest, almost imperceptible noise of a distant conversation behind a door. When I reached the front of the church, I heard the owls in the belfry.

I turned up the side street to the right of the church – as you look at the façade – and took fifty steps in the sooty black. Up that side street, at a spot where I imagined there were houses with collapsed roofs, the path starts to descend. I walked along it gingerly so as not to stumble. As I did so, I realized how little I knew Cadaqués, the numerous corners of the town I'd never seen, despite my long stays there and the curiosity the town aroused in me. The end of my descent left me in front of a solitary house with a crack of light in the door. I went in as agreed: without knocking.

I found myself in a long passageway at the end of which a murky, yellowish light flickered. As I walked down the passageway, Bread and Grapes appeared in the diffuse light. When I came to the end, I saw I was in the kitchen. There was a small fire in the hearth in a back corner. Hearth fires in Cadaqués tend to be meager.

"How are we?" I asked.

"I must say we're well," he replied, forcing a laugh.

I felt, however, that Bread and Grapes wasn't as upbeat as he had been at dusk. I thought he looked depressed and seemed tired. While he helped me take off my sou'wester, he said naturally and calmly: "Sorry to have been such a nuisance. . . It's no night to be tramping the streets. . ."

"Don't worry. . . I always go to bed late. Besides, I can tell you I'm really thrilled to be speaking to a man by the name of Bread and Grapes. It's a lovely nickname, if a little strange."

"What can we do about that? It was my father's and I was stuck with it."

I heard what sounded like a stifled laugh and turned my head toward where it originated. I saw a young woman in front of the fire, looking in our direction; she seemed young and dark with the whitest of teeth and immaculate hair, but was slovenly dressed.

"Maria. . ." said Bread and Grapes, rather embarrassed. "You must know her. Everyone in Cadaqués does. She's my landlady. . ."

I apologized for not seeing or greeting her earlier. Maria got up from the fireside and asked if she could get me anything. Bread and Grapes drowned out my thanks by telling her to bring coffee and a bottle of cognac.

The room had a round table, reed chairs, a corner cupboard, a tiled floor, a stove, the hearth, prints of Naples, a bucket, a pitcher, a lurid calendar and a small mirror hanging from a hook on the cupboard. The ceiling was vaulted and the walls whitewashed. There were two steps and a door in the corner opposite the hearth, the door – I imagined – to the stairs. It was all simple, shabby and ordinary. I felt quite at home after three minutes in that kitchen. Nothing jarred: everything felt lived in, useful and comfortable. There didn't seem to be a draft in the place, an absence which is always welcome.

When we'd poured our coffee, Bread and Grapes told the girl: "Maria, my dear, time for you to go to bed. I've got to talk to this gentleman and tomorrow we have to be up early. . . It's late!"

Maria shrugged her shoulders emphatically, nodded, and with a conniving smile went through the door to the stairs without saying a word.

"Now you'll tell me. . ." I began, when we were face to face.

"Yes, senyor," said Bread and Grapes, livening up. "I've heard you take a stroll to El Jonquet every day. . ."

"Yes, senyor, that's right."

"Please understand that if I could do this myself, I'd not have bothered you. I could, if you like, use a friend from Cadaqués. But believe it or not, I trust you, whom I've known for three or four hours, more than any such person. You are the right man."

"Right man for what? Please explain yourself."

"Right man to keep an eye on the boat in El Jonquet, the one we were discussing this evening."

"But why do you want me to do this? What does 'keeping an eye on' entail exactly? I don't think I've ever kept an eye on. . ."

"Of course, of course. . . I'll ask a question that will help you understand. Did you notice that Fatty Verdera's sloop has a rowboat?"

"Yes, I did."

"Where was it when you left El Jonquet this evening? Tied to the stern of the sloop or on land, on the beach?"

"It was on land, on the beach."

"Do you know what that means? Do you know what it means if the rowboat is on the beach? It means nobody is on the boat, that Fatty and the pilot have disembarked."

"Obviously!"

"That's what I mean by keeping an eye on. . . There are lots of small details concerning this boat I must keep abreast of to make sure they don't do me down. . ."

"So what you want me to do is to look around whenever I go to El Jonquet and then tell you what's going on. . ."

"Exactly. . . You won't arouse any suspicion because you've never been mixed up with any of us. If they spot me in the vicinity of El Jonquet, even though I'm a dab hand at these things, something will go wrong. I'd rather not think what might happen if they see a member of my gang in Cadaqués! We all know each other, right? And have done so from way back, if you get me."

"But what's it all about? What are all these squabbles? Is it to do with smuggling?"

"I told you this evening it would take a long time to explain."

"That's all very well. But you do realize one favor earns another. I promise I'll keep going to El Jonquet, as I always do, and I'll tell you what I see in the cove. But you must understand I don't want to get mixed up in anything unpleasant, particularly anything that might implicate me out of ignorance."

"It's all very urgent. . . I don't know how to put it. . . You're the only person who can avoid a disaster."

"That wasn't what I meant. . ."

"You're asking me to reveal something very sensitive. . ."

"As are you. . . We are level pegging. I think it absolutely fine that you smugglers are discreet and cautious. Discretion and absolute silence are the basis of your business. But you must realize, dear Bread and Grapes, that I know who you are. I've heard people talk about you a lot. Only a moment ago, a man in the café said he'd seen you in Els Jònculs at midday."

"He's wrong there. I was here at midday and at four I was by the En Morell stockyard waiting for you."

"I'm sorry I kept you waiting so long. I just wanted to say that everyone knows exactly who you are. Not the details of what you're up to, of course, but they recognize your face."

"Whatever you say. But we can never be too discreet."

"That's true. And that's why I'm surprised you want to keep discretion all to yourself. I've a right to a bit of discretion too, don't you think?"

"I can see I've got this all wrong, that I've made the wrong choice. . . !" said Bread and Grapes, in an anguished tone, wearily getting up from the fireside.

"No, you haven't! You can assume, for my part, that I have forgotten everything we could, can or might talk about. I've a hopeless memory. How about a drop more cognac?"

"I can see I shouldn't have said a word. . ." insisted Bread and Grapes, in that same upset tone.

"You're wrong. Come on, let's clear the air. . . What's the problem with Fatty? You portray him as a dangerous character. I believe you. But I think you're just as dangerous. I thought you seemed very agitated this afternoon. And I think you're even more so tonight, despite being so cautious. What's your beef with Fatty?"

"None. What do you expect? Business matters."

I stared at him. Suddenly he changed tack and asked: "Why do you need to know?"

"No need at all. I'm just curious. Curious. . . in a literary kind of way."

"What do you mean 'literary'?"

"So I know what's going on and then, some day or other, thirty years hence, I might tell. . ."

"Don't you see I shouldn't have told you a thing?"

But he said that in a very different tone of voice – at least that's what I felt. I sensed he was beginning to trust me.

"Would you believe me if I say I find you very hard going?"

"Well, that's mutual. . ."

I got up from my chair, went toward my sou'wester, which was hanging behind the door, intending to put it on and leave.

"Sit down! What's the rush?" he asked, blocking my way. "What have you got on in the morning? Nothing, I bet. . ."

"This is a waste of our time. . ."

"Why be so impatient? How long have we known each other? Don't be so prickly! We've time to talk about everything, sit down!"

"I prefer things ready and shipshape. You must take your chances when they arise. Blather gets you nowhere."

Obviously, before getting embroiled in any escapade with that individual, however insignificant the business of the boat in El Jonquet was, I wanted clarification, to know more or less what was behind the quarrel between those two men. The presence of Fatty Verdera in Cadaqués was very odd. Bread and Grapes's suppressed tensions, even more so. What surprised me most was that Bread and Grapes, an expert in clandestine activities in the area, notorious for his skill in obtaining secret information – the customs police had never been able to catch him in the act – should try to use me in the matter of El Jonquet. It was a bold step to approach a stranger like myself, hoping for a collaboration that might turn out to be embarrassing and counterproductive. He'd clearly heard good things about me. No doubt, he thought I was an idler who went to El Jonquet to write poems. But there lay the rub: why had he approached me when he himself could have hidden in the cove for a week, confident he wouldn't be seen by anyone? The veil over his intentions was very thin. But what exactly was he planning? What was Bread and Grapes up to in El Jonquet?

I didn't return to the fireside, and it was then, when Bread and Grapes saw I was determined to walk away, that he decided to open up. We had our exchange standing by the door to the passageway. He probably rambled on for twenty minutes nonstop, jumbling things up as people do when circumstances affect them directly. A smuggler lives obsessed by the idea of betrayal. He believes that if he weren't subject to betrayal, he would be invulnerable and could exercise his trade with complete impunity. The source of betrayal is envy and resentment. Sometimes envy assumes a commercial form; sometimes it is spite – namely, annoyance caused by the presence of certain individuals in our environment, gratuitous, unintentional annoyance some people arouse simply by being in our vicinity. Bread and Grapes outlined all that incoherently, in fits and starts, but his verbal incontinence did reveal a few facts. Facts that are important for subsequent events in this story.

He told me he'd been involved in contraband for many years and led a gang that operated along the coast of the Cape Creus peninsula (this was public knowledge). He added that, thanks to his endeavors, he was practically the kingpin in such matters (which was also well known). He said his gang was noteworthy because it was savvy, canny and rooted locally. He was a representative for a company that obtained its merchandise in Algiers. This company faced fierce competition from another Majorcan company that worked out of

Gibraltar and Tangier. One of the ingredients in that rivalry was Fatty Verdera.

Fatty Verdera, who had skippered packets that crossed the gulf, knew the territory and as a result had been made responsible for this stretch of coast. He'd tried to establish a presence but had made no progress. Every partnership he'd set up had collapsed. Fatty Verdera had thus concluded that the only solution for his business lay with Bread and Grapes. He made contact. The men had known each other for years. Fatty suggested very favorable deals with a view to persuading him to leave the other company. Bread and Grapes rejected them outright; he wasn't interested. He was a man of his word and happy with the deal he had with the enterprise he was serving and wasn't prepared to leave it for the first newcomer who came calling. At first Bread and Grapes's lucidity and obstinacy surprised Fatty Verdera. Bread and Grapes believed Fatty would now let things be and leave him in peace for good. Bread and Grapes was a man who preferred to carry out clandestine acts rather than talk about them. He was quiet and reserved. Banter made him anxious and made his blood pressure rocket. However, his rejection wounded Fatty's self-esteem. Fatty wasn't going to give up so easily. Commercially, that type of business was attractive because the territory offered such good prospects. Fatty considered his own failure to penetrate the business a black mark. He wasn't one to accept such a setback lightly. So he believed he had to pursue Bread and Grapes. He entered negotiations with him that lasted months, in the course of which he vastly improved all his original offers. The only result was to increasingly inflame Bread and Grapes. Pursued by Fatty's wheedling charms, Bread and Grapes was at the end of his tether. He felt all those offers, all those conversations, all that interest, were an insult to discretion, to silence, to the absolute reserve that was a basic requirement in their line of trade. He had engineered things so his family never knew where he was and had never been open about key matters with members of his gang; he now considered himself harassed and outraged by the lighthearted insouciance with which Fatty approached their activities. The moment came when the mere notion of Fatty's existence sent his brain into a spin and gave him a strange sense of physical unease. He began to see him as a real enemy and to consider the way he was acting as a criminal, fateful source of rivalry.

However, up to that point things remained on theoretically innocuous terrain. Bread and Grapes could do nothing against Fatty because he had no evidence of wrongdoing. Nor could Fatty do anything against Bread and Grapes because he still hoped to win him over and involve him in his plans. Thus, de facto, each man stood his ground. But the day came when Fatty decided it would be impossible to recruit him to his outfit and that led to a marked change in the situation. After a long period when they had no news of each other, Fatty appeared on the coast in the stern of his old, battered sloop from Marseille. The sloop spent a long time, most of spring and summer that year in Llançà and Port de la Selva and then in the autumn sailed into the waters around Cape Creus. Apparently, Fatty was acting the tourist. On a short trip to Collioure he'd taken a woman on board – to wash the dishes, so he said. Fatty visited taverns, prepared tasty fish stews on board and soaked up alcohol like a sponge. Once when he was transferring from the rowboat to the sloop, he fell into the water and they struggled to drag him out. All that was surprising because it seemed so benign. Fatty was a businessman who never wasted his time on frivolous activity. But what really exasperated Bread and

Grape was the fact that Fatty employed Tanau as his pilot, sailor and cook. Tanau *was* his enemy. He was, or so he said that afternoon, one of the few enemies he had on the coast. He was a persistent, all-out, unwarranted enemy. The two men had never had any serious or major contact; there'd never been any real friction between them, but Tanau hated Bread and Grapes for simply existing. He was Bread and Grapes's enemy number one because Tanau was always talking about him. Given his line of business, talking about him was the worst offense possible; it broke and offended the reserve and discretion that went with the territory. "Talking about me, singling me out, is to betray me, do you see?" said Bread and Grapes. But Tanau had gone further: he'd informed on him openly. He was a real snitch. That was why when Bread and Grapes saw the two men together in the sloop, he decided things were entering a dangerous phase.

"Those guys are much cleverer than the customs police and are on board their filthy sloop looking for proof, all they do is spy on me and try to catch me at it."

"Do you have a clue as to why?" I asked.

"It's hard to say. Maybe to destroy me or make me relent and force me to join them."

"Are you sure tension isn't blinding you, that you're not taking this too personally?"

"I don't think so. Contrary to what people think, business is poor, has gone downhill and is getting worse. There's a lot of competition and that's a disaster. It's not like years ago. I spend my life tramping up mountains, negotiating these rocky coasts night and day, and I get a miserable return. It's a serious matter precisely for that reason: it's shrunk so, it's all about a few wretched pessetes."

"And self-esteem as well, I imagine."

"Of course. But not self-esteem in the way you perhaps think. In terms of Fatty and me, it's not about who will hold out the most, who's the toughest. What I hate about that man is the gross way he handles dangerous, undercover activity, his total lack of savvy. It's so easy to do things badly. Things should be done properly."

"I see that. You are a real pro as a smuggler and Fatty is a mere amateur."

I thought such praise would appeal to his vanity. I was wrong. Bread and Grapes responded with a completely indifferent shrug of the shoulders.

"So, to sum up," I told him, as I grabbed the wooden door knob, "you think it's impossible to reach a compromise. I ought to tell you I'm the kind who always likes to make things work."

"So am I. But in this case I don't see it. This business will end badly. If it involved only Fatty, there might be a way. But don't you worry: Tanau will make sure that doesn't happen. That's why I said it will have to be resolved one way or the other. One of us has to go."

That last sentence brought a smile to my lips – I'd say almost unconsciously. I said goodbye, left and heard Bread and Grapes bolting and barring the door behind me. I glanced at the house. It was not exactly a house that was isolated from the town; it was, however, a house whose back – via the kitchen door – lead to an olive grove. In that sense it was a wonderful place for a man who operates outside the law. It offered easy access to the olive grove – to the mysterious world of the olive groves of Cadaqués – and that's priceless. When I walked up the church lane, I heard the cracked parish bell chime three o'clock.

The weather hadn't changed. There was a very high level of humidity. The viscous sheen seemed to soften the slates, the persistent water seemed to deflate things. A red haze enveloped the street lights. Old

Cadaqués's lanes were completely silent. The silence was even more striking on the beach: the sea gave no signs of life. It was still. The water had a dense quality, like tar, and was just as black. It was a dense, mysterious sea that had lost its lightness of touch, its playful sense of movement.

I slowly walked to La Riba and took a stroll beneath the tamarinds on the promenade. My imagination retained the very real presence of Bread and Grapes. I'd looked at him from all sides as he'd gone on and on. I'd been surprised by the huge concentration of strength suggested by his body. I don't think he'd reached thirty. He was small and stocky, and his flesh was compressed like the ears of a sheaf of alfalfa. His face was round and wanly dark, his eyes black and bright, his nose and mouth normal, his ears big, his teeth splendid, his voice loud and gruff. A face that gave you the impression it could express every possible shade of emotion, that it could be irascible, sensitive, susceptible, suspicious, flattering, affable or taciturn. But you could never imagine it as deadpan. Despite his forceful physicality, you imagined him exuding charm and unctuous politeness. His arms and legs were short, his hands fleshy, his fingers short and thick. His black hair was a touch unruly – hair that rebels against the comb – and his face always seemed stubbly. When he left the barber, he still sported yesterday's bristles. You caught a glimpse of steely biceps under his jacket sleeves, and muscular thighs and large, imposing knees under his trousers. Sometimes, especially when he heard something to his liking, the blackness in his eyes liquefied – I formed the constant impression that he must be a good companion and the sort that will resist to the last, if need be.

Despite the bad weather, I went to El Jonquet on subsequent days.

The light gray of the silvery-green olive trees was a delight. The cove slumbered, solitary and still: exactly as if it were asleep, as if all notions of time had fled the place. The sea was completely calm, as if holding its breath. Occasionally water crept up the soft, muddy sand and seemed to sigh – as if the sea could no longer hold its breath and needed to exhale. The water was a pale white, a morose shade of gray that caressed your eyes. The fjord's still waters, between the purple seaweed and strident green reeds, seemed more opaline, more pearly than the sea. The coast oozed dampness.

The small sloop was still anchored at the back of the cove – on the beach – and its lack of movement brought to mind a drawing rather than any tangible object. The wet had stiffened its rigging, and yet the lines seemed filthier, more fragile than on the first day. The vessel had a small cabin, which must have had a very low ceiling, two portholes on each side and a cockpit in the stern, where I could also see a trestle table and hatchway, near the rope on the prow. Next to the mast was a stove, a few dishes and various cooking utensils. They'd left the boat looking untidy; they'd not even bothered to pull a canvas over the cockpit; the cabin door looked open, though I couldn't be sure about that given the state of my eyesight. The vessel was in the old style, round, broad, with little in the way of sails. Its power of resistance must have been tried and tested. Given its state of neglect, I was tempted to drag the rowboat up and, most of all, to give it a bit of shelter from the rain. But I decided not to, I thought they'd probably not have thanked me.

The rowboat remained perched on the beach like a small frog. I couldn't see any fresh footsteps on sand that had hardened. Judging by what I could see, it had enjoyed a state of unbroken solitude.

Four days after the conversation I've just transcribed, I was on my way back to Cadaqués when I spotted a man leaning on the En Morell stockyard wall; he was smoking a cigarette. I saw the glow from a long way away. It was Bread and Grapes.

"How are things?" I asked.

"I must say things are good. . ." he replied, using that hallowed Cadaqués response, immediately adding: "Been to El Jonquet?"

"Yes, senyor, I've been to El Jonquet."

"Anything new to report?"

"Not a thing. Not a living soul. And what about you? Have you been working these last few days?"

"Me? I've been thwarted as usual. . . Listen: I'd like to ask you something."

I could tell from his eager, anxious tone that he'd come expressly to put that question to me.

"I'd like to ask you a. . ." he repeated.

"Go ahead."

"How is the boat in El Jonquet anchored?"

"It's anchored with its anchors very deep in, as if anticipating a blast of the mistral."

"Two anchors set in a *V*?"

"No, senyor: a single anchor and a single rope."

"Is the rope in good condition?"

"My eyesight isn't too good, but it appeared to be made of new hemp. You don't see many like that around here."

In the meantime we kept walking to Cadaqués. The air was heavy. The stillness of time and place, intense.

"What you've just said," and he accompanied his words with a sly laugh, "is really interesting. There are things you should know. Tanau isn't mad; he knows the territory and knows the nearer a boat is to land, the less it will suffer from the mistral."

"Naturally. And where are the men from the boat?"

"Tanau is in Llançà. His wife is sick. I already told you that. Fatty Verdera must be eating and drinking in Figueres or Barcelona. He can only think about such things and making my life impossible."

"Bread and Grapes, aren't you being rather presumptuous?"

"No, I am not! You know, the way those men have vanished, the air of abandon over the sloop, is all about whether I'll fall into their trap. I'd even say that Tanau's wife's illness is probably faked. They thought I'd resume work if they didn't show up for a few days. What gets their goat most is that I don't react. If only you knew how much money I've lost because of those crooks! Two fishing boats that should have been working around here have been forced to land along the Sant Feliu coast. Since Fatty took Tanau on, I've done nothing and I'm not thinking of doing anything any time soon. If they saw movement, they'd fall on me like flies on honey."

"Are you really doing nothing?"

"I told you: nothing at all. However, something or other must be done. They've prepared a trap for me by pretending they've left. I'm beginning to wonder if it's not time to force them to fall into a trap of my making."

"I don't understand."

"Right! I can do something similar and force them to come back. And when they come, we'll pounce."

"It all sounds very complicated."

"They call it the 'Llançà corporal's strategy.' These people have such a way with words! And don't think I won't: if nothing new happens, I'll probably start plotting now. I intend to go to Jònculs tomorrow."

"And why Jònculs?"

"Jònculs is key to one of the bits of business I do. It really is."

"And what will you do in Jònculs?"

"Nothing. Loaf around, so somebody or other sees me and spreads the news of my presence."

"And how will you go there?"

"I'll go via La Cruïlla, by the shortcut from Cadaqués to Roses."

"What if I come too? I'd like to see what La Cruïlla is like with you as my guide."

"I'll be frank: your presence in Jònculs would be no help at all. If they see us together, they'll think we've just gone for a stroll, and that's precisely what I don't want them to think. We reach Dead Woman's Well and then go our different ways. From there on, you'll have to decide what's best for you, understand?"

"I understand. When do you want to leave?"

"At ten a.m. All right?"

"Rendezvous?"

"Past the En Baltre farmhouse. I'll be waiting. In any case, you will go to El Jonquet tomorrow, won't you?"

"Yes, of course, as I always do."

"I'm very interested in anything you can tell me about the sloop's anchorage. That would be a real help. I'll tell you why some day. . ."

We'd reached Bread and Grapes's public frontier. We said good-bye; I headed toward my tavern, and who knows where he went!

La Cruïlla carries the stigma of the Cadaqués poor. For centuries it has been the shortcut used to transport things to sell in Roses. People have carried thousands of tons of goods, especially fish, wine and oil, along that hellish, precipitous route. The Cadaqués poor, mainly women, transport things on their heads – used as they are to carrying buckets of water like that. The sweaty treks along that path in summer and winter, in all weathers, over the centuries, would create, if ever brought together, a colossal energy mass. It's where people have relinquished their youth, muscles, nerves and spirit. They've relinquished them there, and continue to do so.

The journey from Cadaqués to Roses is possibly not as demanding as the other way around. The climb doesn't seem so steep or abrupt, as does the one you must tackle from the Alzeda farmhouse to the Pení col on the way back to Cadaqués. But it offers little relief: if the path seems easier, loads, on the other hand, are full. When they return, the climb is tougher, the loads lighter. As we said, La Cruïlla is an instrument of torture for the Cadaqués poor.

Now, if the journey is for pleasure, it is magnificent. You must experience La Cruïlla if you want to have the slightest idea of this country. The path offers wonderful, panoramic views. The day they build the Roses-Cadaqués coastal road – a thing we probably won't see – people will be entranced by its beauty.

You start on the path at Llaner, a poor track to the En Baltre farmhouse. At one point to your right you pass the turning to the Sant Sebastià hermitage, the popular sanctuary of Cadaqués. On its saint's day people walk up there, eat omelet and *butifarra* and indulge in violent dancing shindigs. The track peters out by the En Baltre farmhouse and a goat track starts the climb to one side of Pení Mountain through an infernal pile of rocks.

This climb, if done leisurely, with time to look back now and then, is bewitching. As you climb, your vision of the sea gradually expands. A captivating sea spreads itself before you and land shrinks and thins out. To the north, over waters disappearing in a distant haze, you can see the silhouettes of Cape Creus and Massa d'Oros, the fractured coastline of Mar d'Avall, the gentlest curve of Guillola Bay and the aggressively white town of Cadaqués on its silvery-green cushion of olive trees in the depths of the bay. You can see El Baluard, crowned by its flamboyant fortified church, and a sliver of beach. La Riba, El Poal and El Pianc. And like a fugue over the sea, the olive-tree-covered coast, the Colom tower, Ros Beach, S'Arenella and Caials. The windmill's old tower rises above this tongue of land and at a similar height the whitewashed walls of the Sant Baldiri cemetery and church shimmer through the dense green foliage of olive and cypress trees.

That magnificent landscape, like all landscapes, has its days, its hours, its moments. The morning in question offered nothing novel in terms of the weather compared to previous days. Perhaps it wasn't so stifling, but it remained overcast. It was a yellowish-gray day: the becalmed sea was the color of watery absinthe. Geological strata blackened and gleamed like trails of snail slime. Weighed down by humidity, trees seemed depressed by their burden; the olive trees had lost their svelte, airy lightness. There was a muted stillness in the air. The porous murk gave the whitewashed walls of Cadaqués the bland, spongy consistency of runny cream. Smoke slowly spiraled from chimneys and melted into a low sky the color of French chocolate.

In any case, even if it had been a more open, clearer day, the morning has never been the time to see this landscape, in my opinion. Bright morning light is not the best for this countryside. When the light is full on, the black of slates, the white of walls, the green of vegetation meld into a paste and you can see nothing. It is in the evening, when the sun goes down behind Pení, that the details of its warmth emerge, when color and feeling emerge from the landscape. Olive trees become seamless, delicate and vaporous. They gleam grayly. Monotone geological strata lighten. Patches of white shimmer elegantly, humanly, enlightening and ennobling heart and mind. The detail traced over the white is exact, perfect and voluptuous. Reflected in the grain of the sea – sometimes a slightly black-cherry, vinous hue – white shapes seem more fragile than in the medium of the air. The reflections are embellished by the magic of the sea's mirror. The gently waning light imposes on everything – or perhaps extracts – the spirit of the landscape, a spirit that suffuses an observer with a sense of isolation and remoteness.

Bread and Grapes was waiting for me past the En Baltre farmhouse, and though I arrived a quarter of an hour late, he showed no signs of impatience. He seemed very happy. Despite the autumnal season and weather, he wore nothing on his head, carried his jacket over his arm and gave an impression of wondrous strength. He strode along enthusiastically at a speed that was too much for me. I told him I couldn't keep up.

"You must realize," he said, "that I'm in my element now. This is my country. I should really confess how relaxed I feel among these rocks. . . Besides, I'm in a hurry. . ."

"To do what?"

"When we reach the top, I'll add something to what we were discussing the other day. Pity it's such a gray day. . ."

"November weather. . ."

"Yes, senyor, if it were lighter, you'd have a better grasp of what I'm about to tell you."

It was a steep, straight climb, and my sedentary heart raced. Bread and Grapes, on the other hand, had made concerted efforts to slow down. He walked in front and when he planted his leg down, his steely muscles flexed. We finally reached the slope of the mountain – I was exhausted, he was as fresh as a daisy – where that broad incline meets the southern ridge of the Pení mountainside.

Then, to the south, a vast panorama came into view where you could see the misty, green-black mountains of Begur and Gavarra on the horizon; before them, the Medes Islands, the Santa Caterina de Torroella mountains and the wonderful land of the Ampurdan, the silvery ribbons of its rivers (the Fluvià and the Muga) and the blue-white ponds of Castelló; the Gulf of Roses opened opposite the plain, closed to the west by the convulsive shapes of the Garrotxes, a huge, magnificent sweep of a gulf like a somnolent lake; the mountainside dropped seaward swiftly and suddenly and died on the pink-gray granite of Norfeu, the Jònculs inlet and the pine trees of La Falconera. It was an intriguing spectacle, though like all things hazy, not without its touch of melancholy.

"Sit down!" blasted Bread and Grapes, interrupting my reverie.

We sat down on the corner of the Pení ridge. It was a singular spot that allowed us sight, to the north, of the entire coastline of Cape Creus and the Gulf of Lion and, to the south, the Gulf of Roses. The Cape Creus peninsula stood out wonderfully beneath us – the part I'm referring to, that is. Bread and Grapes seemed immune to the spectacle. His mind was full of more tangible matters.

"This spot," he said, with a laugh, eyes lit up by passion and life, "is very pretty. It's the exact place from which I hope you'll begin to understand my trade. If I succeed, you'll see why Fatty Verdera is so interested in all this. You, senyor, are attached to things of the sea and will understand me right away. Imagine any boat, a Majorcan fishing boat, for example, located ten or twelve miles to the east and outside the entrance to Cadaqués Bay. This vessel is waiting for the appointed time to unload its cargo of tobacco or whatever on the coast. As dusk falls, the boat is spotted by vigilant customs police. They pinpoint it perfectly in their binoculars. If this vessel had only one place where it could work, if the nature of the coast and the boat's movements allowed only a single movement, its efforts could be fully observed and controlled. But the boat I've mentioned can keep close to land because it has complete freedom of action. It's been spotted by police binoculars, but that doesn't guarantee they know which way it's going to head to do what it has to do. The nature of the coastline means that the fishing boat, where it is located, is an equal distance from the Cape Creus and the Cape Norfeu coasts. Whether there is a southerly or northerly wind, the boat's position allows it to work in either place, even though by land Cape Creus and Cape Norfeu are separated by a huge distance and difficult, precipitous terrain. If there is a northerly wind, the vessel can sail back up Cape Creus with the yard tied hard to the rode, its sheet down, and slip into Portaló, for example; or it could lower the sheet and go into Jònculs. If it's a southerly, the vessel will reach Jònculs with the yard tied to the rode and the sheet down, or it can head straight to Portaló or Taballera. As you know, the distance on foot along goat tracks between Jònculs and Portaló is so great it's normally impossible to establish a watch in both distant points and all places in between. The vessel is completely free to create its own subterfuge: at twilight it can persuade the lookouts following its movements through binoculars that it is sailing along the Roses coast; when darkness closes in, it can head to its real destination along La Selva coast. The lookouts will decide from the signs they've picked up that they should gather in Montjoi, for example, though the boat will unload in Taballera. Catch my drift?"

"Absolutely."

"I want you to understand how extraordinarily good this terrain is for our line of business. It's unique. The ability to constantly create convincing subterfuges largely compensates for the rotten weather. Nobody can ever guess from land what a boat involved in these operations intends to do. In coastal locations where you can go only one way, boats must keep far out at sea so they can't be seen from land; that's highly inconvenient because, when you're on a job, nights are short. Here you can keep close to land because the fact you've been seen is of no consequence. Additionally, the coast is full of places that are, each in its way, natural havens or small harbors where you can work really well."

"Bread and Grapes, you are an ace strategist, to put it like that corporal in Llançà. . ."

"Don't start using those peculiar words with me! I wanted to tell you what the quarrel was between Fatty Verdera and me, or rather, yours truly. Fatty knows the terrain perfectly, and as he knows it, he likes it. The man from Ibiza is no idiot. He can see the money to be made. . ."

"Fine! But if that's the state of play, why is there only room for one?"

I asked that question completely deadpan, not emphasizing what was behind it. I anticipated that Bread and Grapes's reaction would be hostile. But the need not to pour more oil on the fire, but rather, to pour on as much water as possible, led me to ask. Bread and Grapes jumped up furiously, and with everything he had to tell me, he gawped at me, not knowing where to begin. The veins in his neck stood out and he turned a deep, incandescent red.

"I'll forgive you for asking that," he finally spluttered, "you may know a lot about writing, but you understand nothing about any of this. Do you think this trade is like running a bakery or a butcher's shop or a tobacco store? For Christ's sake! I only have to think of any competition working in a spot like this and I start fuming and my hair stands on end. Working like that would mean immediate betrayal and prison within a couple of days. . ."

"Please, don't get so worked up! What do you expect if I'm at a loss? Please forgive my total lack of savvy. . . What you need tell me about," I went on, changing the subject, "is the nitty-gritty of your trade. . ."

Visibly calming down, Bread and Grapes replied, "I'll tell you later. What if we start walking again? It's late and we've a long way to go. . ."

"Of course."

We took the path on the southern incline of Pení. We walked a long time without saying a word. The slope we were crossing comprised a series of precipitous ravines that flowed into the main artery of the stream down to Jònculs. The path followed almost a straight line, in a slow descent to the Pení col. I contemplated the wonderful spectacle in awe. Bread and Grapes walked on staring at the ground, still annoyed we were going so slowly. We reached the col and found Dead Woman's Well, a miserable pond where animals from the surrounding farms came to drink. The landscape was treeless and barren.

Another vista opened up from the col, vaster than the previous one; to the north you could see the whole coast of Port de la Selva, Cape Cerbère and, on clear days, the French coast. From this viewpoint you got an exact idea of the geography of the Cadaqués peninsula. The baseline of this peninsula passes over the col, a line formed on its northern side by the stream going down to Port de la Selva and on its southern side by the one to Jònculs. In a way, it is the line that marks out tax evasion in this country. The domain of Bread and Grapes. His muscles of steel had been forged on the precipices of those mountain streams.

"To control this trade," he told me, "you must have broken your bones in these hellish places. I know both streams with my eyes shut and have crossed them in every kind of weather, night and day. It's quite a haul from Port de la Selva to Jònculs. At my pace a little over an hour and a half," he boasted naïvely.

"People always exaggerate. . ." I suggested.

"I tell you that's true! I've left the café in Port at eleven at night and been on Jònculs beach by half twelve. Just as I said, I lost my youth on the sharp edges of these rocks. . . And now, if you like," he added, making a sudden leap, "I'll tell you what you were asking about a moment ago. And we won't talk about anything else for now. We must say our goodbyes. I should be in Jònculs. . . And while we're at it, senyor, what are you intending to do?"

"What would you recommend?"

"Are you hungry? If you are, go to any of the farmhouses on the path back to the road and they'll make you an omelet. They are good folk and close friends of mine. Say my name and every door will open to you."

"Do you really know everyone?"

"These poor farmhouses on this side of Pení, like the ones past Bufadors and Puig Alt on the Cape Creus coast, are one of the keys to what I do. It's very simple. Imagine for a moment we land in Jònculs. Well, if the situation suddenly becomes dangerous, for whatever reason, a wrong movement or a mistake, the goods are stored in purpose-built places along the coast. They're probably not as good as the ones on the Torroella coast, but they're not nothing. If the night is looking good, the gang loads the 'bundles' on their backs and starts walking upstream, along tried-and-tested tracks, as far as these farmhouses, where they hide the goods. The gang breaks up as soon as the job's done. Later, at a time that's considered opportune, the goods are loaded into wine vats and these vats are carried by cart along the road to the requisite place. You must know what you're doing. It's not easy. You must be ready at the right moment. You must have contacts you can trust. People look as if they're transporting full or empty vats, when nothing could be further from the truth. Leading a cart laden with goods in this way, from one of these farmhouses to the station in Llançà, requires a certain presence of mind. . ."

"I've no doubt about that. . ."

"And apply what I just said about the terrain where we are now to the other side of the country. . . and you have everything you wanted to know. Exactly. . . though, I'm sorry, you know nothing, in fact, because it's much easier to talk about these things than it is to do them. Talking about them is like talking about the weather: it gets you nowhere. . ."

We said goodbye after agreeing to meet up in Cadaqués the next day. I saw him slip quickly down the bed of the stream to Jòncols and disappear into a dense olive grove. I ate an omelet in the En Causa farmhouse and slowly walked back to the town along the road. By five – it was getting dark already – I was in Plaça de les Herbes.

The following day I went on my usual walk to El Jonquet, but as I'd not noticed anything new in the cove, I didn't think it necessary to look for Bread and Grapes. Nor did he do anything to show himself. I expect he decided it wasn't urgent or necessary.

When I thought about our excursion to La Cruïlla, one thing became apparent: Bread and Grapes had shown a degree of trust in me. Obviously, I couldn't say exactly how much. When I examined our exchanges at a cooler remove, I felt his explanations were more about indulging me than offering any sense of tangible friendship. He was obsessively focused on El Jonquet and had no doubt provided me all those picturesque details strategically, as he'd probably respond to anything I might ask him, even perhaps giving the odd specific detail, to humor me so I'd continue going there daily. What exactly was he after? I couldn't imagine, however hard I tried. My natural attachment to the cove probably did have a role to play. I find it difficult to pinpoint what that role was exactly. I sometimes think this whole to-do was a pure invention of Bread and Grapes's southern imagination. Now, for my part, and for merely speculative reasons, I find the fact I've become an accessory – clearly a very minor one – to a local smuggler quite amusing. In any case, I've always believed that Cadaqués – until not very long ago a home to witches – was always shrouded in mystery.

At this stage, I'd have thought it premature to judge Bread and Grapes and his stories. I thought that I should at least wait to see the repercussions of his visit to Jònculs. He'd assured me with that deadpan seriousness of his that his (you could almost say our) excursion had consequences for what was at stake in El Jonquet. I couldn't imagine what they might be, but he'd talked about it all so assuredly he'd practically urged me to think of the excursion as decisive, evidenced by the seriousness of his own position. I could only await the fallout from his famous "strategy."

I wouldn't say he was unlikable. I will say that I'm from the Ampurdan and used to dealing with people from my country. If this had happened anywhere else, I'd have fled him as the devil flees the cross. If I was more or less intrigued, it was for the opposite reason: people on this peninsula reckoned they didn't really belong to the Ampurdan. When people from Cadaqués or Port de la Selva have to go to Figueres, they always underline the fact they are going to the Ampurdan, as if it were a foreign land. It makes no sense. Perhaps they think they are different because of their extreme similarity. No. All this is trifling. What I liked about Bread and Grapes, what led me to form a favorable opinion of him, was his physical presence. He is a man who gives you the impression that he is *very* strong. It's unusual to find or have dealings with men like that. All of us are quite puny. You know, the strong people I've met have usually seemed relatively sincere and serious. My curiosity regarding Bread and Grapes largely derived from a wish to find out if this view might be confirmed yet again.

The next time I saw him, he was waiting, as previously, leaning against the wall of the shed in the En Morell stockyard. It was a miserable dusk. The succession of overcast, dim days, with such stillness, viscous damp and absence of wind, was over. That weather, so unusual in those parts, had caused a great number of people to catch colds and had put people in bed with the flu. You heard coughing in the streets – something unusual in a place where people rarely have sore throats and usually rattle away ten to the dozen. A southwesterly had set in; movement had followed stillness. It gusted away, fierce and fast and shook the branches of the olive trees. Waves crashed over La Riba. The water was a murky blue. The November cold was damp and insidious. For hours a spectacular mass of dark black clouds had been rolling over the horizon in a northwesterly direction. Lit windows and streetlights gave off a depressing reddish glow.

"How did your trip go?" I asked Bread and Grapes, by way of a greeting.

"I reckon it was all right."

"Well, what do you reckon?"

"If you really want to know, I can say it was perfectly all right. I reckon Fatty Verdera will get here tomorrow. At least that's what I'm hoping."

"How do you know?"

"It's just a hunch, how shall I put it. . . ?"

"You think you saw him?"

"Only from a distance. . ." said Bread and Grapes with a sly laugh that became cheeky and impish.

"You did what was necessary in Jònculs?"

"I saw the folks I needed to."

"Did you bump into your enemies?"

"I don't have enemies. I've enough with the chatterers. . . They were there."

Bread and Grapes didn't like the superficial tone of our conversation. He probably thought I didn't take him seriously. All of a sudden he said: "You're going to meet Fatty Verdera tomorrow. He'll come to your tavern for lunch, if I've done my sums right."

"What do you want me to say to him? I don't think he'll suspect me at all."

"Nothing, as far as I'm concerned. The only thing I'm interested in finding out is if he's alone or is with that bright spark from Port Llançà. If he's by himself, everything will go swimmingly. If the other fellow comes, we'll see!"

"So, in your eyes, Fatty Verdera isn't the enemy. . . The other fellow, however. . ."

"Fatty is a wretched tyke at the mercy of the bottle. The other man isn't. He goes after what he wants with his eyes open... We'll see! And while we're about it, how did you find El Jonquet?"

"As far as I could see, no changes. There was no sign of anyone paying a visit over the last few days. It's totally calm now that a southwesterly is blowing. The boat is well anchored and has drifted toward the opposite side. It's not moving or dipping. Dear Bread and Grapes, El Jonquet is a wonderful inlet, an excellent haven for boats of that kind."

"And don't I know it!" my friend replied.

The image of the house I'll build one day in El Jonquet – if they decide to sell me the olive grove – passed through my mind.

"And while we're on the subject," Bread and Grapes added, "I remember you said it was anchored by a single rope. . ."

"Absolutely. It's anchored to deal with a single worry: the mistral. The anchor is close to land; it has enough slack to shift with the wind and that will keep it near the beach, its main defense against the mistral.

"And is the anchor still so close to land as you say?"

"Don't doubt that for a second. The boat's hardly in the water. I think you could raise the anchor with the water at thigh level."

"Meaning?"

"I've nothing else to report. And if you don't believe me, you're free to go and see for yourself."

"I believe you! That fellow from Llançà is a bright spark, but sometimes the smartest people miss the easiest trick."

He uttered those final words in a tone that's difficult to describe. He employed a mournful lilt which I thought hid a sense of satisfaction he could barely contain. The tone of his words emphasized his hypocrisy. In the course of our conversations, it's likely Bread and Grapes had used many a hypocritical turn of phrase. I'd paid no heed; that's nothing out of the ordinary. But a child would have spotted the thrust of his latest.

I didn't ask him to explain himself. As we walked, I found it most unpleasant out in the open. The wind was sinister and sad. It wasn't cold, but it felt as if it was; the humidity kept mind and body in an empty, uncurious state. It was the kind of twilight that makes you dream of a good fire, an amusing book or pleasant company and a bottle of whisky. So I felt it right to walk faster and reach town as soon as possible, although I was sure I wouldn't find any of the things I just mentioned. In any case the breeze was so unpleasant, simply finding a refuge appealed.

When we were saying goodbye, Bread and Grapes asked: "You busy this evening?"

"No, why?"

"Come and have supper with me. I'm very happy today. I've got partridges and Maria's a very good cook."

"Thanks, but better leave it for another day. It's an awful night. Cadaqués is horrible when there's a southwesterly. I prefer a week of north winds to four hours of this."

"So just come for coffee."

"No, thanks! Any other night would be better."

"That's a pity. Today's been a good day for me. I don't know how to tell you. . ."

"Well, may God keep it that way. Besides, I imagine we'll meet tomorrow."

"I wouldn't be so sure. I could have lots on tomorrow. We'll see. And don't worry about the weather! This wind could blow all night, but tomorrow will be another day."

"Do you think it will be northerly?"

"A mistral! I almost guarantee you that. . . Sweet dreams!"

"Good night."

In the course of our relationship, many things changed. The only thing that didn't was the level of formality in our conversations. He was always very deferential and I was ever polite, as on the first day we met.

The next morning, when I came down to the dining room, which was always so empty, I saw another place laid on the table next to the one where I usually sat. As the mail coach had just come, I imagined it must be a traveling salesman. I'd not yet started on the anchovies – which, in Cadaqués, soaked in local olive oil, are a tasty starter – when a man appeared in the doorway; he was stout and swarthy and walked slowly over to his table. Intuitively, I supposed it was Fatty Verdera. And in effect, it was. His first request to the waitress was phrased in such a strong Majorcan accent I had no doubt who he was. After lunch the hotel owner confirmed that it was so. Even if I'd tried hard not to, I couldn't have stopped thinking about Bread and Grapes. His first prediction had been fully realized.

Initially I might have been put off track because I didn't find Fatty Verdera to be as fat as his nickname suggested. He was on the fat side, but his height compensated his plumpness. He was a tall, large man. He was swarthy, not in a firm or glowing way but in sickly, off-color fashion.

I saw him so close up and had so little to do – apart, that is, from eating lunch – that I scrutinized him for a while. His face was round, chubby and coarse and had no sharp lines: a face made up of small, insubstantial protuberances and drooping flesh. He looked to be fifty-five, though he was probably younger. His hair was scant and graying and his white eyes bulged above huge purple bags; his forehead was broad, his nose normal, his mouth fleshy, his ears large and the back of his neck short and flabby. Everything else was in proportion to his height: broad shoulders, a serious potbelly, thick legs and sizable feet. He was clean shaven and wore a light-colored suit that hung on him: it was ready-made.

Fatty Verdera picked at his food, sipped his wine quickly – he'd ordered a bottle of the good stuff – and seemed to look at the world aimlessly; his whole body reacted listlessly. When he spoke to the waitress, he did so in the outwardly friendly tone employed by people from those islands. His hands seemed to move stiffly, even robotically. His manner seemed to communicate displeasure toward others, if not toward himself. It was a manner that reminded me of recalcitrant drunkards I have known – people whose reactions seem to have shut down, as if the links between the different parts of their organism had been severed. I remembered Bread and Grapes telling me that Fatty Verdera was a drunkard. Possibly. At any rate, a chronic drunkard, one of those who are in their element with the tiniest drop of alcohol. They usually strive to avoid seeming what they are, try to walk straight-backed, but you immediately see the truth of the situation.

Fatty Verdera's lunch was a long-winded affair, not because of an abundance of victuals, but because he chewed everything so painstakingly. He looked exhausted when he'd finished his meal. However, the proprietor brought him a good filter coffee and placed a bottle of cognac on the table, and Senyor Verdera now seemed to wake up to the outside world. He jollied up slightly.

He gave the impression of a man who felt under the weather. He must have been toping for years. He was one of those people nobody has ever seen in a noisy, grotesque alcoholic delirium, but who, by drinking on a small scale every day, manages to achieve a state of befuddled unawareness. Drop by drop the skin fills. Their organism slowly adapts to their sad passion, and a time comes when everything they do, say and vaguely think must be seen through their obsessive, febrile, alcoholic habit. A time comes when everything annoys them, when they find reality to be most unpleasant and they disengage completely. Though they feel compelled to show an interest, in truth, they couldn't care a damn. Nothing impinges on them. They turn into a kind of bit actor in everyday life; their playacting becomes their defense wall, behind which they pursue their puny lives. I thought Bread and Grapes's observation that Fatty Verdera wasn't an enemy most apt. That fellow would have agreed with anyone, just as he would have disavowed anything. His indifference was absolute. However, that kind of passive, merely contemplative man usually has a predator by his side bending him to his will, simply because a manipulator running the show serves as an easy solution. People like Fatty Verdera find the world so complex and entangled they don't dare take individual initiatives. They need someone else to take the lead...

I tried to pass the time looking at the small ads in the newspaper that had just arrived. After his second coffee, in which he poured an amazing amount of cognac, I decided he would fall asleep. His head slumped onto his right shoulder and his eyes shut for a second.

I could perfectly imagine his state of mind at that point. He'd arrived in an exhausted state after his comings and goings over the last few days. The first thing he'd done after alighting from the bus had been to knock back two or three vermouths in the Casino. Then, during lunch, he'd downed a bottle of wine, followed by three coffees mixed with half a bottle of cognac. It was a copious intake. It's likely that if he'd not been by himself and so absorbed in dubious thoughts, he wouldn't have raised the bar so high. However, this was the outcome. The most obvious thing you could anticipate was that he'd fall asleep at that same table. But all of a sudden, his whole body shuddered and he got up gingerly. Now on his feet, he glanced at his watch, after rummaging in his pocket for a moment. (I suspect he had no clear idea of the time indicated by its hands.) He scornfully returned his watch to its place. He then grasped the handle of the plain, black leather briefcase he'd left on an adjacent chair. The briefcase was bulky and must have contained his crumpled pajamas and most private needs. Then, visibly tottering – despite every effort to proceed with a degree of dignity – he reached the dining-room door. The tavern keeper was on the doorstep.

"So you've finished lunch?" he asked, displaying his uneven teeth.

"Yes, senyor, and it was a fine one."

"Will you be here for dinner?"

"No, senyor. That. . . won't be possible! I'll be back for lunch tomorrow. Good afternoon!"

"Good afternoon!"

When I reached the front door of the tavern I saw Senyor Verdera going up the Sa Felipa side street. He walked rather hunched down on rocky legs. At one stage he steadied himself against a wall. Then he disappeared.

I had letters to reply to, and once I'd done that, I decided to stroll to El Jonquet, as I did almost daily. After passing the Creus bend and walking the top part of the path, I saw the southwesterly had abated. The sea, which I could see beyond the roofs and walls of Cadaqués, was unpleasantly choppy as it usually was after the southerly wind dies down. As I walked, I stumbled over stones and leaves from the olive groves. I found everything quite hard and jagged. The weather was dry. There wasn't a cloud in the sky. The procession of clouds over the sea had come to a halt, and the horizon was clear and bright. To the north, over Bufadors, to be exact, the sky was an icy, metallic blue. It was a pleasure to walk. The air was seamless and light. My heart and mind seemed rejuvenated. The mistral, still far away, was within view.

Before I reached the En Morell stockyard, Bread and Grapes appeared from behind the wall of an olive grove. He seemed very pleased with himself. It was the first time I'd seen him laugh so gleefully.

"So he's come?" he asked, rather jokily.

"Yes, senyor! Your prophecy came true. You're an ace, Bread and Grapes!"

"And hey. . ." he responded immediately, clearly anxious: "Did he come by himself? Did you see anyone else?"

"I couldn't tell you for sure. He spoke to nobody in the tavern while he was eating lunch. But I've no idea whether he saw anyone before lunch."

"That bright spark from Port de Llançà always makes me nervous . . ." he added, his face clouding. "He's always capable of appearing from nowhere . . . We'll see soon enough! Meanwhile, Fatty Verdera *is* here . . . Did he drink a skinful in the tavern?"

"I imagine he drank as he usually does. You know him. On the other hand, you must have seen him walk by not long ago."

"He was a couple of yards away, but he didn't see me. I thought he looked well plastered. He's a man that likes his drink! Now he's gone to sleep it off on the sloop, till tomorrow morning. He doesn't usually eat supper, and if he does, never very much."

"So you think Senyor Verdera is in El Jonquet?"

"I'm sure he is. And he'll have gone to bed hours ago. If you go, you'll spot something new."

"I was intending to spend a while there. . ."

"That's up to you. Let's meet up when you come back. I'll be waiting. I'd ask only one thing. See if anyone else is in El Jonquet apart from Fatty Verdera. You can tell just by looking at the footprints on the beach. Fatty leaves very deep prints. The fellow from Llançà is skinny. On the other hand, if Tanau is on the sloop, he'll show signs of life. He'll cook something or other to eat on deck. . . you get me?"

"I get you perfectly. . ."

Bread and Grapes disappeared into the olive grove and I slowly resumed my walk. When I reached the barren waste of S'Alqueria, I felt the mistral's first faint gusts. A yellow and black streak of cloud scudded across the sky over Puig Alt, almost always a symptom of the wind's presence. The bluish black of the sky had turned glassy.

It was deafeningly still in the cove. The rowboat had gone from the beach and was tied to the sloop's stern. There were no signs of movement on the sloop. The last downpours had transformed the sandy beach into a uniform, compacted mass, where footprints were clearly visible. When I examined them – something I did after lingering in the olive grove – I decided they were all made by the same feet: rather fat feet. Fatty Verdera's. Then again, I felt it was almost impossible that that man in his state could have reached the sloop on his own steam. He could have fallen into the water, for example. But the man from Ibiza must have been so expert in things of the sea he could surely have done everything related to the trade with his eyes shut.

I stayed in El Jonquet for a while. The wind was gradually settling in and almost made me anxious to start back. It was a benign shelter. Wind blew from a funnel created by the small fjord. It rippled the water in the depths of the cove. There was a rapid succession of bluster and calm. When there was a sudden gust, the water seemed to rush as if impelled by a brief tremor, as if it were seething. The calm gave the water a pale, wan color. These variations were visible near the coast, from the shelter given by the rocks along the strand. Thirty fathoms in, the choppy sea foamed, the wind created a lively current that disappeared into the sea. The waves made for an undulating horizon beneath a cold, metallic sky.

I was thinking about how the sloop had been anchored so close to land. Given where it had been positioned, if it had a good strong rope – and everything indicated that was the case – the boat ran no danger. When it was hit by a gust, the mast swayed a little; very little, what was normal in such situations. The anchor rope remained taut. That said, the small sloop's cabin was possibly not the ideal place to spend the night in these conditions. However, it was very likely that Senyor Verdera, when sailing in the Gulf of Lion, had experienced rougher weather.

I waited to see if the ever-wilder gusts of wind led to any movement on deck. They didn't. As I was leaving the cove, I thought I saw a vaguely reddish light shining out of the portholes. Night was beginning to fall. Perhaps the Ibizan had lit a lamp and, in the darkness of the night, the light began to give out unsteady signs of life.

My walk back was most unpleasant. The wind gusted with insane fury across the high, unpopulated, barren wastes of S'Alqueria. Every step I took was a real effort. It was a solid, heavy, tangible wind – a wind you could almost lean on like a wall. As dusk fell, its fury mounted. It blew clouds away like bits of rag, blunted the first stars, brought trees to their knees; pounded by the wind, the twilit sea was an immense expanse of tumultuous, uncontrollable foam. The howling wind brought an elemental savagery to the air. It was a night to shut your door and stay home.

Bread and Grapes was waiting for me, hands in pockets, cowering slightly, in the shelter of the En Morell stockyard wall.

"What's new then?" he asked, walking toward me.

"I don't think there is anything. . ."

"Is it one or two people in El Jonquet?"

"Only one: Fatty Verdera."

"Are you sure the other fellow isn't around?"

"I'm sure, sure. . . I'd say almost a hundred percent."

Bread and Grapes grinned on the sly, but I registered it.

"Time for a cigarette. . ." he said, handing me his tobacco pouch. "What do you reckon? You have to be daft to spend a night like this in El Jonquet! Did you actually see Fatty Verdera?"

"No, senyor. He must have been asleep in the cabin. When I left, there was a small light on inside."

"A small light, you say. Why did Fatty Verdera need a light?"

"I thought it might be a signal left for someone he was expecting."

"You mean the pilot? I don't think so. If he's not here now, he won't come until tomorrow morning. It doesn't make sense to be abroad at night, especially on nights like this."

"Of course. . . And, by the by, what are we going to do? I was thinking that maybe it was time for us to make a move. . . what do you reckon?"

"I really can't accompany you today. . . and believe me it's the weather to be inside rather than out. But I've still got a job to finish off."

"Very well, I'm going back to Cadaqués. Good night!"

The mistral howled like a rabid beast. Against the black night, the stars twinkled brightly. They seemed to have moved closer. At times, the branches of the old plane trees on Plaça de les Herbes shook so violently I thought the wind might have blown off a roof or two in Cadaqués. I watched all that from behind the windows of my tavern balcony at around half past ten just when I was going to bed.

The next morning, after lunch, the proprietor came over and declared rather anxiously: "That gentleman from Majorca, or so he told me, was going to come for lunch, but he hasn't shown up." I tried to tell him anything was possible in that kind of weather.

I didn't go to El Jonquet that afternoon. The mistral continued to gust wildly. It was extremely dry. When that weather goes on for a long time, people start to get edgy. It's as if their nerves were on a short fuse. I spent a while in the café, but there was such a nervous hue and cry in there I quickly left. I spent most of the afternoon reading in the tavern kitchen. I had no news of Bread and Grapes that whole afternoon.

The next morning, tired of being still for so long, I went to El Jonquet, though the wind was still gusting. When I arrived, I felt the wind was scraping my skin off.

I was dumbfounded: the sloop was gone. I couldn't see any trace of its previous presence.

I found it hard to think it through coldly. In the first place one thing seemed beyond debate: the boat hadn't left the cove of its own volition. In any case, I decided to go by Port Lligat on my way back, in case the boat had taken shelter there, which I felt was a very remote possibility.

"If the boat has disappeared," I told myself, as I turned over what had happened, "it can be due only to two possible reasons: either because the anchor rope didn't withstand the fierce wind or because the rope was destroyed, severed, cut or snapped – whichever word you choose to employ – in an iniquitous, criminal way. If that were the case, the wind would have swept the sloop away like a fallen leaf to be swallowed up by the sea. No cock or hen will ever sing from its decks again."

I pledged to return to the cove on a calm day to see whether there was any trace of the anchor or anchor rope on the seabed. Such a find would clarify what had happened.

On my way back, I walked through Port Lligat. The fishermen told me they'd seen no boats and didn't even know there was a sloop in El Jonquet.

When I reached Cadaqués, I went to the magistrates' court to make a statement. It was closed and wouldn't open until the following morning. The clerk listened to me with a pen behind his ear, smoking a cigarette. Then he exclaimed indignantly: "But who could be so stupid as to anchor a sloop in El Jonquet in this weather!"

I discussed it with the tavern proprietor.

"In a nutshell," concluded this gentleman, after a lengthy exchange, "I have lost money, a bottle of wine, half a bottle of cognac and three filter coffees. . . And they slander us innkeepers! What do you reckon? What a country!"

I sent a message to Senyorita Maria who lived in the house where Bread and Grapes stayed. Maria told me her guest had left a good few days ago and hadn't said when he'd be back.

When the mistral died down, a gentle southwesterly set in. The temperature became more benign. I went to El Jonquet. After the fury unleashed over the last few days, a delightful convalescent peace reigned over the cove. The olive groves, which seemed to have molted, came back to life. The sea was still. I thought I could see a becalmed piece of cork floating in the spot once occupied by the sloop. Given it was winter and the place was so isolated, it couldn't have been from a net or creel. I used a bamboo reed to pull the cork inland, to within two yards of the beach. It was a cork attached to a rope, one of those corks people attach to an anchor rope to indicate where it is and facilitate handling. I took my shoes off and went into the water up to my knees to get it. I held it up and saw it was attached to a hemp rope, the rope that had probably belonged to the sloop. I examined the rope and noted someone had cut it in at least two or three places, seeking out the easiest places for a knife. . . until that person had found the right one and severed it by applying the knife with steely strength.

OUT TO SEA

We set sail from Port de Sóller in *Rufí*, a small six-yard-long yacht; it was very early on a September day in 1920. . . the sixteenth or seventeenth, if I'm not mistaken. We were planning to reach Barcelona after dusk. There are roughly some ninety miles from Sóller to Barcelona, as a bird flies. Nothing extraordinary. Perhaps the boat was marginally on the small side.

Before we set off, Martinet, our skipper, offered us black coffee of the highest quality. Unless you're truly exhausted, you usually sleep very uncomfortably in these small craft. Everything is narrow, poky and unyielding. Out at sea, only breezes blowing over the stern are gentle; if there are head winds, they're most unpleasant. Apart from which, everything, especially the water, is impenetrably hard. That coffee stiffened our backbones and put to rights our aching, empty stomachs.

How wonderful coffee is at sea! It's one of the finest discoveries of seafaring folk: starting the day drinking a cup of strong, barely sweetened black coffee on an empty belly. That beverage makes an almost immediate impact: your mind projects itself onto the outside world, you are fascinated by everything around and a gleam comes to your eyes. It's quite the opposite of the sickly, palsied depression generated by milky coffee. Your heartbeat accelerates, your senses are fired up. You go from that limp, tottering murk when you climbed out of bed to a vigorous state, feeling ready for anything. You stop wondering whether life is wearisome, meaningless and a total waste of time. As you look out to sea, those two mouthfuls of coffee encourage you to start the new day – a mysterious new day.

The sun had yet to mount Puig Major. A predawn light in the tiny harbor glimmered over the circle of houses around that liquid shell, a gentle, tender, limpid light outlining everything in delicate colors, as if projected through the most subdued magnifying glass. Things had an infantile freshness, a quiet, passive presence that was nevertheless full of life. All was calm. A profound silence floated in the air, melded into the light, hanging there, waiting for the sun to break, the mute hum of things about to enter the flux of life. The port waters were a greenish purple flecked with red and blessed with the stillness of paradise. It was a palette reflecting the arid terrain around the harbor – rock faces the color of thyme. Fishing smacks anchored by the shore seemed so drowsy they could have been inside a glass cabinet. A brushstroke of vegetation splashed in front of the houses added a dense, moist green verging on black. To the east, above the high mountains, the sun's invading glow echoed across the clean, gleaming sky. But it wasn't yet a summer sun. It didn't yet have the shimmering blue heat of a summer sky. It was brighter and greenish.

The water opposite the town was so flatironed, one image hovered above another: the real port, the cadaverously white houses, the trees, pines and encircling rocks, the rigging of the smacks at anchor, the wave of movement of the early risers – which seemed robotic from a distance – and the port reflected in the waters of the mineral gulf, a wealth of detail in a liquid film that seemed oily, morose, and static, the reflected image sometimes (just for a moment) drawn on tremulous water and then immediately given material form in that strident calm, livelier than the tangible image, more elegant, more seductive, purer than the reality – perhaps because of its very own extreme transience. It was truly bewitching, and there we were, all those on board *Rufí*, holding our cups, gawping at the wonders offered by Port de Sóller. Panxito, the cat sailing with us, put its front paws on the side of the boat and joined us in observing those fine things. For some spirits – and I mean mine, not the cat's – the mere presence of the sea is enough to sink into the deliquescent bliss of the contemplative life. What are you contemplating? Nothing, in the end. Shapes that come and go, are made and unmade, are won and lost, transform and change. Everything at sea is fleeting, except the fascination generated by its resident instability.

So we drank our coffee and set sail. It was six thirtyish. In the narrow harbor mouth the soft buzz of crickets on the coast thrilled our ears for a second. We'd heard so many crickets in Majorca these seemed more like the spontaneous surfacing of a half-faded memory – memories of summer that return in winter. It was a fine day, but September is not the time for crickets. We negotiated the harbor mouth and entered a white, becalmed sea – oily, foaming waters the color of molten silver. A breeze blew from inland but was almost imperceptible. In any case, we were suddenly hit by a delicious, warm breath of air from the island's soil, tasting of toast suffused with an intense aroma of dried herbs. Pure delight that lasted only a moment, because once the engine was switched on, we were hit by the acrid smell of burnt gas – and the vista of garages, inhospitable streets, elegant ladies and gentlemen, the miserable tedium of routine life passed before our eyes, evoked by the pituitary, like something bordering on the malevolent.

We decided to head straight on. Using chart and compass, we turned our prow toward Barcelona. We hoisted the mainsail and jib. The breeze was so slight the sails merely fluttered as we picked up speed. As the sun invaded land and sea, the calm turned stiller and duller. Joanot, Martinet's son (an eighteen-year-old lad who had worked on trawlers out of Barcelona) took the helm. The rest of us were absorbed by the weather. Deep down we were all quite unsure: we had lingered too long on the Majorcan coast, we were behind schedule, it was late to be crossing in such a flimsy craft. In September you can take nothing for granted at sea. The autumn equinox is implacable. It can hit ten days before or ten days after you were expecting it. Those ninety miles, which at the beginning of August you could sail as easily as eating a peach, were now a huge conundrum. We sailed in silence. Only the engine chugged loudly. Martinet was sitting on the stern side of the boat and when he saw me approaching he grinned.

"For the moment, the weather is on our side. It's calm. . ." he said.

"So I see."

"We can only wait. The day's not got going yet. . ."

"Outlook uncertain. . ."

"Right! We'll have to see how the day turns out. . . We can't say anything for sure."

Martinet wasn't in the mood to talk. He lit a cigarette, got up and walked toward the prow. A short while after, I saw he'd lit our small cooking stove and was about to gut a dentex we'd bought in Sóller. He threw its innards into the sea and then something unexpected happened: although we were two or three miles from the coast by now, we saw a small band of herring gulls flying behind *Rufi* like an aerial escort. Martinet smiled as he saw them approach. He threw some guts into the sea and the birds dived down as eagerly as ever. Their main occupation must be tailing ships. They followed us for ages. They came close to the boat's side, apparently keeping us company.

A herring gull is not a pretty animal. A white-headed gull, even less so. It's a powerful, ravenous bird, which I personally like because it gives me a feeling of freedom – a feeling of freedom I would have liked to experience firsthand and never could.

I was spellbound by those birds. They followed us, flying slowly, sometimes gliding, staring hard in case a tidbit fell into the sea. When that happened, or when Martinet simply looked as if he was about to throw something, they all dove frantically toward the water. If there was prey, they eagerly fought over it amid swirling, frothing waters. Almost always, the prize was carried off by the wiliest bird, the one who had only watched the skirmish engaged in by two others. The wiliest would retreat and fly away in order to eat in a more relaxed fashion. But often another swooped down from behind and forced the morsel to drop from its complacent beak. It wasn't an edifying spectacle. When the birds dove as a result of a gesture that led to nothing, they emerged from the water resignedly. The deceit hadn't discouraged them. They continued to follow *Rufi* as if one had to rely on mere appearances.

I looked at the herring gulls and thought of the huge literary trail those birds had inspired. They may not have filled as many sheets of paper as nightingales, because the nightingale has been sung by every literary school, and the gull only by the Romantics, but the gull has been used to express all manner of superficial sentiment. Then, on a lesser scale, come swallows, and on a par with them, owls. If a library of the texts inspired by these birds were to fall on us, we'd be in a parlous state, even though their subject is so wingèd. Images of these birds have helped to enlighten human feelings. Naturalists have described them with their customarily cold lexicon. But we still know very little about the lives of birds – not a scrap, in fact.

In my view, there are three kinds of gulls, though that's only my humble personal opinion.

White-headed gulls – the biggest, with long, sturdy bodies and a huge wingspan – are the most becoming, and nothing much is known about them. It's not right to say they are marine birds, that they live exclusively in the sea. More precisely, they are birds that belong to maritime and land areas. They make their nests in the most recondite, remote, inaccessible places on the coast and are totally antisocial. It's true that they're visibly parasitical to boats and hunt fish, but that doesn't mean they don't also head inland. If they fly above an olive grove, when the olives are ripening, white-headed gulls will devour them in large quantities. The people of Cadaqués know this only too well. If olive groves are in their flight path, you'll find a large number of olive pits on coastal areas frequented by these birds. They like fish and they like olives; in this way, they are the forerunners of individuals who like to sit on a café terrace at aperitif time eating olives stuffed with anchovies.

Obviously, people aren't necessarily aware of this, because these gulls are obsessively eye-catching over the sea, so clearly profiled you want to sketch them, whereas on land, in the depths of an olive grove, they aren't so visible. Conversely, our eyes are so used to seeing them fly over the sea, as part of the horizon's furniture, that we can't imagine what they look like when they're pecking olives on land.

Their most aristocratic – or literary – moment is when they pursue ships like decorative predators. Their resilience in flight is surprising; they can follow in a boat's wake hour after hour, especially when gliding on a tail wind. Their loyalty to shipping is not all romantic, even though any bird in flight arouses a drop of romanticism within us: their fidelity is fostered, in fact, by the scraps thrown out by vessels. In this activity, white-headed gulls have achieved a degree of guile that I have repeatedly observed. They manage to adapt their lives to the timetables of the ships that pass across their field of vision. All sailors in coastal vessels have acknowledged this. If a vessel appears in their sights in the morning or at noon – I mean at breakfast or lunchtime – the gulls abandon their rocky hollows and throw themselves into the chase. If a vessel passes by midafternoon, they take no notice, don't budge, don't shift, because they know they won't find anything succulent in the foam from the screw and rudder. And that is no fantasy but a reality that's been confirmed time and again. Poets are duty-bound to ignore this, as is the poet manqué in every sailor or passenger, because, after all, nothing can be more agreeable at the end of a long sea voyage than the appearance, just before land hales, of gulls flying through the air. It's as if they have come to welcome us personally, to tell us that family and friends will be delighted to see us again. They come to eat, but they seem to come to welcome us. Splendid! It would be folly not to accept appearances. Keeping images, symbols of hope, alive is a sensible, practical activity.

Fishermen love these large, lean birds, with their steely cartilages and their bitter-tasting flesh and the forlorn, cynical stances they adopt when resting, for the same reason: they bring hope. Their presence in a specific area of sea is almost a guaranteed sign of fish – of great shoals of fish swimming near the surface. If dolphins accompany the gulls, then there are fish for sure. However, dolphins are such stupidly greedy animals, are such a blind, disruptive force, eat in such a noisy, disorderly way, that they scatter the shoal and make their capture tentative and precarious.

In the placid calm of June, a joint attack of dolphins and gulls on a mass of sardines or anchovies swimming close to the surface is a spectacle that helps one to understand the meaning of life. Dolphins attack head on, swoop in viscous spirals, gobble savagely. Their path, three fathoms under water, is marked on the surface by a trail of bubbles and white froth and the oily outline of the area where the fish swim as they feel themselves under attack and scatter in every direction. The shoal disintegrates and the fish escape in a frenzy. In the meantime the gulls, with one wing folded and the other in the air, at a forty-five-degree tilt, make the fish leap like silver coins, amid the turbulent, swirling, foaming water.

But all this is a frantic spectacle that's hardly edifying or exemplary. It is nature unleashed, shamelessly displaying itself, in all the biological glory of animal might. For a fisherman, it is a spectacle that leads to scant profit and brings little hope.

Dolphins spoil everything, like too much tomato in a stew. When gulls operate in isolation, released from the predatory dolphins, they offer more potential. Thus, when they swoop vertically, at dawn or dusk, on an area of sea not scored by fins, a nearby longboat can live in hope. "Now we'll be able to pay," thinks the fisherman, affectionately eyeing nature, "our most pressing debts and the one hundred eighty-seven coffees recorded in the IOU book." These are the expectations of well-minded folk. And when the gulls resurface with a couple of fat, silvery sardines in their indistinctly yellow, gilt-tin beaks, appearance becomes reality. The sardines are like flaccid, drooping mustaches on the aging faces of those big birds – mustaches that give them each a sinister, scowling aspect.

Then there are the herring gulls, from the less precipitous coast. They appear with their offspring at low tide, when an intense aroma wafts inland from the many reefs jutting out of the water. Even in the most crowded parts of the shoreline, you can often see four or five young herring gulls, the size of a year-old partridge, carefully poised on a microscopic, glazed archipelago, while the parents, on sterner, bulkier rocks, seem to watch assiduously over them. That's when the youngsters experience their apprenticeship in cunning and patience. They spend hour after hour – if the parents don't signal danger – fervently gawping at nearby occurrences. The soporific, trusting progress of a small, aquatic monster swimming close to the surface makes them nervous and lively. Any movement in the sea – a fish, a shadow, a glint in the water – makes them move their legs and wave their wings. If there is a real possibility of a catch, they shift from contemplation to a dive in a second. They catch it or don't. It makes no odds. It's about learning the trade, honing their skills. . . Suddenly the old parent birds signal to their chicks – a sign I've never been able to pin down (maybe a faint, almost human cry of distress) – and the little ones fly up and after their parents with a swiftness and sense of obedience those papas and mamas on land who spend so much on educating their children would envy.

Then there is the third class of gulls, a kind of degenerate white-headed gull that lives out at sea, if it can earn its keep there, and, if it can't, in the lakes and lagoons of the hinterland. Like those intellectuals classified as alimentary empiricists, as yours truly was, from an early age by the high priests of puritanical rhetoric, a category I will never be able to throw off, however many years go by.

In the spring, when the sea abounds in fish swimming on the surface, these birds could be mistaken for heroic, upstanding white-headed gulls. However, when the sea empties out, their resistance is weak: they look for waters that can feed them. In barren periods of autumn and winter, they fly inland and you often spot them in murky inland marshes, sewer-fed harbor waters and mudflats. If pickings are slim, they fly farther inland, following the course of rivers. You might even see them in inland cities, as long as they have even the slightest bit of water. When the weather is poor, you'll glimpse them in small farmyards mingling with the most stupidly tame and well-drilled domestic animals. Then you observe the strangest sight: faced with unbridled nature, the farm animals go wild in a way and make a bid for freedom, while the gulls, who are usually self-sufficient, embrace a more domesticated livelihood. You get that curious mixture of geese, ducks, gulls, hens, chickens, pigs, cows, mules and horses that you encounter on land that is close to the sea. The mix is short-lived: when the land dries out, the gulls fly off.

These birds are pulled by two opposing incentives: freedom and domesticity. Like humans they face an unpleasant, insoluble, eternal dilemma, and like humans they resolve this dilemma based on two factors: their mood and their level of hunger.

The white-headed gulls distracted us for a good while. Then they took flight and abandoned us.

Meanwhile, we'd sailed a number of miles amid the most extraordinary stillness. The day had turned cotton-woolly, silent, atonal. A low ceiling of white clouds had covered the sky. The blue of the sea had grayed. The light had dimmed. The lines of the horizon had shredded and disappeared. We could no longer see the coast of Majorca: the island's lofty northern coast had floated for a time between sky and land, like a purple cloud, and now it had disappeared from sight. But the becalmed sea was literally astonishing: there wasn't a breath of air, the yard was still and *Rufí* moved with limp sails, driven by a noisy engine that clattered annoyingly.

Martinet sat on the stern side smoking cigarettes. He was watching the weather out of the corner of his eye. He seemed content, and then not so. When I glanced quizzically his way, he said: "It's so calm!"

My presence on *Rufí* had its justification: I was a guest. When my friend Mascarell invited me to spend a month or two on the Majorcan coast in his tiny craft, it was somewhat of an effort to accept. They say the sea unites people: that's a myth from a bygone era. Solitude, in the long term, never united two people. It separates them, puts them face to face, makes them inflexible. I accepted because, in the end, new experiences in life, as they randomly offer themselves, are beneficial and useful. The moment I told Mascarell I accepted his invitation, I thought it would be the last adventure we'd share. I was wrong on that count.

Mascarell was a colossus as far as hospitality went. During our stay on Majorca, the last thing we thought of was making each other's life impossible, being a nuisance: he went his way, I went mine. Sometimes we'd converse for seven or eight hours on the trot and at other times we'd not see each other for two or three days or would just meet up at mealtimes in *Rufí*'s stern. He never tried to force his ideas on me and I never felt the need to force mine on him. We had left

Barcelona together and would return likewise; generally the opposite happens. These adventures usually end up with people at each other's throat, scowling, one in the stern and the other in the prow of the mail boat.

Mascarell was a rich bachelor (he and his brother owned a textile factory) but was sickly and his doctors had suggested a long period of rest. An old fan of the sea, crazy about angling, he decided their advice was almost providential. What they were proposing was precisely what he'd been wanting to do with no success for fifteen years. So he purchased *Rufí*, had her refurbished unpretentiously and invited me to go and spend a few weeks in Majorca.

"And what will we do in Majorca?" I asked.

"I'll fish with my rod, and if I feel like it, I'll use the stay to hawk some of our products. We've got customers in Palma. . ."

"I imagine you do. And in Manacor, Sóller and maybe in Andratx. . ."

"If it's of interest, I'll look into it. . ."

"Don't bother. And what will I do in the meantime?"

"What you always do: write, chat and idle. . ."

I found myself on board *Rufí* as a direct result of that comment. . .

Mascarell had said very little on our return journey. He had complete confidence in Martinet, to whom he attributed, as a good Majorcan, perfect knowledge of the waters we were sailing. He'd not even taken the trouble to look at the weather.

He'd started reading *Nautical Instructions* for the western Mediterranean, and I glanced at the page he had open and saw he was reading a description of the Gulf of Lion.

As the day gradually became gray and soporific, a time came when I thought the weather too straightforwardly reflected the way *Rufí* was sailing and the behavior of those on board. I sat in the cockpit intending to chat with my friend for a bit.

"Hey, Mascarell!" I said.

"You'll have to shout. You can't hear anything above that engine. It's most annoying. . ."

"I just wanted to ask you a fairly foolish question. Do you really like the sea?"

"Come on, of course I do! What do you expect me to say?"

"Right. I expected you to say that. Now, do you mind telling me why the people who live around the Mediterranean like the sea so little? In fact, they've never liked it. If we go by what the books say, and without wishing to play the pedant, this pond is very important. All the basic elements of our civilization have emerged from its byways. And as you know, the people who now live along these coasts like the sea only for two or three weeks in the summer and always on the basis of gazing at it from terra firma."

"What are you implying?"

"Let's just analyze the situation for a moment. We've just left Sóller for Barcelona in this small yacht, which is a very plucky, but quite tiny, nutshell. We've been sailing for a few hours. We're twenty or thirty miles off the coast of Majorca. We can see only sea and sky. Probably because we're sailing so carefreely and the weather is so good, we aren't really worried about our boat's size. Even so, it would be a real pity to be devoured by one of those big or little monsters that live in these waters. I know if I thought about that, I'd get goose bumps. . ."

Martinet – who was quite close – looked at me and smiled. Mascarell first looked serious, then burst out laughing when he saw Martinet's smile.

"Let's continue our analysis. In the first place, the sea is scary. Nobody can deny that. Then, I'm sorry to say, it prompts something very like disgust. Even in the best of times when you are about to eat a delicious dish of rice on deck, the sea is horrendous. The sea gives us a precise idea, a physical sensation, of the elemental nature of the cosmos. From a specific point of view, that colloidal slime you find in the sea, the plastic viscosity enveloping things in this medium, is like the quintessence of life. Now, from the point of view of human life, the epic nature of the sea's boundaries, our puny smallness in comparison, has the same impact on us as molecules scattering in the void. That's why every reflection on the sea is like a reflection on death, on that tremendous disintegration. 'The most startling wonder of its depths,' wrote Conrad, 'is that their cruelty can never be plumbed.'"

"You ought to know, you were once in a shipwreck. . ."

"Let's proceed objectively. The instinctive terror the sea produces seems to me derived from the possibility of being devoured by fish. Some of these animals have big heads and mouths. These must bite off flesh in big strips, but there are many different kinds of fish: some with tubular mouths and minute teeth. These must eat as they breathe, calmly, delicately, as if sucking on a straw. They're the ones that disgust me most."

"I quite agree."

"It horrifies me to think that the hearts of many men, their encephalic mass, might have been sucked down the tubes these little fish have, tubes like the barrel of a musket. You'll tell me it's foolish to worry like this, and that it's all the same whether you are consumed one way or the other. In any case. . ."

"The sea is sacred."

"Absolutely. It's what they believed in antiquity. When they were facing anything frightening, they decided it must be sacred. You could make an anthology of what the ancients thought about the sea and it would be huge fun. Socrates, an important fellow on the shores of this sea, systematically refused to step foot on a boat. On terra firma he played a role at the battle of Plataea, which today we might even describe as heroic. However, he was a complete coward when it came to adventures at sea. He used to say he could understand humankind's turn to seafaring only as a result of potential profit: the prospect of making lots of money made it a human inevitability. This idea has endured in our world, even now when vessels are propelled by engines. Pliny the Elder, who sailed the seas of the Roman empire as a colonial administrator, maintained that man's fatuousness is so great that, not satisfied with being buried under the earth, he decided to test out what a grave under the waves might be like. There's also something striking in the life of Saul of Tarsus, later Saint Paul: the ease with which he set sail, the way he resisted storms and shipwrecks. This was a new phenomenon in the ancient world, and it provoked an immense revolution of the mind."

"The sea is an immense cemetery. . ."

"Of course. It is an immense cemetery and, what's more, it is the only cemetery that's never been violated. It can never be disturbed beyond a certain depth. Men and women's bones are the target of the most violent, unforgiving polemics in every era. We have seen so many violations in our day! In the sea, everything is untouchable and beyond human grasp. Everything disperses and is untraceable. The sea is sacred because it inspires terror, because it offers invincible resistance, because it has a mysterious, impenetrable dimension.

Thus, dear Mascarell, three or four yards from the side of *Rufí*, on which we sail, that mystery is real and palpable."

"All the same, there is another side to all this. I recall hearing you once say. . ."

"I will repeat it word for word. I've often said that on the matter of food, the sea is a likable mystery. These waters that throb with a mysterious, diffuse life-force produce monsters we call fish, which, if seasoned in the ancient manner (a hundred percent Homerically, if possible), can offer huge potential. A fish, which can in itself be quite repugnant, is easily redeemed once grilled, stewed or casseroled. To an extent, this humanizes the mystery, and even though its secrets are not uncovered, at least it's lovable. . ."

"A mystery you love practically ceases to be one. . ."

"In truth, nothing changes. Everything is simply more likable. It would be ridiculous to deny that the sea can be pleasant. It has some features that are literally mouthwatering and others that are extremely intriguing, if you can forget the disassembled nature of its boundless darkness."

"But that isn't only a prerogative of the sea. That goes for every-thing: the sea, the earth, men, women, air. . ."

"That's very possible. . . But what do you expect? It may be that a straight hit from the sea is harder, that it teaches lessons that disman-tle human arrogance quicker than any other challenge. No swagger can fool the sea. It all leads you to conclude that life is a string of hurdles to show humans, most tangibly, how infinitely puny they are. If they don't use their vague, equivocal smallness to form a clear idea of their shocking insignificance, what use is it? Ignoramuses, yesterday and today; ignoramuses, tomorrow and forever. And the greater the ignorance, the greater the shallowness, emptiness, lack of consistency. 'God knows the depth of human understanding and knows that all is vanity,' say the Psalms. Sometimes it seems that the sea, which always dwarfs us, for which we can never find the right adjective, always confirms the truth of that line most tellingly."

"It's a terrific school."

"The best there is. It's admirable because it always puts us in our place. Intellectually, it's so efficient because it teaches humility and modesty. . ."

The first part of our conversation interested Martinet. The second, much less so. He didn't reckon it was worth delaying suppertime to listen. He walked to the prow, lit the stove and soon had supper underway in style. Meanwhile, he brought us some really delicious martinis.

I've always had a fondness for a few high-caliber alcoholic drinks, but I've never been able to stand cocktails. With one exception: a dry martini. That is a truly captivating mix. It's a drink that out at sea works the same wonders as aperitifs, and black coffee in the morning. Coffee arouses the receptivity of the mind at that hazy moment when the dawn breaks. A martini has the same impact in the midday sun or when the stars begin to twinkle.

Martinet was a Majorcan from Portopetro. He had sailed as a young lad in local smacks and handled the Mediterranean in a way that was nourished by his lively fount of memories. When he married a water diviner from S'Alqueria, he immigrated to Barcelona – to the Barceloneta, to be precise – bringing quite a family in his wake: his mother-in-law and a bevy of sisters-in-law. However, the family couldn't adapt. The Barceloneta air didn't suit Martinet's mother-in-law, sisters-in-law or wife, who in the meantime had given birth to a son, Joanot.

Given the excessive noise, the price of food and the cramped nature of their apartment, they went back to La Roqueta. On this return voyage, only one sister-in-law became lopped from the family tree: Mariagneta, who had started to court and then married a sailor from Torrevieja who worked on salt-transporting boats – a short, swarthy lad with dark round eyes, curly hair, a mariner's bandy legs and strong expressive features, like a young monkey's. That lad's presence in the life of the pallid, languid lass with bags under her eyes made the air of the Barceloneta more acceptable. When the man from Torrevieja arrived in Barcelona, he ran to his wife and never left her side, day or night. He changed his clothes – donning a blue-striped suit with a double-breasted jacket, a silk cravat and baggy trousers that barely hid his yellow shoes – and the couple went out (he'd be smoking a cigar) with panache. They liked to go to the cafés that offered entertainment – above all, Set Portes. There they'd eat oranges and peanuts while, at dusk, the establishment's windows steamed over with the spray from a southwesterly wind and were turned a melancholy yellow by the café lights.

Martinet was now on his own in Barcelona. He sailed for a good few years. He spent the entire campaign of the First World War in the small packets that plied the ports of southern France. He met danger – the northern blasts in the gulf shook him up more than once – but he earned his bread. His son had grown up and Martinet sent for him. Martinet's ambition for his son was that he shouldn't be a sailor but a fisherman. The first large trawlers were leaving Barcelona and proving highly profitable. The vessels were strong and their engines powerful, and business appeared to be good. Meanwhile, Martinet left the merchant navy and entered the service of a yacht-owning gentleman – a very curious, aimiable individual who suffered from seasickness, a girlfriend he didn't like and a couple of automobiles that gave him horrible headaches because his sons risked their lives in them every day. A rich gentleman with few pretensions who enjoyed life only in his office on Carrer Ausiàs March – a small office, served by minute windows, with a table, a settee, three chairs, a calendar and a reasonably large safe; however, although he liked it so very much, he was rarely there, as he was busy fulfilling unavoidable social obligations.

For Martinet, meeting that gentleman was like winning the lottery. The *patron* – as Martinet called him, in memory of his contacts in the south of France – went out of his way to use his yacht. First he tried not to vomit by following advice from motley doctors and swallowing a variety of pills that brought no cure. Then he tried to get used to being seasick, but that didn't work either. He finally decided that his natural state warranted having terra firma under his feet. He had his craft firmly anchored in the waters of the nautical club and made Martinet responsible for keeping up its appearance. Martinet did this with all his good faith and all due care – with genuine *esmero*, to use a word he liked – though he was convinced that the small vessel had entered a long, agonizing, stationary death. He spent his time painting its timbers and polishing its brass and keeping it in a perfect, orderly state. These tasks, which were next to futile, were well paid, as if they did make a difference – the *patron* always refused to consider any of the offers to sell that came his way – giving Martinet a sense of security he'd never experienced before. He became more of a loner than he was in the years when he sailed. When his old shipmates – who he sometimes met on Passeig de Colom – said he was working as a watchman, he half grinned and left that as his only response. Though his family life was almost nonexistent, it was the only thing he, like all loners who might have enjoyed some company, felt passionately about. Joanot, his son, led his own life on board a Barcelona-based trawler from Sant Carles de la Ràpita – a life Martinet accepted but didn't understand. The lad was too fond of doing his own thing and Martinet judged that to be a sign of aloofness. But then he had his wife, his sisters-in-law – his family! – parked in the rather barren, lackluster outskirts of Portopetro! He sent them money – almost everything he earned with infallible regularity – from the Barcelona post office in Plaça d'Urquinaona. After he'd sent his money order, he left those dingy offices and felt the high point in the month had just passed. He kept back only the minimum he required. He left in reserve ten pessetes, in case Joanot was "cheeky enough to ask him for money." This precaution never failed; Joanot was ever ready to ask for a handout.

"I'll cook the dentex my wife's way," Martinet said, when he'd prepared all the ingredients. "No seasoning, two potatoes, *a la marinera*. . ."

While we stayed around Majorca, Martinet always cooked thinking of his wife – precisely how she would have done it. Whenever Martinet mentioned his model, Mascarell winked at me.

Mascarell had persuaded Martinet's *patron* to let him accompany us. He and Mascarell were friends and worked in the same line of business. His *patron* agreed, emphasizing, however, that he didn't like his boat being abandoned for too long. Obviously: it hadn't moved from club waters for four or five years. It was beginning to display a grayish stubble and was slowly aging. The sailor was clearly pleased to embark on *Rufí*. It proved easy enough to bring his son on board. They both went to visit their family. They returned earlier than either Mascarell or I had anticipated. Joanot showed up looking blank, Martinet, gloomy. When he talked about their visit, he spoke lugubriously: "Those women are never satisfied. . ."

Perhaps he'd pitched his hopes too high and things hadn't turned out as he'd dreamed. Distance breeds such disappointment. Seen from close up, things *are* disappointing and usually quite exasperating too. Their only true allure comes from the fiction of remoteness.

When the fish stew began to show signs of life, the air was impregnated with a delicious smell. The stove was in the prow and *Rufi*'s passage sent the aroma from the fish wafting our way. Mascarell, who was deep in a book, suddenly looked up and asked for another martini.

"What's that you're reading?" I asked.

"Do you know Maupassant's *Sur l'eau*? It's lovely. . ."

"I do and it's one of my favorite books in *Rufi*'s library."

Mascarell carried on board fifty or so volumes that were more or less directly related to the sea. It was a library with one strange feature: it had no fixed location. Its volumes were scattered around the boat, and you were always finding one or another in the most unexpected places. The downside was that if you were looking for a particular title, you could never find it.

"Maupassant has a special touch when he's writing about the sea," said Mascarell.

"Absolutely. And I can tell you that it's very hard to write about the sea. It's a strange phenomenon, you know. The sea produces a kind of enchantment that doesn't allow for any unpicking – that's to say, it doesn't favor anyone remaining sufficiently lucid, when faced with the spectacle, to apply the right adjectives. Maupassant's book seems so simple but really demonstrates the novelist's power to unpick things."

"Even so, the sea, the sea was like a drug. . . That's obvious from the book. . ."

"I'm not sure. . . Perhaps it was less of a drug for him. I understand he was interested in only one thing in life: women. He looked for women everywhere, even when he was sailing, alone with his mariner, on his small yacht. His libido controlled him. I'm interested in the sea for itself. I'm not a novelist and I don't think novels exist in real life; there is only a flow of unconnected, random, fortuitous events that develop, pass and vaporize. Novelists have to believe that memory is man's strongest faculty, otherwise they'd have no room to play; in truth, man's strongest faculty is his forgetfulness. Personally, I reckon the sea represents the essence of life, because I'm unable to see any meaning at all in its eternal movement. That's no doubt why the sea makes me a contemplative soul. We spectators of life construct novels and dramas when we discuss the things happening before our own eyes, when we apply a dialectic to them, when we strike a stance. What stance do you want to strike before the sea? You must gaze at it or let it be. There's no other option. For me the sea is a path that leads to disinterest, to an indifference toward things, whether real or fictitious. . ."

"I'm really not sure. . ."

"But of course! The moment you embark, you have that pleasant feeling of seeing things from a different perspective. While you are at sea, things on land seem small and insignificant. Mountains still command a degree of respect. Plains become a more or less light or heavy brushstroke of haze, grayer, then brighter. Towns look surprisingly insignificant the second you're half a mile away. Houses assume derisory shapes and sizes. Roofs and walls immediately meld into the earth. The smaller things on land are, the more absurd they seem seen from the sea – the more poisonous they become, the more stupidity, lunacy and monstrousness they contain. In this sense, sea voyages are most useful, because they help put things in perspective. All kinds of nonsense and idiocy lurk under those trifling roofs – including one's own. If the roofs are so insignificant, imagine how insignificant the things beneath the roofs are! Just test it out. After you've been in a seaside town, try gazing at it from three or four miles away. Forget the narrow streets and the arcades in the square. From out at sea you'll see the huge quantities of foolishness and madness that contribute to making our lives unpleasant. You'll be shocked by the pettiness of all that your eyes take in. It will make your life freer and less constrained. . . And if one day you climb a mountain, try to catch a glimpse of the village spire from the nearest peak. You'll see it looking so small, like a postcard village. It all helps sweep the shadows away from life."

"Which is to say that the sea cleanses, which seems obvious enough."

"Yes, things seen from out at sea are put in their rightful place, and that's really valuable. But then comes a second stage when you immerse yourself in the sea's variety. The Mediterranean, I mean! The other seas are pure geography to me. And personally I'm happy to be limited in this way. I can never understand words like 'eternity,' 'unity,' 'universe,' 'infinite'. . . If the ancients were distinguished by boundaries, I believe I'd have been a decent ancient. And after all, everything in the Mediterranean *is* local: the weather, cuisine, dialects and people. Everything here is constantly changing. A few miles to the south or to the north and everything varies: the direction of winds, the taste of fish, the amount of garlic in a stew, accents, tastes and feelings. These shades can be astonishing. At the same time of day, the southwesterly can be blowing in Cape Creus, the north wind in Cape Leucate and an easterly in the Tinyaus in the Camargue. Do you remember that day we met a northeasterly in Sa Dragonera and a southwesterly in Andratx? That was the day when Martinet said a northeasterly makes for a white sea and a southwesterly a blue. . . There's no doubt that the constancy of these contrasts reinforces a permanent nitpicking of dogma. These differences mean that a voyage across this sea is ever intriguing, if you have an open mind. Everything is changing and transient, which implies a degree of discomfort that finally trans-forms into mere vagabond caprice: the clouds, the sea, the wind and the color of the sky. The lightness surrounding us is so striking you yourself end up transmuting into a light, levitating being. You let yourself go in the same way you secure the sheet when it's too windy. Any other attitude would make little sense. What else could you do, if not that? Object? Argue?"

"And then contemplation begins. . ."

"Indeed. Even though I've sadly concluded that the most sublime contemplation doesn't provide a living and that to live this life com-fortably, you need a steady income. Once you have that, you can enjoy the life of an impenitent idler. You'll become a spectator spending a couple of hours watching how the clouds are made and unmade, how the blue of the sky turns pink, then mauve, then crimson, how the waves and their burden of sun pass monotonously by. All this becomes the most natural thing in the world. In this state it is unthinkable that you might decide to write a letter, that you might want to meditate for a moment. Everything slips over your senses and leaves no trace. It's as if your thoughts liquefy and the most solid thing they contain is light, color, air and wind. Sailing is never relaxing, but nothing could be lighter and more weightless for your thoughts. Nothing could be more mentally pleasing than a suggestion of sirens, colorful sirens, surrounded by air but, fortunately, bereft of anything carnal and firm, or persistently present."

Mascarell signaled his disagreement. I understood he had a more tangible conception of sirens.

"In any case, to sail at the mercy of winds and the intrinsic frivolity of our own nature is indeed something subtle, because it leads you – or at least leads me – into states of contemplation with little in the way of obligation. This is feasible on days and nights when the weather is good and the sky clear. Obligations set in when the sea unleashes and smashes a parcel of water into your face, salty and hard as stone. That is most disagreeable. Then the sea becomes a tangible, direct challenge. Everything begins to swirl devilishly and you're persuaded, once more, of the smallness of humans. When you're on board a small craft, a strong northerly is blowing, and you're trying to fry a couple of eggs, and you see the absurd way the eggs dance in the pan and you realize you can't in fact fry them – *that* is when you get a clear sense of what exactly you represent."

Martinet put the stew on the table. We lunched with the usual appetite one has between the sky and the sea. Then coffee was served. A lot of table talk ensued. Mascarell spotted the last bottle of Courvoisier and we paid our respects copiously.

The look of the day hadn't changed at all: rather, every feature had been reinforced. The ceiling of pale-gray clouds seemed to lower as the afternoon set in. The sea, amazingly still, was blue-black. Horizons appeared to shrink. As day began to fade, the light tended toward a ghostly hue. There was the slightest breath of wind. Now we sailed in a more relaxed style. Joanot hoisted the sails before lunch. Mindful of the weather, I glanced at Martinet now and then; he was probably thinking along similar lines as he stared at me, but we said nothing. A good day at sea – whether you want to make your escape or tackle the day head on – is one that frankly asserts itself, that has a palpable, visible shape. This was an imprecise day, in a state of suspension, an embryonic moment. The strangeness of the weather was clearly affecting us: the silence on board deepened, nobody felt like talking. We looked. . . but what were we looking at? What could we have looked at, if there was nothing to see? Only water surrounded by low, thick mist. The engine was making a tremendous racket, but apart from bothering us on board, I don't think it annoyed anyone else. It was a noise that didn't carry three hundred yards, that vanished into the immense void.

"What's the barometer saying, Martinet?" I asked, lighting a cigarette. "Is it going up or down?"

"Neither!" answered Mascarell, laughing. "We're sailing without a barometer. It was an oversight – we forgot it. When I get back to the office, I'll find one inside an elegantly wrapped parcel with the other things we omitted on this trip. However, if we don't have a barometer, we do have Panxito on board, and he might give us a hint as to what weather to expect."

"A cat doesn't have much meteorological sense. Or if it does, it modestly hides it. Panxito won't help us. That's a pity! Just look how he's dozed off next to the stove once he ate his fill. His digestive juices must have brought on cold shivers, and now he's warming back up. Cats are like prudent folk: they don't need advice, and they do whatever the hell they want to."

"In that case," said Mascarell, "we are a ship abandoned by the hand of God. I mean to say, we're at the mercy of nature's dark forces. . ."

"That's not quite right. We can rely on Martinet, who really knows what's what. Over the last few years he's expanded his own seafaring nous with that of his *patron*, which is vast. He's been sailing for four or five years without his vessel budging an inch, as if he were on board a transatlantic liner, painting and polishing brass. You really must agree, Martinet; yours is an ideal life for a sailor. . ."

"You can joke as much as you like," retorted Martinet, pouring a shot of cognac into his coffee and granting his vowels all the grace of the Majorcan lilt, "but you have hit one nail on the head. I haven't met a single sailor who liked the sea. The sea is just another way to earn a living, a fairly unpleasant way at that. What sailors and mariners like most about the sea are its ports, and of the things in ports or thereabouts they most enjoy the cafés. There's nothing prettier than the sea seen through a café window, especially when the weather's poor and the coffee is warm and delicious. . ."

"I'm sure your *patron* shares your view. . . !" said Mascarell, slapping Martinet on the back.

"Senyor Mascarell," said the sailor, "that's a view shared by many amateurs. I've learned that in the years I've worked at the club. If you'll allow me, I'd like to tell you something. . ."

"Go ahead, Martinet. . . We're all equal here."

"Oh, please don't say that. . . ! We're not all equal here. You, senyor, are the master and give the orders. I'm the sailor on board. I meant something else. In Barcelona I've observed that people's affection for the sea can be quite intense. . . but I can tell you, here and now, that affection can disappear in a flash. The sea brings lots of headaches and peculiar ideas. It can seem lovely in your head but not so lovely in reality. Sometimes it can be mean and nasty. If you want to keep your love of the sea, it's best you don't catch it when it's unleashed and raging. I've often seen how the most unthinking, boisterous lovers of the sea are the first to tire of it. If they catch it on an off day, are for a second scared, upset or alarmed, their fine words dive underwater. And the oddest thing is that all their fancy notions disappear totally, without a trace. There's no chance they'll ever come back. Ever. . .""

"That's very well said, Martinet. . . What I'd like to know is why are there such sudden changes. Is it discomfort? Is it the sense of unease the sea often triggers? I don't mean the people who suffer from sea-sickness, which explains why millions of human beings are horrified by the sea. We'll leave them out of it. Let's speak of the others. In this regard, I think it's vanity that leads the rest to wrong conclusions. When people experience the least bit of unpleasantness at sea, they think they look foolish. It's ridiculous, but that's how it is. For people living in this country, things are all the more hateful in proportion to how foolish they think they've been made to look."

"I probably wouldn't go that far," Martinet replied, rolling himself a cigarette. "What I will say is that if you want to keep your love of the sea, you should try to avoid experiencing it at its worst. It's lethal if you happen to be out there when it's scary. You must take every step not to let that happen, and if you do get caught and trapped, you must bear up, and bear up like the bravest."

"Martinet, what do you mean by 'bear up like the bravest'?" asked Mascarell solemnly.

"I mean, on this craft, as on any ship, keep quiet. . . You can't play games with the sea. The first thing you need to handle these small craft is basic cunning. If, despite all your efforts, you're caught out, you must put on a brave face. When you go to a dance, you must dance. Today, for example, I. . ."

"Out with it, Martinet, out with it. . ."

"It's something silly. I just wanted to say that when we left Port de Sóller this morning, when it started to get overcast, I'd have bet five hundred pessetes it would all end in mist and a southwesterly, which would have been the best for our voyage. And look what's happened: it's gotten more and more overcast and becalmed. The wind hasn't rippled the sea for a second."

"And what do you deduce from all that?" asked Mascarell.

"Very little, nothing much at all. All I can say is that I understand nothing. And as doctors like to say: time will tell. The day will play out as it pleases. . ."

Joanot had his hand on the helm. Martinet took over and told him to go and wash up. Mascarell handed Joanot a cigar, which he lit with evident delight. He started to smoke. . .

Before lunch I'd found a translation of Goethe's *Italian Journey* under a cushion in the cockpit. There were several Italian books in *Rufi's* small library – Mascarell knew Italy and liked to read in Italian – as well as a number of sailing charts from the Italian Cartographic Service. In 1786, the date of Goethe's first trip to Italy, he had never seen the sea. I tried to find out what that first contact had led his brilliant pen to write. I jotted down some quick notes.

Goethe arrived in Venice toward the end of September 1786. On the night of the thirtieth he writes in his diary: "Today I purchased a map of Venice and it's much bigger than I'd imagined. After studying it for a long while, I went up the campanile of San Marco, which gives one a unique view. It was almost noon, the sky was wonderfully transparent so I could see both far and near without needing an eye-glass. The tide was covering the lagoon and looking toward the Lido, a narrow strip of land that encloses the lagoon, I saw the sea for the first time and some sails in the distance."

"I saw the sea for the first time. . ." That's all he says.

Over the next few days, Goethe wanders around Venice, where, strangely, he doesn't seem to have a single friend. He behaves like a typical tourist (although that word had yet to be invented) in the city: he goes in and out of churches, he gazes at works of art, he rides in a gondola, at night he goes to the opera – especially opéra bouffe. On 8 October, he writes in his diary: "At first light this morning I went to the Lido, the strip of land that closes off the lagoon and separates it from the sea. After getting off the boat, I walked across the strip of land. I heard a loud noise created by the sea crashing on the beach, and I realized it must be high tide. And so my eyes finally have seen the sea!"

After describing what he did on the Lido (he collects small sea shells and snails), Goethe writes of his visit to the tomb of Smith, the English consul, author of an edition of the works of Palladio, in the Protestant cemetery. Goethe writes: "All in all, the sea is a great spec-tacle! I will try, as best I can, to sail in a boat, because the gondolas don't dare venture into the open sea."

"All in all, the sea is a great spectacle. . ." This is Goethe's memo-rable comment on gazing at the sea for the first time. It's absolutely a statement of the obvious, a kind of obviousness that this German genius, influenced as he was by Greco-Roman culture, very rarely fell back on. Some people have noted it is quite a commonplace state-ment. I'm not sure. . . I think that Goethe rises to the occasion with a reasonable flourish, which is, in any case, typical of Goethe.

I have always found it very difficult to write anything general and overarching about the sea that was worthwhile saying. There are many analytical descriptions of specific moments of the sea, and some are excellent. English literature about the sea is extensive and, at times, unsurpassed.

Few things exist on the subject of the sea that can rival lines of Byron's poetry (in rhetorical mode) and pages of Conrad (in realist mode). But overarching judgments about the sea miss the mark.

Mascarell, whom Maupassant seemed momentarily to be sending to sleep, asked me: "What are you doing?"

"Not much. I'm taking some notes on Goethe's *Italian Journey*."

And I read him what I had written. Mascarell opined that Goethe displays the circumspection of a true intellectual.

"He could have launched into a speech in poor taste," he told me, "but he merely writes a comment that is banal and ordinary. His was a good reaction."

"I agree with you," I responded. "Have you ever witnessed reactions from men or women seeing the sea for the first time? It can be highly amusing. There are usually two kinds. Some opt to burble in a grandiloquent, incoherent, exorbitant manner. They lard their perorations with the inevitable words 'grandiose,' 'sublime,' 'immense,' 'eternal,' 'enormous' and the whole gamut of shock troops of the most facile, predictable adjectives. The same sort of verbiage the starry vaults often produce. If the individual embarking on this sonorous rhapsody has the misfortune to be at all educated, he will add alongside these resonant adjectives the Latin race, the Parthenon, the canon, the classical arch, Pericles, Alcibiades and even, if he's not careful, Roman law. Generally, however, people seeing the sea for the first time don't usually say a thing: they are overwhelmed and they stay silent. Not very long ago I engaged in conversation with a farming lady from the Plain of Vic, who was contemplating those briny waves for the first time. She reacted by saying: 'Perhaps there's too much water for so little meat. . . !'"

"That's typical of us," Mascarell observed, "her sentence typifies our way of being, which always aspires to keep its feet on the ground."

"Perhaps. In any case, there is poetry in our literature that, in my view, is some of the best that's been written about the sea. Like the poem by Don Joan Alcover entitled 'Miramar' that goes like this:

> *I've always lived by the sea*
> *but got to know it only today;*
> *suddenly, in Miramar,*
> *it showed its face to me.*
> *Seemed to smile and breathe*
> *like a sleeping maiden,*
> *seemed to flow from one world to another*
> *like an impetuous current.*

"The final four lines are apparently simple but contain a wealth of knowledge. When Alcover says the sea seems to 'smile,' he's embracing the solar world of the Greeks before the sea, perhaps the Homeric moment, because it was Homer who said those words that are so beautiful: the sea's 'ineffable smile.' The word 'breathe' contains the whole Romantic tradition of the sea, the idea that it is a blind, cosmic force in perpetual movement, in the eternal movement of breathing and living. And the last two lines,

> *seemed to flow from one world to another*

like an impetuous current.

inevitably bring to mind the figure of Ramon Llull, to whom we owe one of the most beautiful, most profound, most modern things ever written about the sea:

The sea, current of the world. . .

"Things must be seen, if at all possible, in their time and place. The usual adjectives the ancients use to describe the sea are 'cloudy,' 'foggy' and 'dark' – the most precise meteorological adjectives – because the Mediterranean, as a result of the predominantly southern winds, often appears this way. On the other hand, their knowledge of the sea's expanse was limited, so that to venture beyond a few capes – beyond *finis terrae* – was to enter an unknown world, pure darkness.

"But at the same time, divine, ideal marine moments come now and then. This is especially the case in June, when, luminous and placid, the water's surface, rippled by a breeze, under a dazzling sun, is flecked with glinting white foam, like a broad, ineffable smile. The people of Majorca call it the blossoming sea. It happens on days when the weather's straightforward, when a northwesterly picks up just as crickets in pine groves on the coast start to sing, and that dry, cool scent is in the air. It can even happen at twelve thirty, with the sun at its zenith, when a blue southwesterly blows. The two adjectives used by the ancients ring exactly true. Just as the notes given by Ramon Llull and Alcover couldn't be more precise when you gaze at the sea from a great height, panoramically – in a word, from Miramar. Then the sea appears like an immense current, like an unbounded flow.

"Mysticism about the sea exists in the countries of northern

Europe and is particularly reflected in Scandinavian novels. Faced by its astonishing power, northern Europeans tend to endow the sea with spiritual might – a force of something infinite. 'This dark, blind power,' says Conrad, 'knows no feeling of generosity.' In the Mediterranean, terror before the sea has led men for twenty or thirty thousand years to imagine divine protectors who are able to save us from its ever imminent attacks. As a result of successive layers of cultures, the Phoenician Astarte and the Greek and Roman Venuses have each been displayed and represented in old hermitages along our coastline."

The compass watch pointed to five p.m. It was at that point, on the dot, that *Rufí* began to pitch. We were so used to calm that when the prow dipped, then surged, it took us all by surprise. Martinet handed the helm back to Joanot and positioned himself on the prow, where he stood and observed the change with one hand on the jib halyard.

"What's happening, Martinet?" asked Mascarell, intrigued.

"Choppy swell to prow, Senyor Mascarell. . . A heavy, fast swell."

"And what does that mean?"

"It means that the wind pushing it, driving it, will soon. . ."

"And which wind might that be?"

"From the way the sea is turning, I'd say the wind we could well do without."

"Meaning what?"

"I mean it's a head wind that, if I'm not mistaken, is the mistral."

"So what must we do, Martinet?" asked Mascarell nervously.

"I think we should keep quiet for starters, then see how it develops. . ."

Martinet ordered Mascarell to take charge of the tiller. He, Joanot and I tried to put some order into things on board. Everything not thought indispensable was stored and shut up in the hold. The mainsail was taken down and secured. Just in case, Martinet hoisted a small storm jib. We tightened rigging and ropes. The deck was quickly clean and tidy. We put a blanket and tarpaulin over the engine.

"What frightens me most," Martinet whispered to me, "is that a shower of seawater will soak the engine and stop it. If that happens, we'd soon have to decide what to do. . . So that's really important."

"Do you reckon we're far from Barcelona?"

"No, we've made average progress. We must be off Garraf."

We filled the gas tanks and carried a jerry can of oil to the stern just in case we needed it. Sailors believe that if you spread oil over the sea, it will reduce the strength of the waves and they won't hit so hard. And it's true enough.

Apart from the swell, the weather was as usual: the same opaque air and stillness. Martinet kept a sharp eye on the area of sea in front of the ship's prow. If it had been clear, we'd have had a perfect view of the coast. But the horizons were quite invisible. It was a real pity not to be able to see the Montserrat mountains, which are so magnificent from out at sea! When we'd secured *Rufi*'s small lifeboat, we all went to the poop deck. Previously, Martinet had ordered Joanot to bring him bread, a bottle of wine and a slice of dry sausage and to store it there.

"Have you people got oilskins?" he asked.

Mascarell looked at me; I looked at him and we both laughed. I'd brought a raincoat; Mascarell said there was a heavy-weather coat in his cupboard. We were ill prepared.

"If the weather turns rough, please do your best not to get wet," Martinet advised us grimly. "If you get soaked, it will make life even more difficult. Please stay inside the cabin."

At the onset of twilight, the swell got choppier and more violent. Occasionally there was something like a breath of fresh air. In any case, the wind was taking its time to settle in.

"We can't be very far. . ." said Martinet, untangling his oilskins. "When the wind kicks in, it will blow all the stink from the sewers in port. . . You just wait and see."

And with that – it was a quarter to six – a bright-green eye appeared on the horizon ninety degrees west. This eye described a perfect arc – an arc of light that first showed as a narrow, flattened crack in the dense, opaque haze and then gradually spread. A quarter of an hour after that crack appeared, the whole of the northern horizon had cleared wonderfully. A metallic-green sky had emerged, across which blackish-purple streaks of clouds sailed, driven by the wind. Garraf surfaced, the lower coast of Llobregat, Montjuïc, too, and much hazier, the Montseny mountains in the distance. We thought we were so close to Barcelona that we would have heard the buzz of the city, if it hadn't been for our boat's engine.

All of a sudden, the sea began to turn green half a mile from *Rufi*'s prow. Beyond the swift-moving, undulating green, we could see a line of white that was also advancing. Martinet – now suitably dressed – had taken charge of the helm. Joanot was at his side, also adequately attired. Then came the first gust, followed by a second and a third. They were relatively gentle, though they came as a shock to the system after nine or ten hours of becalmed sea and left us nonplussed. Then calm returned followed by a lashing wind that hit the boat like a round of grapeshot. The mast bent; *Rufi* heeled over. That whiplash of wind brought the first waves, squelching with foam that the wind blew away. A huge shower of water fell on *Rufi*'s deck, which the scuppers struggled to sluice away. Mascarell was drenched. I'd have been too if I'd not sheltered behind him. Martinet was scowling.

"Senyor Mascarell, get below decks! Stay in the cabin. . . And you, senyor, if you want to stay on deck, put your coat on. And don't make me have to repeat that!"

Mascarell disappeared, looking fed up. I went to get my coat. Our small craft was tossing and pitching like a nutshell. You had to grab the first thing at hand to walk a single step. The way the prow dipped deep into the collapsing waves was disturbing; *Rufi*'s stern rose, showed its ass and screw in the air. All the craft's timbers began to shake and vibrate like the leaves of a tree. Then the prow rose up, casting down two huge beards of water that bubbled and frothed ferociously. I had to crawl to the cabin. When I stood up, *Rufi* suddenly pitched over and sent my knee crashing into the side of the bunk; I saw stars. I looked awful. Mascarell, who'd struggled to take his clothes off and was lying on his cot, asked me: "What's wrong?"

After a while I went back on deck and walked over to Martinet. I found him in fine fettle, flexing his muscles, face tensed. He half laughed – though it seemed slightly for show. Joanot was observing things with total indifference. He was used to trawlers riding out a storm.

"How's it going, Martinet?" I asked the second I reached his side.

"Shout or I won't hear you. . . ! The wind blows everything away. Speak up!"

Squalls of water continued to hit the deck, flooding the sides, washing over the decks, and spray and rivulets soaked our faces. The salt burned our eyes. Now and then you had to wipe your eyes with your elbow to see anything.

The onset of the wind had cleared the haze in a flash. The sky was limpid and bright – a September sunset, autumnal, cold and bluey gray. To the west, over Montserrat, the horizon was a spectacular yellowy red. Only small blackish wisps raced over the open expanse of sky, the typical ragged streaks blown along by those winds. The coastline stood out and Barcelona's urban sprawl could be felt behind Montjuïc. Factory chimneys in Clot and Badalona stuck out in the distance.

"I smelled the stink from the port sewers. . . Did you, senyor?" asked Martinet, with a laugh. "Can you see Martell? It's clear enough."

No, I couldn't make out Martell. Over *Rufí*'s prow you could see watery spray scattering over the sea. Sometimes there was a clear spell and you got a vague glimpse of something. Generally, the spray stayed dense and opaque. The gusts came thick and fast; on each side of our craft they swept away the crest of foam like gleaming feathers. The swirling, roiling sea boomed thunderously.

"The wind," remarked Martinet, "is blowing real strong. Our only hope is that it won't last long. Sometimes if it's strong, it soon dies out."

"And what about *Rufí*? Will it survive?"

"She's a brave little boat. Look at her prow pitching! She's a real boat! But really too small for this kind of squall. When she's hit full on by a blast, she's paralyzed. . . And that's natural enough."

With a north wind or mistral, the sea's surface is unmistakable. The wind speed makes the water surge like a swollen river, bubbling, splashing, rushing. Beneath that flow comes a series of long, tall waves, with deep troughs and high crests. The waves make boats pitch and heel, raising and lowering them as if on a set of scales. The sea's current and the wind's force heave boats one way or the other, depending on the direction of the gusts. Thus, if they sail into the wind, boats sway as they edge forward, like a wheel leaning this way and that. Martinet gripped the tiller tight trying to steer *Rufí* through the eye of the harshest, most unnerving onslaughts, but the blows from wind and sea were harsh and dramatic, and everything was beginning to suffer the pressure of the unleashed elements.

It all seemed a matter of patience. It was all about reaching Martell eventually. We were level with Llobregat. To reach Martell we were dependent on our engine. If the engine was fine, we could assume we'd reach the harbor mouth, though, obviously, we couldn't be sure when. This was the lay of the land as Martinet saw it. It was true to his mariner spirit.

I tried to persuade him that along with what you might call his frontal tactic there was another strategy that was possibly dangerous, but might be more sensible and practical. I was used to sailing in even smaller craft, and my experience had taught me that sometimes being pig headed, turning things upside down and trying to pass through the eye of the main hurdle didn't work.

"Martinet!" I said.

"Out with it!" he replied, wiping away the water streaming down his cheek.

"You're intending to head straight to Martell, straight into the wind and sea?"

"That's right. What would you do in my place?"

"I see that. But we could also sail closer to land and seek shelter from the coast."

"Don't talk to me about the coast. Ships need water."

"I agree. But the closer we are to land, the less we'll feel the wind and the sea."

"No, forget it. I don't want to lose this boat. I'm not familiar with the sandbanks. What I want is water."

"Fine. You're in charge. Just think, on the other hand, that if the engine breaks down, we could reach Martell along the coast simply by using our sail a bit."

"You're suggesting something that fishermen do," he answered curtly. "And you know only too well I'm no fisherman."

"I won't mention it again. You're the boss."

Martinet, who was already – one might say – organically immersed in the situation we were confronting, seemed obsessed with a single thing: the purr of our backup motor. But at a quarter to seven – I remember it well – after a buffeting from the sea that rocked *Rufí*, the motor missed a beat, and after a few spasmodic splutters, it stopped altogether. Perhaps it was soaked. Perhaps it stopped because of the beast's inherent evil, because one thing you can predict about a motor that's up and running – especially in circumstances like that – is that it will stop. Once *Rufí* had lost its driving impetus, she was like a feather at the mercy of sea and wind, which were carrying her away at top speed.

Martinet didn't think twice – and his was a saintly reaction, for any attempt to sort out the motor, or simply to tarpaulin the cover off, would have been effort expended in vain; he turned the tiller and gave our poop a tail wind. For the moment, any idea of reaching Barcelona was dismissed.

"Are you hoping to make it to Garraf, Martinet?" I asked.

"We'll see. . ."

"Maybe Tarragona?"

"For the moment let's just try to keep our heads down."

Martinet ordered Joanot to hoist the storm sail. When the wind hit the small sail, *Rufí* started speeding apace. It's not easy to sail with a tail wind, and it's not without its dangers. But Martinet showed himself to be a mariner with lots of experience and skill. *Rufí* sailed well; the small sail we were carrying in the prow seemed to raise its head and allow the boat to float energetically. The vessel slipped over the water like a seagull, lurching from side to side, sometimes leaning to starboard, other times to port. That twisting and turning, leading the boat to heel over this way and that, forced Martinet to keep the rudder tight, and created such a swirl of water it sometimes swept over the stern and soaked the boards where we were standing. Meanwhile, dusk fell. After half or three quarters of an hour sailing with a back wind, sight of land had almost vanished. Streams of white light from the Montjuïc lighthouse punctured the air.

Martinet gave the tiller to Joanot, cut a slice of bread and sausage and took a swig of wine. He seemed much less nervy and uptight than an hour earlier. Making an escape always brings a degree of mental peace. A shower of water occasionally hit the backs of Joanot and Martinet, who were sitting in the poop. The water thudded against their hard oilskins and streamed down them.

I went down to the cabin. Mascarell was lying on his mattress. He'd managed to pull a blanket over his body. He looked pale and sickly. I told him what had happened, and when I confirmed what was going on – namely, that we were heading back – he listened in total resignation. I was expecting him to tell me he had to be in the office in the morning, but he said nothing.

"Aren't you well?" I asked.

"Don't you worry about me. I'm just feeling under the weather. This craft is too small. I must buy a bigger one."

"Don't get worked up. It's unpleasant, but nothing we can do about it. Just bear up."

"Will you believe me if I tell you I've never suffered so much mentally?"

"Of course. It's only natural."

I went back on deck. Martinet was holding the tiller again. Joanot struggled to light the two sidelights – two sad fireflies that at least made us feel we were in good company.

As there was no way to light the compass binnacle, I couldn't work out the route we were taking until the stars appeared and I located the polar star. I was rather astonished to see we were heading sharp southeast, over the Menorcan channel, to be precise. Martinet had given up on Garraf, Tarragona and Sóller as possible safe havens. He must have decided: "As we're in flight, might as well do it as quickly as possible, the best way the wind and sea can take us." One theory is as good as another.

Rufí was making progress like a steamship – to use a sailorish cliché. Wind and sea were driving us forward. We always sailed in the same style: suddenly lurching and heeling over. Fortunately, it wasn't a cold night; it was dry and the stars were twinkling. Martinet didn't budge from the stern the whole time. He ordered Joanot to go and get some sleep until midnight and I stayed at his side. I later stretched out on my bunk, and his son took my place.

When I walked into the cabin, Mascarell asked: "What's happening? Where are we?"

"Why don't you try to get some kip? It's a quarter to one. Do you want anything to eat or drink?"

"Is it still as windy? Is the sea still so rough?" my friend asked dreamily.

"Not so much now. . ."

"Where are we? Are we in sight of the light on the headland?"

"We're sailing along the northern coast of Majorca, but I couldn't tell you exactly where we are."

I added one or two other things but soon saw he wasn't responding.

I struggled to get to sleep but finally did so out of physical exhaustion rather than real sleepiness. I could see the red glow from the side-lights on the water through the porthole next to my bunk swaying up and down, and that made me anxious. *Rufí* was pitching and swaying like a drunken boat, which stopped me from really sleeping.

The next morning I opened my eyes and was surprised by the sense of peace surrounding me. The first thing I realized was that they hadn't called me at four as we'd agreed. Why hadn't they? It was quite dark in the cabin. And so peaceful! There was a palpable, physical peace, a force that closed my eyes again. I reacted and, looking out onto the quarterdeck, saw Mascarell dressed for city life and putting things in his suitcase.

"Where are we, Mascarell? What happened?"

"As you'll see, we're in Portopetro, one of the biggest ports on the Mediterranean."

"Why didn't you give me a shout?"

"You were sleeping so soundly nobody dared."

"So where is Martinet?"

"He's gone to see his family. He said he wanted to sleep at home tonight, as the north wind had brought us back here."

"What about Joanot?"

"He's in the bow, catching beltfish."

"But what on earth happened, Mascarell?"

"Martinet will tell you at his leisure. All I know is that when the north wind began to die down in Alcúdia Bay, at dawn, given that we were off Alcúdia, Martinet decided to sail on a few more miles, and so here we are. We sailed here, with a light northeasterly."

"And what are you doing now, Mascarell?"

"I'm packing my case. We should reach Palma before evening to catch the mail boat. We'll be in Barcelona by the morning, even though there's a north wind blowing. I've hired a small cart to take us to S'Alqueria, where we'll try to find a taxi. Come on! Get your things together, we've no time to waste."

"What about *Rufí*?"

"Martinet will bring her to Barcelona, if that's what he decides. And if he doesn't, they will take the mail boat when they feel like it. In that case, she'll stay anchored here. A relative of Martinet's will take charge of her."

"Mascarell, I can see you've been busy."

"You bet, my boy! I've convinced myself that dry land is the thing. The sea's not worth a puff of tobacco smoke."

Mascarell showed he was an admirable organizer. The next morning we disembarked in Portal de la Pau.

Two or three years after these events, I bumped into Martinet one day on the Pla de Palau.

I asked after *Rufí* and Senyor Mascarell.

"*Rufí* is still in Portopetro," said Martinet. "In the summer the kids dive off her. Apparently there's a man who wants to use her to breed mussels, if Senyor Mascarell agrees to a deal. He's yet to get round to it!"

"It's been ages," I said in turn, "since I knew the whereabouts of Senyor Mascarell. He spends his summers in the mountains. He doesn't want to hear any mention of the sea. His obsession was a flash in the pan. . ."

"That's how it goes. . ." said Martinet, with a laugh.

"Anyway, Martinet, I'd like to tell you one thing, now that we've bumped into each other. We should have sailed close to land the day that north wind started to blast."

"No, we shouldn't have! I couldn't do that without risking losing the boat."

"In any case, the boat was lost. We could have reached the harbor mouth with a small sail."

However, Martinet was in a hurry: he had to go and paint the factory owner's boat. When we said goodbye, he looked at me rather standoffishly: the way a mariner looks at a beach angler. I accepted that with good grace, because only a fool moves things from their rightful place.

SMUGGLING

That house in the neighborhood of El Pianc in Cadaqués was one of the first I ever rented. There are people who remember the various abodes they've had, the houses where they've lived, in minute detail. I wish I had that kind of memory. Curiously, nonetheless, I do remember the house in El Pianc very clearly for a series of circumstances quite unrelated to the house itself.

It was clear that the *americano* who built the house had been been nurturing that dream for some time. It was a large house, made from first-rate materials and in a visible location. When something is a long-standing focus of dreams, it ends up assuming a lavish air. Situated in the highest point of El Pianc, this house enjoyed wonderful views over Cadaqués Bay, the town and Pení mountains.

The basement rooms, cut out of the slate, were spacious and dark, with a big cistern in their depths that collected roof water. It must have been a huge cistern, because when it rained and water sluiced in, it made a dull, sepulchral sound, a scary, thunderous boom. Obviously, the *americano* had intended to use those rooms to lodge (in winter) his boat, fishing tackle, firewood, barrels of wine and drums of oil. Unfortunately that fine fellow never saw any of his hopes fulfilled because he died in Argentina before making his definitive return. Nor did his children ever come back, so the house became a property rented out over the years to a succession of tenants.

It was, then, a fine house, though there was little in the way of contents: simply whatever people had left behind. To live there, you had to bring the indispensable – which is what I did – the few belongings I possessed in L'Escala. They didn't fill the place; rather, they seemed out of place and pointless. Most rooms continued to be completely empty; I don't remember ever opening their doors.

On the first floor there was a large, luminous central dining room, with one bedroom on either side. That suite opened out onto three magnificent balconies on a façade that looked expressly built for a life of contemplation: they framed such intriguing vistas.

One of the dining room's side walls had a rather pretentiously curved fireplace, and its mantelpiece was home to a pseudo-artistic clock that was perpetually halted at 5:25. That figure of 5:25 remained etched in my memory as a result of a later coincidence I shall describe in due course. It was a curious clock: the outside was normal with a bronze frame, face and hands, but it lacked any inner mechanism. Somebody must have removed it and then abandoned the fictive clock, a disemboweled clock. A white wooden table stood in the center with four reed chairs, beneath a wire hanging from the plain ceiling supporting an electric bulb inside an arty pink glass capsule, like a small engraved bell. That bare item, hanging in too large a space, struck me as rather depressing. It was all that remained of the magnificent light installed by the *americano*.

But that dining room did have one good item: a settee, a Cadaqués settee, of carved, light-brown mahogany, which had probably come from Italy, a somewhat shabby, appealing settee, with a small couch upholstered in frayed green cretonne. It was a perfect size and really comfortable, adapting as it did to the human body, and even aroused feelings of genuine affection. But the odd aspect of that piece of furniture was the way it belonged to the house's jetsam – things people had in turn forsaken. I asked the owner's agent who had made the mistake of leaving the settee, but he couldn't enlighten me.

The walls would have been bare too, if it hadn't been for the previous tenant – a Swedish painter – who left three or four unframed canvases he'd begun hanging there, attempts to represent olive trees that were in a process of coming into being, in a hazy, intangible state yet to emerge from the murk. If it hadn't been for some vivid green brushstrokes over the haze, you might have concluded that they were canvases that had been erased rather than just begun. When I gazed at those abandoned attempts, I sensed that the painter had decided to say farewell by leaving a memento in the house, but the memento was timid and inchoate, like the memory of the features of someone you saw walk by years ago, just that once.

The first thing I did when I went to live in the house was to drag the settee over to the balcony and place a table in front of the window so I could work there. As the house faced south and received the sun full on in summer, I hung a gauze curtain over the window to soften the glare. When the weather cooled, it was an ideal place to be. Ideal for idling rather than working. Between one thing and another, however, I spent many engagingly solitary hours on that settee with my papers and tomes on the table. Toward the end of September, clear of summer haze, the Pení mountains regained the purple, bluey-mauve of flowering thyme. Against that backdrop, the whiteness of the houses seemed to blanche and become a light tawny gold or pale brown. Toward dusk, the waters of the bay were streaked with the pink of new wine. It was a time when Cadaqués was silent, peaceful and still. From my balcony I could see a few small figures strolling along the Baluard quayside. The air turned purple. The southwesterly breeze died out on that path. I had visited the Oberland of Bern, that flower of the Alps, in the spring of that year and felt the Alps were radiant. When I compared these memories to ones I had of the Pyrenees – and in Cadaqués I was in the midst of the Pyrenees – I felt the Alps were mountains with clear, uplifting strata while the Pyrenees were a depressing purple. Though that's purely a personal opinion.

It was at the start of one of those autumnal twilights – early October – when, stretched out on the settee, contemplating the thyme-hued Pení, I heard a whistle that shattered the calm as if someone had just fired a rocket. People were harvesting and working in the olive groves, and Cadaqués seemed empty, if not deserted. My senses had pleasantly dozed off in the silence, and that strident sound so close by startled me. I went out on the balcony. Nobody was on the promenade. I couldn't see anything special. A sailing boat was slowly entering the bay on the evening sirocco. I thought it was a foreign vessel and stared at it. At that exact moment they tightened the downhaul and were furling the jib sail after steering into the wind. I heard them cast the anchor into the sea. The vessel was in the entrance to El Pianc, directly opposite the house where I lived. There was no better place to keep your boat in Cadaqués harbor.

I soon realized the boat was the *Mestral*, a small thirty-footer I'd had built in L'Escala and later sold to a Roses fisherman by the name of Baldiri Cremat. This Baldiri was the bravest, wildest sailor in the port of Roses. I immediately knew the whistle I'd heard was his way of greeting me. Baldiri was good company but could be disconcerting.

However, all that rushed to the back of my mind as my eyes affectionately watched the *Mestral*. She was a small Majorcan keelboat with a bridge, excellent for sailing, one Vadoret had built with exquisite good taste, a boat that had given me so much joy and one I had sold because I'd had no choice, very, very reluctantly. The *Mestral* is the centerpiece of my memories of life in L'Escala.

When the master carpenter was making it, I spent many an hour in his workshop in La Punta. I even lived in the area. Spending time with shipwrights and caulkers is such fun. That is, in small workshops on the coast. When they are too big, boats become bulky affairs, part of heavy industry. The construction of an iron vessel creates an infernal racket and is best seen in a movie house. Now, small shipyards are a delight. Timber brings a lovely smell. The saw drones monotonously, albeit musically. The tar spitting out from the fire arouses your appetite and, if you have a cold, cleans out your tubes. In winter, the sawdust and wooden chips warm your feet. The caulker's hammer isn't deafening. It's a sharp, cheerful, almost rhythmic tap that never annoys. It's enthralling to see a boat of human proportions being constructed. It requires specialist knowledge – they are true tradesmen. It is a pleasure to see artisans at work, much more of a pleasure to see an artisan at work than a regiment of workers lifting picks or spades. Artisans have created the most beautiful, most graceful, most decorous things in this world. What machines make is nasty, horrible, depressing and fatally coarse.

When a customer appeared, the shipwright would say: "What do you want, senyor? A sailing boat or motor-driven boat? A Majorcan keelboat or a flat bottom for trawling? There are many kinds of boat, but no two are ever the same. Tell me the length, width and depth you require, I'll make a model and then we'll see whether what you want is a vessel or a frog. Because it might be that what you're really after is a tin crate. Individual whims usually get it wrong."

"Oh, come on!"

"It's obvious. . . It's what I was just saying: there are no two boats that are identical, not even those that are mass produced. Even machines can't produce units that are the same. On the other hand, it's extremely risky if you want to make something different to rely on individual fancies, because you never know what the end product will be. You and I can tell a beautiful woman from one that is not. And that can help us see whether what you have in mind is a vessel or a tin crate."

"So there are no rules?"

"Very few. As few as there are for predicting how a marriage will turn out. Tell me what you want and I'll make a model. We can discuss it and then proceed. A boat must be built to sail, and that is no fantasy: it's for real."

Once he obtained what he'd asked of me, the shipwright set to work, took out his sheets of paper, made his drawings and calculations. That was his craft, linked to innate insight and the experience he might have accrued sending boats, in any weather, out to sea. "In any weather" goes without saying because you rarely ever sail in complete calm. The calculations and drawings are the practical demonstration of the insight the artisan will call upon when he is actually building the boat. Later, those calculations will be transferred to the timber – which, preferably, is always oak – or the frame timbers, or ribs, as summer holidaymakers call them, that make up the structure. Everything will depend on the grace and solidity of that structure, of the assembling of the frame timbers: the boat's seaworthiness, its safety, elegance and comfort.

The frame timbers must come before the keel. If you want to build a boat in scatter-brained fashion, first put the keel in place, then attach the frame timbers as best you can. But if you want to build the genuine article, first build the structure and then mount it on a firm, stable keel. In any case, the keel is important. It's always best if it's made from a single piece of wood. I've seen a thirteen-yard keel made from a single trunk – from a magnificent tree. The wood must be from a first-rate tree. The keel is mounted on the teeth of two pine-wood pivots that have been sunk into the ground. This is known as "laying" the keel. Then the timber frame is fitted, like reconstructing a sliced melon. I use the melon simile because I think it is most apt. At any rate, try to ensure the boat doesn't look like a melon, especially a watermelon.

Fitting the frame is a very delicate operation and requires great precision. The ribs, in the center of the keel, have the open, arrogant shape of the horns of a well-endowed ox. Near the prow, they are at a sharper angle that gradually closes as you draw near to the stem. On the stern side, their form will depend on the shape of stern. What kind of stern do you want? If the boat is motor driven, it will end in a flat surface vertical to the water. If you want to sail and win regattas, you will try to eliminate as many surfaces that involve friction as possible. In a fishing boat, you will shape the stern so it is best fitted for fishing. "England is a country," said Voltaire, "that has a single sauce and many religions." A vessel is an object with a single keel and many kinds of sterns.

Once the timbers are fitted to the basic tree and prow, from stem to stern, the ends of the ribs must be attached at the height of the deck – or bridge – using the strake. The strake runs at a height that depends on the boat's depth. This strake is the thin, curved timber plank that seals the frame from stern to prow at the top. Once the strake of a boat has been laid, you have a perfect sense of its future shape. You mustn't confuse the strake with the gunwale. The gunwale is what covers the strake. The strake is what secures the deck and the bridge. Once it is in place, the boat looks like a cage made of curved bars. Then you can see the vessel's structure and say whether it has turned out to be a frog or a thing of grace, whether it pleases the eye or not. That's the time to make changes. It will be too late after.

If the boat's shape is acceptable, then the planking is put in place – that is, the cage formed by the timber frames is covered. There are outside and inside planks: generally they are pinewood and are fixed to the timber ribs and layered in order. Once the vessel is covered in that way, you can say it is finished. Then the building of the deck and gunwale require careful attention. As well as the caulking. Applying tar and paint are entertaining activities.

Once all that is ready, the innards of the vessel must be created, and that's the job of the master carpenter: the engine must be put in place together with berths, storage cupboards and the infinite elements a well-made vessel must have. It is useful to consult catalogues from England. All these features will reveal the owner's good taste and seafaring ability. You only have to step foot on a boat to see whether the owner is a man of the sea or simply wants to use it to go out and eat a paella once a year with his friends in some corner of a foul-smelling harbor.

A boat must carry rigging and masts. When the hull is finished, they must be hoisted. Getting that right is a matter of grace and style: each boat is different and, consequently, its tackle is distinct.

I stayed on my balcony and gazed down at the *Mestral* until the light faded altogether. The presence of that fine, elegant craft reminded me of my stay in L'Escala, the long periods I had spent in the small docks of La Punta, when she was being built. So many enjoyable hours! The building of the *Mestral* still brings me so much pleasure! Now I was watching her slender silhouette in the crepuscular light of the bay, a whitish patch on water tinged with gentle twilight purple. I reflected how the *Mestral* had vanished from my life as that glow faded from the absolute, rocky stillness of Cadaqués Bay.

Back on the settee – which was so pleasant! – more memories surged that were extraordinarily precise.

We launched the boat in Perris harbor with quite a bit of difficulty, because it's a filthy area with very little water. But the experienced Vadoret managed all that. We decided to make our first crossing to Cadaqués to test her out. She was still unnamed. The fact was I hadn't a clue what to call her.

We enjoyed a few very agreeable days. A moment comes at the height of summer when, even though you know you're taking a real risk, you feel a tremendous desire to do nothing at all. Sky and earth, sea and mountain, wind and calm, urge you to spend your time on less painful occupations than filling page after page with petty, even irritating, paragraphs. There is this contradiction: the best way to while the time away is to do nothing. Writing is a complicated trifle that in the end wears you down to the bone. Any excuse is good to put it aside for a period. Intellectual work has that drawback: it can be very taxing, but it doesn't make you sweat and never eliminates the excess toxins from the body's tissues. Your inevitable, sad mental imaginings wear out the fibers but don't restore vitality: physical effort rejuvenates; mental effort ages. You feel an irrepressible urge to sweat, to pull on a rope, to lift paternoster lines, to row. At night you're sleepy; the brain repels all obsessions, you sink into a blissful swoon. You can't wish for a more useful form of escape than a boat.

When I was walking along La Riba in Cadaqués, I saw Senyor Víctor Rahola coming toward me, with that quiet, unbelligerent air of his. An older gentleman, over sixty, who radiates a wondrously iridescent warmth of feeling. He was dressed in nineteenth-century fashion: buttery drill and a perfectly starched shirt. When I see this gentleman, my memory springs into action. We were blessed by so many friends in common (many now dead), loved so many remote, solitary heaths on this and other coasts, and are united by such a love of the sea that I spur on his imagination and he sparks a wealth of memories and experiences in me. His character combines, on the one hand, insights from the his most complex medical knowledge and, on the other, from the most appealing poetry. I'm thrilled to meet him; it's a genuine pleasure. His character allows him to be totally natural with unlettered people and always suggests a vast expanse of uncharted territory.

"So then, it seems we have a boat. . ." he told me, with a laugh.

"Yes, senyor, I have a boat we can use to go wherever you want."

"And what name have you given her?"

"It doesn't have one yet. I don't know what to christen her."

"Why don't you call her '*Mestral*?'"

"That's a name with a certain pedigree."

"It's a lovely name. It's the name of the healthiest of winds. Personally, it cures all my aches and pains. People across the Mediterranean use this name; it's part of the lingua franca. That's what it is in Catalan and Spanish. In Provençal and Occitan, it's *mistral*. In Italian, *maestrale*. The same, in modern Greek. I believe the word is very similar in Turkish and Slavic languages. 'Mistral' is even used by the English. I've never understood why club boats are given such rare or exotic names. Names in French are the most common."

"It really is a lovely name. . ."

"Besides, the word '*mestral*' brings to mind one of the most extraordinary crossings I ever made. It was a dangerous, rapid, astonishing crossing. You'll probably not believe me if I tell you that I went from Cadaqués to Civitavecchia in under forty-eight hours in a schooner. It was because the mistral blew us along."

"Tell me more, Senyor Víctor. . ."

"When I was young, my health was poor, so my parents decided to put me on one of their sailing boats that went to Italy. They generally went to Anzio to transport chestnut wood used in making wine vats. I've known Anzio for over fifty years. My parents thought a sea voyage would strengthen me and give me an appetite. So I embarked. We left Cadaqués in a family schooner with a crew of excellent local sailors. It was winter and we hoisted the sails with a sharp mistral – the best wind, as you know, to leave this bay on. By the Cucurucuc in S'Arenella all the sails had been spread and the vessel advanced at a swift pace. Once out of the bay, the skipper asked his crew, as usual: 'What shall we do? Straight on?'

"In the winter, with tail winds from land, it wasn't usual to cross the sea in a straight line from one side to the other. Our destination was Civitavecchia. We could go straight, via Boques de Bonifaci, running off the wind or head northward, via the Hiéres. The crew replied: 'Straight on!' And the skipper agreed. So we headed toward Boques de Bonifaci. I was a thirteen- or fourteen-year-old youngster and it all seemed wonderful. We gradually left the coast. Then the wind picked up. Small ragged clouds scudded across the cold, blue-black sky over Pení. A moment came when the white blotch of the Sant Sebastià hermitage seemed to float on the waves. Given the weather and the wind's gathering strength, the skipper ordered all topsails to be furled and strapped down. They dropped in turn with a din: the main jib, inner jib and forestaysails. However, as there were still too many sails, the main and mizzen sails fell too. The brig looked like a huge, plucked bird. We were sailing only with the square sail, to keep the prow up and nimble. It was such a smooth ride: the waves pushed us strongly, sped us rapidly forward; the tensed masts and rigging whistled, seemingly overwhelmed by a nervous, crackling energy. Water surged over the stern; salty spray drenched us. The piercing whistle of the wind on the shroud, stays, rigging and topsails remains etched on my mind to this day as one of my most vivid memories from those years. The brig proceeded, its prow digging two huge furrows of foamy water, now this side, now that. I wasn't at all safe or stable on deck and the skipper locked me in the cabin. It had a lamp in one corner – we had set out in the afternoon and it was dark now – and soon it was as dark down below as in the sky. The brig swayed and pitched violently along. But what I remember most clearly from the first part of the voyage are the waves, the wild horses of the Gulf of Lion, waves shaped like caverns, inky black and crowned by tall, fast, furious crests of white foam. They rushed at our stern and seemed about to engulf us, but the vessel was well steered – the skipper didn't budge from the helm until we reached the end of our voyage – and always flew in a cloud of spray, on the edge of a breaking wave, to the din of bubbling, roiling water. The wind was taking us away. We sailed past Boques, and the lighthouses of Corsica and Sardinia paraded by and were out of sight amazingly quickly. The wind was less impetuous in the shelter of the Sardinian coast. Forty-eight hours after leaving Cadaqués we anchored in Civitavecchia, holding our watches. The effort of keeping on course and the nervous tension had exhausted the crew, but the second they saw the first tavern, they all revived. . ."

"No need to say another word, Senyor Víctor. The keelboat will be called *Mestral* in remembrance of your voyage."

So that was why the little boat – which had just arrived in Cadaqués – was called "*Mestral.*"

I'd just finished supper. There was a knock at the door. Baldiri Cremat walked into the dining room accompanied by a man he introduced as his brother-in-law, Pau Saldet. Baldiri was as open and chatty as Saldet was reserved and deadpan. Baldiri came in still wearing a cap; the other man was holding his.

"Have you had dinner?" I asked.

"Yes, senyor, we have."

"What can I offer you?"

"Whatever is to hand. . . We don't want to cause you any bother. . ."

"Are you planning to go fishing in the *Mestral*?"

"No, senyor, we're off to France."

"She's a good little boat to go anywhere, as you well know."

They sat around the table: Baldiri, comfortably; Saldet, with a bit of his rump up against the back of the chair. I brought in coffee and white rum.

"We'd like to have a word," said Baldiri, lighting a cigar.

"Fire ahead. . ."

"Would you fancy a trip to France? We'd thought, 'Perhaps he'd like to go to France and then write one of his witty chronicles.'"

"Of course. . ."

"We've loaded up with cans of olive oil here in Cadaqués. You know how it's the best. . . We'll transport it hereabouts to pay for the voyage. On the way back, we'll load up with bicycle parts, valuable stuff that takes up no room. We have to meet a man in the Salses Ponds. You could say it's a business matter. In fact, we're just going for a laugh. . ."

Baldiri was doing the talking. His brother-in-law stared at the ground. He sometimes nodded in a way that suggested he was in agreement. Pau Saldet seemed misanthropic and self-absorbed.

"I don't understand what my role might be on such a trip. . ." I said, after a lull in the conversation.

"I'm not suggesting you should have one. . ." interjected Baldiri abruptly. "You should come as a man of leisure. You'll be there to put people on the wrong track. We'll say you're the owner of the *Mestral* and you hired it out to us to sail along the Roussillon coast as far as Leucate. Do you understand? You should act as the owner, go to the café and read the newspaper. . . We'll be your crew, if you like, your servants. . ."

"Baldiri, you're a wily old fox. Tell me the truth: what are you really after in France?"

"What I said. Just what I said. I'm not lying. Or shall we say I'm not lying on purpose. . . though on this occasion it amounts to much the same thing. What do you expect? We all have our ways of working."

"That's fine, and thanks for being so candid. . . How long will the trip be?"

"If everything goes to plan, let's say a week. Today is Saturday. We must reach the Salses Ponds in a week's time, next Saturday at dusk. Once we've loaded up, we'll head fast round Cape Creus."

"If the weather is fine. . ."

"It will be. . . In the meantime, you'll have all that time to visit the Roussillon. If you don't know the place, you'll like it. If you're agreeable, we're all set."

"When do you intend on leaving?"

"We're ready. Right now, if possible. We've got to see a lad from Port de la Selva early tomorrow morning. He'll be by Prona Cove with his longboat."

"So who is he? Baldiri, I know you're sensible and a live wire, but I get the impression lots of people are involved. . ."

"The lad from La Selva deserted when he was a youngster and has fished for years around Leucate. He's a pilot. He'll inform us about the channels."

"What channels?"

"The ones into the ponds."

"Will he come with us?"

"No, senyor. He'll just give us the info. . . Do you own a gun?"

"And why would you need a gun?"

"Because there are lots of geese and coots in the ponds, and all kinds of birds are passing through at this time of year. We can say we're going to shoot geese in the ponds, if the French challenge us."

"I see you'd like to turn me into a true hunting gentleman. But the truth is I've never shot a gun."

"If you own a gun, don't worry, I'll shoot it."

The truth was I didn't own a gun and wouldn't have known how to find one in Cadaqués at that time of day.

I'd known Baldiri all my life. Hermós had introduced me to him years ago. Hermós thought he was one of the cleverest, most courageous youngsters in the port of Roses. Perhaps he was a man who liked to overindulge – too fond of women, booze and cards. But Hermós said he was a dab hand in the stern of a ship. When Hermós said anyone in any trade was a dab hand, you could rely on that person.

The *Mestral*'s presence in Cadaqués, after such a long separation, had set me thinking. I was really delighted by the idea of spending a few days aboard her beloved timbers. Though we weren't connected in any way now, I'd never been able to forget her. Besides, I'd nothing else to do in the coming week. There was nothing urgent... So I said I'd go with them to the Salses Ponds.

"What should I bring, Baldiri?" I asked.

"We have all we need on board. Bring a couple of blankets because it gets coldish at night. And some money, of course... We don't want to look stupid, you know? You won't be wasting your time... If everything goes well, we'll even have a little present for you..."

"Bah!"

When I walked into the street, with blankets under my arm and a small suitcase with my personal things, it was a damp, misty night, cloudless and windless. If there was a breeze, it came from the south, was very gentle and was ideal for sailing. Total silence reigned over Cadaqués. Streetlights were flickering like exhausted fireflies. There wasn't a soul about. The church's cracked bell rang ten o'clock. The

Cadaqués church bell doesn't ring solemnly and slowly; it chimes too quickly and skips a few beats.

When we reached El Pianc beach, a young lad emerged from under a skiff and joined us. It was a friend of Baldiri's, probably the one who'd supplied the olive oil he'd bought. He seemed half-asleep. He said hello and didn't say another word. This lad rowed us silently to the *Mestral* in his skiff without lifting his oars out of the water. When he'd dropped us off, he grabbed his oars and left, also without a word.

"It's so nice to meet someone around here who doesn't talk nonstop," I told Baldiri.

"That lad is a one-off. He's an ace when it comes to working at night."

Hermós would have said he was a dab hand.

We raised the anchor, started the engine and left.

It was a noisy engine. A wonky car engine. Baldiri took the tiller and turned the prow toward the small Calanans lighthouse, no doubt to make people think he was going back to Roses. Although there was no danger in Cadaqués, his prudence reassured me. We sailed like that for a while. As soon as we were in the mouth of the bay, Baldiri told Saldet: "Hoist the sail!"

While the sail went up, Baldiri raised the tiller and pointed the boat toward the Cape Creus lighthouse. There was still a gentle breeze, the sail swelled slightly, just enough to take out the side sheet. But the *Mestral* responded gratefully, and though that helped only a little, we were happy. She was built to sail and a little breeze was enough to display her excellent qualities. When sailing, she always carried her head high, her prow straight and slender.

I glanced over my old keelboat. She wasn't as clean as when I left her, naturally enough. She could have done with a lick of paint. The to-and-fro of fishing gear had left its mark. However, the boat was intact and seemed to have gained to a degree: she seemed more shipshape and used.

Once past Port Lligat and Guillola Bay, Baldiri hugged the coastline. He knew the lay of the land. It was a pitch-black night, but he moved along it with the eyes of a cat. We found a calm sea by Claveguera, though the current was coming from Mar d'Avall, and the *Mestral* quickly left the rocks behind. The splendid glow from the indistinguishable beams of light from Cape Béar appeared in the northwest.

When we had navigated Cape Creus, the boat entered the gulf of La Selva, where the water seemed clearer and deeper, the winds stronger, and nature freer and more powerful than anywhere else along our coast. Past the inhospitable plain of Tudela, the wind seemed to pick up. Sailing with the lateen over placid waters barely ruffled by the breeze, the *Mestral* carried herself wonderfully. You could hear the glug-glug of the water splashing against the bow.

We reached Prona Cove at two a.m. Paraffin lamps were burning on a rowing boat outside the inlet. A man was there with his jacket collar up, holding oars, lit up by the bluish-white light. A boat was anchored right behind the rocky entrance to the inlet. As we passed close by, the light from the greasy lamps allowed us to see people asleep on deck, wrapped in thick blankets. We anchored next to their boat.

It was so humid, the damp penetrated our sheets and blankets. I thought it was high time to retreat to my cot under the prow. I squeezed onto the thin mattress and was soon comfortingly warmed. I must have fallen asleep quickly. When I woke up, the sun was already high in the sky.

The moment I poked my head up above the bow, my bones felt depressed by that measly mattress. I saw the sea was still calm and that the longboat had gone. Prona Cove is perhaps the most characteristic geological incision in the gulf of La Selva. It is a purely rocky inlet. There's no trace of vegetation, only a tragic-looking, derelict shack. The sea was growing lively with a strong swell. The geological blackness seemed to turn gray in the damp, dense air. I spotted a motionless seagull, looking slightly shrunken, silhouetted on the rock in the entrance to the inlet.

My companions had lit the stove and were preparing garlic and onion sauce for a fish stew. The stove was giving off smoke. The onion smell was delicious. A dozen mackerel lay by the side of the stove with the electric-blue lines they have when they've just been fished out of the water. They must have been a present from the lad in the longboat. Mackerel isn't a fish you'd want to eat every day. It's too oily. But if you eat it now and then in a stew on board ship, when you're feeling ravenous, it's pleasant fare. Mackerel stew makes an excellent second supper and, if you're an early riser, a succulent breakfast.

A stranger stood next to Baldiri and Saldet by the stove and I assumed he must be the man from La Selva who was familiar with the channels in the Salses Ponds. He was on the old side, gray haired, olive skinned, with a mourning cap that contrasted with a left eye that was white, dead and swollen like a pigeon's egg. He was tall and stout, and sported a large, drooping, French-style mustache. They told me his name was Quimet, Quimet de la Selva to his friends.

Quimet was holding forth. Baldiri smoked while he listened. Saldet was holding the ladle.

"When you leave El Racó," he was saying, "you'll enter the gulf's big beach, which will seem never ending. Then you must head north, by night, toward the polar star, five or six paternoster lines from the low-set coast. If you meet easterly winds, move away from the beach, because the sandbanks break up and you might be turned over. If you keep on in this direction, on a clear day, you'll see Cape Leucate, which is white, is not particularly high and looks as if it's been basted in flour. A semaphore post is located on top of the cape. . ."

Saldet must have decided the sauce was just right. He threw eight or ten mackerel into the pot with a sprig of parsley and quickly poured water over the lot. Then he put the lid on and took out his tobacco pouch.

The day was struggling to find itself. A white murk floated over the sea. The weather was wet. A mixture of seawater and sand sluiced down the *Mestral*'s deck. You could see that the wind would either settle in to the south – or drop. The rocky inlet's silence seemed endlessly deep. Now and then a small fish leaped over the smooth mirror of water.

"Then you'll sail along this coast," resumed Quimet, "from Argelès, via Canet, Perpignan's beach, as far as Barcarès de Sant Llorenç de la Salanca. Although it's a frighteningly open, exposed stretch of land, you'll see pairs of oxen moving over the sand. Past Barcarès the coast turns into a thin strip of sand, behind which you'll find the pond stretching as far as terra firma. It's a huge pond. The strip of sand to Leucate is some ten miles long and encloses a large expanse of water. It's an area of shallow water, teeming with fish, a kind of dead sea, unless the north wind is blowing. And for heaven's sake, steer clear of the north wind!"

"If the water is so shallow, can we sail this boat there?"

"It'll be hard, particularly if you don't make sure to keep as close as possible to the far north of the pond, I mean, as close as you can to Cape Leucate. Keep out of the pond itself as much as you can. I should tell you that all the boats used on the pond are flat bottomed, like coffins. The advantage is that if you hug close to the cape and are caught by the *cerç* – the name the Frenchies give to the north wind – you can escape via the breach in the bank and take shelter in the cape."

As Quimet de la Selva offered his advice, Baldiri's scowl darkened. As ever, Saldet nodded, but I couldn't make out whether in response to what Quimet was saying or his brother-in-law's anxious expression.

"But is the water really that shallow?" he asked nervously.

"It *is* shallow. As shallow as you could ever imagine. But if you get good weather and are patient, you'll find ways through. Sail slowly, test the water with a stick. Sometimes you may touch the muddy, sandy floor and you'll have to clean the mire off. You'll not have to do that much if the weather's fine. . . Just one question: where are you supposed to meet the man you mentioned?"

"On the sand bed by Cape Leucate."

"Just what I thought. That's the only place possible. It's the only stretch you can reach in this boat, if you're lucky and have the patience."

"So how do we enter the pond?"

"Via the breaches in the sandbank. There are a few that are stable. Others that aren't. Now and then heavy seas breach the sand wall and create a channel – one that may last, or may be filled when the weather changes. The water in the pond can also rise, breach the sandbank and pour into the sea. Winds, currents or the fury of the sea creates these channels. There is a stable one hundred fifty or sixty yards south of Cape Leucate – at least there used to be when I lived in those parts. That's the entrance you should use."

"You said a hundred fifty or sixty yards?"

"Yes, go in with a tail wind, a northeasterly, if you can, and head straight for the shelter from the cape."

"Do people live around there?"

"Not a soul. The people from Leucate fish much farther into the pond, to the east of the village, using their black flatboats. In the place I mentioned you might find a coot or geese hunter at this time of year. Some people spend their lives among the reeds and bamboo, in high rubber boots in the water, taking aim with their guns."

There was a pause as Saldet lifted the lid over the stew slightly, and a delicious aroma wafted from the pot.

"Quimet," said Baldiri, "none of this is very good news."

"Well, I didn't want to pull the wool over your eyes."

"I know you didn't."

"To be frank, I don't understand," the man from La Selva continued jauntily, "why you agreed to collect the goods in that spot. . ."

"We were given no choice, Quimet! In the first place, the man I have to meet lives in the village of Leucate. There was no way I could persuade him to transport the goods to Port-Vendres or Collioure. As they always sell out, they call the shots. You can be sure that if I hadn't agreed to pick the stuff up, he wouldn't have brought it to me."

"Be that as it may, that spot is no Shangri-la. Luckily you. . ."

"Quimet, I'm just a beast of burden. And there are still people," he added, squinting at Saldet, "who throw it in my face if I have a glass to drink. . ."

Pau Saldet brought out plates and forks, wine and bread, and we ate the tasty mackerel stew. It was spicy and you could feel the impact of a tangy red pepper, but at that time of day with such humidity in the air anything else would have seemed bland. It was October, which meant that the mackerel did not have (nor did any blue fish) the tender meaty flesh of springtime. Still, they were filling and quite delicious. The Roses wine – thirteen-degree proof – they'd brought along would have been unpalatable at any other time, but it slipped down easily. We emerged from breakfast positively revived. A strong, aromatic percolated coffee with a drop of rum put us all in the mood to get a move on.

We set sail. Quimet disembarked on a beach beneath a stone quarry by the entrance to Port de la Selva. We watched him walk off up the path with his basket on his back. When he reached the top, he waved to us.

We hoisted the flag high again, stopped the engine, and turned toward Cape Cerbère. There was a good, if gentle, wind. We were in no hurry. Saldet took the helm. Baldiri stretched out. We gradually left the gulf of La Selva, and its dark geological formations glistening through the damp, opaque air. The Albères massif floated in a misty haze that kept the sun at bay. The *Mestral* made slow progress. The coast was deserted. It was a Sunday. We had a bite to eat at one and by two were anchored in the southwest corner of Cerbère, opposite some highly colorful closed shops and a café that seemed full of life.

Baldiri said he was thirsty and jumped on land. Saldet, on the other hand, declared he wasn't intending to leave the boat. I disembarked with a view to taking a short stroll.

If Cervera weren't a frontier and international station, not a soul would live there. It would be little more than Colera's beach. It is a dark, charcoal-colored rocky inlet with a funereal, black-pebble beach. At that time – three p.m. – the sun was already behind the mountains, and shadows were engulfing the houses. Tucked in the narrow strait of the inlet, its buildings seemed constricted. The deserted streets had a deadening effect.

Cerbère is a theater curtain. And I don't say that because of the presence of the railway station, customs and police. Those venerable institutions project reserve and chill over the town – a very visible circumspection. Mystery seems to be in the air, as in all frontier settlements. People hide their indifference behind polite gestures. Everyone is lead footed, but going their own way. Everyone is quiet, nosey and playing a secret role distinct from the role they appear to be playing. If you're not a local, you understand nothing. All frontier towns are the same: sealed boxes. But there seems to be less awareness in Portbou.

No, Cerbère is a theater curtain because people have tried to prove that a frontier really does pass through and really does separate them out, even the locals. No genuine frontier exists between Catalonia and the Roussillon, and that means that a stagey frontier has been created: houses have created a settlement that dramatically signals it is different. As nothing separates them, they have built different houses and roofs. The roofs are really French, I mean from inland France. Farther up they become Catalan again, the tiles are like our tiles. But in Cerbère they just had to be different.

What happened to Cerbère's roofs and tiles happened to language throughout the Roussillon. The centralizing French state quite deliberately emphasized a dialect with the intention of creating a patois unrelated to the language of the area, aiming to show that the language had been corrupted. The aim was to hollow out the mother tongue of the inhabitants of the Roussillon. If that had disposed them to speak French better, one might understand the state's actions to a degree. But they can be spotted a mile off when they speak French. Their accent triggers uncontrollable hilarity. Thus, the state has created people deprived of their real, genuine means of expression. It has turned out to be a wretched, antiquated, unnatural linguistic policy, suited only to render people second rate and strip them of their individuality. However, languages, even when they reach extremes of degeneration, are difficult to kill off.

As I had nothing to do in the station, at customs or with the police, a moment came when I felt I was in a Normandy hamlet that had been painted on paper. I spent a while counting train carriages passing by. In such places, there is little else to do. However, after counting the carriages of five or six long trains, I felt bored to death.

When I arrived back at the beach, darkness was falling. I walked past the café door and saw Baldiri speaking excitedly to a man. The latter looked like a grocer, and what's more a grocer from our country, in the sense that you could see no signs of French cooking about him. If any element has been forged that differentiates Catalans and the inhabitants of the Roussillon, it is their cuisine – much more than any political or administrative measures.

When I walked past Baldiri, he seemed extremely animated. He winked at me. I suspected the shopkeeperly individual at his side, a gray, plump fellow, was saying exactly what he wanted to hear.

When I was back on board, I saw that Saldet was peeling potatoes.

He was going to boil up some potatoes and beans. The inevitable winter dinner. Saldet grunted, grinned at me and went on with his task. After a while Baldiri sloped over the wet, black pebbles toward us.

"One job done. . ." he said, as he jumped aboard, whispering as befitted the spirit that reigns over frontiers.

"Ah!"

"I sold the oil to the man that runs the shop over there. One always does these deals with shops."

"Did you get a good price?"

"I made a profit. What else can you ask for?"

At that hazy moment, just before the streetlights came on, I spotted a man approaching the breakwater, opposite the *Mestral*'s stern. It was the shopkeeper. He was wearing a cap and overcoat. Baldiri and Saldet quickly unloaded the drums of olive oil – which anyone might have mistaken for drums of petrol. They carried the dozen eight-liter drums to the nearby shop, the door of which was ajar. No light was on in the shop. Five or six minutes later my colleagues arrived with the empty containers.

"When do you want to have dinner?" I heard Saldet ask.

"We'll have dinner in Banyuls. Raise the anchor!"

Baldiri started the engine, but only at half speed. It was completely calm. Not a breath of wind. As soon as we left the inlet, a train passed by above the houses along the beach and flashes of light from the Cape Creus lighthouse appeared to the east, distant and submerged in the fog.

Baldiri was whistling. He seemed happy. Perhaps he'd had a drink or two. He took his cap off, unbuttoned his shirt collar and lit a cigarette, exhaling noisily. He was trying to restrain himself, but his bliss was there for all to see.

"The sooner these things are concluded. . ." he said, as if talking to himself.

Baldiri seemed to be content duty had been done.

We hugged the coast, which was black as a wolf's maw. The sky was low; the humidity intense. You could hardly hear the sound of the sea on the edge of the coast. Everything seemed swaddled in silence. The air was murky and tepid. Timbers, clothes, hair, all damp.

Would you believe it was my first time in Cerbère? It's a place where you could easily get lost. . .

It's quite a long way from Cerbère to Banyuls. I squeezed into my den in the prow and must have fallen asleep. I slept for hours. When I woke up, I saw the town of Banyuls, the *Mestral* anchored by the harbor wall and the first light of dawn glimmering. Saldet was boiling up coffee on the stove.

We were anchored by the wall in the east corner of the harbor, the only spot slightly sheltered from the graceful sweep of the bay. The ugly bulk of the Aragó marine biology laboratory stood at the other end of the beach. The town lay in between: opposite us, the fishermen's quarter was steep, bustling and picturesque; beyond that Banyuls becomes bourgeois, with an array of fine houses and cafés. It seemed to me that the tall plane tree – now rather shabby – in front of Madame Py's café must provide delightful shade in the summer and be the right place to have an aperitif. Beyond that is the channel made by the *riera* and several buildings that looked like wine warehouses.

So just as Cerbère is a theatrical backcloth, the part of Banyuls that overlooks the beach is a Catalan town bereft of old features – a community displaced from the interior to the marina when the sea became a safe place.

We drank coffee and I shaved on deck. While shaving, I looked at the mountains surrounding the funnel of Banyuls. The geology of the gulf of La Selva never changes: a scattering of dark slate with a reddish glow, bovine-shaped mountains, long, gentle humps, covered in scree, vineyards beautifully cultivated on terraces supported by drystone walls. When I'd finished my shave, I washed my face in the fountain in the lower part of the harbor wall behind the sardine boats that had been pulled up on the beach. A seventeen-year-old girl stood by the fountain, a splendidly curvaceous young woman. She was waving her hands in the air and her clothing was extremely skimpy.

"Aren't we cold?" I asked.

"I'm never cold!" she answered, a broad smile on her white teeth, moist lips and almond eyes. She had a magnificent head of dark golden hair that radiated youthful energy. I thought she could have served as the model for the Venus of the Pyrenees that people had always dreamed of. She filled her pitchers while resting her arm on the rim of the fountain, with her back to me. What a marvelous back! What Fustel de Coulanges said about the Venus came to mind: that the whole of ancient culture simmered on her flanks.

I reckoned it was extremely pleasant to be in a country where you encountered a Venus by a fountain in the early morning.

When I returned to the *Mestral* with the melancholy produced by a vision of total beauty, I found Baldiri and Saldet arguing. Or rather, Baldiri was launching into an angry tirade against his brother-in-law.

"This coffee you've made," he was telling him, "is like bilge water. It's worthless as coffee. It's all very well your killing off your wife and children with catarrh so you could buy an olive grove and vineyard, but you should show a little more consideration toward me. . ."

Saldet smiled at him in agreement, slyly so; you couldn't tell if he was actually agreeing with Baldiri or if he was defending himself.

"What's more," added Baldiri, "what you've cooked so far has been disgusting. You're a terrible chef. Everything you've prepared has been overdone or burnt. You're a pot burner. Are you trying to save on the water that boils over. What do you think you're playing at, you miserly sod? I want to eat and drink. . . If you don't cook a decent rice dish today, I'll throw you off the boat and you can walk home. . . Do you hear what I said? I'll throw you off. . ."

I could hear Baldiri's pontificating from the quayside. It's quite hopeless; it's absolutely impossible to imagine two people who must cohabit ever getting along in our country. In this case, Baldiri was right. Saldet was a poor cook, but even if he'd had greater qualities as a cook, Baldiri would have found some other excuse for churlishness in his character. The lengths people in this country go to so they don't get on are amazing. It's their favorite pastime.

When I came on board, Baldiri shut up and lit a cigarette. Although it looked as if the day would clear up, I thought I'd need something thicker. I pulled on a sweater. There was a steady breeze but the sea remained calm, and the sky was cloudless. In the autumn, you sometimes get periods like that: no real wind and a becalmed sea. It's the time when olives are ripening.

"That's what I like!" shouted Baldiri. "You should go for a stroll now and be a gentleman of leisure. Go and play a hand of fives. . . I suppose they still play that game in Banyuls. Are you going to jump on land? I'll keep you company for a moment. . ."

There was a group of fishermen on the shore, looking as if they'd just eaten breakfast, standing full of good cheer gawping at the *Mestral.*

"That's a good *bateau, mon brave,* I'm telling you!" said one old man. "It's just the one I'd choose to sail the waters around here! Look how roomy it is! Ours are too skinny and narrow!"

Baldiri walked with me as far as the fountain, he said the coffee had been so watery he needed a tavern. His legs were giving up on him.

"Is the wine of Banyuls any good?" he asked. "They say it's a wine that's worth a mass. . ."

"That's what people say. . . However, believe me, wait and try it this afternoon. It's going to be a long day and it's only half past eight. . ."

After glancing in the direction of the fountain to see whether the Venus of the Pyrenees – or if you prefer, the Venus of the Albères – had returned, I went for a stroll around the fishermen's quarter. Extremely picturesque and far from hygienic. The streets are steep and narrow, paved with sharp pebbles from the *riera,* which is how they used to pave streets before people wore real shoes – paving for the rope-soled sandal era. The wealth of cages with pets, the profusion of fishing tackle and fish boxes and the odd wandering goat made those streets even narrower. There are vines in front of many houses, as in old Cadaqués. The rain that had fallen over the last few days made the street slimy and slippery.

Although the vines were bare, I'd like to have seen the girl with the pitchers beneath them. But Venus had disappeared.

I walked down and back to the beach and strolled past the cafés. Before reaching the *riera,* I turned up the road to Puig del Mas. This road takes you past a succession of residencies with delightful kitchen gardens toward the Rectoria – that is, old Banyuls. At the time of the French Revolution, Banyuls had very few houses by the seashore. They were concentrated around the Rectoria – a small Romanesque church (shut today) that remains standing only because God so willed it – precisely because a cemetery is next to the church. In the ideological system of centralizing France, the Romanesque and Gothic were not valued at all and were deemed to be coarse, barbarian styles, deriving from an obscurantist, outmoded and sickly populism. What was worshipped was Versailles, the life in Versailles, *la cour* and its wan geometrical gardens. The end result was that the French – socialists and communists included – will bow most grotesquely before a marchioness.

I'd like to have entered the small, intimate church, gilded by the centuries, but it proved impossible. A man said there might be a burial that morning and they'd open up. However, I felt that very unlikely.

I walked on up the road and under the railway viaduct to Puig del Mas, a small country hamlet perched on a conical hump by the side of the *riera*. Puig del Mas is a rural hamlet typical of our country: silent, sleepy and reserved – the mysterious reserve that a life of smuggling projects on frontier communities. It is like being in a perpetual state of confusion, sensing you're being watched but not knowing by whom or from where.

Past Puig del Mas, the path continues up the valley as far as Col de Banyuls (that is, the frontier), following the *riera*'s lethargic twists and turns. As you walk on, the sides of the mountains rise up, but never lose their long, gentle contours; their slopes are covered in vineyards and olive groves; it is a dreamlike, luminous, recondite, ecstatic landscape, dozing to the buzz of bees. A geological expanse without wild shapes or blood-curdling boulders, with a spontaneous, delicate, bucolic sensuousness that isn't at all histrionic. This is the way Maillol came and went from his tumbledown Les Abelles farmhouse to Banyuls, a path that may have led him, after so many wrong turns, to conceive genuine sculptures.

It is this landscape that produces the best wine, the best oil, the best honey in the Roussillon, the three graces that Banyuls has on offer and the town's source of prosperity.

From a bend in the path you can sometimes see a distant farmhouse, and however tiny your knowledge of the importance of Col de Banyuls in the frontier's clandestine, contraband nightlife, your imagination leads you to shroud it in mystery. You feel you can still dimly catch the noise of beasts of burden passing along those rocky paths. You glimpse the stubborn sangfroid, the wealth of knowledge, the cold, controlled resistance of solitary old fellows, as wily as feral animals in the night. The human history – both secret and forgotten – of this earth I now tread becomes a real obsession.

As the sun rises, the air warms and the humidity fades; the autumn air is pleasantly tepid. Shrubs and plants give off an intense smell. Under the bright sky, by the light of noon, golden vines glitter and shine. People are tramping amid the olive groves. A sleepy cart climbs the quiet road. The sun silvers the water rushing down between the pebbles in the *riera* and turns the cool grass a liquid green.

Back in the *Mestral* we eat a plate of rice; small helpings of fish and chicken. Saldet is sad; he's probably thinking we could have got by with less. Baldiri gives him the occasional withering look.

That afternoon I visit the Institut Aragó and spend a while admiring the splendid aquarium. It is significant; perhaps not as important as Monaco's, but well worth a visit. It's expertly built and the imitation of nature has that touch of fantasy an aquarium requires.

However, though my experience in the matter is strictly limited, I've always thought the life of an aquarium fish is notably different than the life of a fish swimming freely in the sea. Because it realizes its food is guaranteed, such a fish becomes simply decorative, a tame, insipid, completely innocuous creature. It looks dozy, takes a nap even when swimming. I suspect it's the result of the silence behind those huge windows, the inane somnolence reigning there. I'd like to eat an aquarium fish. What flavor can these fish on full board have? I suspect it's bland and eminently forgettable: a taste endowed by excessive urbanity, what a purely decorative, well-fed lifestyle fosters.

After that, I visit Maillol's monument to the dead, a flattish monument located on a rock – a small island – at the end of the bay. There is a dying athlete in the middle of the stone frieze and tragic scenes on both sides. The sculptor planted the humblest local shrubs at the foot of the shrine. The demise of the athlete makes a great impact, even though the monument's Hellenic spirit is seen through German erudition. Maillol wasted half his life ridding himself of eighteenth-century France, and then he had to rid himself of erudition from German academic journals. Fortunately, he lived a long life. If that hadn't been the case, he wouldn't have had time to sculpt anything decent.

When I get back to the quay, I see Baldiri in conversation with a tall, robust young man who is full of energy. Initially, I think I've seen him before somewhere. Baldiri, who has imbibed a good amount of Banyuls wine, introduces me falteringly.

"He's a construction worker – a good one – and they call him the gang master. . . And he's a good friend."

"I think I know you, but I can't think from where. . ." I tell him.

"I'm a big friend of the old man. . ."

"Which old man?"

"Maillol."

"Now, I get it; you, senyor, are the model for the dying athlete on his monument. . ."

"That's right. . ."

It's quite distressing. It's like coming across a man who has resurrected – a man who'd been declared dead with a fanfare, but who'd only suffered only a bout of typhoid fever.

"Your death, dear gang master, will be the making of the monument."

"Why?"

"Because it's always a shock to see dying athletes turn into construction workers."

"Well, I'm not intending to die any time soon."

"And I too hope you live for many a year."

There was a light mistral that night. From my den I could see a marvelous, pure blue sky, full of glittering stars.

After lunch the next day we set off go Port-Vendres with a southwesterly. Once out of the bay, we hoisted the sail and the *Mestral* moved wonderfully.

The coastline from Banyuls to Port-Vendres isn't as wild as from Portbou to Banyuls, but it is long. The Coll de les Portes is huge. Cape Béar, which makes up the southwest entrance to Port-Vendres is an immense, forbidding promontory with a very powerful lighthouse. The cape conceals Port-Vendres, so once you've sailed around it, the town comes as a surprise. It's lovely to reach Port-Vendres by sea. The approach by land cannot compete.

There are only two genuinely natural ports on the coastline of historic Catalonia: the bays of Cadaqués and Port-Vendres. When they belonged to one nation, no great building works were completed in either. Collioure was the port for the Roussillon. Now Cadaqués, as a port, has remained at a prehistoric stage, while a magnificent harbor has been built at Port-Vendres.

Before stopping off in Port-Vendres, I'd have liked to spend a few hours in the Palilles cove, which is so solitary and full of trees, but Baldiri refused point-blank. There is a dynamite factory in Palilles that I gather belongs to the Nobel group – the famous Swedish manufacturer of dynamite who established the prizes. Baldiri said he had friends in the small docks in the harbor just before the spot I'd suggested and that he was quite apprehensive about this kind of factory, because they sometimes set off explosions and cause the earth to quake. So we simply sailed past Palilles.

Once we reached Port-Vendres – a town I know well – I told the skipper that our entrance into the rectangular dock might seem pretentious, and that we could drop anchor on the corner of the dock a few yards from the pharmacy owned by Monsieur Forgas, the town's radical-socialist mayor and an acquaintance of mine. But Baldiri said that the rectangular dock was the best place to anchor. His last intake of wine had made him cantankerous.

In the evening, I walked along to the end of the quay and dined in the Hôtel du Commerce. They were still building the Compagnie du Midi hotel, and the Commerce was thought to be the best of its kind in town. Above all I was looking forward to the bouillabaisse, which I'd found to be excellent on previous visits.

However, that evening my expectations were soon dashed. Great expectations are dreams of a shadow, which is why they last so long. Small ones, on the other hand, die one after another. . . It's sad to acknowledge that certain exquisite things that have become associated in memory with various stays in diverse locations have, in actuality, vanished forever. In Port-Vendres, my memories of the town, its sky and water were linked to a particularly classic, delicious bouillabaisse. You came there hoping to eat, maybe even to partake more than once. Now it is no more. The gentleman who made it has retired from the culinary art. He has rented out his establishment to people who cook like barbarians. This is the melancholy fact of the matter.

What is the fascination with bouillabaisse based on? I think that a dish becomes popular only when in one way or another it meets the demands of human greed. It's sad to say, but everyone, however normal they may appear, hungers for something spiritual or material. Ambitious or sensual, greedy or spendthrift, imaginative or voluptuous, human nature is never passive, is always hungry. So, then, a bouillabaisse contains an element a diner will always appreciate, for it is at one with the very essence of that noble vice: a bouillabaisse invites you to eat solid things with a spoon, and that explains eighty percent of its glory. I'm not usually hyperbolic, nor do I let myself be carried away by nostalgia, but I do think that the bouillabaisse cooked by the gentleman who has now retired was the best in the world. Those who had tasted it retained such fondness they had it dispatched to the remote places where they lived. And canisters of bouillabaisse were sent to Paris and London at top speed. Its reputation was such that people carried it, as they say, with kid gloves. And even if it had to be reheated on arrival, it still preserved the taste, aroma and lightness of the bouillabaisse as if served on the spot, which is what most resembles the unforgettable light of Provence.

The ground floor of the Hôtel du Commerce was home to a café of the same name, the favorite haunt of the great and the good of the town. After lunch or dinner – because the Roussillon retains the custom, shared by so many towns on the other side of the frontier, of going out after dinner – three or four tables were set up to play *piquet* or *belote*. Monsieur Forgas was the lead figure in that heady gathering. Monsieur Forgas, a tiny old man with bulging, bloodshot, tortured eyes, wears a large rosette of the Légion d'Honneur in his lapel. He is the town pharmacist and, from time immemorial, its mayor. He belongs to the party of Monsieur Pams. I was once present at a public meeting chaired by Pams and Forgas. The former said in the course of his speech that Port-Vendres was Monsieur Forgas and that Monsieur Forgas was Port-Vendres, because Port-Vendres couldn't be understood without Monsieur Forgas, in the same way that Monsieur Forgas couldn't be understood without Port-Vendres, which meant that if you embraced Monsieur Forgas you embraced Port-Vendres and if you embraced Port-Vendres you embraced Monsieur Forgas, because Port-Vendres was inseparable from Monsieur Forgas, in the same way that Monsieur Forgas was inseparable from Port-Vendres, because you couldn't separate Port-Vendres from Monsieur Forgas or Monsieur Forgas from Port-Vendres. . . In a word, there was such a fervor that the audience was overcome with emotion, and Monsieur Forgas was so moved he literally hung from the neck of Monsieur Pams like a couple of scapulars, and tears and sobs came to every eye and mouth and the meeting ended in a sea of tears. That's the way of political oratory: it sometimes has its way with the tear ducts.

All is peaceful at nine p.m. in Port-Vendres. I once befriended an old, lame man who carried a stick and dragged a leg. He worked as a night watchman, and I used to sit next to him on a wine vat for two or three hours at a time or we'd stroll along the solitary quayside. I still think I can hear the noise his leg made as it dragged over the cobbles. Deep into the night we sometimes heard tunes from an electric piano in a house of dubious reputation – loud and clear. The old man would stop for a moment and wink at me like a tired, old dog and then we'd continue on our way.

Another thing that thrills me about Port-Vendres is the to-and-fro of ships from Africa. Two large mail boats link the town to Algiers and Oran. When they hoist the green flag over the harbor light it means a vessel is approaching. People look out their windows or walk down to the quay to watch it entering. It's a splendid, natural harbor, but very enclosed and inland. The vessels that enter it do so like horned snails returning to their shells. The maneuvers of the boats from Africa are more drawn out and entertaining. What's more, on deck there is usually a mass of North Africans, Arabs, blacks and other people. Half an hour after the boat has docked, bands of greasy, shabby men inevitably wander the streets. Others start playing cards on street corners. From one steamer to the next there is always an odd straggler wandering the streets in a haze, the whites of his eyes bulging.

Apart from the days when there is a mail boat from Africa, a pronounced calm reigns on the Port-Vendres quayside. Sometimes a packet boat arrives from Marseille or Sicily laden with carob beans or sulfate for the vineyards. When the crew is unloading sulfate, the clouds of dust thrown up make your hair stand on end. The carobs perfume the air, and the carts transporting the seed carry the warm aroma around the town and rocky outskirts, wafted by a dry, crackling north wind.

The magnificent, sheltered bay of Port-Vendres was never used in the days of the counts of Empúries and Roussillon, nor was it used in the era when the nation was one. The first time the name of the present town appears is in a document from the reign of King Jaume: a few down-at-heel houses. Nevertheless, that corner was one of the safest in the western Mediterranean. No heavy *riera* ever floods down, so there is no danger of a mudslide blocking the port. In the Middle Ages, Coullioure became the port for the Roussillon, and Port-Vendres never amounted to much, despite its superior conditions.

After the Treaty of the Pyrenees, one of the first and best governors of the Roussillon, the Count of Mailly, took a great interest in Port-Vendres. The renowned Vauban fell in love with the place for its military potential. When this interest was born, according to Vidal's *Guia Històrica i Pintoresca dels Pirineus Orientals*, Port-Vendres had a population of forty-five. In the course of the reign of Louis XIV, the monarchy spent a million and a half francs on military installations. The town took on an inevitably French look. Port-Vendres doesn't look like a stagey backdrop as Cerbère does, but it is quite different from many other Roussillon towns. It is a town of the new order, somewhat cold and geometric, with an excess of color that is so pretty in the grayness of northern France but in the bright southern sun sometimes seems overlarded. If I'm not mistaken, when you come from Catalonia, Port-Vendres gives you your first sense of being in France.

To celebrate Louis XIV's generosity, the Count of Mailly had a magnificent obelisk built in the rectangular square they had deliberately located at the right angle formed by the town's two harbors. It is a twenty-five-yard-high gray needle made from Estragell marble on a pedestal of red Vilafranca marble. Before it was damaged in 1793, the obelisk supported a terrestrial globe decorated with fleurs-de-lis. The base was also pompously inscribed with phrases lauding the memory of the Roi Soleil, which nowadays can be read in the Museum of Perpignan.

Maillol's monument to the dead is on the edge of this square opposite the harbors, and it includes a lady with an eighteenth-century hairdo wearing a Versailles-esque blouse, apparently made of tulle, and holding a palm frond. Given the style of the square, the sculptor must have thought his sculpture was in keeping. The old man likes to adapt his sculptures to the places where they're going to be erected. Perhaps he exaggerated in this instance and proved more papist than the pope. The monument to the dead of Port-Vendres isn't one of the best that Maillol has sculpted.

Was *Portus Veneris* – Venus's Port – *inter Pyrenei promontoria* (Pomponius Mela, AD 43) really the site of Venus's temple in the Pyrenees? Writers declare, with characteristic geographical insouciance, that the Romans raised a temple to Venus at the entrance to the Pyrenees, and that the site was called Portus Veneris. Strabo seems to connect this port with the temple to the Venus of the Pyrenees, as does Pliny.

But where was this temple located? A segment of the Peutinger Table seems to suggest (very vaguely and speculatively) that this temple was on the island that's now joined to land by a three-hundred-yard breakwater that closes the bay of Port-Vendres to the north. However, there is no trace of any ancient building on this island and likewise nothing has ever been found on Cape Béar. Like any other citizen, I also have a right to conjecture and I believe the temple to the Venus of the Pyrenees would be found on Cape Creus (Crosses), because its name can be explained as the hallowing of a pagan site. If there'd been a temple to Venus in Port-Vendres, the town would be called – and you can be sure of this – Sant Pere Nolasc or Mare de Déu dels Dolors, as a result of the natural palimpsest of cultures across the centuries. Whenever I am in Port-Vendres, I try to find a trace of that famous temple, and I've never found a thing. Once I asked a man who cultivated a local vineyard about it. He stared at me at length and then said: "This must be down to Monsieur Forgas. If he doesn't know, there's no need to be taken in by such rubbish. . ."

Over time, the implications of the town's name, combined with the apparent lack of any truly mouthwatering trace, spawn a certain amount of disenchantment. I felt this more than ever on this particular occasion, because after the disappearance of the Venus I'd glimpsed for a second by the Banyuls fountain, after the metamorphosis of the dying athlete into a local bricklayer and the vanished bouillabaisse of the Hôtel du Commerce, I'd have preferred something positive and more substantial.

I thus spent a couple of morose days in Port-Vendres. I saw little of Baldiri, because he needed (especially when away from home) someone or other to fawn over him, even if he was always footing the bill. Saldet did not deboard the *Mestral*, saying he really disliked France as a country. The excessive generalization displayed by such a judgment revealed that, had he ever studied and read the necessary literature, he could have become an extremely distinguished philosopher.

An hour before we left, Baldiri appeared with a big gramophone horn under his arm. He said he'd purchased it from a loitering North African and was intending to recoup a little profit on it because they always pay well for such horns in Roses, especially if they are big ones, because a big horn always goes down well in one's sitting room. There's no denying that gramophones with a horn have become very fashionable and that everyone who can tries to exhibit such a strangely shaped object.

We brought the horn on board and set off.

It's no distance at all from Port-Vendres to Collioure. You pass Cape Gros and Mauresca Cove and then the wonderful sight of the French Catalan town immediately comes into view. In the course of the journey the coast mellows, its face is set against the gulf, which is in turn swept by the north wind. Altogether, it forms an astonishing panorama.

Collioure is the egg's yolk of the coast of French Catalonia. Cerbère and Port-Vendres are modern French creations, where Banyuls and Collioure are two ancient Catalan towns. Collioure is spectacular, especially when viewed from the sea.

The bay of Collioure is open to the north and northeast, but the town is built on the horn of the bay, sheltered from the mistral. Coming from the gulf, you first encounter Port d'Amunt behind the isle of Sant Vicenç, which has been joined to land in modern times by a wall that fends off crashing waves and is extended by a breakwater that ends in a large crucifix. There is a chapel dedicated to the saint on the isle. Then comes Port d'Avall within the bay and its curved beach. These two ports are separated on land by the huge building known as the Templars' Castle, whose high walls fall precipitously into the sea. At the foot of this impressive bulk flows the channel of the Dui *riera*, which creates a delightful beach opposite the most ancient part of the town. This is the best-sheltered area of the bay and the center of activity for sardine fishing. The town has a small fleet of sixty or seventy sardine boats.

The strange, squat fortress built by Charles V looms over the town: Sant Elm. Later, the Watchtower Fort was built on the hills south of the town. This whole place is a crisscross of fortifications wrought by the opposing interests that ravaged local communities. Today those stones are dead, indifferent witnesses to past sorrows. The only danger now is that you might mislabel a fortification and be identified as an outsider.

Seen from the road that connects Collioure to Port-Vendres, or seen from the sea, the town is a magnificent sight. Collioure is small, but has a grandiose aspect. The Templars' Castle is dramatic. The town buildings, the colors of the ancient tawny, toasted stones, the antique, gloomy, rather dilapidated tone lends everything an impressive noble aura. Nothing, perhaps with the exception of Sant Pere de Rodas, can compare to Collioure along the coast of the gulf of La Selva.

Collioure is deeply rooted in history. Nowhere along this coast have so many traces of antiquity been discovered, including Iberian and Ampurian coins. Collioure was the Roussillon's port during the Middle Ages and its importance is evident in Perpignan's Loge de Mer. The bay was ideal in the era of small vessels. Ships began to move to Port-Vendres when they grew in size – though this didn't happen until much later on. There was considerable trade in Collioure throughout the fifteenth century, probably because its port gave closest access from the sea to Perpignan and the plain of Roussillon.

"What a great place!" exclaimed Baldiri, throwing a rope on land after casting the anchor into the sea, as he inhaled the strong smell of salted anchovies coming from the beach. Baldiri is like that: on board, he's always scowling, but when he sees houses he suddenly cheers up.

"Don't you tempt fate!" responded Saldet, frowning. "It's in such *great* places that they always want to inspect your papers."

"So what? We'll show them the gramophone horn. . . I don't think we've anything else on board. . ."

I told them that the best thing would be to keep a low profile.

Baldiri was the first to jump on land. He said he was off to buy a fish.

"I expect we'll see him one of these days. . ." said Saldet.

Baldiri was tall and thin, fair and blue eyed. His hair was wiry and wispy and he moved nimbly along; his Adam's apple protruded. He leaned to one side as he walked, giving his silhouette an off-kilter appearance. We watched him walk along the street that followed the *riera* and go into the first tavern. Saldet contemplated his every step with a mixture of curiosity and indignation.

No doubt to show me that they were two very different temperaments, Saldet grabbed the pitchers and went to get water from the fountain by the beach. He must have imagined I was looking at him, because he adopted the stance of a victim the whole time. The contrasts between the two brothers-in-law were amusing but also worrying. The needles they kept sticking into each other drew blood. The riskiest part of our business was still unfinished.

The afternoon was on the wane, and as the light dimmed, I was delighted by the whites, blues, ox-blood reds and tawny golds of the stones of Collioure against the dark backdrop of the surrounding countryside. It was a riot of color from an unlikely mix of urban cubes, ancient stone walls, washing hung out to dry and salt-and-pepper trees. All that added to the smell of the sea, the taste of salted fish in the air, the hustle and bustle and messy array of small boats that made for a lively scene. Everything seemed naïve and pungent, a tad wild, in your face, covered in salt and the smell of shellfish: a melodramatic, excessive presence. Collioure is an *ensemble fauve* – to put it in French – and it is hardly surprising that painters of that tendency are infatuated with the town.

When he returned from the fountain, Saldet whispered cautiously in my ear so nobody would hear: "I'd like a couple of words. . ."

"Go on, my dear Saldet, use four if need be. . . What is it you want to tell me?"

"I wanted to say that Baldiri is a dead loss. . ."

"You think he's a dead loss before we reach the Salses Ponds? What will he be like when we get there?"

"You always put on a bold front."

"How'd you expect me to act?"

"I just mean he's too fond of women and the bottle. . ."

"And don't you like women?"

". . . and can be rude."

"Yes, he's on the rude side, but what can we do about that? The other things you mention are nothing new. . ."

"You say they're nothing new?"

"That's right. Tell me who's not fond of women and the bottle? That's been the case for thousands and thousands of years."

"I don't know. . ."

"You don't know? Perhaps you're not really aware of the situation we are in. Baldiri is the skipper. He's responsible for everything. You and I are simply two items. I am, shall we say, a voluntary item. You've got some reason to be here, I imagine. What's he promised you?"

"A thousand pessetes. . ."

"I'd think it worth your while keeping your head down for a thousand pessetes. Don't you agree? It's only a matter of a few days. Be patient. We'll see soon enough. . ."

"If you say so. . ." he muttered in a falsely obsequious tone.

"No, Saldet. You mustn't keep your head down because *I* say so. We don't have a choice in the matter. We are committed to this galley.

We must see it through. Keep our heads down. That's the least we can do. . ."

Saldet looked at me askance and mumbled a few words. Then he shut up.

"Would you like a smoke, Saldet. . . ?" I asked, offering him a cigarette.

"That's very kind of you. . ." he answered, forcing a sad smile.

A few minutes later I jumped on land.

The wind had died down. The air felt damp. The black pebbles on the beach glistened. Early dusk created an opaque, gloomy atmosphere. A smell of salted fish wafted by. I felt the need to try the renowned anchovies of Collioure.

I walked along the seashore. In ancient times, the grandiose building of the Templars separated Port d'Amunt from Port d'Avall. The sea pounded its very foundations. Now they have built a walkway that allows you to cross from one side to the other close to those old stones. They've put in an iron rail along the side, which helps you to walk when a fierce north wind is blowing. That's how I reached the road and the beach at the back of the bay – which I followed as far as the evangelical chapel. A broad street starts out in front of this building and goes behind the Templars to the Dui *riera* and the shady lane that runs alongside it. This street is the center of Collioure and home to bustling cafés and shops.

I went into the Templars restaurant and ordered anchovies and an aperitif at the bar. I was served by the owner, Monsieur René Pous. Later Pous and his delightful wife became among my best friends in the Roussillon. That friendship originated in those anchovies.

"These are good anchovies, but the fish isn't local. . ." I told him with a deadpan expression.

He responded spiritedly. He denied what I'd said. Then, in a less abrupt tone, he asked if I was a fan of anchovies.

"I live in a place that often has very good anchovies."

"And where might that be?"

"Cadaqués."

"Ah! I've heard that too. And how did you know the fish wasn't caught locally?"

"It has a slightly bitter taste. All fish from North Africa is bitter like that. Not to mention their lobsters. . ."

He said that Collioure anchovies, like wine from Banyuls, was so marketable they had to have recourse to fish from other parts, though they prepared the fish in the local manner. If the wine of Banyuls was only from grapes picked locally, there wouldn't be enough to meet the needs of early morning mass.

Obviously the quality of anchovies depends on the way they are cured, but the time taken to cure them is as, if not more, important. An anchovy that hasn't spent at least a year in the jar doesn't quite make the grade. It is a raw, bitter, soft anchovy that doesn't have the creamy tartness of one that's been properly cured. Once out of the water, an anchovy must be put in brine; it must be salted, preferably without ice, because ice ruins everything: ice separates the skin from the fish's flesh. The fish must marinate in salt for just a day or two. Then it must be cleaned, its head and guts removed, though without cutting it open and while preserving the red thread that runs from its head to its guts. Apparently this artery is crucial in the marinating process. After that, the anchovies must be stored in jars, one above another, separated by layers of salt and good pepper. The pepper must be of the *best* quality. Then a broth of water and salt must be prepared to fill the jar of anchovies. You know if the broth is thick enough if you throw in a spud and the potato doesn't sink. When the broth is ready, the jars must be filled and hermetically sealed. Then they must be left alone for at least a year. If they're opened earlier, it does the customer no favors. This period of time is much more important than the labels that are usually stuck on the outside of the glass jars, which serve only to con people. This process, followed by the maceration period we have described, produces anchovy fillets as good as any from Norway.

That exposition of mine won me the friendship of Monsieur Pous. It's been a very pleasant friendship, because the restaurant's cuisine is good and can cope with the presence of demanding palates in convivial mode.

We then wandered around Collioure for a few hours. The town, sheltered within the fortified walls, comprises narrow sailor streets, old streets, with large old houses, washing hung out to dry, and you'll sometimes spot at a window the face of an attractive blonde or the anxious, sad, pale face of a dark-haired girl.

Baldiri appeared on Thursday night with a bottle of firewater under his arm – calvados, I think. He looked tired but calm. He said he was sleepy. Before stretching out on the boards, he announced we would set out tomorrow, Friday, early in the morning.

I stayed on deck for a while gazing at the bright, autumnal moon – the old moon – shining on the stone of Collioure. The massive castle, imbued with an unreal, turbid luminous yellow, could have acted as a backdrop to a high drama. The water in the bay was phosphorescent. The sky was low and murky. Everything was soft and limp. The moon shone on the *Mestral*, which was drenched by the drizzle and glowed lugubriously. The weather was depressing and made you dream of the shelter of a roof and a welcoming fireplace. Dampness and the southern wind in the Mediterranean have helped man emerge from prehistoric times much more than any factor listed in history books.

At seven the next morning, when I poked my head out of my den in the prow, I saw Baldiri staring at the sky. Saldet was lighting up the stove, which gave off an acrid, low smoke. Baldiri seemed worried: he'd put on a thick, wine-colored jersey. There was a brisk southeasterly and the sky was overcast.

We ate toast covered in olive oil and drank coffee bolstered with liquor. I liked French *eau de vie* – and especially a dry calvados – as much as Italian grappa. Baldiri stared at the sea and sky and seemed far away. He must have sensed my quizzical gaze, because all of a sudden he declared: "I don't like this weather one bit. It will rain in the ponds. It's been like this far too long, but then what has to be, will be..."

"You're afraid a north wind will blow up after the rain..."

"Of course I am! We've been unlucky. I expected the north wind in Port-Vendres. I was expecting to watch it blow from the café. On other occasions, with the humidity we've had, everything would be just right; it would have rained and the wind would have blown... But the weather is dragging, it's all still to come, while we must be in Leucate at the time agreed. Otherwise, we'll have had a wasted trip..."

"What Baldiri says is spot on...!" Saldet grinned.

"Yes, it is, but what I don't understand is why the north wind has to blow at an appointed hour..." I said, to counter any onset of depression. "It might come late and give us time..."

"Fear and anticipation make me say that, you know."

"We'll see when we get there. It makes no sense suffering on account of what might happen tomorrow. We've enough to worry about here and now."

Baldiri reckoned we were showing too much sail and ordered a tightening of the middle reef. He gave the *Mestral* the once over and decided everything was in order. He thought the poles we had taken on board on the advice from the man from Prona Cove might have been on the short side. But they were the only ones we'd found. Then we set out. It was a quarter to eight.

Baldiri manned the tiller, and once we'd swiftly departed Port d'Amunt, he steered the vessel out to sea. When the black bulk of Cape Béar appeared to our stern, the cloud-covered peak of the Sant Pere de Roda mountain came into view in a murky haze at the back of the gulf of La Selva. The coast gradually lost height, and once we'd passed the small Racó beach – which in terms of history and geography is the last flourish of the Catalan Costa Brava – the beach of the Gulf of Lion appeared with Argelès in the distance, beneath the proud heights of the Albères mountains cloaked in the greenish-gray of cork oaks. At the start of the great plain of the Roussillon, the contrast between the slender Albères and the infinite horizontal expanse of sand is a magnificent sight.

When we were level with that great beach, the belfry in Elne became visible over the green plain and the wind picked up. We had little in the way of sail, but with a tail wind, we still had too much. So Baldiri ordered the yard to be furled, which was done soon enough. The *Mestral* now sailed more smoothly and elegantly. The wind was monotonous and constant. We sailed level with the beach, less than a mile out from the gray sand. A brushstroke of dark green stood out on the barren sand and died at the foot of a misty, sublime Canigó.

The *Mestral* sailed sprightly on. To the north, the horizon was cloudy and the Corbères range, a faint outline.

It had been barely two hours since our departure from Collioure when Torres de Castell Rosselló appeared high above the autumnal green and, on the beach, the first signs of what would later be the town of Canet. Oh, if only it had been sunny, and the air hadn't draped a haze over that distant prospect, it would have been such a pleasant sail! The coast passed quickly before my eyes, but with just enough stillness for me to follow the many sights of the plain of Roussillon. Amid the flaxen-green vegetation I glimpsed a spire, a tower, the white patch of a farmhouse, a clump of houses, the smoke from a train. . . But it was a gray day with a low, overcast sky.

Suddenly Salanca appeared, and Barcarès de Sant Llorenç. Pairs of oxen stood on land in front of squat houses the color of the sand. It was a desolate, empty, inhospitable sight, a landscape devoured by a huge expanse of sand. Barcarès made me think of some Van Gogh paintings of maritime Provence. Every expanse of sandy beach in the Gulf of Lion, under the harsh light of summer, brings to mind Van Gogh.

We also left Salanca behind and gradually the sandbank of the Salses Ponds came into view. Behind the strip of sand, which seemed muddier and darker than the sand on dry land, the haze seemed to thicken as it slumbered. The pond water was almost white, a faint blue. Meanwhile, the purple barren rocks of the Corbères gradually emerged. The Corbères obstructed the landscape to our west and north and tended to descend slowly over the sea; the mountains gradually lost height over the ponds, covering them with the point of their scythe. Finally Cape Leucate appeared, its whiteness melding into the damp, murky atmosphere. Seen from afar, surrounded by low-lying land, Leucate looked like an island, which it probably once was. The horizontal panorama suggested ancient attitudes.

As we sailed by the sandbar, the pond narrowed and shrank. The town of Salses and the old frontier fortress stood out against the stony, brownish earth, dotted with mallow, of the Corbères. Salses is the advance guard of the Roussillon, the frontier of historic Catalonia. Leucate is the advance guard of the French. Between those two extremes you could see a handful of houses or Cabanes de Fitó, which they write as Fitou, in other words, *la fita*, the boundary.

I would like to have taken my time contemplating that landscape charged with history, an extraordinarily harsh, mysteriously water-logged terrain, but the time had come to end our journey; we couldn't continue on the sandbar, which extended as far as the cape. Baldiri had moored the *Mestral*; we heard the waves splashing the blue-black, slanting beach. Saldet suddenly held out his arm and pointed to the breach in the sandbar. That was the way through. He reckoned it was under a mile away. The man from Prona Cove had gotten it right. We lowered the flat sail and started the engine. The northeasterly we really needed in order to make it through the channel was not there. You just can't have everything in this world. When we reached the waters around the entrance, Baldiri didn't hesitate for a moment: he tried a risky maneuver, telling Saldet to put the engine on full and head for the center of the breach. We held on so we wouldn't be tossed about like dolls if we hit a sandbank, but we hit no obstacles and sped into the still water of the pond. Baldiri slowed the engine to the minimum. Saldet and I kept testing the depths with the poles from Collioure. There was little in the way of water, and the pond was packed in places with weeds and reeds.

Baldiri seemed to disappear. It was work requiring enormous

patience. We had to find the path – a path none of us knew – which had to be established yard by yard. The *Mestral* got stuck several times on mud and sandbanks. We had to reverse, we had to move forward. . . We entered the pond at one o'clock, at two we had advanced two hundred yards toward Leucate. We persisted for another hour and a half. But eventually the pond decided enough was enough. The pole gave us only a yard. It was impossible to progress any farther. Meanwhile, the reeds had grown dense, which must have convinced Baldiri not to go any farther. Those yellow feathery plants made a perfect hideout for our craft.

"Cast the two anchors to our stern in a *V*. . ." the skipper instructed Saldet. "I'm afraid of the north wind, and we must make sure we can make our escape. . . Cast out both of the anchors from the prow. It will be dead calm within the hour. . ."

Three yards from where we'd anchored, we found a boat, flat bottomed and painted black like a coffin, tied to a stake. We imagined it must be the lair of some passing bird hunter. The presence of that funereal cask felt odd in the porous, blue-black haze of twilight. We pulled it toward us with a hook and Baldiri stepped aboard. As we didn't have oars, he grabbed the poles from Collioure. Then we watched him squeeze between the reeds until he was out of sight. In the meantime Saldet lit a fire and started to prepare to fry fish. It was four p.m., and the light was very dim. The light in the air had turned gray.

When the fish was fried, Saldet and I ate in silence. We left the skipper's helping by the side of the fire for when he got back. After we'd downed three or four glasses of wine, Saldet declared: "This is a very strange spot, and a miserable rat trap."

"If a north wind blows up, what do you advise?"

"We should make our escape. Go back to the breach and scarper. . ."

The wind never came. There was an eerie silence. The water was totally still. The *Mestral* made not the slightest movement. The air weighed heavy. It was as if we were part of a still life. Saldet lit a lamp and hung it from the yard of the lateen sail.

"So Baldiri can see us when he comes back. . ."

That was a good idea.

It was past eight o'clock when the skipper returned. He said he'd reached dry land. Three or four hundred yards farther on, at the end of the pond, there was a small harbor with very shallow water, made from stakes that had been driven into the earth. That was the exact spot where, tomorrow, Saturday, he had to meet punctually the fellow who was bringing him the goods. I felt he seemed lifted by the results of his exploration.

"It was a foul trick to force me to come to this place," he went on, "but though it's horrible, we'll probably survive. That black boat is a jewel. . . It will come in very handy tomorrow, unless the hunter comes to claim it."

He then added that he'd almost gone to Leucate, but had decided against it as a precautionary measure, so they didn't begin to be suspicious of a foreigner.

He ate his fish with gusto. Drank copiously. Then downed two or three coffees he fortified with liquor. He was jolly. I suddenly realized he was actually a bag of nerves. We each retired to our respective corners. Before doing so, Baldiri ordered Saldet to hoist the jib with two strong sheets, the best ropes he could find.

I struggled to get to sleep. All of a sudden I heard the rain drumming down on the timbers that were my ceiling. I went on deck. It had begun to rain, a steady autumnal stream. The air was warm and still.

Saldet was talking in his sleep. I heard him say: "The olive grove. . . the vineyard. . ." Baldiri had stretched out under the passageway, facing the sky, his hands on his neck. It was very dark, but I thought his eyes were open.

The next morning when I stuck my head out, it was just brightening. Day was dawning painfully. To the east there was a purple streak on the horizon; above that, a dark-red streak faded into the pallor of the sky's gloomy, gray vault. It had been raining almost the whole night, everything was sopping, stifling and wretched. There was an oppressive muteness in the air.

"If you like, we can make a canopy. . ." I heard Saldet suggest.

"You'll do nothing of the sort. . ." replied the skipper curtly.

"Where are we going to have breakfast then?"

"Wherever. Right here."

Saldet carried the stove down the passage and boiled up coffee in the bilge in a cloud of smoke.

I'd been looking forward to spending those idle hours visiting Salses and the castle. This was now out of the question. After I'd drunk my coffee, I returned to my den, where I spent the morning nodding off and reading a book by candlelight. It rained, then stopped, and there was a long period when nothing happened. The skipper and Saldet had donned their waterproofs, and I heard them coming to and from the bridge, without saying a word.

As the day went on, the showers lessened. Daylight seemed to gather strength within the opaque sky. We ate a cold breakfast: a slice of bread and a slice of sausage. Baldiri ate mechanically. He was obsessed with the weather. He stared at the horizon to the north, at the depression accumulating between the final buttresses of the Corbères and the white Leucate promontory, toward Narbonne and Languedoc. For a moment a bright clearing seemed to open up at the back of this vista, where sky and earth intersected, like an arc of light from a bridge, and a livid, bright-green ray filtered through that arc. Baldiri snarled at this apparition and said: "Where we come from, that would be a north wind. . ."

For hours the skipper had been convinced we were heading toward such a finale, but I was surprised to see how conjecture was now turning to reality, potential depression giving way to firmness and calm.

"We should make our escape," Baldiri said calmly, weighing his words. "It's dangerous and there's no shelter. But I gave my word I'd be there this afternoon at a set time and I intend to keep my pledge. If this man shows up, we'll wind up our trip successfully. If he doesn't. . . for whatever reason. . . our voyage will have been a waste of time, and we'll be slightly poorer than when we started out."

Saldet listened as if he were an oracle. I was smoking. It had stopped raining. The sky was still very low cast and misty, but the light wasn't so murky. The air was fresher even though it was so still. The sea was white and placid. The stillness in the air seemed to spread a strange anxiety everywhere.

"So then," said Baldiri, after a pause, as calm as ever, "I intend to be in the agreed place at the agreed time, whatever the weather and however dangerous it may be. If the fellow I'm expecting keeps to his word, we'll be done straightaway. Then it will be time to load up, come back on board and flee this place. . . If he doesn't appear, I intend to wait for an hour. When that hour has gone by, if he still hasn't shown up, I'll come back, but I do intend to wait that hour for him, even though we might lose the *Mestral*. . . You'll say it's all very risky. That's true, but in this business your word is sacred. . ."

In the lull that followed, he looked down and then summed up, calmer than ever: "This is the situation: as Saldet is in a sorry state, I expect he won't want to leave the boat. Now, you can do what you want. If you like, I'll take you to the shore. You can go to Port-Vendres and I'll come and pick you up some day next week. I don't want to force you to suffer what's coming, which will be most unpleasant. . . So what. . ."

"Baldiri, I trust you, but I also trust the *Mestral*. . ."

"Yes, she was a good buy, no denying that. . . And now we know what's what, we can't waste a moment. Saldet, organize things on board. Put everything in their proper place and secure them tight. Lower the quarter sails, cover the boat. Not a drop of water must fall down below. Put a tarpaulin over the stern quarter. We must keep the engine dry. Furl the sail and tie it to the yard. You'll have more than enough with the jib sail. . . If the anchors strain too much when the north wind starts to blow, run the *Mestral* onto the first sandbank. When I get back, we'll see if we can use a piece. . ."

Baldiri hauled in the black flat boat and made for land. It must have been half an hour later when the mistral set in with all its grandiose ferocity.

A person who hasn't experienced a northwesterly gale in the area of the Corbères massif and the Salses Ponds can't claim to know what that astonishing phenomenon is like. When the Corbères reach the sea, they are low flung and bare. They seem like a small obstacle put there to arouse the fury of the wind. The immense watery expanse of the ponds is an invitation to gust uncontrollably. The terrain is mysterious and gloomy, even under a summer sun, as ends of frontiers usually are, and that helps give the spectacle a sinister touch. And so this invasive wind, which penetrates the most hermetically sealed openings, whose gusts can only be stopped by a swath of masts and rigging, finds here the ideal territory to display itself with complete freedom.

The wind blew up suddenly, without a single warning gust. It may have been preceded by a drop in temperature and a dryness in the air. When Saldet felt it lash his face, he shouted: "That's it!" and ran to the stern, clinging to the rail like a cat in order to keep an eye on our anchors. The *Mestral* slightly heaved over on her starboard side, but the anchors resisted, and straightening her back to the wind, the ship returned to her natural position. When I saw that first sign, I lay down on deck up against the side of the boat, because it would have been a waste of energy trying to stay vertical in that wind. The first gusts were accompanied by a deep, heavy roar, like a dull, distant thunderclap, and streams of spray whistling through the air. The reeds surrounding the boat began to whip the hull above the waterline, creating a chaotic din. The water began to bubble and fizz frantically. Meanwhile, from my relative haven, I began to observe the rapid changes all around us; the sky cleared, a dense cloud of white vapor formed over the pond's surface that soon placed a floating wall of mist between the Corbères, the plain and our spot, blocking our view of anything in the distance.

Half an hour after the wind had settled in, the previous rain's thick, low-cast haze dispersed. Part of the mist over the sky was reabsorbed in space; blue-green, sometimes faint-pink or purple patches began to appear in the early twilight burnished by an icy chill; the wind blew away another section of clouds extraordinarily quickly.

Meanwhile, the air went on drying out, and small, black clouds, jagged, tattered and typical of the mistral, scudded across the cold, clear sky, fragments of the bank of cloud still filling the northern horizon, a cloud the wind had elongated like a monstrous lizard.

The fierce blasts pounding the pond water created a choppy swell, which threw up streams of water. The wind combined these streams with whirls of fine muddy sand from the pond's banks and the sandbar separating it from the sea. Gusts of watery spray with myriad grains of sand rapidly covered the boat's bridge and our puny bodies with the thinnest layer of slime. Coated by a wet mineral mange, our hair, eyes and faces were sore and irritated beyond belief. We were immersed in a haze of small, solid, floating particles, which the wind then swept away to create a low curtain of fog no eye could penetrate.

On the other side of the long ribbon of the sandbank, the sea churned the mass of froth and foam in long crashing waves.

The atmosphere gradually darkened, and twilight seemed to lodge the first, unimaginably bright stars in the sky. The smooth, wan metallic sky gave the stars the magnetic brilliance of luminous splinters.

Meanwhile, the wind blew with the blind tenacity of dark forces, tense, wild and incomprehensible, a dull, dark roar over which spirals of streaming spray whistled intermittently.

It was pure prehistory, nature in the raw, totally haphazard, a transmutation of land and sea. You could do nothing, say nothing: only ardently remember things that were motionless and comforting.

Baldiri was taking his time. He'd left over two hours ago. Although it would be tricky for him to get back – so I thought – the delay implied his encounter hadn't taken place. The man he was expecting must have decided that weather freed him from any commitment. You have to be so poor, possess such vitality and have a tremendous spirit of adventure to engage in those small – terrible, obscure, unknown – tragedies of wretched daily life!

It must have been almost eight o'clock. The mere acknowledgment of the time sent me into the deepest depression. . . We didn't hear him come. We suddenly saw him haul himself over the side rail and heard the rubber soles of his Wellington boots scraping over the sand the wind had scattered across the bridge. He looked exhausted, eyes bloodshot, hair disheveled – almost unrecognizable – but I noted he was acting serenely. He said good evening absolutely normally. I saw he was carrying nothing, hands in pockets. The man had clearly not showed up.

He opened the cupboard under the bench by the mast, rummaged and extracted some clothes – a red jersey and a jacket (an ill-cut, half-length overcoat) – which he put on after taking off the leather blouson he was wearing. He shouted his questions at Saldet so the wind didn't blow his words away: "Everything stored properly? Everything battened down?"

Saldet nodded several times.

"Start the engine. First in neutral. . . Then when we move off, open it up slightly."

He started the engine. It was barely audible, even though it was from an old jalopy and very noisy. The screaming wind blotted everything out.

"Now let the prow rope out. Save as much as you can. Then cut it!"

When Pau Saldet returned after completing that operation, the skipper said: "Now raise anchors. That's yours!" he ordered, pointing to the starboard. "This gentleman and I will try to lift the other."

We went to it. It was a long, tricky business, hampered by the way the sandy, salty spray forced us to squint. It irritated our eyes and paralyzed our arms. It was a waste of effort and Baldiri ordered Saldet to put the motor in reverse. The anchors yielded at last and we hauled them on board. The *Mestral* was released and the wind carried her down the pond. Baldiri jumped and grabbed the tiller and Saldet put the motor into forward.

Now we've reached the point in the story I find difficult to tell at all coherently. I could never manage an accurate explanation of our exit from the pond. Was it chance? Was it luck? Was it the skipper's extraordinary sense of direction, which enabled him to remember the path we'd taken the previous day? Was it the wonderfully clear night sky that helped Baldiri draw on his talents? I don't know. We did hit a sandbank, but the moment he felt the obstacle on our keel, he ordered the motor on full. The screw threw up a formidable flurry of water, but Baldiri was set on completing the maneuver and the *Mestral* progressed through. When analyzed coldly, it seems absurd, even though the skipper said he was an expert on sandbanks in the Gulf of Roses and sensed resistance the very first instant the prow heaved. I never really swallowed any of that. The *Mestral* lurched violently, but it was the power of her engine that carried her through. . .

How did he find the channel out of the pond in the pitch black of night? I couldn't explain that either. I simply remember that when the prow was in the breach, its back to the wind, he howled like a wild animal: "Lengthen the jib, Pau!"

The jib sail was lengthened, the prow of the *Mestral* rose, and we passed through the strait in a cloud of sand, as if the current carried us out in its arms. Once back in the sea, he let the boat be driven by the tail wind for ages. We sailed out to sea, and suddenly to the south, a quarter to our west, the beam from the light on Cape Béar appeared.

"Ah!" said Baldiri, taking a deep breath, waving his hand in the air. And while he steered the boat toward land (I imagined he was heading to Sant Pere de Roda), a huge squall of rain crashed over his back. He was unmoved. I suspect the worst was over from his point of view. The key moment had been getting out of the rat trap of that pond. A difficult journey lay ahead, but the contest was won.

We sheltered by his side. There was a driving wind and huge sea current. The *Mestral* sailed using all her wonderful qualities. She descended from the crest of a wave like a frail feather. When she came down like that – and the prow lurched – we felt an emptiness in the pits of our stomachs, and our hearts thudded. The skipper was alert to such lurches. He had tied a rope to the helm to keep it straight and controlled the rope with his hand. It was a real effort for his amazing arm to keep the vessel on course when the current was battering her. But he rarely failed.

All of a sudden he asked for coffee and liquor. We'd passed on supper. It was a peculiar longing that was difficult to satisfy. However, Saldet couldn't resist trying to appease him.

"I suppose you won't mind waiting half an hour. . ." replied Pau.

"Or even an hour. . . You make the coffee as best you can, and God will reward you."

Soon we could see thick smoke wafting over the deck by the mast area.

The problem was always the same: there was nothing you could do or say; you could only long for the pleasant things in life. Squalls whipped our faces; bundles of water keeled us over; we felt a kind of nighttime, salty cold in the marrow of our bones. . . and could only longingly recall those pleasant things. The pitching of the wave-battered *Mestral* forced us to hang on to those memories of past comforts ever more intensely.

Our mugs arrived half-empty, but the emptiness was compensated by large shots of a dry, metallic liquor. Baldiri reckoned it was sweet and bland. "It tastes of palm fibers. . ." he said. "On land all drink seems strong. . . but men have yet to invent a drink to match the blasts of the mistral."

Wind and the sea carried us along.

Baldiri stared toward the southeast. When you're sailing on a night like that, your mind dreams of lights on land, longs for the lighthouse that must be coming – the lighthouse of hope.

"Did you see it?" he shouted excitedly, all of a sudden.

"See what?"

"It's Cape Creus. . . !" he said, putting the tiller aside, abandoning Sant Pere de Roda as our destination and pointing the prow to the light he'd just glimpsed in the distance.

A few minutes later, the glow was confirmed.

"Hey, Pau, my friend, take the tiller for a while. . . Now we know where we are, I want to have a smoke. . . And you, my good mate. . ." he said, ramping up his chumminess toward me "Don't you move one inch. You'll be fine under the prow. Don't be afraid of leaks. . . The *Mestral* is well caulked. . ."

It would have been absurd to congratulate him. Meaningless too. Anyway, I was quite exhausted. I retired to my usual lair – the funnel-like hole that's so comfortable when you're familiar with its rough corners and that cossets me on good nights and bad. As I took off my sopping clothes – bumping my head now and then – I felt a pleasant sensation of comfort. The *Mestral's* pendular swaying no doubt helped me sleep like a log.

The next day, when I woke up, I wasn't sure whether it was morning or afternoon. When I poked my nose outside, I saw we were anchored by El Jonquet in Mar d'Avall in Cadaqués and sheltered from wind and sea. The wind was still gusting; you could tell that from the silvery, white-foam color of the olive trees in Guillola Bay and the limpid, bright-blue sky.

The immediate air I breathed was full of a delicious aroma. Saldet was preparing a sea-bream stew with a few potatoes. The skipper had caught the sea bream fishing with a rod. Rod-fished sea bream is the most delicious fish in the ocean. Saldet alternated his ladling maneuvers with a careful polishing of the gramophone horn purchased from the North African in Port-Vendres. The skipper had asked him to give it a rub with a cloth. It was a splendid, exuberantly green, white-striped horn – the only item we'd brought back from our voyage.

When it was lunchtime, Baldiri said: "We could have gone to Port Lligat, but given last night's weather, I'm sure they'd have assumed we were coming from France. . . So we've landed up in El Jonquet, a solitary spot, except for the flies, naturally. It's a bit farther for you to go, senyor, and a rougher ride, but it's what there is. . . and won't take a day."

We said our farewells midafternoon. Baldiri planned to leave soon after in order to reach Roses in time for supper. I grabbed my small suitcase and blankets and set out on the path to Cadaqués. I reached the town via the slate of El Poal. I didn't meet a living soul. Darkness was already falling. I enthusiastically welcomed the silence.

As soon as I reached my house in El Pianc and switched on the light in the dining room, I saw the fictitious clock on the mantelpiece. As usual, it said 5:25. How odd! I thought. That was the exact time the *Mestral* had entered the Salses Ponds.

In any case, that vessel had been christened, inspired by the mistral that had blown Senyor Víctor from Cadaqués to Civitavecchia. Now she had received her confirmation after a similar phenomenon had blown us home, in fits and starts, from the Salses Ponds.

STILL LIFE WITH FISH

∽

Then, my dear friend, we lived in Fornells – not in the Fornells that is in Menorca, a shabby, squalid spot, but in the Fornells in our country, a sheltered, delightful place. After wandering the world for so long, after so much futile, wearisome activity, it was time for me to stop for a moment and rest awhile. It was the right decision: I went for a couple of weeks and was still there a year later, far from hunger, work and stress.

At the time Fornells had no church, no public clock, no local government office, no embodiment of legal authority. There wasn't even a cemetery, which is surprising, given there are so many cemeteries in this world. It meant those of us who lived there thought we would never die. If in the event anyone did, tears prompted by the presence of death turned to icy anguish and the coffin was carried along the most unlikely paths. There was an excellent source of water, under pine trees, with a large wash place where young girls with gleaming teeth and moist gums went to bathe. In winter when the gods brought downpours, there was a rush of water like a woman's translucent thigh, green-blue veins under a pinkish body of water.

Small, nondescript houses were scattered around, connected to a distant hamlet by a series of tracks and shortcuts. There wasn't anything one could describe as an appreciable urban mass. Men and women, old and young, all told we must have been some thirty-five individuals, and the houses we occupied were detached and separated by some distance. It would have been an exaggeration to call it a village: they were simply fishermen's houses set on a rocky landscape, in the most sheltered spots, surrounded by evergreen mastic trees – small, whitewashed houses clinging to the ground, roofs touching the rock face, doors open to the sea, pine branches giving a little shade to their façades. Rather than a strategy to communicate with others, those houses represented a way of living extremely solitary lives.

Everything that goes with human life was there: no house was without a cat or two; three or four dogs, of complex, mongrel stock, had settled in the area; a cockerel heralded our dawn; two old, shaggy, good-natured asses seemed like remnants from a past long destroyed. Culture – what people generally call culture – was little in evidence. There were no teachers and the laws related to state education were ignored. If they wanted to study, children would have had to cover seven to ten or twelve miles there and back: common sense dictated that they went when they had nothing else to do, and even then it wasn't a foregone conclusion. We didn't even have a single wretched volume of the Espasa-Calpe dictionary to consult. We received one or other of the daily newspapers, very late, in the form of wrapping around rice, noodles or beans, which we would skim or daydream over – if their dense pages didn't first disappear into the kitchen stove or the fire in the hearth. Women, in particular, had no respect for the printed page and were always short of paper. It is undeniable: Fornells, in that era, was no hotbed of culture. Nevertheless, if you wanted life with the taste of oblivion and remoteness that nervous exhaustion craves, it was a wonderfully mellow place.

Sheltered from northerly winds by the Cape Begur cliffs, the land sits there like an earthenware dish on its geological base – a sunny dish, open to the sun rising across the sea and closed to the sunset by the mountains. The land is poor but has been admirably cultivated with the noblest of crops: ancient, silvery olive groves, carob trees, cypresses, evergreen pines, almond trees and vines. Contemplated through these majestic forms, which sometimes would bend under the richness of their sap, the sea was something bright and beautiful, like an unexpected, reassuring gift from nature. In early February, when almond trees blossomed above the small ears and beady eyes of broad bean plants, the sea loomed across a pink haze. Bathed in the wintry sun, the honeyed yellow of the mimosas gleamed. Bronzed green oleanders had a reddish glow. Agave plants on rocky ridges were streaked with an egg-yolk yellow. A scent of rosemary, gorse and lavender floated in the air along paths melding with pine resin: it was a refreshing smell, a tangy, innocent delight abroad.

As there were once lots of vineyards in the area, there are still remnants of drystone walls. Among the old stones, in ravines and gullies, were small, exquisitely kept gardens with small fences to keep off the wind, where a golden light seemed to linger willfully. The produce is first rate. Peas are particularly sweet, subtly so. The Fornells asses labor slowly away in the bright light that hangs over the fenced-off plots. Sometimes, toward dusk, their loud, spectacular hee-haws fill the air, as if a force of nature is being unleashed. Then everything wakes up from its earthly, vegetative slumbers. The asses' braying reaches to the sky and the small, spongy clouds sailing by appear to halt for a moment. Everything tenses edgily. It is but a moment. . . When the asses decide their performance is at an end, they let their ears and tails droop, gaze sadly, if benignly, at the outside world and return to the juicy grass.

In such off-the-map byways, existence moves between two extremes: on the one hand, there are lethargy and tedium; on the other, your curiosity is sparked by next to nothing, by the tiniest things, far removed from your own interests. As life passes by, you realize how important lethargy is. Nobody knows how to resist tedium. Life has shown you that some of the perennial sources of anguish are futile agitation, gratuitous movement and other people's involvement in your life. Even so, you are unable to resist that numbing sensation in your heart when you feel time passing by. Men and women cannot resist lethargy because they think – for no reason at all – that lethargy is like a slow death. Thus, we escape by opening the door to invasion by others. We escape, only to suffer more. That is why I believe that one of the surest touchstones to measure a man's strength is his ability to resist the onset of lethargy. In Fornells you needed to possess that strength, and openly so. It was an astonishingly tedious spot.

The moment would come in March when you felt the fire in the hearth was an irritant. It was time to build the pine-branch shade over the front of the house. Green was the pine, and pungent its aroma. The operation signaled the start of good weather. The first becalmed seas arrived after the spring equinox. Sometimes that stillness was so profound it lent the lacquered water a soft bluey green. With the sun on your back, your eyes dazzled, you'd be fascinated by the fabulous underwater shapes you could see from the coast. These were rare, unforgettable moments curtailed by the onset of Lenten winds and choppy seas. Human life flitted beneath the shade from the pine branches. Braziers were good company. It was an excellent place to live and let live, to watch things of the land and the sea. Everything invited you to lead a tranquil life and never rush. The sun warmed; the wind caressed. Sometimes you put the noisy old alarm clock in a prominent spot and looked at its hands now and then. How satisfying it was to look at a clock and be able to say: "Only five minutes have slipped by!" It is so pleasant to feel that time isn't marching on so speedily. It isn't easy to enter that state. If you succeed, it helps if you want to lead a life without stress. The person who can say: "It's been a wonderful day. . . I've been delightfully lackadaisical. . ." is wise, full of insight and first-rate company.

In Fornells, that fantastically lethargic place, I came to embrace the charms of tedium. Giving time a slower rhythm can be sweeter than honey. Feeling you are alive is to feel you are dying, and awareness of the heart's ticktock prompts unbearable anguish. In the deep lethargy of a small backwater, that ticktock is barely perceptible. The slightest thing catches your attention and sparks your curiosity. I remember so many things that have entirely vanished. I remember the mystery in the air created by a bright January moon; the voluptuous light of spring on the almond trees' pink blouses; the progress of a lateen sail across the bay; the look in the eyes of a man facing a plate of plump grilled sardines; glistening water streaming off pine trees after a night of slow, silent rain; cats dozing by the fireside at winter twilight. But perhaps my most vivid memories are connected to the world of fish and fishing. In my memory those things are inseparable from the way fish were cooked – the simple, delicious Fornells way of cooking fish.

The dusky grouper is the best fish in the Ampurdan. The first time I saw one swimming – in the waters around Cape Begur – I was fascinated by its shape and power. It has a huge head, a muscular body and dark skin covered in yellow blotches. It swept across the limpid water like a phosphorescent flash of lightning – as if the friction from its viscous form had created a beam of light in the luminous water. Dusky groupers can be caught on a longline hook or with a line with bait trailed strategically in front of their lairs, because, it is worth noting, those groupers always live in hollows and caverns along the coast. The depth of their lairs varies constantly: they can be very deep but are often very shallow, three or four yards down, and little more. That's why on days when the water is clear, it is relatively easy to contemplate the fascinating spectacle of a grouper swimming. They are difficult to land, if they're not hunted with a creel, because they are so strong: when they sense they've been hooked, their first reaction is to enter their lair or squeeze into a crack in the rock. In such cases the danger is that the line hooking them will be severed as it chafes against a rocky ridge. When you feel that first powerful tug on your hand, you must land it quickly if you are to stymie the fish's stratagem. There is a complete division of opinion about the best way to prepare a dusky grouper. Fortunately, it is excellent however it is cooked. Some reckon the best rice in the world is that cooked with a grouper's head. I'm also of that opinion. A grouper's head and a handful of rice is a thing of beauty. Others prefer it stewed. In any case, it is such a meaty, tasty fish it can't be bettered fried.

In Fornells, the common dentex is highly prized. Is it as good as they say? I don't think so. In stews – with a few potatoes! – I almost prefer the white, or common, sea bream. Its flesh is scant and a tad tough and stringy. If it's cooked in good quality oil, it tenderizes. Anyway, it's not a fish one should at all disparage.

In the local taste-bud hierarchy, brown meagre comes between the dentex and sea bass. It isn't as good as sea bass but has a subtler taste than dentex. And that is exactly right. Sea bass – that is, one hundred percent sea bass, nourished in good, rocky waters – is an extraordinary creature. It's first rate however it is prepared: boiled with a potato and an onion; in a stew; roasted, or simply fried. Fishermen say a sea bass is the wiliest fish in the sea. When it finds itself surrounded by a net on a sandy seabed, the sea bass is amazingly adept at burying itself; that way, the net passes over its back and it escapes capture. It's compelling to watch the subterranean fish keep a sharp eye on the movement of the net, and no sooner is it out of its grasp than it quickly twists, throws off the sand and shoots off like a rocket. Guile doesn't make it any less tasty. It retains its name – *llobarro* – along most of the coast except for the northernmost stretch in Cadaqués, where they are called *llops*, *loups*, as in France. Conversely, in Fornells we call the red scorpionfish of Cadaqués a *rascassa*, like the French *rascasse*, though we are much farther from France, and in England it is a hogfish. Life is variety. I have heard it said that the best bass are caught by rods or a trident, but I don't believe the implement by which they are caught affects the quality of their taste. The quality of a sea bass comes from the cleanliness of the water and the food within its reach. A sea bass from dirty or turbid water isn't tasty: it's almost a different fish.

Gray mullet often live side by side with sea bass. Generally speaking, mullet isn't highly rated, it always likes mud and one can taste the poor quality of its often wretched diet. However, there are many kinds of mullet: there are freshwater mullet in ponds and rivers. This fish indicates the great variety one can find within the same species. It's a similar situation with *roger* – red mullet – which is called *moll* in Barcelona and other parts of the coast and *rouget* in French. Red mullet is so delicious. It is one of the highest points in marine cuisine. I think everyone would agree it is a good fish. Obviously, it's always a vexed issue when one discusses what taste buds like and dislike. One could probably create a list of fish based on their objective qualities. It would be necessary, however, for most people to accept such a list. The question of position and hierarchy has always been a difficult, delicate source of contention. For example, I adore grilled sardines when they are fresh and plump. Others believe it to be a vulgar, commonplace fish. If a friend were to ask me what you should eat in May, I'd answer straightaway: thirty sardines per head, fresh out of the sea, fat, gleaming and grilled, and four tender local lamb chops with a spring salad seasoned with oil, vinegar, salt and mustard. That makes a total of thirty-four items. That's a goodly number. Accompany the sardines with a dry white claret, made from Macabeo grapes from L'Escala, and the chops with a mellow red, and you see how they just slip down. . .

Red mullet is a high-grade fish, but you must apply immortal principles based on experience when choosing your fish. There are at least five kinds of red mullet that I know of, even though I know nothing – and not forgetting the huge ignorance that exists when it comes to the sea and fish. The variety of types in nature can't be pinned down. Besides, nature tends to fake its products constantly. Many fish have their ersatz: the common squid is a substitute for the veined squid; the John Dory, an ersatz sole; there is an infinite variety of gray mullet, most of which are worthless, but the red-cheeked gray mullet and the rock mullet, at specific times in the year, and always with an element of good will, rival the excellent sea bass. There are also many kinds of sea bass, some of which, like silt and estuary sea bass, are frankly inferior; others are top of the range. Whenever possible, I think it's a good idea to dispense with these obsequious, servile fish that aim to imitate the refined class. It's a sorry business replacing veined squid with common squid, or sole with John Dory. . . Sometimes, it's difficult, because one's purse doesn't stretch that far. We poor people have to be extremely patient and often have no choice but to use the fakes created by nature. It sometimes seems that nature and capitalism have signed an eternal pact of friendship. . .

So then there are five kinds of red mullet. Does that mean there are five different species of these fish? I don't think so. The category of red mullet depends on where it lives and what it eats. It's a very active, rather stupid, highly carnivorous fish – lobsters also eat meat if they can find any – and it digests in an immobile, dreamy state, drowsing on sand. However, at dawn or sunset, it emerges from its slumbers and driven by hunger throws itself into a hunt for food, abandoning all balance, caution and common sense. As if blinded by hunger it enters a state of frenzy. If, on its travels, it comes across a fine-mesh net, it attacks it without thinking twice and commits suicide, an inglorious, unlamented suicide. Such is the life and death of a red mullet. There are less tasty fish that are infinitely more intelligent.

As we said, the category of a red mullet depends on where it lives and what it eats. There may be cases – this is a hypothesis – when a red mullet of good stock, one of those first-rate specimens they call *juliolencs* in Tossa de Mar, perhaps the best along our coast, migrates from its group, abandons its family and ancestral watery pastures and goes to live with red mullet of a different class, like the prodigal son. In such cases, don't pin your hopes on that red mullet. Its qualities are suddenly diluted. It takes on another color. It becomes another kind of fish. Seventy years ago, materialists declared with impressive gravitas: "Man is what he eats." That could be said, and much more reasonably, of red mullet.

There is a lower class of red mullet – the so-called *ombradiu* or shadowy mullet – that is found in less than clean waters in commercial ports or spots near fishing villages, and it's a greenish hue. Then there is the mud-loving mullet that trawlers catch very deep down; a small, pinkish mullet with a long, narrow head and thin scales. It's what they feed you in rural boarding houses and taverns and, of course, in big cities. It's not very nice. Red mullet that live near sand or seaweed are tastier and plumper, their flesh firmer. This progression in quality really runs parallel to the quality of their watery habitat, and it's a well-known fact that the saltier the water, the better the fish that swim there. Shadowy mullet live in water that isn't very salty, in waters professors and naturalists call – excuse my pedantry – lentic. Top red mullet, the glory of the species, the aristocrats in the family, live near seabeds where there is sand, seaweed and rocks – that is, swim in areas of white coral reefs, where you'll often find lobsters. Such are the *juliolenc* in Tossa, the one on the Torroella coast and the one in the waters of Begur. When you encounter a large red mullet with a round head, strong rough scales and strong compact slices of flesh, you know it is top class. Don't hesitate for a moment. The bigger, the better. Grill them with a drop of vinegar. They're also good with garlic and parsley. Moreover, the cooking process will enhance their colors. Red mullet on the bottom rungs of the ladder will turn a wan pink on the flame. Conversely, the best red mullet will turn an intense, sumptuous cardinal red, that red we all know, which is so like the immortal reds Velázquez used in his portrait of Pope Innocent X in Rome's Galleria Doria.

Mullet sport a beard. Their beards look like small, vibrating hooks, which they use to scratch the sea floor where they live. Mullet use their beards to eat. Well-respected gentlemen may also use their beards to the same end.

The best fish soup is the one made from a *burra*, of the sole family, which are called *somera* on some parts of the coast. It is a small, black, round flatfish, a bit larger than a silver five-pesseta coin, with lots of bones. In itself it is inedible, but when boiled in a broth, it produces the most intense, delicate-flavored soup any fish can provide. Generally speaking, the best fish in the sea are those that least taste of fish, those that don't give your stomach the unpleasant turn you get from the smell of fish in the market, or fish when it's being salted, or even an empty fish box. *Burra* soup is the soup that least smells of fish of any that you can make. A rich soup can also be made from the broth of those long, multicolored fish that go by the name of tub gurnard or, in some places, shortfin or naked-belly sea robin. It brings such an intense, subtle taste to the palate, which is what one expects from a good soup.

I can't seriously claim I have ever been a fisherman – of the professional or amateur variety. However, even though I've never established myself in the terrain in my own right, it is undoubtedly true that I have helped to catch lots of fish.

I began conscientiously, the way things should begin if you want to do things properly: I began by learning to pull on a line. At the time, dragnet fishing was practiced in Aiguablava, a beach in Fornells

Bay with very fine sand and no reefs. Dragnet fishing is a nighttime activity, and as I've always liked going to bed late, I discovered it was quite in tune with my character. It was wonderfully elemental and easy! The skipper on land gave us a loop of rope – a grommet – which was attached to one of the dragnet's pull ropes. And it was all about walking along and pulling on the rope with the loop over your shoulder until it was all out and then starting back from the water's edge. As this kind of fishing was usually practiced by the poorest men and women around, people have expressed doubts as to whether it was they who kept the rope tensed or whether it was the rope that stopped them from falling over. They were excellent men and women – people who'd never had an opportunity to reach a minimal degree of respectability or had lost it with the passage of time. They weren't fishing folk: they were simply the rock-bottom poor, the out-and-out, genuine *misérables*.

My God, what nights they were! Dragnet fishing – like all operations that use light – was a nocturnal activity in periods of darkness. It commenced with the old moon and finished with the moon in the sea. When the moon was full, people enjoyed a break and disappeared from the beach.

On dark nights, under the high cliffs over the cove, Aiguablava became a pitch-black grotto. The shadows were dense. Often, in the distance, you could see the boat with its sad speck of damp luminous yellow hanging in the blackness of the bay. If there was the slightest swell, the light hopped and skipped so comically it made you weep. The old light from pinewood sparking in iron braziers had been replaced by acetylene. The beach sometimes stank unpleasantly of calcium carbide. When it was dry and the sky was twinkling, the acetylene gave out a white-to-bluish glow; on damp, misty nights it turned a fine yellowish red. While we waited for the moment to loosen the rope – that is, the moment to let out the net – the beach was profoundly silent, a silence scented by an intense aroma of pine and seaweed. Sometimes we saw a vaguely human form wandering around holding a poor, spluttering lamp. The silence was so total it felt theatrical.

The boat with the acetylene lamp, in which the dragnet skipper had embarked, was moored between two boats with lights. The lamp would go in search of fish. Nothing is dogmatic in the fishing world. If the lamp discovered a shoal of blue fish, sardines, anchovies, chub, horse or common mackerel, it tried, making the least noise possible, to lure it closer to land. If the attempt looked as if it might work – which was always difficult to predict – someone would signal with a green lamp to the person in charge on the beach. It was all about coaxing the fish to the beach shallows. When the signal was given, the biggish boat was moored, leaving one rope on land, which, in turn, pulled the net under the water so as to leave its sack behind the boat with the lamp. Once the sack was closed, the biggish boat brought the other rope to the beach. When this operation was concluded, the sack was dragged as far as the breakwater. With the loop of rope over your shoulder you then walked up the beach into the thickest of shadows beneath the front line of pine trees. By the water the sand was damp; it then became fine – sand dust – and pleasantly and warmly tickled the soles of your feet.

There were two ropes: the southwesterly rope and the easterly rope. The orientation of our coast, from Cape Creus to Alfacs, is marked by the path of the winter sun. East is the rising sun and southwest the setting sun. These points of reference are the touch-stones when it comes to locating yourself on our shores. The net would be slowly dragged toward land. Sometimes a crazed, dazzled fish jumped under the light. In the incandescent, metallic water, the fish made bubbles that rose from the depths and died on the surface, like lips melting in their own breath.

It was imperative to keep the cork float around the mouth of the net in a vertical position behind the lighted boat. Sometimes the southwesterly rope would be pulled harder than the easterly one or vice versa and the net's mouth appeared to curl and snarl. If the easterly rope was pulled too hard, a man on the lighted boat shouted through hands cupped like a loudspeaker, shattering the deep silence over sea and beach:

"Pull southwester. . . !"

Responding to that solemn cry, an elongated shout came up from land:

"Southwester it is. . . !"

"Pull southwester. . . !" the voice on the lights boat often repeated, trying to straighten the net.

"Southwester it is. . . !" answered the beach.

The resonant drawn-out phrases, like the end of a psalm, slowly vanished into the shadows, as if disappearing into the water.

"Pull easterly. . . !" the gruff, distant voice suddenly bawled from the sea.

"Easterly it is. . . !" cried those on land.

Those pulling on the easterly rope with the coil round their shoulder upped their effort, bent their backs, sank their bare feet into the sand.

As the sack of the net drew nearer to land, curiosity was piqued. It would have been an exaggeration to speak of emotions. Those people were too downtrodden to feel emotion. That belonged to past, ravaged things.

The sack landed full of water, like a monstrous black excrescence. However, once on the soft sand, it soon deflated. If there were no fish, it lay like a dark, tired, dead blotch under the white light from the lamps. In that situation, people ran their hands over their shoulders, yawned and ate a hunk of bread. But there was always something or other. The fish died – it was a net for catching blue fish – in a series of frantic convulsions that created a stream of diamond-like droplets of water. Those frenzies were short-lived: our eyes were bewitched by the glitter. Then we opened the sack and saw the fish, a mass of molten silver, still alive, a glittering blue and tremulous light green. Like all fish that swim in shoals, they died in line, gregariously, as if anchovies had had a premonition of their jars and sardines of their boxes. You could watch the last gasp as they choked, the sad grimace of their final flourish. Then the surface of the blue fish was covered in that sticky, colloidal film that covers living beings in water, which slipped through your fingers and gleamed mournfully.

I tried my hand at many other things. I joined in a lobster campaign in the channels off Fornells. We fished with creels, often at quite a depth. There are infinite ploys that can be used with those wicker baskets, inside which bait was hung. Fish are generally hungry, and when driven by hunger, they are blinded and commit suicide. It is easy to go into a creel and difficult to get out. There are huge creels to catch the amazing spring conger eels. There are creels for lobsters and smaller mushroom-shaped ones, called prawn creels, which catch many different kinds of fish. The best bait for prawn creels is the female sea urchin. Lobsters eat all kind of bait, fresh or salted.

Creels must be dropped in suitable places, and to know where they are, you need a clear, or at least approximate, idea of the underwater orography. It is vital to have a precise knowledge of depths. Besides that, you must be able to feel those depths in the palm of your hand – namely, by being sensitive enough to feel that small, often barely perceptible bump made by something thrown into the sea when it touches the seabed. You must have that sensitive touch even if a creel descends one hundred twenty fathoms. Those places are determined by the lay of the land, because everywhere in a coastal sea is a product, the vertex, of an angle drawn by specific land formations. It is futile to lower lobster pots onto sand, seaweed or mud: you won't catch a thing. Fish – every kind of fish – live in their own geographical habitat. In the months when you are allowed to fish them, lobsters live in the sides of underwater mountains, in the valleys and hollows within those mountains, in rocky or stony areas covered in bushes of deepsea seaweed. The signs that point up fishy zones are often known to fishermen via the oldest family traditions, by empirical detail accumulated by their forebears. The only wealth many fishing families possess is the knowledge of these indicators, sometimes recorded in a notebook, sometimes preserved not so accurately by memory. However, knowledge of all these connections is fading, and will in the end be lost. Human life is being mechanized.

The hunger fish feel isn't that languid hunger some humans feel. It is blind, frantic, active hunger. When fish are hungry, they start swimming, they rush around in search of potential food and tend to ignore obstacles. At such times, their sight fails them, their wily, beady gaze is gone. Nets are there to take advantage of such moments of madness. There are many kinds to catch sardines, sand smelt, bogues; fine mesh, long and wide. And many others.

Fish go hunting for food – like most animals – twice a day: at the break of dawn, as the song goes, and at dusk, as the sun is setting. That is the ominous time when a net must be sunk and ready. Fish circulate, swim by, swerve, cleave the water like spears, turn around and, eyes clouded by the hint of prey, are caught in the net.

Nets must be set down in strategic places because the hunger that drives fish crazy to the point of killing themselves never makes them stray from their usual habitat. Nets are dropped to cover their pastures, small coastal straits, the bottoms of cul-de-sacs, and the mesh must be strong and resistant; holes must be mended and suitably tinted. They must be lowered following the twists and turns of underwater rocks, because straight lines are few and far between in nature, and they must be brought up at the right time. They must never be left indefinitely in the water but be raised at turning points – namely, at dawn or dusk. If not, every fish caught in the net will ineluctably be devoured by predators. A sucking, gasping fish is on track to becoming defenseless prey.

Nets capture the tastiest fish along our shores: scorpionfish, red mullet, hogfish. . . Animals with monstrous heads, eyes bulging as if they were about to have an instant heart attack. However, nets aren't only dropped where the seabed is ridged and difficult; sardine nets are hung over sand in bays and gulfs to catch blue fish that are migrating. . . supposing they do migrate. These fish swim – or toil, as fishermen say – at the same time as other fish, but they can also do so at odd moments, when fascinated by a glimmer of light or chased by a hungry predator.

Dragging nets along the seabed, across sandy or muddy flats, along the floor of underwater ravines, is an ancient art. This kind of fishing used to happen only in winter, and would be carried out by pairs of fishing smacks. Each boat dragged the rope on the net, sailing windward or with a wind from land. Fishing smack skippers at the time were considered to be first-rate fishermen, the aristocrats of the trade. Their boats carried a lateen sail and a jib and, though they didn't have keels, they resisted well in wintry weather. They were expertly handled. Moreover, the skippers had to be familiar with the underwater geography to avoid snagging their nets. Even the cleanest seabeds have potential snags: wrecks, rubbish, the tops of rocks where the net can catch. Apart from severely damaging the net, such snagging can lead to the loss of a whole catch. Land formations indicate the precise location of these perils. Trawlers have replaced those pairs of boats, and one boat now does the work of two. The two ropes of the net drop from the trawler's poop and the mouth of the sack is kept open by two doors, pieces of wood the progress of the boat tends to separate, keeping the bag wide open. These highly sea-worthy boats have keels and powerful engines and stand up to the sea phenomenally well. Trawled fish are excellent, especially in winter, but apart from a few specific species – like monkfish, for example – they can never rival species that feed in less muddy spots, that receive more light and coastal sun.

There is much more to say about fish in Fornells.

We were talking about mullet, and mullet is one thing and forkbeard another. Mullet, caught by rock faces, are top rate; fork-beards are lured into creels. The forkbeard is a deep-sea fish, and when it comes to the surface and meets much lighter pressure in the atmosphere, it swells apoplectically, dramatically inflating with air. Atmospheric pressure is relative: an excess kills many animals; a lack of pressure kills deep-water fish. A forkbeard is dark gray with a vaguely ferrous tint on its slimy, colloidal skin. Its flesh is on the bland side, but a slice fried and accompanied by a tomato, pepper, onion and escarole salad makes for the loveliest summer breakfast imaginable. If you wake early one day and toil for a few hours, the moment will come when you'll really fancy breakfast. A dozen – or two – grilled sardines are a welcome prospect. However, a breakfast of sardines on a sweltering summer morning, when a bumblebee is buzzing a few feet away, induces a sense of being stuffed. In a benign climate that is so devilishly predictable, sardines make you sleepy, stiffen your joints, sap your will. Your touch becomes haphazard and images turn lascivious. A breakfast of sliced forkbeard is infinitely lighter, if not as tasty; in any case, much subtler.

Creels can catch conger eels, spiny lobsters and *llobregants* – the common lobster – which are called *llongants* or *llobegants* on other parts of the coast and *homards* in French. If you want to follow my advice, cut a conger into thick slices and ignore the tail, which is too bony for human consumption. This sea snake is always good to make a substantial, if frankly insipid, rice dish. It tastes its best in the spring. Then slices of conger, cooked with tender, sweet Fornells peas, constitute an objectively delicious meal. Human malice tends to pass off the moray – another sea snake – as a conger, or at least as its ersatz. It's an abominable comparison. Apart from the fact that they are two quite distinct fish, one can't compare their quality. The conger is the color of sinuous, slippery, snaky things: its skin is streaked white and gray, an almost bluish gray. Whenever painters want to create an image of a fleeting form, they must have recourse to the thin sinuous cylinder of a conger eel, the color of which is but a faint hint in water. A moray is a very dark, earthy color dotted with yellow and gold spots. It is a fish that belongs in gloomy hollows, dark caverns, a malign beast, like a handful of gold coins lurking at the bottom of a secret vase.

In the age-old dispute between supporters of the common lobster and supporters of the spiny lobster, the former always win out, as shown by the difference in price these crustaceans fetch in the market. Although spiny lobsters are rarer than the common variety, they are always cheaper. No sight is more scintillating than a creel of common lobsters rising to the surface. These crustaceans convulse, shake their tails, spasmodically jump, beat their breasts, bend their erect, vibrating legs over the coils of their body. The noise their drumming makes sounds like something hollow, as if the flesh they contain were separating from their pink shells. But they usually subside, let themselves be covered by a cloth and reach the tank full of life. It is best not to keep male and female together in the tank, because they sometimes kill one another. They must be kept separate, though that's not so easy because it's generally hard to guess the sea creatures's sex. When they surface captive, common lobsters aren't so frenzied; they are stronger and, consequently, more self-confident. They die all the same. The issue as to which crustacean is more delicious is a matter of taste. Both have arguments in their favor. The *homard*'s flesh is sweeter and softer, the spiny lobster's more compact and firmer. In my humble opinion, they must be eaten grilled, passed over embers, with a light vinaigrette, that should be slightly stronger for a spiny lobster. No sauces. It's wrong to boil them: boiling destroys their divine essence, their spirit, transforms them into something vegetable, passive and diluted. Only embers and a grill enable the aroma to be retained on the toasted, calcareous shell.

The great family of scorpionfish – with their monstrous, apoplectic heads, poisonous sting, bright reds, coagulated-blood reds and motley colors – produces, in a higher state of evolution, the circle of hogfish, which is one of the finest creations of the sea. The scorpionfish is a hungry, nay gluttonous, fish that is caught with small mesh nets: it has little edible appeal – except for making soup broth – because of a surfeit of bones. A hogfish, on the other hand, is first rate: it is good however it's cooked: boiled, stewed in its juices or casseroled. It can be caught with hooks on a long line, or with a trammel net. The true adepts of eating fish – who are few and far between – think that a hogfish's head and gills are out of this world.

Sea bream, white bream, goldline and big walleye are rock fishes that feed on the flora on the reefs and rocks near the surface that receive intermittent sunlight. Such pastures give them a rocky, rather bitter taste, which could only be described if a palate had clearly literary inclinations. In any case, one could establish a hierarchy between all those fish: perhaps the goldline is poorest in quality, the one with the rockiest flavor. It's highly entertaining to see a shoal of goldline devouring the vegetation on a reef, churning the water, making it simmer, as the lightning fish turns on the blue of its back and then on its silvery belly. Fishermen catch them with casting nets and use them as bait on longlines or rod lines. Dentexes also like them. They too can be caught at dusk, on a corkline baited with sea lice or hooks with bread pellets that are left to drift.

Perhaps white bream should be ranked at the top of this hierarchy; it is better than dentex in my view because it tastes so much fresher. Pink bream is also delicious, especially if it is on the weighty side. It's very likely that the pink tone of this fish – a marble pink when it comes out of the water – is the most refined, delightful pale red that exists on this planet. Both breams are good prepared in whatever way and are quite unrivaled. The other rock fish I mentioned a moment ago are nothing out of the ordinary but can act as a worthy accompaniment to greens at dinner.

One could say a lot about king prawns, cuttlefish, langoustines and crayfish. These crustaceans are fished here by trawlers dragging a net across a muddy or sandy seabed. The quality of their flesh varies a lot according to the area where they feed. If their flesh is muddy, crumbly and pasty, they cannot be compared to those bred in pure, fast-flowing water, which helps produce a hard shell and compact flesh. It is crucial for fish to be fresh; environment is key to quality. A poem by the Rector of Vallfogona has been preserved and is dedicated to "the wild dragon of Tortosa, the symbol of the city's guild of fishermen. . ." It is one of the few poems in Catalan that adjectivize fish.

Fleshy pompano,
tender, milky mullet
and compact sole,
with sinuous conger eel.
Rowing lobster,
Goliath crab,
inky squid
and silvery scad.
Freckled moray,
gilded bream,
with mother-of-pearl langoustine,
and glassy corba.
From freshest mullet
to driest, saltiest bass. . .

There are three kinds of adjective in this list: the totally gratuitous, the approximate and the precise. The latter – the "tender, milky mullet" – relates to fish that live in muddy waters, to the species in the estuaries of the River Ebro, to pinpoint their habitat exactly.

I'm suggesting by all this that crustaceans are at their best when they are stiff and firm rather than limp and flaccid.

They are used to give flavor to rice, and that's fair enough, but they are much tastier grilled with a dash of olive-oil vinaigrette. In my opinion they are never on par with the common or spiny lobster.

The spider crab is a wonderful crustacean that can sometimes be caught in the spring, when laying its eggs near the waterline on empty beaches. It can also be caught with a trawling net or creel: a spider crab is like an upturned pot, a raw-red beast that walks using its joints like a system of levers. Fans of the shelly species say the spider crab is the best of all the crabs caught around here. That might be taking it too far. Though it is a large creature, it is home to scant flesh, more a figment of the imagination than real, but those who are adept at scouring the shell – that is an art like any other, an anatomical dissection like any other – maintain that the flesh you do find in the shell cannot be surpassed. When they speak of grilled spider crab, their eyes almost pop out of their sockets. Also, when good weather comes, rice with spider crab has a very good press, with a scattering of freshly picked peas, the right sauce, not too dark, to the point that I have heard people claim it's one of the best rice dishes there are. It adds a strong, concentrated flavor to things and leaves a sweetish aftertaste that's certainly surprising and original on the palate. At any rate the spider crab is one of the most delicious elements that spring brings to our coast, although it's often forgotten nowadays.

Hake fishing along our shores has entered what may be a terminal phase. Hake used to be fished with special longlines a long way out to sea. It's an excellent fish and much liked, particularly inland. It has little in the way of fishy odors and is easily dissected because its bones are transparent, and so it's become the ideal fish for people who don't really like fish. Hake is a fey, twilight animal; it belongs to the menus of convalescents, of individuals who can eat very little, and those who stay in inns and taverns in our country: commercial travelers and fly-by-nights. One of the things that make traveling so sad in this country is being forced to eat round hake steaks every day, accompanied by a leaf of escarole. The decline in hake fishing means it is quite hard to say if there is a lot of hake in our waters. In Barcelona they've tried to invent a kind of "quality hake," which usually refers to hake fished on a longline, but in reality they're catching the fish with trawlers. As a result, there are a lot more consumers of so-called longline hake than longline hooks cast into the sea.

The last few days of March. As part of the starry, rather cold fascination of those spring nights in Fornells, I watch the twinkling white lights switch on in the longboats, the *trainyeres*, that had disappeared from sight in October. Their appearance in the monotony of Fornells life is such a novelty that everybody is quite astonished by those fleeting, errant glimmers. People talk for a good two hours about those lights that keep me company and excite those who do business from the sea. Money, money, money. . .

A man in a group sitting by the line where they hang nets up to dry or mend tells us about his thoughts on sardines.

"Those people in the longboats will make a pile. Now's the time when huge shoals enter through the Strait of Gibraltar and swim up the peninsular coast, with a southwesterly wind, the Lenten wind, as far as the Gulf of Lion. This mass of fish, sometimes instinctively, sometimes fleeing from predators, swims along the line of the coast as far as the sea of Genoa. Then, in late summer, the beginning of autumn, sardines and anchovies follow the reverse route. As the sun dips, they come down the coast, always searching for pleasant water temperatures, through the straits and off to warmer, tropical seas. Such are the perceptible migratory moments of sardines, anchovies and perhaps blue fish in this country," says the fisherman. "As they move up and down, these shoals never reach the coast of Italy. That's why Italian farmers who want to eat good saltwater fish must buy it here... By the time the fish reach the coasts of the Italian Riviera, the water is too cold and they turn back..."

What do we know about sardines? We know nothing. Biologists have struggled to unravel the mysteries of the life of blue fish, to track their precise habitat, yet to this day haven't come up with anything clear. Is it a migratory fish that moves from one area to another, driven by currents, winds and dangerous predators? Only doubts exist on that front. Is it an animal that goes intermittently from waters near the surface to the hidden depths of the sea? I mean, does a blue fish migrate vertically? Does it swim from top to bottom or from left to right? According to the latest studies there are masses of local blue fish that are sedentary and reproduce in places that have nearby pastures, independently of the huge shoals that migrate. So the results from these studies are nonexistent: we know nothing at all.

One placid summer afternoon I climbed the coast by the Cape Creus lighthouse and saw the largest shoal of sardines I had ever seen. At the surface of the water it occupied an area of over three hundred square yards and constantly changed shape. It was a mass of fish turning in on itself, a cosmic silvery-blue swarm suspended beneath the surface, touched by the setting sun, drifting with the wind – a light southeasterly – and the waves, which were monotonous, mechanical and persistent. The drone of a southwesterly... The shoal was visible for hours, indolent and passive, before it finally disappeared into the shadows of twilight. If a predator had appeared – tuna, dentexes, not to mention dolphins – that entire mass would have been terrified, become self-aware, and fled in seconds. But where would they have fled to? Horizontally? Vertically? From top to bottom, from right to left? Do we have a clue? We may really know nothing after all...

On tranquil nights, from the light boat of a longboat – where I often happened to be as a recalcitrant bird of the night – one can often see small bubbles in the illuminated area of water; they rise from depths perceptible to the eye, like points of a needle crossing the glaucous mass, eager to reach the surface. Some reach the water-line exhausted; some are livelier, iridescent, glinting with life. Those bubbles are evidence of the existence of fish at a lesser or greater depth, near the sea floor. The fish are fascinated by the light and come to the surface; sometimes, despite the attraction of the lights, the fish remain invisible in an unknown zone. In the first instance, the fish wants to die bewitched by the movement of the *trainyera*. When that is the case, there are multiple signs of fish. First, isolated sardines swim through the water like tiny crazed snakes; sometimes they splash furiously above the waterline. Those first sightings increase until a shoal coalesces under the light, a swarming mass in translucent waters.

So then, sardines – and blue fish generally – live intermittently at the bottom of the benthos and in plankton zones. Naturalists use these two words to name the two essential elements of marine geography. The bottom of the sea as a whole, from the coastal plain to the abyssal depths, composes the benthic system. The waters supported by the seabed make up the pelagic system. Creatures of the benthos live in the former and plankton in the latter. In the former there are mainly underwater flora and small living organisms, while fish live in the latter.

The penetration of light creates another division as regards these two systems. First, there is the diaphanous zone, which is affected by the penetration of sunlight; then there is the aphotic or shadowy zone, unreached by the rays of the sun. How far down do sunbeams penetrate? Apparently, sunlight has made an impact on photographic plates at depths of between five hundred and a thousand yards. In reality, however, from two hundred yards the strength of light becomes so weak and the density of the water offers such resistance to penetration that vegetable life dwindles at an astonishing rate. It doesn't stop entirely: it becomes scant, and a large part of the benthic platform is formed by sand or viscous slime.

In Fornells we thought that mullet belonged to the benthos, but to its diaphanous zone. We attributed the fish's bright colors to the fact that its scales were touched by the light of the sun. On days when the water was still and limpid, we would see them motionless and sleepy eyed above the sand between two mounds of seaweed, as if they were listening to a lecture. They sometimes stayed there for hours until they started to swim at dusk. Naturalists tend to give light a key role in underwater life. It is remarkable that fish usually swim at the sun's two critical moments: dawn and dusk. In any case explaining the color of fish by their contact with light would occasionally make us look foolish. How could you explain the pink, delightful red of the blackbelly rosefish we caught with kite-fishing lines at a depth of two or three hundred fathoms?

Similarly, we believed that forkbeards, monkfish and soles belonged to the benthos and its aphotic zone. Their dark, muddy hue, their flattened shape, which we attributed to the pressure of the water, and the stupid airs suggested by their flat form led us to believe they had never wallowed in sunlight. We thought their scope for movement was small, that their swimming organs were scant and feeble. But what did we really know about these creatures? Soles do not abound along our coast, but it would be wrong to think there are none. Sometimes when a storm stirs the sea, the odd one is caught not in areas of rocks and seaweed but in zones of mud and sand. This means that soles can live at a depth, and can live there all the time, because it hasn't been proven that when they are caught by the coast it is the egg-laying season. No. It can happen at any time of the year. Now, as soles are always the same color, whether caught in the diaphanous or aphotic zone, we had ineluctably to conclude that our knowledge about them was pure hypothesis, devoid of consistency or evidence. Sole is ersatz brill. Brill is a high-quality fish: it isn't as muddy colored as sole, it is darker, stronger, more intense.

The sardine – to return to the sardine – is, then, perhaps an animal that inhabits both surface and deep water. Sometimes it sails and splashes along the waterline; at others, it shows signs of living in the depths. From the point of view of a fish's life, the demarcation line between sunny and shadowy zones is quite imprecise. It is very likely that most of the fish who contribute to our nourishment and live near our coast are animals of an undetermined zone. There are migrating fish that pass our country by. Others migrate from the surface to the depths and vice versa. Others move from the diaphanous to the aphotic zone, in other words, migrate from the coast to the sea's abysses, slipping down the sloping plain that is the Mediterranean shelf. These shifts and migrations happen in one sense or another according to the time of year. Fish have their set, fatal moments, which nothing can trigger or delay. Don't count on groupers in January. . . But apart from all this, which is quite peripheral, what do we really know about things of the sea and fish? Theories proliferate. Hypotheses are endless. But there is little specific data. In brief, our knowledge derives from what we have learned as fishers of dishes. We know that sardines, mullet, soles, groupers are delicious and that, when spring comes, conger eel with fresh peas is a tasty dish with an exceptional flavor. . .

Hooks are items that man must have created the second he learned how to manipulate metals. It is such a simple shape and so practical and efficient that its prehistoric nature is quite evident. The hook is an invention like the wheel: a wonder of guile and skill. The hook is behind an infinite number of fishing methods: from those that use a fishing rod, which is improved yearly, those without a rod – like the longline or kite-line fishing – or those based on traps for predators. For a hook can catch a fish with or without bait.

Rod fishing has created a huge bibliography, activated the pens of distinguished writers and produced delightful commentaries on fresh- and saltwater anglers. Freshwater anglers are everywhere reputed to be peaceful, thoughtful, stubborn and averse to raucous behavior. They'd deserve a habitat that makes their lives easier and increases the likelihood of success. At the rate we are going, however, anglers will soon enter the category of heroes. They will seem beings struck by adversity. Because in our country, where there is so much water in the sea, every day there are fewer fish, and in rivers that are so full of fish, every day there is less water. These contradictions leave a sour aftertaste. In any case, the number of rod fishers is increasing exponentially, especially freshwater ones. There were two or three great anglers in Fornells who specialized in catching fish in stormy weather. As homes were short on food after two or three days of storms, those anglers were highly regarded.

Anglers are totally misunderstood by the population at large. People think they are simpletons trying to while away the time, escaping the boredom of family life on the pretext of mindless distraction. But that's a mistake. Although it may seem incredible, an angler is above all a most sensual individual. Hook fishers strive after a stupendous physical sensation, the one experienced when you catch a live being, through a series of fascinating tugs that directly impact the person fishing. A rod fisher, like the longline fisher with his kite, feels the electric tug of his prey in the palm of his hand. It is an ineffable experience: it is pure bliss, a sense of physical control mixed with sensuous ecstasy, the fisher's own startling will for power affirmed through the palm of the hand and communicated to the fisher's every sense: a feeling that cannot err.

No fishing device communicates so directly the tug, or if you will, the fish's bite, on bait and hook as the line an angler holds in his hand. So we shouldn't be surprised by the perennial popularity of this type of fishing or the growing prestige it accrues on all sides. It is an intense assault on the nervous system – direct, unique and spectacular.

We should note that the intensity of feeling doesn't depend on the weight or size of the catch. It depends, in essence, on the fish's energy, on its rampant hunger. At the moment of the bite, even if every fish has its individual way of biting, hunger can make all fish seem a similar size. It does not matter whether you are fishing small, brightly colored rainbow wrasses, whose mouths are shaped like the barrel of a musket, all set to suck, or blackbelly rosefish with wider, greedier mouths – the angler with a kite line feels strong pulls, stunning, electrical frissons. Obviously, the moment after the bite, the size and weight of the fish *are* registered: once caught, the small fish's reactions diminish, it becomes moribund; on the other hand the fifth or sixth tug of a grouper or sea bass can have the same striking intensity as the first. Some fish seem more delicate, they bite more directly and languidly. This does not depend on the animal's size either. It depends initially on its level of hunger; then on the resistance it puts into its final struggle against death.

The fishing rod dulls these sensations. When you hold a rod, the dramatic thrill of the captured prey is felt more by the rod than its owner. When you fish from a skiff, with the line in your hand, the feeling is much more immediate.

However, everything in this world has its checks and balances. Just as the angler feels excited by his catch, all his cunning rushes to his brain to ensure he secures it. These flights are mental and, consequently, less pleasant. An angler isn't a gratuitous collector of fleeting sensations that vanish as quickly as they appear.

The bite is where hook fishing begins: then comes the pleasure of possessing the animal that has bitten. Not all fish that have been hooked are landed easily. Some are difficult to land. Some swallow the bait without the hook catching on its tissue; a quick movement and the hook is dislodged and expelled. When a grouper, a really vigorous fish, feels it has been hooked, it enters the first underwater hollow it can find and stays there; if the fisher isn't skilled, there is a risk, as we mentioned before, that the line will be severed when it rubs against the ridges around the lair. Other fish break the line with a frenzied, furious tug. It's quite common to catch a fish and find a hook in its entrails when you open it up.

An angler's skill consists in slowly tiring the fish in order to avoid a line break and its loss. You have to know how far you can let the rod bend, and tense the line without it breaking. That way the fish tires and lets itself be hoisted to the surface. When that moment comes, it is still very easy to lose your catch, because as the pressure of the water stops affecting the fish's body, its flesh tends to swell and slacken, and if the hook isn't properly embedded in its tissue, it can easily be vomited out. When the fish reaches the surface, you must have at the ready your landing net – that is, a net with a circular top. You must place the net expertly under the fish and, with a quick movement, land the fish. There is nothing more exciting than a good landing. It gives the same feeling of uplift that some financial and banking operations produce.

In any case, this is the only kind of fishing that gives the fisher direct, firsthand experience. Pulling on the rope of a seine, a trawling net or a creel and hoisting a longboat's fine-mesh nets by hand or mechanically raising a trawler's nets trigger curiosity, economic calculations and culinary hypotheses. But those fishing devices will never give you the sensuous elation generated by rods, longlines, kite lines, snaglines and troll fishing. Even so, of all these devices we have just named, a rod implies the presence of an element that distances the angler from the immediacy of a tug. The angler's ideal is the line in the palm of his hand, and the easiest way to get that is the longline, basically a line with a series of hooks, which allows the fisherman to feel simultaneously three or four fish biting.

A hook can be used without bait, as a simple ploy. And that isn't a modern form of fishing (spinning and jigging are contemporary with sailing boats), though it's also true that this approach to fishing has been considerably refined.

The sea is home to all manner of predatory hunters. Big fish eat small fish. This is a fact that could be proved geometrically using the same method that Spinoza used to demonstrate his theorems. Watching a pod of dolphins following a shoal of anchovies or sardines for hour after hour isn't what you'd call an edifying spectacle, even if it is an unforgettable sight. Watching a family of dentexes in mad pursuit of a string of sand smelt, driving them into the cul-de-sac of a bay is a similar spectacle.

Making the most of this instinct, anglers attach a feather to a line, conceal a hook and let it run through the sea. Sometimes, instead of a feather, they use a spoon that spins when pulled through the water, creating the impression of a swimming fish, or a small tin fish that gives a similar effect. These ploys are now efficiently manufactured. Then there is trolling: a line with a feather that hides the hook; previously, it was pulled from a sailing or rowing boat, profiting from a favorable wind. This kind of fishing is now much more productive because a motor-powered boat can give the line a steadier speed. The dragline shouldn't be too loose or too tense; it should give the fake fish a realistic speed. The result is that by dint of the predatory nature of fish that we've mentioned, when a fish sees the fake fish speeding through its waters, it pursues it, devours it and is hooked.

The key to this kind of fishing is to ensure that you pull the line through suitable places. You will catch sea bass by the edge of a beach; dentexes or white bream near a reef or underground rock, in an underwater strait, in an area of guaranteed nourishment. You must know how to pull the lure through the middle of the water and avoid dragging it along the seabed, and that requires someone expert on the rudder who knows the lay of the land. If lines catch on rocks, all will inevitably be lost.

This method will give the fisherman an immediate reaction if he is patient enough to hold the line. That's not usually the case, and he often ties the line to a handle or oarlock, sometimes attaching a small bell to signal a bite. I don't mean to say that it's not exciting to hear the bell ring; however, if you don't keep hold of the line, you miss out on those strong tugs. Once the prey has bitten, you must be able to control the line, allowing it to slacken and pull so the fish tires and can be landed. At the end you should have the landing net poised.

And that's the system of fishing with a hook without bait, the success of which is based on the predatory instincts of the fish themselves.

In Fornells I always thought that fish caught on a kite line or in a wicker creel – rainbow wrasse and rosefish – are infinitely subtler on the palate than sea bream, big walleye, picarel and turbot. Those fish have wonderful colors. A painter could never replicate their obsessively eye-catching variety. They are excellent in soup or fried in the pan. Some think their juices make a better soup than swallowtail sea perch; they make subtler broth, but never as intense. The big-mouthed, brightly colored rosefish isn't as delicate as rainbow wrasse, and has a mass of bones that makes it quite unapproachable. But by the sea, in the morning, at breakfast time, one is so hungry!

When October comes, people fish using a *xarambec* – which is a rather more intricate kite line – with giant sea snails or slugs caught in dragnets as bait to hook axillary and green wrasses. These fish have fascinating colors and, considering their size, are more sumptuous than the smaller fish we mentioned previously: axillary wrasses are a velvety deep blue and green wrasses are lighter, the color of a freckled brick. They should be eaten fried in good olive oil, leaving the skin pink, toasted and *croustillant*. This word "*croustillant*" hardly seems adequate. It is used to suggest the most exquisite heights that can be reached by a fish that is roasted or cooked on a spit. Now people think that frying fish is something anyone can do. But frying fish is a difficult art and very few have the right touch. A fish that is fried properly is one that preserves tender, succulent, delicate flesh under pink, toasted, *croustillant* skin. Few people can find that point and most serve up almost raw or completely burnt and dry fish. And that's what I want to stress: the great challenge of fried fish is the same as that posed by grilled lamb's leg or shoulder.

The sardine is the best of the blue fish. In spring, when it's plump and oozing fat, it is one of the best fish in the sea, provided you don't have to eat it every day, of course. The best times to eat sardine are at breakfast when they're freshly caught and in the evening, as a second supper, when caught late at night. Freshness is the key to this fish: if it's been kept in ice, it inevitably loses flavor. Moreover, even though fresh, a sardine changes its flavor in proportion to the distance from the sea one is eating it. By the water's edge it has all the delicious taste and virtues possible. Three miles inland it almost keeps up; by seven it is not what it was at source. All things being equal, the best sardines are eaten by the sea, grilled on embers and not gutted. That is the eternal, ancient way to prepare this blue fish. It is crucial to know when the flame is just right: sardines that are too dry or too smoked are worthless; the skin should be cooked and the flesh white and never bloody, so the skin easily comes away from the flesh: that perhaps is the perfect moment.

Could anything be tastier in spring than a plate of grilled sardines? Fat, fresh and full of life. . . the oil gleaming with mute intensity on scales seared by flames. The light creates small glittering pinpoints on the bluey scales, like a swarm of fireflies. You can eat a lot: one leads to another. This nourishment sparks an intense stream of feeling in my body. Sardines make me experience a liquid flow of emotion. Feelings and effusions of goodness, love of justice and humanity. And beauty, of course. Fortunately, these feelings tend to be abstract and that renders them quite innocuous. This reaction on my part is so predictable I've sometimes wondered whether Celtic states of emotional, poetic density aren't down to the important role sardines play in their diet.

Other blue fish: anchovy, mackerel, chad and horse mackerel. In Fornells, the myth reigned that Cadaqués anchovies preserved in olive oil were something exquisite and unrivaled. I would later verify the truth in the myth of those remote anchovies. Big common mackerel is richer than the smaller varieties commonly known as *quintos*. The same thing occurs with mackerel as with sardines, though more intensely: they are excellent one day, especially when cut open, with garlic and parsley, but better to space them out than repeat. All blue fish are a bit stodgy, and if they are to maintain their standing, they shouldn't be visited too frequently. In any case, a mackerel broth in the early morning, when the fish have been freshly caught, is excellent. Scad and horse mackerel are inferior blue fish.

People who've been to France praise to the skies *maquereaux au vin blanc*. Our cuisine is still primitive with regard to fish and hasn't managed to raise the tone of mackerel. Anyway, that French dish is apparently the highest degree of perfection a fillet of blue fish can attain. Here, anchovies are never eaten fresh, always tinned or bottled.

Contrary to what many think, the bogue isn't a blue fish. It is a rock fish that's caught with a bogue net and creel near underwater rocks at a reasonable depth. It is a skinny fish best eaten grilled just after it's been caught, served with a strong vinaigrette. The sand smelt is a small fish that eats the vegetation along the shore and has a slightly bitter flavor, the bitter taste of sunny pastures. The dentex, which hunts sand smelt, consumes them nonstop, encircling them in coastal hollows, where they can be caught by making a din from your boat, with a cast net, in a rather crude, Tartarin-style of fishing.

Sometimes, in winter, nature becomes quite providential with impoverished folk who try their hand with a seine. In the theological system of the world, this must be the origin of the rather average kind of fish – bogues and small rays – that are caught with a seine. In any case, when you've not eaten ray for some time, fried in the pan, with an endive salad, it makes a very pleasant dish. Conversely, sand eels are always delicious. They are a very small serpentine fish, long, thin, streaked with blue, with eyes that bulge out like the eye of a needle. A big fry up of crispy sand eels is one of the finest dishes you can eat along our shoreline.

Of course, everything I've said about fish is up for discussion: I'm not pretending it's gospel. They are mere personal opinions that sometimes chimed, sometimes dissented, with opinions generally voiced in Fornells at the time. While I'm at it, I should say that disagreement was more common than not. In some areas, there was always obvious unanimity. For example, as regards groupers. And rock mussels as well. We reckoned local rock mussels were first rate, unrivaled. We knew that rice with mussels, snails and limpets could never go wrong, was always a safe bet. When we are certain of something, we are happier. Mussels from Cape Creus, the Torroella coast, Begur shoreline and the Formigues Islands, you are a blessing from God. Now that human might and the general disarray have almost wiped you out, I am pleased to remember you in a melancholy mood as one of the tastiest dishes of my youth! In my view, limpets don't have the same quality as mussels: they are much inferior and taste rather insipid. Sea urchins caught in the January low tides, eaten with bread and red wine, are loved by some and loathed by others. In my book, their intrinsic sweetness makes them uninteresting and tasteless.

All these Fornells debates generally refer to fish caught by anglers known as landlubbers, those who work close to terra firma. Issues around fish caught by fishing smacks – people still used smacks at the time – in more remote areas, in winter, weren't the subject of our conversations. The odd old fisherman who had sailed in those boats would talk of monkfish garnished with a few potatoes as something spectacular. I did notice, however, that fishermen had a different diet in winter and summer. Obviously, it is the same cuisine, but in winter they always add a spoonful or two of aioli to fish stews and broth, which enhances the flavor and makes your body euphoric and your throat thirsty. Wine increases the euphoria, and all that creates a state of mind to withstand the cold.

The first days of June. Now is the time to go and enjoy some relaxed fishing. Yes, that's what's new: *relaxed* fishing. In this country, this month is the best month to live by the seaside and enjoy the delights of its murky mysteries. Becalmed seas and gentle winds are traditionally long and persistent in the summer months. The water is transparent, the immediate seabed visible and the sea's texture flecked with wonderful, soft tints. It's as if nature has grown tired of the contrasts and inconstancies of spring, and enters a period of comforting convalescence. The sun begins to warm, the light to dazzle; the body finds everything slightly disturbing. Wintry rigors give way to expansion. Everything takes on a sheen, a pertness – wants to affirm itself – in the fleeting vagaries of life on land. Not yet overwhelmed by summer's oppressive heat, each day, swept by long, gentle winds, moves like a woman in love: like a series of transfigurations. Moonlit nights – the light of the moon on white walls glimpsed between olive trees – have a mysterious charm that sometimes seems secretive and sometimes, depending on your state of mind, incomparably uplifting and noble. Dark nights, under twinkling stars, vanish into the luminous blue. Then comes the heat and a thirsty yellow drapes the earth.

Now, the life of the sea is exciting in these summer months. It is the moment when fish come close to the shore to lay their eggs in clean, sunny, warm waters. The water is filled with dense life. It thickens with tiny beings and glows with phosphorescence at night. It is the moment when fish are in heat.

Lots of ploys have erotic origins and obey the implacably universal need to self-perpetuate, to which fish, like all live beings, are subject.

Like many animals, fish are sensitive to color. Farmers put blotches of white on their vines because they know that rabbits are scared by that color and instantly run off. That's how they save the green tendrils on their vines and the early grapes.

If you drag a white cloth through an area of shallow water, you'll see how octopuses – if there are any about – will wildly throw themselves on it, clutching with their sinister tentacles. Before they can let go of the cloth, they are so blinded by their frenzy they are easily caught. Squid are caught with the infantile lure of a snagline. The lure is a piece of shiny lead studded with nails. You keep it oscillating from the surface downward and the squid embraces the nails, covering the lure with its desperate body. There's a sharp tug on the line and the fisherman simply has to pull up the line quickly. The faster he does so, the deeper the lure's metal points will sink into the squid.

There have been interminable arguments about the edible qualities of squid. They generally live in beds of seaweed or sandbanks and are very sedentary; there are areas of the sea where you will infallibly catch squid. Be that as it may, these creatures have become important to life as we know it and to the menus of inland taverns. Some people think that a plate of fried squid is delicious. For people who care about smell, squid have the advantage of barely carrying a scent. However rubbery, squid can be improved by being stuffed. The best stuffing is minced pork. We should be grateful for the opportunities offered by a squid's empty pouches. Some eat squid in its ink and even octopus with potatoes, when the going's hard, after beating its flesh with branches to soften it up. These are dishes that must be seen as a last resort. Nature was so enthused by the act of placing squid in the sea that it created an imitation: the larger, wine-colored common squid. The common squid has a tendency to displace the better smaller squid from markets and tables for the same reason that good money is chased away by bad. On the other hand, young squid, like young octopus, with a good sauce (which requires patience to make) constitutes a delicious dish. The key lies in establishing a perfect osmosis between fish and sauce.

Both young squid and octopuses are highly sensitive to light and are fished in the summer, almost by chance, as they gather under the lights from longboats. These small beasts, especially in shallow waters, are dazzled by the incandescent blues of the fumes from the petrol and swarm to the surface in a daze. Modern theories in marine biology give a lot of importance to light in the lives of fish. I have only an amateur's experience, but I also believe in the importance of light not only in the lives of fish but in all manner of lives. The attraction humans feel toward the light leads them to agglomerate in big cities with their bright lights. So then, there are two extremes: young squid and octopus are delicious. The rubber chewed on in taverns is common squid, the poor relative of the squid family; true squid should always be eaten stuffed... naturally, if the stuffing is of a high quality.

When it was this time of year and there was talk in Fornells of the need to eat a modest rice dish, the problem was sometimes quickly resolved. Cuttlefish give rice a pleasant taste. They're huge, shapeless, monstrous animals, as stupid as squid, if not more so. They usually stay on the benthic platform. To defend itself, the cuttlefish has an orifice on what we might call its forehead that spurts out a liquid aimed at blinding any adversary. Squid do likewise with the dark ink they pour out, which turns the water murky and facilitates escape. But squid clearly occupy a higher rung on the biological ladder: they defend themselves with a smokescreen, like a modern army unit, and cuttlefish, with a spurt of clear, crystalline water. Its short legs hang down like the arms of the war wounded. Its roundish shape makes one think it is a squid manqué. However, it does make a tasty rice dish. End of argument.

When the weather is placid as now, you take a female cuttlefish, put it on the end of a piece of string and slowly drag it from a skiff along beach areas of sand and seaweed at a depth of no more than two or three yards. The female must be alive and the boat's speed must move languidly to create the illusion that the animal has freedom of movement. And suddenly the show will begin: a male cuttlefish emerges from a thick forest of seaweed, swims above the ridge of an underwater dune, out of a rocky grotto, and frantically embraces the female cuttlefish, blinded by the most mindless of passions. The first day one sees such theater, one is so astonished by such a display of amorous appetite in nature that one almost forget to pull on the string. But as one becomes accustomed to the sight – as one's experience of life deepens – the prospect of that plate of juicy rice quickly displaces any surprise or respect one might feel toward the mysteries of the cosmos. In brief, when one registers that the female cuttlefish has completely disappeared beneath the male, one quickly pulls the string and the male is easily caught. Then one throws the female back in and repeats the operation. There is often competition. It's really infantile. It really couldn't be more so. Eventually, any fisherman endowed with a sense of responsibility tires of such manipulation: he begins to feel he is living, like other beings located on a higher rung of the biological ladder, off a real female. . . however much it may be a female cuttlefish.

Something very similar happens with lobsters: if you are lucky and a female lobster enters your creel, you can be sure that all the male lobsters in the vicinity will pile in through the hole. That's how you get the best hauls of these crustaceans. That was how we came to have a notorious problem in Fornells – since the sea was full of these beasts – and it was profoundly worrying: the problem of the longevity of lobsters in relation to their reproductive energy. The idea was abroad that a lobster weighing four hundred grams had reached a venerable, quite biblical age: four score years. That opinion is based on tradition; on the fact that some macaronic books state, a belief that fishermen hold, that lobsters grow only at the moment they shed their shells, something they do once a year. When they shed them, the crustaceans are left in their shirt, a short, pink-white shirt covered in a layer of sticky, viscous matter. If all that was true, the generative powers of a lobster would last for years, and it would imply a protracted youth. We would be in the presence of a really fortunate creature. However, in my opinion – without committing myself at all – lobsters don't live so long. The idea that their shells are fixed and their bodies are variable has no basis in reality. They grow quickly. The struggle to survive in the sea is hard and predators are everywhere. Mutual consumption is everywhere in the sea, but that is why there is so much food on offer. Granted, fish are voracious. If they didn't have that continuous obsession, they wouldn't fall so easily into the simple traps set in the same places. But that obsession with food ensures reproduction and that abundant first course of ours. Lobsters live as long as the struggle allows in their environment: a few years. The issue is that, as these animals aren't registered and look so alike, we mistake the children for their parents.

There were two or three noteworthy trident fishermen in Fornells. When darkness fell on calm days, they'd rig a light up at the back of their skiff and go out to do their reconnaissance along the coast. One man rowed slowly and silently, merely dipping the oars in the water. Another man, trident at the ready, leaning over the boat's side, surveyed the illuminated seabed. The craft would skim the coast, enter caverns and most out-of-the-way corners, the light fantastically streaking the crags and pines that grew between rocks near the water. The floor of the sea was visible through the transparent mass of water.

The light revealed small static underwater seascapes: beds of sand bedecked with tiny reddish dunes, bushes of shimmering seaweed, mysterious hollows, rocks covered in slimy moss, black, hirsute sea urchins, greenish limpets, bald crabs and mineral deposits. The fisherman went after one fish or another that was blissfully asleep – or at least immobile on the ground – in one corner or another of that seascape. Sometimes his body could be seen above the sand bed or between two rocks in a tiny opening; often only part of his body, as the other was hidden by a clump of seaweed or the shadows from a grotto. The presence of the light didn't usually scare off the fish; rather, the light seemed to coax and hypnotize it.

Then, the moment came in the deepest silence to throw the *fitora* at the sleepy, motionless prey. The *fitora* is a trident that has been adapted. A trident can have three prongs; a *fitora* can have more or less. The prongs are on a long handle, a four- or five-yard-long pole, which can be lengthened – if the prey is farther down – by a rope attached to the handle. The fisherman grasped the handle in both hands and, standing up in the skiff, sent the trident hurtling at the fish's body, throwing it forcefully, as if it were a javelin. You have to take into account errors caused by refraction in the water and that's why you must have had lots of practice. Sometimes it went wrong, but if the fish was hit, then came the second step, the moment to be ferocious. Gritting his teeth, the fisherman finished off his prey by putting all his weight on the trident so the prongs penetrated its flesh. Then he hoisted the trident aboard as the writhing fish convulsed frenziedly and lashed its tail.

If that maneuver were carried out in the light of day, you can be sure that the hurling of the trident – *fitora* or *trall* – would have led to one or more sculptured poses: an Apollonian moment with great artistic potential. However, luckily or not, it is a night operation, helped by darkness, in places where access isn't easy. . .

Naturalists, collaborating with individuals involved in the agrarian economy, have classified birds according to the benefits those delightful creatures bring to agriculture. Some are very positive, in the sense that they destroy lots of parasites; others don't destroy them, but their presence means that more parasites are devoured; others keep a balance between what they produce and what they destroy.

Classifying fish according to their quality on the palate – one more way of being generally useful – is much harder than classifying birds. Issues of personal taste are thorny. Firstly, because lots of people have never thought seriously about such matters, and many others have thought about them far too much and they can never agree, even with those who live next door. In the bland language of the schoolroom, it is often said that fish have their merits and their defects and the best are those whose merits outweigh their defects. But what exactly are these merits and defects? Establishing that: there lies the rub.

In my humble opinion, the best fish in our seas, in the Mediterranean, is what we call a "*corball*" in Catalan. It's what naturalists call the black corvina, a blackish, long, broad fish with bluish tinges, that is fished most in the cherry season – May and June. It can be fished throughout the year, but that's the best time – "cherry time, corvina time" as they say in Menorca. They can be fished by line and hook or with a three-net trawl. When it is put on the table, however it's been prepared – roasted or grilled – not only does corvina not give off the smell that other fish usually do, particularly if they come by the dozen, but they hardly smell of fish at all. Everybody knows what I mean by a fishy smell; it's the sensation of this particular flavor in the mouth, which is rarely pleasant, that's why so few people really like fish. The fish in these waters that barely produces that taste or odor is the corvina, and that's why I place it at the top of my list. My modest criterion is that a fish that hardly tastes of fish is impossible to beat.

Second in my classification would come the sea bass, also called "*loup de mer*" in the south of France, Italy and the north of Catalonia. And I'd put it there for the same reason I argued for the corvina, because it is not as "fishy" as other fish, although more so than the corvina. On the other hand, there are many kinds of sea bass and it is one of the fish that fall foul of lodging houses. So just as there is only one corvina, the good sort, there are many sorts of sea bass, and those with bland, stringy flesh are poor quality. Besides, the sea bass is a wily, cunning fish that is hard to catch, particularly in clean, flowing waters with readily available, healthy food. The sea bass with a soft, muddy, heavy taste that inhabits stagnant or murky water is almost worthless. The sea bass whose habitat is flowing water, the rocky coastline and places with good pastures does live large in my ideal league of delectable creatures.

I would put third the red scorpionfish, or hogfish on the north coast, or the fatter variety found on the south coast called "hen" on account of its color. The countless varieties of scorpionfish, of diverse colors, that live on our rocky coast are inedible because they are so bony. They are malign, monstrous fish. Conversely, they are excellent in a broth and, once boiled, produce broth for wonderful soup. What's strange about the vast family of scorpionfish, which are often of such poor quality and which possess venomous sharp ridges that can leave nasty cuts, is that there is an excellent subset with few bones and exquisite flesh. The horrifying monstrous head, bulging eyes and incandescent red color conceal one of the best fish in these seas, although on the surface it seems only good to be painted. The hogfish is very unfishy and that's the key.

My number four would be the grouper, a fierce, sedentary loner that usually inhabits the same rocky lairs and hollows. It is a powerful fish, with strong colors, a gilded black, splashed with yellow, that seems phosphorescent when it swims. A grouper head makes a fantastic rice dish; it gives real substance to soup. Grilled or roasted, it is succulent. The strange Spanish rhyme "De la mar el mero y de la tierra el carnero" – "From the sea the grouper, from the land, the ram" – is based purely on the rhyme, on the sound. The grouper isn't the best fish and mutton isn't the best meat. Who could ever compare lamb to ox, beef or some kinds of game? In fact, and always respecting their different traits, sea bass, wrasse and grouper should perhaps be placed at the same level. Of the three, the grouper is the one with the toughest exterior.

In Fornells they said that there are five kinds of mullet. And it is quite true. In any case, I'd definitely put mullet fifth in my listing. You can say the same about mullet or "*roger*" ("*moll*" on the west coast and in Barcelona) as we said about sea bass. It dislikes still or murky water, sandy or seaweedy beds, and thrives in flowing, clear waters with a strong current. Small, pale mullet that go in swarms are usually caught by trawlers dragging their nets over sandy seabeds and are next to worthless. Conversely, fat red mullet with a firm flesh under firm skin is really tasty, especially with a touch of light vinaigrette. It is, however, much fishier than the fish we have previously mentioned.

The Atlantic is the sea for sole. Atlantic sole is big, fine and thick. Mediterranean sole is smaller and can't be compared in terms of size. Nevertheless, strangely enough, Mediterranean sole can be very tasty – even as tasty as Atlantic sole. When seasoned in the northern

French style, it is excellent. It's thinking in this vein that I'd place this fish sixth: objectivity demands that. Besides, it's a fish that's not very fishy, which is important.

In my modest opinion, these six fish constitute the lead group produced by this sea in terms of taste. In any case, I think that my criterion, by which the best fish is the one with the least taste, shouldn't be dismissed. The fact that all can be eaten, to their advantage, with the simplest preparation – grilled – speaks in their favor. They resist the dry heat from the embers, and, indeed, improve as a result.

The fish that come in their wake – common bream, sea bream, white bream and dentex – are located on that frontier where qualities are balanced out by defects, and consequently, it is always best to prepare them with a sauce or garlic, onion and parsley, to improve their level. Cuisine, the art of transforming one thing into another, often at a higher level, must be the most suitable in these cases. There is no doubt whatsoever that simplest is best, but that is only true when the fish is at the highest level. The fish in the group we have described benefit from the most elemental preparation.

Naturally, there are other fish that taste delicious: grilled sardine, when it's big and juicy, is unrivaled. In the pea season, a conger eel is an exceptional item. A fry up of sand eels is hard to beat. However, the quality of these fish is limited to particular times of year, especially spring. Mackerel with garlic and parsley, what more could you ask for? The truth is that when the blue fish's moment has passed, it's best left alone. They enjoy a wonderful moment and then fall by the wayside.

So this is my Fornells roll call of fish. It was the one that sparked the least argument. I wouldn't dare to claim it is a definitive list or champion it dogmatically. It is a list produced as a result of the experience of individuals who more or less know what they are about – the list could, of course, be challenged in terms of personal taste rather than from any general perspective.

Simple, modest, unconventional and straight talking, the people of Fornells would finish their long discussions of fish and the best way to cook them with a single, inevitable conclusion that someone or other would utter: "All in all, the best fish in the sea will always be meat."

People inland love fish. Fishermen and maritime folk in general prefer meat, and the meat dish they like best is beef stew with green peas. They also love sweetmeats: anything sweet and sugary.

"I could live on beef stew with peas, cream sponges and strong wine. . ." I once heard a fisherman exclaim emphatically.

That's not as farfetched as it seems.

CORAL AND CORAL DIVERS

As a child, like everyone of my age in my part of the world, I first heard about the coral business as if it were a mythical activity linked to a love of adventure and the fascinating freedom of a seafarer's life. The ancient substrata buried deep in the national consciousness has always held within it a maritime perspective. The presence of the sea in our forebears' memory is still deeply felt today, and most intensely in the countryside . Even so, this memory is beginning to fade among people along the coast. When Catalans were able to work out at sea in the past, pursuing that spirit of adventure and fabled dream, their role was rather modest. When it came to involve sailing without the old freedoms and subject to the new factory regulations, Catalans abandoned ship. In our collective life today, the sea doesn't carry the slightest weight or have any importance – except in summer when people go for a swim. Catalonia is no longer a country with any real relationship to the sea and has become a country of earthbound, sedentary, prickly folk. The last vestige of this part of our past are the soporific snipe regattas.

Senyor F.S.'s father, whom we all knew as the old Cardinal, a fat, ruddy, sarcastic fellow, who could be very pro-church and very pro-usury, owned a bakery in Plaça Nova and was himself tied up in the coral trade. Many said that the Cardinal made most of his money through that line of business. It could be that legend prompted such talk, as legends can sometimes outlast the truth. When Senyor F. S. was appointed the Cardinal banker in Palafrugell after his father died, he had to declare himself bankrupt. This news shocked large swaths of the less educated in town. Susceptible to legends, they couldn't understand how a fortune made from coral could vanish so quickly.

Some well-known families were purchasers of coral from the small reefs on our coast whose boundaries are Cape Béar at the entrance to Port-Vendres and Cape Sant Sebastià – the Formigues Islands, to be precise. The Ponts of Cadaqués; the Forgases of Begur; the Elieses of L'Estartit; the Sunyers of Port de la Selva; the Alberts of L'Escala; possibly the Riberas of Palamós, who were always very involved in trade with Italy – each of these families bought and exported coral. Port-Vendres was another very important center for the trade – perhaps the most important.

The legendary aura surrounding the coral trade has its origins in a really sensational fact – that at its peak people paid an ounce of gold for an ounce of top-quality coral. People today are astonished that such a derisory amount – an ounce of coral is the smallest of handfuls – of a substance that later lost most of its value could command such a fantastic price. An ounce of gold! An ounce of coral for an ounce of gold – for sixteen gold duros! It beggars belief. When I was a child, an ounce of gold could buy you a fine working animal – a young mare or a five-year-old horse.

We should perhaps set aside our astonishment and find a plausible explanation for this situation. It's crucial to try and shed light on the enigma. It is hard to study this country's real history, the things that have happened, the factors that have stirred people's passions – even the most basic – because there is a dearth of case studies that could help us grasp the general situation. If we had access to the accounts or correspondence of one of those families involved in the coral trade, we might be able to clear up this peculiarity. But families in our country generally bring nothing at all to our historiography.

If a tiny handful of coral came to be worth an ounce of gold, it was down to a series of reasons.

In the first place, coral has always been a rare substance. Good, ox-blood-red coral is found only in the western Mediterranean and only in very few areas on the sea's perimeter. Firstly, along the coast of historic Catalonia* between Cape Béar and the Formigues Islands. Coral is nonexistent beyond those rocks as far as Gibraltar, and beyond there, to the Portuguese coast. It can also be found on the north coast of Majorca, from Sóller to Cape Formentor, but apart from a small space around the Sant Vicenç – the Gorg Blau inlet sung by Costa i Llobera and painted by Joaquim Mir – the coral growing on the north coast is poor quality: it is coral eaten away and damaged by voracious microbes. There is an area of coral on the French coast east

---

* The remains of the medieval principality of Catalonia were split up by the Treaty of the Pyrenees, which was signed on 7 November 1659 to end the war that had raged between France and Spain from 1635 to 1659. France was ceded the Roussillon with Perpignan and a new border was established at the Pyrenees. Catalan continues to be spoken in "northern" Catalonia.

of the Rhône estuary and east of the Gulf of Saint-Tropez, way past Esterel. The Italians have coral on the west coast of Sardinia and in an area between Livorno and Civitavecchia – as far as Santa Marinella to be precise. Corsica, the Tyrrhenian islands, Sicily and the Adriatic are completely barren in terms of coral. Not a gram of coral has been discovered beyond the Messina lighthouse – in fact, no known coral exists along the Greek coast or in the sea around the Greek islands. There is one last area: the Barbary Coast, the stretches facing Italy as well France: Tripoli, Tunis and Algiers. In the Red Sea, white coral, which is worthless, creates reefs that have the same formation as those in the tropics, Pacific or Caribbean. They produce very little coral for making jewelry. So that's all there is. Coral-growing areas are few and far between, and some – like those along the French coast – have been practically exhausted.

So there is scant raw material and for centuries the small portion of coral gathered by ancient coral-fishing devices just about supplied the needs of the market. Coral always had an outlet as a luxury item. It was considered decorative and fashionable and was only within the reach of wealthy people – aristocrats, courtiers and clerical dignitaries. Ancient Mediterranean poetry – Catalan, Provençal or Italian – contains numerous allusions to coral as a quality good, the equivalent of a luxury jewel, for the most sophisticated decorative ends.

Then all of a sudden there was a fantastic increase in the demand for coral. As soon as the bourgeoisie began to take ownership of property and goods belonging to the Church and the aristocracy, its first move was to imitate the dying class: their style, their way of life and, naturally, their jewelry. That's when nascent capitalism invents wealth creation that can be hidden and external signs of wealth begin to burgeon. Jewelry is an ancient, distinguished phenomenon;

jewelry as a sumptuous sign of riches is the creation of the bourgeoisie. In ancient family inventories, one finds coral by the side of gold and precious stones but given an inferior ranking. Much inferior, to be sure, but it's always there.

The establishment of free trade, the onset of industrialization and consequent destruction of the simplicity of the artisan and guild life, created a working class that had a degree of acquisitive power and sufficient freedom of movement to increase it. The working class was imbued with the same tendencies as the bourgeoisie. Just as the bourgeoisie had displayed a style similar to the defeated traditional classes, the working class felt the same love of luxury and the same drive to imitate, but as the petty bourgeoisie and working classes on the rise couldn't aspire to buy gold, diamonds, pearls or amethysts, they bought coral jewels: bracelets, necklaces, earrings, crosses, broaches and rings. Coral became one of the jewels of the poor, which explains the sudden surge in demand and the fantastic prices obtained. When trinkets make their appearance next to real jewels, the value of coral rockets.

It would be inaccurate to say that the growth in demand didn't lead to an increase in what the market offered. When the volume of buyers grows, the old device for coral extraction – *la coralera* – is replaced by the first attempts at submarine exploration and gathering, carried out by divers wearing deep-sea diving suits. Production increased but never enough to satisfy the market. Prices inevitably soared. The coral that is highly prized continues to be rare. The sea is full of coral: white coral can be found in abundance; it forms the atolls in tropical seas, but those polyps have never been valued or valuable. The only coral with a high price is red coral – *corallium rubrum* – which is found only in the areas of the Mediterranean we have mentioned and in the tiniest amounts in the Red Sea. Within the vast range of existing corals, the families of red coral are rare, which explains why the appearance of trinketry increased coral's value at an astonishing rate.

Conversely, there are many degrees of quality of red coral. Coral that has been eaten away by microbes has little value. Average, thin, basic coral is worth slightly more. Thick, whole coral with hints of ox-blood red and angelic pink – as coral gatherers say, with pink adolescent cheeks in mind – is what caused coral values to soar.

As well as the clientele we might describe as "Christian," customers from more exotic climes have always existed. In Arabia they bury their dead with coral necklaces. Hindus and the indigenous peoples of Australia hold it in high esteem. The peoples of the Orient, generally speaking, use it to decorate their clothes, abodes and weapons. It was an object of exchange used to negotiate with the caravans that came from the depths of Asia to the markets of the eastern Mediterranean. When the ports of China and Japan were opened to trade with Europe, it was discovered that wealthy and sentimentally inclined Chinese and Japanese placed wreaths of coral on the tombs of their ancestors to commemorate them. When European merchants offered them red coral from the Mediterranean to make these wreaths they were taken aback. Their astonishment translated into excellent sales. Wreaths of flowers last only a second on tombs, because even those flowers we call immortelles, in a leafy leap of the imagination, droop after one night. When those peoples from the East entered the "civilized" market and surrendered to its claim that the most expensive is the best and longest lasting, they decided that coral's evident eternity made their feelings toward their dead all the more durable.

All these considerations perhaps help to explain why, at a certain point in time, an ounce of coral came to cost an ounce of gold. When coral's value reached that level, it was quite natural for the lady or young woman bedecked with its subtle shades to think she was wearing proper jewels – or at the very least, that her coral was much more proper than the ugly tinkling tin trinkets now worn on avenues, side streets and squares.

Anchored in the small harbor of L'Estartit on an early September afternoon, we are settling down to eat lobster in the poop of a coraling boat. The Greek divers on board the small craft have invited me to their table to eat crustaceans they've caught by hand in one of the underwater caves of the Medes Islands, where they have been gathering coral. They are at the end of their campaign and about to return to the port of Cadaqués, where they will winter this year. The Greeks seem very happy: they've curled their hair finely, gleamingly so. They like to adapt to popular taste and stylize themselves by emphasizing the glamorous profile we all cherish of ourselves, presenting themselves in the guise of a photo taken by an arty photographer, a photo complete with skylight, art object and potted palm. With them is their Cadaqués crew, poor folk dressed poorly, rather melancholic but excellent company.

It's a magnificent autumn afternoon. The delicately filtered luminosity seems to bring things closer to one's eyes and underline their wealth of sophisticated shades. The placid, pale-blue sea seems to be relaxing, languid and voluptuous. Sunlight has lost its dazzling summer strength, and everything can be seen more exactly. At noon, Begur Castle stands out against the sky as does the white ribbon of the road winding obliquely down the steep landscape to Sa Riera Beach. The sand on Pals Beach covers a broad arc – at once slender and gentle. The sand is lightly toasted, a honeyed gold. The dark-green pine groves of Torre de Pals float above that gilded brush-stroke, and farther away, a silvery haze hangs over paddy fields and marshes. The foliage over the slow-flowing, haughty River Ter weaves a wall of greenery that autumn dashes with salt and pepper. The spire of Torroella's church soars above the trees. The blue buttresses of the ancient and sedate Gavarra mountains, with the white splash of the Angels hermitage on its peak, make up the horizon to the west. The arid Montgrí sierra, in contrast, is purple gray. A bright-red expanse of flatland extends above the long, white strip of houses that is L'Estartit. The warm, blue sky is high and pristine.

The cook is grilling the lobsters, and the aroma from their singed shells is a delicious presence in the fresh air that the sun's heat transforms into pure joy. I ask an old diver sitting next to me what he knows about coral. He says it is a peculiar stone that fattens and expands in response to the sea's mineral deposits. Another diver, Costas Contos, the craft's skipper, also getting on years, disagrees. The skipper's son, a tall, thin lad, blond and straight-backed, with a sharp eye and mustache, agrees with his father and says that coral isn't stone. He backs his claim with a few arguments.

"So what is coral then?" my neighbor asks. "Is it a plant?"

"No, it's not a plant."

"A plant. . . !" comments the sarcastic fellow from Cadaqués. "Don't rely on pruning the fresh sprouts from that plant this summer!"

"It's an animal!" said old Contos, with the gravitas conferred by his skipper status, folding his arms over his chest.

This clash of opinions immediately took me back to the ancient world. If the old diver had read at all, he could have recalled the wonderful mythological fable. But I think he'd read very little, because I'd only ever seen him with one book: a book on the winds of the Mediterranean and the best way to sail them. After Perseus killed the Gorgon, a monster that turned to stone everything that met her gaze, he went to wash his hands on the beach and threw the fabled animal's head into the sea. The blood from the Gorgon's head and Perseus's dirty hands turned to stone when it touched the water, though it preserved its original color. This petrified blood was coral.

The first diver was closer than the myths. He didn't believe, as did the ancient Greeks, that coral was the petrified blood of the Gorgon. He simply believed that it was an underwater stone, a compound of the salts of the sea. The other diver and his son were more advanced in history. In between those two opinions lay the one defended by Theophrastus and Pliny the naturalist who argued that coral was a plant.

In 1700, Tournefort, in a paper addressed to the Academy of Sciences in Paris, stated that the vegetable nature of coral couldn't be questioned. Confirming his conclusion, the renowned Réaumur maintained that corals were stony secretions produced by plants in the same way that seashells were stony secretions produced by animals. Réaumur was a man of the eighteenth century, which was in so many regards an enlightened century.

The collapse of piracy in the Mediterranean and the conquest of the North African coast by the French at the time of the Restoration coincided with the early enrichment of the bourgeoisie and the beginning of industrialization (and the increase in the size of the market) and allowed coral to be gathered and studied with relative tranquility. Those scrutinizing the coral then analyzed whether it was stone, plant or animal. They declared it to be an animal – to be precise, a cylindrical polyp in its oldest, mature parts and generally in a trihedral form in its newest areas, as a result of three branches spanning out around a common axis. Sometimes the angle is tetrahedral. If you examine a branch via a series of transversal cuts (the moment coral comes out of the water), you can observe a soft, vertical system of ducts surrounded by the hardest accretions. There is constant contact between the polyp and the system of deep ducts, which means that the calcareous branch can't be considered to be alien to the animal's nature. Now it would have been really pointless, pedantic and out of place to speak of such things to those men whose state of knowledge was so precise, fixed and unshakable.

The real nature of coral was discovered relatively few years ago, when the volume of trade, for the reasons mentioned, became considerable. Conversely, as I understand it, coral fishing is one of the oldest, most ancient activities off our coastline. Coral was sought in our seas especially throughout the Middle Ages. There is a stanza by Anselm Turmeda that goes:

Near the royal throne
all hewn
from a single piece of coral
and a majestic red. . .

There are innumerable references to coral, coral gatherers and the coral-catching device in medieval Catalan writing and official documents. There is a verb "*coralar*" for gathering coral and there was a lot of legislation around the activity. Verdaguer experienced the last years of the ancient manner of coral gathering, because in the final third of the last century coral was still collected in the same way as it had been since the time of Jaume I.

In his *Canigó*:

> *The coral gatherers of Begur*
> *fish coral from their barks...*

There is also mention of the Begur coral gatherers in the song about the coast:

> *In Begur live yokel bacanars*
> *who gather coral from La Brama...*

La Brama is an underwater mountain range that starts by Cape Begur and heads south, thus forming the so-called Fornells channel that all lobster catchers in my country know so well. The range forms a sharp angle with the coast, the vertex of which is the cape itself; its location is signaled by the name La Brama and the southwesterly facing cliff. The people of Begur – *begurencs*, whom we, their neighbors, dub *bacanars*, perhaps taking liberties – have fished coral around La Brama from time immemorial. Old local government documents are full of bans against foreign coral gatherers working in our waters, and those bans were predominately aimed at the Provençals who dominated the trade for centuries – though they yielded dominance to the Italians in the nineteenth century. One can say, then, that coral has been gathered along our shores for centuries, an area closed to the north by Cape Béar and the south by the Formigues Islands – that is, by the rocks and cliffs on the coast; don't look for coral in sandbanks or silt.

Coral grows in caves and underwater gullies, in crevices in rocks, in hollows, and it tends to flourish under what we might call shelves or eaves jutting out from rock formations. Generally, it grows from top to bottom, like stalactites. It requires a strong geological base, hard granite rock, pounded by currents in dark, shadowy places. The polyps embed themselves in areas of stone deposits crawling with bugs and dense underwater fauna. Growth is extremely slow. They don't thrive in stagnant water. Naturalists say that the polyps aren't hermaphroditic – that is, they are separate sexes that are fertilized by marine currents: the sea brings the male seed to the female cells, in the same way that the wind transports pollen from male stamens to certain plants. However, any reference whatsoever to such complex processes would distract us from the taste of those grilled lobsters, and I decide that the most sensible thing is to leave them in abeyance. It is a very tasty lunch enjoyed in the best of company and with the best of appetites.

For centuries coral was gathered using a device known as a *coralera*, made up of two short staves of good strong wood in the form of a Greek cross, tied together by an iron ring, with a large stone or lump of lead on top to give it the necessary weight to ensure it would sink. Nets were hung from the four ends of the staves; they were broad meshed at the top ends and formed a much finer meshed bag lower down.

Gatherers anchored their craft by the cliff and lowered the *coralera* by rope over the side, so that the device rubbed against the wall of rock in an attempt to break off coral embedded in the underwater crag. The four ends of the staves, in the form of a cross, broke off branches of coral, and pieces fell – when they fell – inside the net; sometimes the nets got entangled with branches of coral and detached them from their base; other times the current took the *coralera* into a shelf and that could be very productive. When the coral was gathered in the open sea, the lay of the land helped gatherers determine the whereabouts of the coral and the underwater geological strata they must ravage, and then they would throw in the *coralera* and seek the help of nature through powerful currents. In all cases, part of the coral broken off was caught in the bag created by the nets, though it was too primitive a device to salvage everything and a good amount fell onto the seabed.

It was really too clumsy a method to ensure the coral fishers exhausted any one location and too imprecise a means of exploring the reefs for them to be completely stripped bare. If the coral was thought to be within easy reach, a man would be lowered three or four fathoms down to help activate the *coralera* by pushing it as far as he could into the caves within the cliffs. This made the friction against the reef more effective and brought it closer to the coral. These deep-sea swimmers are still called "chest divers" by the Greeks. They dove down like sponge or pearl-oyster divers. They were strong swimmers with powerful lungs. But it was a crude, primitive method and brought profitable returns only because there was such an undeniable abundance of coral. That can be the only explanation since so much coral was lost to the seabed and so little was caught in the net.

The *coralera* was also dragged and rubbed against the line of submerged rocks, within the undulating subaquatic orography, pinpointed perfectly by the lay of the land. In our view, coastal fishers were much more familiar with the ups and downs of that submerged geology than with those of the real mountains they could see against the line of the horizon. It is very likely that the true discoverers of our coast come from an ancient coral-gathering tradition that poverty stubbornly preserved. Their geographical knowledge of an invisible geology, established by groping in the dark when maneuvering the *coralera*, allowed them to trawl, longline fish, use lobster pots and catch painted combers.

The *coralera* was a clumsy, heavy device to handle. If coral fishers didn't lead a dog's life for centuries, they didn't fall very short. The precipitous nature of underwater geography, the abundance of jutting shelves, rocky tailbones and peaks, meant the device often snagged on rocks. The small craft often had a pulley on deck to hoist up the *coralera*, but generally speaking it was of little use. It was hard to detach the device from rocks using purely mechanical means. It was an operation requiring strong arms and all the guile that comes with human sight. You had to use the strength of currents, call on past experience and a sensitive manual touch. It was long, exhausting, heavy toil – the staves weighed a lot – with no guarantee of positive results. A sudden change in the weather, wind or current might frustrate the operation. It would have to be abandoned. The rope would have to be cut, a cork buoy attached and the *coralera* left anchored where it was until the situation improved. That moment might or might not come – or come too late, given the archaic means people had on hand. I believe that hundreds, if not thousands, of *coraleras* have been lost on the subaquatic orography of our coast, an unbelievable number of wooden crosses the sea has destroyed leaving only the iron ring, lead piece or stone used to ensure immersion, objects that corrode more slowly. Perhaps today not even those vestiges of such forgotten efforts remain. The sea is an implacably corrosive cemetery, and a cemetery that remains unviolated.

The craft that specialized in coral fishing were small. It's perfectly natural for Verdaguer in *Canigó* to speak of small craft in relation to the coral fishers from Begur. . . Verdaguer had sailed in the transatlantic ships of his day, and he must have found everything in the sea to be tiny by the side of those huge hulks. The fact is they were really tiny. They were eleven *gúes* – that is, thirty-three hands, because the *gúa*, an old measure used for boats, a measure still in use when I was a child, represented three hands. These boats hoisted a lateen sail and were long and narrow, with gangways and bridged prows and poops.

The crew's berths were under the prow, and the wood and coal cooking stove next to the mast. Everything was squidgy, scant, uncomfortable and extremely hard – a real instrument of torture for those living on board. These craft used to carry four crew members and one ship's boy. The skippers of these coraling craft haven't left behind memoirs like the ones trawler skippers have written. With their black silk caps tilted at a rakish angle and a rather swaggering manner, trawler skippers were the aristocrats of the lateen sail. Their courage and willingness to take risks weren't in doubt, nor was their liking for tasty fish stews in winter, healthy shots of *roquill* and racy songs or their ability to find a café despite the weather or blowing wind. Coral-boat skippers were like furtive dolphins: landlubbers, stuck between reefs and underwater rocks, and indefatigable toilers. Theirs were heavy-duty labors. Trawling was a joy ride, but coral fishers risked their lives less and their shoulders were thicker skinned against the wind.

In some towns you can still find remains of ancient *coraleras*. The one drawn on page 512 of the third volume of the Borja Moll dictionary is a faithful depiction of that age-old device. It is a very clear, useful dictionary drawing:

As I was saying a moment ago, the *coralera* was a heavy, cumbersome tool. It clipped off the tops of branches of coral and caught only a fragment of the broken polyps, the youngest, softest and least valuable. The thickest, oldest, most compacted coral-bearing excrescence, what we might call the trunk of agglomerated polyps, was difficult to dislodge from the stone wall sustaining it. Obviously, it was possible for one of the stave ends to give the coup de grace to the basic membrane, to the body of coral. In that case, the arborescent creature might fall into the net or be lost forever on the seabed. Generally speaking, however, they collected only the thinnest, flimsiest outer branches, which were worth very little. Even so, if the trade in coral was not of much importance in the minds of gatherers, it was profitable for those who sold coral on an industrial scale.

At the end of the coraling campaign, the skippers of the small craft brought the unrefined coral to the towns where they were based – to Begur, L'Escala, Roses or Cadaqués – and their haul was auctioned in the market place like a catch of fish. Local traders bought the coral, and Italian buyers often appeared, which was not to the liking of local speculators. If the Italians didn't come, local traders would send the coral off, first to Marseille and then to Genoa. Later, the European center for the coral trade moved to Livorno, with a subcenter in Torre del Greco, in the Gulf of Naples, just as when Marseille was in control, there was a smaller hub in Port-Vendres. Today Livorno retains its dominance over the coral trade, and the most powerful buyers are based there.

Curiously, some of the industrialists in Catalan coastal towns involved in the cork trade were also active in the coral market. Branches of families from the Ampurdan still live in Marseille and Genoa, and coral was the original reason for their moving there. Livorno became the center for the trade after the Greeks and Italians visibly began to dominate the industry. Livorno was well located to receive coral from Italy, Sardinia, Catalonia and Provence, and it was a good point of call for the Greeks.

When demand for coral began to rocket, both buyers and local agents invested in the small coral-gathering boats. The brilliant heyday for coral gatherers were the years 1840–1900. In my country there are many reminders of that fact:

There are so many people
who don't mind giving
for a piece of coral
half a year's earnings. . . !

It was the era of coral jewels and coral similes in poetry. Verdaguer will write of coral lips and coral's various colors:

Lips are coral,
Cheeks rose. . .

The moment came when the demand for coral was so strong that local coral gatherers, backed by speculators who invested in their ramshackle barks, moved to other seas on a scale that seems quite beyond belief in the cold light of day. Those small craft worked close to land, by the rocks along the coast today known as the Costa Brava, even going out of the strict coraling area, past Béar and the Formigues, abreast of Cape Planes. If you have the experience to draw on, it is perfectly possible to get a grip on this coast and know it inch by inch.

And, at this juncture, I want to make a small aside that the context demands. The name "Costa Brava" given to these shores stuck rapidly. The title has been around only for a few days. It was first proposed in the dining room of the Paradís restaurant in Fornells, then owned by Don Bonaventura Sabater, by Don Ferran Agulló in the course of a lunch to celebrate an electoral victory. But, quite frankly, the adjective "*brava*" as applied to this coast has a small drawback that became obvious as soon as the importance of foreign tourism for the area grew: "*brava*" is untranslatable, and all the translations made into the different languages of Europe are inadequate, not to say fanciful. In French you can't say the Côte Brave, because that epithet in that language is used to describe the heroic actions of gendarmes and the military and cannot be applied to geographical locations. You can say *le brave caporal*, but not the Côte Brave. Shall we translate it as the Côte Fière? That sounds horrendous, gives one the shivers and is unacceptable. It's the same in English. Shall we dub the Costa Brava the Wild Coast – that is, the savage, untamed coast? It's excessive and imprecise. So what should this coast have been called? I believe the most appropriate name for these shores would have been the Costa del Coral. People will object that only part of the coast is coral bearing. They'd be right, but so what? The issue was to find a name that would be intriguing in every culture and interchangeable in every language, one that would have been profitable internationally and lent a touch of exoticism somewhere between the Pacific Ocean and the opera house, undoubtedly attracting tourists. After all, when a country wants to exploit its beauty spots financially, it has a perfect right to adopt the name it feels will be most effective.

Catalonian coral gatherers' travels to remote countries stem from ancient tradition. In the past, the old coral fishers of Catalonia – and this is a real, historical fact, not a myth generated by the lyrics of local choirs and written by old café hacks with only a smidgeon of musical talent – fished over hundreds and hundreds of miles away because the small craft they used received financial suppport from what today we would call the powers that be. They worked in Sardinia, Italy,

Provence, in every corner of the Mediterranean, because these were our seas.

In the course of the past century, at the peak of the industrializing of the merchandise, when the memories of past dreams had faded, those small coral-gathering craft went on the most amazing journeys. They were able to do so because they used long-distance sailing ships, which in the Mediterranean were generally merchant vessels. It would have impossible for small, thirty-three-hand craft to reach, by their own means, the Cape Verde islands (where they worked), the Civitavecchia coast (where L'Escala coral fishers traveled) and the coast of North Africa. They were tiny, frail, defenseless craft without bridges, and even if they had sailed in summer, in periods of becalmed seas, the voyage would have been too long, too unwieldy, and with crews who were too inexperienced to embark lightheartedly on such an adventure. So instead, the coral gatherers' minuscule boats were loaded onto larger vessels going to the Americas or distant Mediterranean ports, which deposited the coral gatherers along their routes in areas close to where they intended to work. That explains their presence in Cape Verde, among other places. If not, it would beggar belief that those derisory craft, crewed by men who knew practically nothing about sailing, could have reached such remote spots. Those seas were virgin, and anticipated earnings promised to be great: it was worth their while to leave home, especially when the voyage could be made without taking dangerous risks, and with all the guarantees of normal commercial trade.

Some of those campaigns in distant seas were highly profitable, as demonstrated by the existence in Begur of Carrer Vera, a street newly built with the fruits of coral campaigns in the second half of the last century and sheltered by the old castle from the mistral. It was a campaign conducted on the coast of North Africa that made the Begur coralers wealthy men. Other towns could provide examples of bourgeois architecture that originated in the coral trade. On the other hand, Begur at the time was also an important center for the cork business – much more so than nowadays – and the international, outward-looking mindset generated by that industry influenced the coral trade.

When it is coffee time, the sunny afternoon still seems to be warming up. In the afternoon silence, the presence of the houses of L'Estartit continues to be striking: a cart rattles along in the distance. The water's surface in the small port is as motionless as a mirror. The white, gelatinous umbrellas of jellyfish float two fathoms from the boat. Seated on the quayside, an angler looks to have dozed off, silhouetted with startling precision in the fresh air. A human figure sometimes walks by the white houses.

"A Greek from my homeland, the Dodecanese," says old Contos at that point, "played a role in the coral trade. His name was Constantine Papaoekonomos. He was a sponge fisher off North Africa, and one fine day arrived in Majorca ready to explore the potential for sponge fishing around the Balearic Islands. He had brought along a band of professional fishermen. At the time, the islands of the Dodecanese were the domain of the Ottoman Sublime Porte, so those men were officially Turkish nationals, though they were all one hundred percent Greek. They were strong, highly skilled deep-sea divers. A deep-sea sponge diver enters the sea holding a piece of smooth marble weighing twenty pounds. That stone helps him sink and reach a decent depth. When he lands on the sea floor where the sponges live, he puts the stone under his arm and uses his free hand to wrench out sponges. Sponges live on flat areas of the seabed and are easy to wrench out. A deep-sea diver can go down two hundred forty hands, stay underwater two or three minutes and bring to the surface three or four sponges. If the plants are good quality, two or three plunges are enough to bring in a good day's income. There are lots of good sponges on the Barbary Coast. The type known as *melati* – its Greek name – fetches a high price in Port Said.

"Papaoekonomos found poor quality specimens deep off the coast of Majorca, so-called elephant ear, which is used by printing machinery. In view of those poor findings, he moved his men and business to Ibiza, where they found better sponges, the so-called Venetian sponge, which is delicate and good for bathroom use. However, there was very little, and all in all, the campaign was a failure and the gangs of deep-sea divers returned to Greek and North African waters with the sheepish look of men who left home to earn money and came back with nothing.

"In the course of the campaign, Papaoekonomos wrote my father on the island of Symi, in the Dodecanese, lauding the Majorcan coasts as sponge paradises. I don't know if he was intending to trick him or was still confident that his expedition would be successful. The upshot was that my father arrived on those shores with his whole family, but must have realized immediately that prospects were minimal. He had no choice but to strike out for himself, which is just what he did.

"In the meantime, Papaoekonomos moved to Barcelona, where he entered into partnership with a Barcelonan by the name of Carrascal. Now that they had exhausted their search for sponges, they turned to coral. They came here, to L'Escala to be precise, from where they waged a very successful coral-gathering campaign along the

Torroella coast. They were responsible for the first use of a diving suit to fish coral. After so many centuries using *coraleras*, that was the first really important innovation.

"Diving suits produced excellent results and the old coral gatherers in L'Escala adopted this new procedure. They bought diving suits and the machines for injecting air. Extraordinarily, the crews of the coral craft refused to adopt the new method. On the other hand, a number of small farmers from the surrounding area – from Albons, Viladamat, Bellcaire, etc. – did opt to go down to the bottom of the sea wearing that monstrous attire. Such cheek had never been seen before. They knew absolutely nothing about the trade. They were people who worked on the land – farmworkers – the lowest of the low, according to sailors. They led the campaign quite blindly but earned money.

"Papaoekonomos and Carrascal liked living in the country. Carrascal married a girl reputed to be the prettiest girl in town at the time: her name was Marina. They became so well acquainted with the area that one day they appeared with a small steamboat, apparently to fish coral. It was absurd: that was no boat for maneuvering between the rocks on our coast. Scandalmongers said the steamboat was intended for wholesale smuggling – which is a smuggler's ideal set up. L'Escala boasts a long, admirable tradition of smuggling. Those foreigners – the Greek and the Barcelonan – tried to participate in the *genius loci*, to enter the most genuine local traditions. I don't know how their new business went. But the competition from local divers using diving suits certainly greatly annoyed them.

"At this point, my father had gotten established in Barcelona, worked for himself and set up a company sponsored by the royal family and peninsular grandees – the Marquis of Comillas, the Count of

Villar, etc. He explored the east coast as far as Cape Leucate looking for sponges but found none. By Leucate, he found a few dead,
rotting sponges. These seas don't breed sponges. Maybe because
they're too clean. The sponge is a plant whose alveoli are filled with
a rich fauna of insects and microbes. The alveoli of sponges along
our coast remain empty, and the sponges stay stiff and hard. Spong-
iness doesn't develop, as in the *melati* of the coast of North Africa.
This fact could trigger only one outcome: systematic coral gathering
by diving-suited divers, with *psikefalea*, as we say in Greek – which is
what my father decided to do with diving companies from the Greek
islands."

Three complete diving suits are drying on board the small craft.
Honestly, I find them quite alarming. It's a curious fact that diving
suits were first used in the Mediterranean at the beginning of the
industrialization of coral fishing, between 1830 and 1840. These
innovations developed alongside the aforementioned appearance
of the middle classes and the onset of industrialization. Everything
joins up. A diving suit comprises two parts: the helmet – that is the key
element, a tin sphere with a window to allow you to see out, attached
to which is the air-injection tube and the breathing valve – and plates,
also made of tin, attached to a rubber suit that covers the rest of the
body: the plates cover chest and back, and the rubber, belly, legs and
arms. The helmet is screwed to the suit as tightly as the screwing will
allow. A man inside that apparatus is transformed into a strange,
monstrous being, as if viscous shapes from the sea have been tamed
by mass production. However, there is one thing worse than a diver
dressed as a diver, and that is a deflated, flaccid, dead diving suit hung
to dry over the railings and gracious lines of a tiny craft. In the gentle
autumn afternoon light in the port of L'Escala, that sphere with its

turbid glass window, tin chest and languid, soft-rubber shape, at once wet and hard, is enough to make your hair stand on end.

That's why, when the diver, dressed like a synthetic octopus, sinks into the sea, you wish – quite inhumanely – never to see him again. The machine for injecting air starts up. Those small devices were simple enough but onerous to operate. You had to keep turning the wheel nonstop, and as the diver gained depth, turning the handle became ever more strenuous. At a specific point of pressure – triggered by the diver's depth – you had to activate the handle every minute. Those machines are now powered by small electrical motors, which can be controlled according to air requirements the diver signals by means of a guide rope.

When the diver is immersed, responsibility for his life is in the hands of the guide. The guide is the man who understands the language communicated by the diver via the rope joining him to the boat. The diver and the guide exchange an international – primitive, if intelligible – language. One touch – a pull – on the rope means: more air. One pull and short tug signal: bring me up. Two tugs: decrease pressure. Two pulls and short tugs: send down a hammer, etc. The guide must be alert. He can't daydream, because a good part of the success of the operation depends on him.

The diver carries a bag on his chest, where he puts the coral and objects he thinks worth collecting along with the fish he catches, if catching fish is at all feasible. If he does catch a fish, he must first kill it, because fish – so foolish when free, to the point of approaching any unusual presence they encounter – when trapped, will defend themselves. Carrying a live fish to the surface in a diver's bag would be a difficult feat.

A diver in a diving suit can work for half an hour at a depth of thirteen or fourteen fathoms. A fathom is about eight hands. Twelve fathoms is twenty yards. As the diver gradually sinks down, the pressure increases and the length of stay at any depth shrinks proportionately. This quick sketch gives some indication of the revolution the use of a diving suit represented in coral fishing compared to using *coraleras* or deep-sea divers.

Diving suits solved the coral gathering problem to such an extent that an area systematically explored by those divers became totally barren for years. Coral grows a centimeter every eighteen years. It is an animal that grows so slowly it would be impossible to breed – if anyone decided, at their own expense, to risk doing so.

As coral thrives in hollows, caverns, stony roofs and eaves, and tends to grow from top to bottom like stalactites, the problem is obvious enough: a diver must be able to reach cavern ceilings. If the hollows are low roofed, it's feasible to work standing; if they're too low, he must wriggle inside like a fish. However, caverns are sometimes high and inaccessible. In such situations, the diving suit solves the problem, because the diver can control at will the air pressure inside the suit. When the air inflates the suit it helps draw him back to the surface. An absence of air inevitably makes him go down. He can thus hang under the cavern vaults asking his guide for more air and working on his back under the ceiling, or on a level with the cavern by opening the air, or expiratory, valve. The diver activates this valve, located in the tin helmet, with his head. It's all about being skilled enough. It's part of the trade. In any case, I know few intellectual workers who can weave so delicately with their heads as those suited divers.

That expiratory valve is very useful, as we have just seen, but it has one drawback. The caverns and caves where divers work tend to be covered by a layer of mud left by sea squalls, a muddy silt that the air expelled by the valve stirs up, thus clouding the water. The diver's body movements agitate the mud even further, making the watery space where the diver must move and work cloudier still. This means the divers carry out the task of severing the coral with a suitable hammer from the ceilings of underwater caverns with poor visibility; in fact, they must grope their way, because the water becomes extremely murky. This phenomenon happens not only in the hollows in zones with light but also in those deeper down, more so in the latter, which aren't affected by squalls as much as by the action of currents. Of course, the latter offer a natural obstacle, their intrinsic lack of light. If divers nevertheless succeed in producing positive results, it is because as they grope around, intuition and experience help them orient themselves in the water; it's not infallible, but it's usually effective. They manage to explore pitch-black caves and water that is so churned up and dark where people not in the trade wouldn't be able to move, let alone work. A diver must orient himself before entering those dens, before the water has been stirred and the air expelled from the suit has disturbed the layers of mud. The clear waters allow him to locate coral and all the fish to be found in the area. In such places you can find lobsters and corvinas. The crustacean is one of the few sea animals that hide from the presence of a strange body, it slips into crevices in walls and shelves in rocks. But theirs is a strange way of hiding: they always do so leaving their two long antennae sticking out. Sometimes you only have to pull on the antennae and the animal emerges, because the place offers no source of self-defense. In those situations, the diver kills them by twisting their heads and puts them in the bag over his tin breastplate. But sometimes they don't emerge, even though their antennae are visible. The corvina is a fish that likes dark hollows. It is a dark, silvery fish that, in my opinion, is surpassed in taste only by sea bass. It is also a foolish fish that swims toward the glass in a diver's helmet when he is hammering away at the stone base inhabited by swarms of little insects where the coral grows.

Coral is a very sensitive animal within its habitat. As long as it can't feel any contact with a strange body, it remains quite hard and secretes a viscous substance, covering itself with a kind of fatty plastic. As soon as you put a hand on it, it hardens further, shuts itself off to a degree, absorbs that plasticky layer and seems to petrify. While it is under water, the level of petrification is less hard than when it is in contact with air: then petrification is total. In July and August the coral buds open and a kind of small white flower emerges. The coral secretes more juices. It is the moment when the animal is at its most firm and plastic – though, clearly, that plasticity is quite relative. It's the moment when divers say the coral is blossoming and looks like tiny almond trees in bloom, a wondrous, charming sight.

In the end, what really makes work difficult for these divers in their suits is the scant, often nonexistent, visibility where they are operating. I am sure the day will come when their labors will be made easier by the presence of a powerful light attached in some way to their clothing. Perhaps the new physics will solve that. But they don't seem enraptured by innovations. When I tell them of the efforts being made to bring light to their underwater explorations, they shrug their shoulders. They remind me of the way deep-sea divers were ravaged by the introduction of individual breathing apparatus. Those devices made divers overconfident in their powers. They went much deeper and remained under water too long. Many died when they resurfaced, with burst veins, arteries and blood vessels, and with blood spurting from noses, ears and mouths. Pearl fishers, whose work is heavier than gathering sponges because they have to shift through kilos of oysters before they find the jewel they're after, have always refused to use that innovation that, conversely, has been adopted by divers in many ports. Perhaps it's all to do with a desire not to facilitate their trade by making it accessible to any amateur, as well as the need not to wipe out coral reefs entirely.

Given the obstructed visibility that the mere presence of these men produces at the bottom of the sea, particularly in the more geologically fantastic places near the sea floor, divers usually grin wryly when people tell them about underwater wonders and incredible seascapes – especially now that there are so many shotgun fishers. The sea – they tell me – hardly ever comes with the still transparency of an aquarium. It is possible to see the colors and shapes of underwater seascapes as long as you remain in the lit zone and the area is sheltered – say, in an unexposed cove. If the water is quite shallow, the sun is shining brightly and the surface is like a mirror, you don't have to enter the sea to observe fascinating subaquatic vistas: you can contemplate the view without moving from the side of your craft. However, the open sea is affected by currents. Along this shoreline, currents from the east muddy the water; currents from the southwest increase transparency. On the other hand, the presence of an alien body underwater – of a diving-suited diver, the only person who can gaze at the view before him with a degree of calm and serenity and, thus, the only one who can take it in – stirs up all the deposits in the area, disturbs all around him and, consequently, muddies limpid waters and destroys visibility. However much an area may resemble an aquarium, an alien presence changes the medium, waters churn, becoming murky and agitated. These are sights you see only from a distance: if you draw near, your movements generate clouds of matter in motion that fly up before your eyes and blot out the spectacle. Divers believe all those scenic wonders have only ever been perceived from open air by people in sheltered spots.

The sea has a top layer of water that is invaded by daylight, where these fantastic spectacles can appear: viscous, repellent, unsuspected shapes, sometimes so malignant they send a shiver down your spine, amid colors the human imagination could never conceive: the ochers, magentas, mauves of the petrified reef, the reds on the viscous brown of some reptiles, the faded, deathly yellow of languid jellyfish, the unreal gray of small slugs, the liquid, deliquescent green of wrasses, the carnival speckles of five-beard rocklings the color of grilled salmon. Sometimes the fish swim by, undulating so slowly they seem to caress the slimy skin of lethargic seaweed. Small, round saddled sea bream, blue and gold stripes over white scales, swerve and flatten out like rolling silver coins. Dreamfish and spring minnows sometimes spark a blue flash when they swerve over a long stretch of sand. Snails proceed slowly in fast-running channels; whelks slide over tiny flora on rocks; hairy sand crabs go in and out of their lairs; deep-crimson mullet seem to slumber between sand and weed; while a shoal of mackerel, all green and blue, swim by switching their tails. Sometimes, a brushstroke the color of quince jam on the back of a swordfish recalls an autumnal sunset. However small fish may be, their eyes look straight out of hell; in the water, almost all eyes bulge out of their sockets, some over a purple circle, like a circle of exhaustion and tedium, which is the case with gilthead and white sea bream; they are amusing fish because their hellish eyes seem to harbor a strange, melancholy fury. Common pandora are a luminous salmon pink, and blotched picarel are characterized by pale gilt on dark scales. But no fish has the rich colors of the rainbow wrasse, especially its mahogany, peppermint-green and clerical-purple streaks, the reddish gray of its belly and pinkness of its fins. If you scrutinize a square centimeter of geological strata, you find an animated microcosmos, dotted with alveoli and holes, inhabited by insects, minuscule crabs, diluted-wine-colored slugs, small orange monsters like drops of a technicolor pus. Fish swim by opening and closing their gills: their exposed insides glitter like tiny rubies. At surface level, sea urchins appear to suck the water and tense their spikes, a funereal black, though never really pitch black: males are reddish black; females are flatter and purplish black. The water's movement makes the surface of the rough, barren, grayish rock shimmer.

How far down does this layer of luminous water go? It is impossible to say. There is no day of the year when the light has the same intensity. Winds change the surface of the water; currents can be dirty or clear. The luminosity of an area depends equally on its latitude and the surrounding geology. Sandy seabeds are more luminous than seaweedy ones. Limestone and granite rock attract more light than veins of slate.

It is also true that at a certain depth, you enter an area of dull light, of monochrome, motionless light. Light must pass through the huge blue filter of water. It is a thick filter that seems to paralyze the light. Reds and oranges disappear; yellows tend to turn green – light green – intermediary colors are demolished, a monochrome stasis invades everything, the light isn't strong enough to penetrate the filter's glaucous mass, and colors evaporate, everything turns a flat greenish blue. Underwater photographing is almost impossible from twenty yards down if you don't have a stream of artificial light. The best photographs of the sea are always taken in aquariums. The becalmed monochrome of those luminous areas is impenetrable.

The dim, uniform space slowly shrinks as you get deeper. Through that imperceptibly darkening zone, you enter a zone of total blackness. With the means we now have at our disposal, fifty to sixty yards represent new frontiers, just a fraction of the sea's expanse of shadow.

So the afternoon passes pleasantly chatting to those fine folk. As the light begins to dim, objects touched by the sun turn golden. The breeze picks up, but the humidity has a soothing influence. A light southwesterly blows along the beach at dusk and ruffles the sea. The flatland above the sand is covered in a fine bluish mist. Golden light touches the liquid green tops of the pine groves in Torre de Pals. As the sun goes down, the foliage around the Ter assumes an elegant, solitary, autumnal splendor.

I sit and gawp for a moment at the strange aspect of the helmets and rubber suits lying on deck, and old Contos invites me to put one on to see how I'll look in it. It's an amusing suggestion but I am *not* amused.

"My dear Contos," I tell him, "we talked about lots of things this afternoon, but I reckon it must be quite tiresome to work inside that peculiar garb."

"Of course it is. This suit carries a hundred forty pounds of lead to facilitate immersion. It's indispensable. But when you've reached the spot where you want to work, it feels like a dead weight and makes moving freely difficult. It requires a grueling effort to stay down. Surfacing is simple enough: you only have to ask for more air. Dragging that weight along is exhausting. To try to delay the onset of exhaustion, we rarely work in a vertical position. We drag ourselves along the sea floor like crawling beasties. We grip hard on rocks or whatever is around. There are many kinds of diver, and their ways of working are different depending on what they hope to achieve. Clearly it's one thing to pull up sponges or collect oysters for their pearls or salvage iron from a shipwrecked vessel. I've worked as a diver in this country doing every job imaginable. During the First World War, I brought up coal for Senyor Fortó in Sant Feliu from a vessel that had gone down on the underwater reef by the Aro beach. That was very different work from what we're doing now in those islands over there. I think the best, least tiring, way to gather coral, especially if you have to descend to a substantial depth, is to move like a lobster, which always goes up and down by clinging to jutting eaves, balconies and shelves of underwater rock faces. Other people work in other ways. As I was saying a few moments ago, it would be hard to regulate work at the bottom of the sea, because it's not like factory labor. I've seen wonderful, extremely strong divers who have been competent at one task and not at another. Italians make good divers in diving suits for working on wrecked ships at a great depth. But nobody can rival the Greeks for working underwater. They're the best in the Mediterranean in this line of work."

Contos pauses, runs his hand over his shoulder and declares rather sententiously: "On the other hand, the diving trade, or *oitis*, as the ancient Greeks called it, isn't a bad business. It's not very comfortable being under water; it's very pretty, but not what you call relaxing. I'd be lying if I told you otherwise. Nevertheless, it *is* very peaceful. I don't recall ever being attacked. . . Even those thieving dolphins that eat the fish caught in nets are completely harmless. In that sense I'd much rather be twenty fathoms down than walking in many a street or square."

SHIPWRECKS:
A REPORTAGE

Years ago I went through a phase where I loved reading about shipwrecks. People who are thought to be sensible and to prefer a quiet life react to disasters at sea as they do to wars and revolutions. These are events they don't ever want to experience in the flesh. Conversely, narratives about the bloody catastrophes that intermittently have rocked this world make for pleasant reads, particularly when they are well written and are read during the winter, by the fire or in bed, as you listen to the rain splatter and the wind howl. In bellicose, irrational times, such thoughts may upset individuals who are professionally involved and their friends and relatives. In peaceful times – which do exist too – they entirely reflect what people generally feel.

Disasters at sea have prompted the noblest expressions of heroism and human tenderness. And in that sense the pages that describe them are uplifting and inspiring. However, they have also acted to expose in a naked, violent and grotesque manner the most abject acts of human selfishness, the instinct of self-preservation, which is a much stronger instinct than any ethical posturing and moralizing verbiage – an instinct that permanently keeps people who weren't born with a saintly vocation on the implacable terrain of potential criminality. Often individuals who have had the misfortune to be shipwrecked, in the course of the catastrophe, have committed acts they'd never have carried out in normal conditions, acts we must describe as absolutely horrendous, even though we too might have reacted in the same way in the same circumstances.

On the other hand, shipwrecks along coasts have also unleashed, from time immemorial, pillaging, thieving and depredation on a grand scale enacted by those living near the disaster. Vessels have been sacked and the shipwrecked parties have been robbed. There is huge documentary evidence on that front. The worst enemy of the shipwrecked was the local landlubber. The sinister climax of their misfortunes was the sacking of their sinking vessels by the peaceful, sedentary folk living along nearby coasts.

Nowadays there has been a decrease in the number of shipwrecks. Engines provide a defense against the sea that sails never could. In Europe there are few remote beaches. Lighthouses, meteorological services and radio-telegraphic communications have increased safety levels. Over recent years, more crashed airplanes on barren heaths have been sacked than vessels.

"What would be the point now of debating whether the disaster we've just experienced was the result of carelessness or whether the careless elements influencing our acts were as significant as they seem at first sight? I am one of those who believe that we act rashly in life all the time – perhaps, if you think about it, life is just one continuous rash act – and that not even people thought to be careful, cautious and cold-blooded are exempt from such behavior. Rash acts are committed on land and sea, but perhaps the latter seem more dramatic and spectacular because there are always fewer people involved at sea than on land. I must recognize one thing, quite unreservedly: in the whole of this regrettable business we displayed total ignorance of the local sea and weather. . ."

My interlocutor was a young French gentleman. Well built, fair, red cheeked and sturdy, he had all the traits of a French northerner in his midthirties, wearing a sailor's outfit that hung loosely on him, which he'd bought the day before, upon reaching Cadaqués. These clothes did not detract from his magnificent male profile. This gentleman and his yacht had gone down by Cape Creus, and he was waiting for his repatriation papers to come through in order to return to France. Meanwhile, we were enjoying an aperitif on the terrace of the Bar Marítim in Cadaqués opposite a becalmed bay – with a sea that was so wonderfully placid you couldn't hear the water breaking on the sand. It was twilight in early September and the sea had gone from that afternoon's silken blue to a deep spongy gray, which was now changing with the last glimmers of light to the characteristic dark slate of the geology of the Pyrenees. Dim ripples of light from the town were beginning to shine on the still water, which seemed ironed flat.

The shipwreck had occurred at dusk on 4 September 194–. . . that is, two days earlier. The yacht – registered in Cannes, thirteen yards long, fitted out as a ketch, equipped with a twenty-four-horsepower engine – had been lost completely. The three-man crew, after lots of woe and chaos, managed to reach the coast in the vessel's tiny dinghy, carrying their possessions in bundles. A curious detail: they took their most indispensable effects but forgot the money, which went down to the bottom with everything else the boat was carrying. When my interlocutor mentioned that, he didn't fail to emphasize that this was one of the most careless acts of that scary evening. When they disembarked on the rocks along the shore, their abandoned dinghy was literally shattered to pieces by the sea and thrown onto the coast, and they had to claw their way painfully up crags, in complete darkness, constantly imperiling their lives. After an hour and a half of crawling they finally reached the entrance to the Cape Creus lighthouse, where the keeper on duty welcomed and helped them and communicated the incident to the authorities.

While we conversed, that gentleman seemed bewitched by the placid sea before us.

"It's very difficult to square this calm," he told me, "with the weather yesterday and the day before. I mean, it's surprising how quickly and suddenly the weather changes in this country, and the sea along with it. It's quite extraordinary. Perhaps the weather is worse to the north, but whether it's bad or good, stable periods are much longer and I think the changes are much less sudden."

Old Captain Gibert, a merchant seaman, was sitting next to me. He was very old and long retired from the sea, where he had sailed in the era of sailing ships. He lived in Cadaqués, where he'd been appointed secretary to the local magistrates' court. Gibert listened to the owner of the shipwrecked yacht attentively, concentrating hard, not moving a muscle on his face.

"So your yacht was registered in Cannes, but you all come from northern France?" I asked my interlocutor.

"Yes, senyor, that's exactly right. The seaman on board and my friend Burgoing, a professor of archaeology at Caen University, and I are all from Normandy. I was born in Honfleur and live there the whole year. We registered the yacht in Cannes because I don't like taking my holidays in the north. I like the sun and I like sunny holidays. Personally I adore the Mediterranean. I think it's unrivaled as a place to spend three weeks. And, as we're on the subject, I'd like to make a confession. Do you know what the problem is with us northerners? We have a completely false idea of what the Mediterranean is like. We think it's a picture-postcard sea – that's why we like it so much – and we believe that the weather here is benign and placid. I think this leads to carelessness. We are much too trusting. That was probably the cause of the disaster I and my colleagues suffered."

"You're quite right," interjected Gibert, in a natural tone that precluded any riposte.

"Our ignorance led to the disaster. It's the key to understanding what happened. That, and that alone."

"Where were you coming from when you found yourselves opposite this shoreline?"

"Tarragona. We'd been anchored in the port of Tarragona for a few days because my friend Professor Burgoing was interested in visiting the Roman city."

"Did you come straight from Tarragona to Cape Creus?

"No, senyor. We spent the afternoon of our third day in Palamós, stocking up on gas and provisions. We set out from Palamós at seven a.m. on day four."

"Did you set out with a southwesterly?"

"No, senyor. It was completely becalmed. The southwesterly blew up when we were off the rocks known as the Formigues Islands on that coast. By these islands we hoisted the mainsail and jib and sailed with a tail wind for a good stretch. When we were opposite Cape Begur we noticed the wind had dropped."

"So when the wind dropped, you lowered your sail, I presume?"

"No, senyor. We started the engine and progressed with sail and engine power toward Cape Begur. When we were by Cape Begur, the wind had completely dropped, but we met. . ."

"Go on, go on," Gibert urged, ever more intrigued.

"We met a heavy sea, with a quite unexpectedly violent swell. A windless sea that was exceptionally fierce."

"Against the current, naturally. . ." said Gibert, with the hint of a smile.

"Yes, senyor. A head current, a northerly, as they say in Cannes."

"You met the *marrutxell*," said Gibert, using an old sailor's term. "What did you decide to do then? Did you at least lower the sail?"

"No, senyor, we did not."

"But given there was no wind, and a head current, why didn't you?"

"I expect it's because we didn't realize what was happening. In effect, we thought that swell was a sporadic occurrence, linked to the cape, and that once we'd passed the cape, we'd meet calm waters again. In fact, when we'd left the old Begur semaphore building behind, we sailed into what the chart called Pals Beach and found the sea to be more manageable."

"Fine, fine. . ." said the old seaman. "In any case, that 'we didn't realize' sounds rather odd. In my humble opinion you ought to have lowered the sail. If I might ask another question, I'd. . ."

"Ask as many as you want, captain. . ."

The French gentleman's mouth relished that word "captain." Gibert was totally unimpressed by the word. He was such an impoverished captain he was forced to run the local magistrates' court to eke out an existence.

"I was saying, that if I was allowed one more question, I'd like to ask if, with that swell head on and the yacht pitching and heeling, you didn't lose any tackle. . ."

"Yes, senyor, we broke a mast. The yard of the mainmast dislodged and fell on deck. It quite exhausted us trying to sort out the mess of ropes and rigging. It was quite a shock."

"A shock up to a point. If you'd been sailing in your country's seas, you'd have furled the sails and secured them properly. As you were sailing in the Mediterranean, you sailed lackadaisically, taking no precautions. . ."

"That's perfectly true," replied the Frenchman, despondently.

There was a pause. Old Gibert spoke a French you could understand: when he couldn't find the right French word, he used the lingua franca that he knew well because he'd spent years crisscrossing the Mediterranean. If he couldn't find a word, he looked at me for a moment, smiled and waited for me to help out. If I couldn't, he continued.

"When the mast came apart," said the old man, "you must have had to furl the mainsail."

"Yes, senyor. It was a struggle because, as I was saying, the yard falling created a huge mess."

"Once the sail was furled, it felt as if the sea wasn't so rough. . ."

"That's right."

"Of course! That comes as no surprise at all."

After brief lull, Gibert, very quietly, and making a real effort, said: "Now let's examine your situation once you'd rounded Cape Begur. The wind was almost nonexistent, nothing out of the ordinary. But the swell of waves was too heavy for your craft, was too rough and difficult to handle. Did one of you look at the sky at the time? You did? What did it look like?"

"The south," replied the Frenchman, "was a mass of clouds. It was a sky brought by a rainy wind. A procession of clouds was passing over Cape Sant Sebastià. To the north, the sky was clearer, but it was a glassy, livid blue, with shreds of clouds blowing the opposite way to the clouds on the coast we'd just left."

"So then, you were in a spot where there was no wind, though with obvious signs that the wind was gusting to the north and south of where you were. What did you think was causing the heavy swell hammering your yacht so violently? How did you explain the swirling waters that coincided with the drop in the wind, the rough sea that stopped you from moving forward? Did you think that was something normal?"

"We never gave it a moment's thought! We believed it was summer and that in summer, in the Mediterranean, hypothetical turbulence could only be sporadic. We believed the roiling sea would last a few moments. . . However, the barometer was tending to rise as we advanced."

"That's possible. Often when the north wind settles in, the barometer rises. Of course, where you really got it wrong was thinking that in early September along this coast you'd meet summer conditions. By early September, summer has come and gone. In fact, it has long since gone. . ."

"In your opinion, what are the limits of summer?"

"Ancient mariners used to say that there are three great ports in this sea: June, July and Port Mahón. You can work out the consequences of such a view, which I believe is quite accurate."

"That's a very short summer. . ."

"What can we do about that? It's what there is. . . Just one more question please. . . Didn't you notice the current in the sea? Were you sailing a long way from the coast?"

"No, senyor."

"So you must have come across a set of lobster creels. What current did the cork buoys marking their location reveal? In which direction were they being pulled? I'd almost swear the current was going in the opposite direction to the swell. That's why the sea was so rough and choppy."

"The fishermen in Cadaqués told us as much. The truth is that we paid them no attention. We were overconfident. It was summertime and we were on holiday."

"Yes, overconfident, that's for sure."

And Gibert suddenly changed tack and directed a question at me in Catalan: "They were on holiday, maybe with a bit of northern swagger. When out at sea in a boat, you can never be on holiday. You know that. You've always got to be on the alert. They're the only holidays you can have."

The Frenchman ordered another absinthe; I did too. After a brief exchange, Gibert agreed to drink a glass of water.

"I'd like," he went on, after taking a sip of water, "to tell you the situation you were in, drawing on my long, if meager, experience. The swell came at you from the north, head on; the current that was driving you was from the south – that is, the opposite direction. The clash of those two forces, in key parts of the coast, like the capes, creates swirling, roiling waters that can exhaust the patience of a saint: a tremendous swell meets an extremely rough sea. On the other hand, in more inland gulfs, the clash is less violent and the water much calmer. You met the same turbulence by the Medes as you did in Begur. When you were in the gulfs between Montgó and L'Escala, the swell was much less dramatic."

"Exactly so."

"Now I'd like to know what you put that conflict of forces, that roiling water, down to. . ."

"I think I already told you, we didn't give it a thought. . ."

"You never suspected. . ."

"We never suspected a thing. . ."

"You never suspected that the choppy waters might be a clear signal, a warning of a northerly gale settling in somewhere or other in the direction you were heading?"

"We didn't think at all!" said the Frenchman, downing a copious amount of icy absinthe.

"That's why you were lethally trapped. I've often seen it happen. When local fishermen told you that your experience by Cape Begur should have put you on your guard, they couldn't have said truer words. You were sailing without a wind, but the presence of the sea hitting your prow was signaling to you that a wind was settling in from the same direction. The sea was acting like a special kind of messenger."

"What would you have done?" asked the Frenchman, a touch anxiously.

"If I'd have been in your yacht, I'd have made for the first port I could find and laid anchor. I'd have let the squall blow over my deck.

You had Roses within reach. You had Cadaqués, which, however ignorant you are of local charts and waters, offers a splendid safe haven. When you're out at sea, you must always be weighing up the forces at play and making decisions based on experience. What made you decide not to head for a port?"

"It's very simple. We reckoned that the drop in the wind meant the sea was mellowing. When it was windless, we forecast a becalmed sea."

"That was a very odd calculation to make, devoid of any basis in reality."

"I agree. But at the time, it was the only clear conclusion we could draw. We didn't even think about putting the state of the sea down to the conflict between the current and a distant wind, do you see?"

"Yes, senyor. I see you only too well."

I was astounded. I'd never seen Captain Gibert say so much in a conversation. He usually spoke so sparely that I'd sometimes walk the whole length of La Riba practically without hearing his voice. He was a small, fair, thin man with tired, bloodshot eyes and a singed mustache, who gave you the impression he was in full control of his every gesture; he was quietly spoken and looked rather suspicious, and his age meant he walked slowly. When anyone asked him something, he wouldn't necessarily say anything in reply: he'd wave his hand, which he must have thought sufficed. That's why I couldn't understand why he was being so talkative now. I later decided he took such an interest in the exchange because he wanted to ensure the French gentleman didn't experience further misfortunes. I decided that because one day I heard him come out with a very strange statement in the café. Namely: "The same folk always sink out at sea."

"So then," said Gibert, picking up the thread of the conversation, "you passed the Meda strait battling against an adverse head current and a choppy sea, and when you entered the gulf, it was much calmer. . . You were powered by your engine. . ."

"Yes, senyor. We'll talk about the engine later because it was a decisive factor in our disaster. When we entered the gulf, things visibly improved. That was another element our ignorance reinforced, because it gave us a false perception of reality. However, now we've got to this point, I must confess something else: we were in a rush, our holidays were coming to an end and we couldn't afford more time."

"When you're out at sea, it can be very dangerous to be in a rush. . ."

"Besides, we'd grown rather tired of life on the yacht. The seasick professor was always throwing up. Our mariner said he was longing to be on land and was getting increasingly belligerent. He was a nautical club sailor. Sometimes that kind of man is excellent; but they're often pure armchair mariners. I was bearing up as best I could. I was upset by the way our craft was pitching and constantly afraid the rigging would come down. What's more, I can tell you these small yachts look so pretty anchored by a nautical club, are so slim lined and attractively painted, but they are incredibly uncomfortable and exhausting when the weather and sea are rough. I'm sure if we'd been in a local fishing smack, we'd have had a safer voyage and enjoyed a greater level of stability."

"Please, do continue. . ."

"When we were by the Roses coast, sheltered by the coastline, the sea yielded a little and we became complacent again, as I mentioned.

However, as soon as we left the bay, in the precise spot on the chart called Cape Figuera, the swell became heavier and we felt the first gusts from the north in our faces. I glanced at the panorama before us and saw, beyond Cape Creus, a heaving line of wind and spray that sometimes looked like dust, and frankly I was totally flummoxed. I was sure the weather wouldn't change. The fishermen told us they couldn't believe it when they saw us sail past Cadaqués Bay. . ."

"Of course they couldn't," said Gibert. "They were astonished to see you sail past and not take advantage of the safe haven of Cadaqués. . . Much sturdier vessels than yours would have done so, are always doing so. . ."

"Well, we didn't and that's why we are in the pickle we find ourselves. The number of miles to Port-Vendres had diminished and we sailed on blindly, one might say. We wanted to finish our holidays as soon as possible, because the sea rusts and corrodes everything and can drive you irresistibly on to make your escape. It had been exhausting ever since we left Palamós, and the politest word heard on board was '*merda*.' We were at our wits' end; we couldn't stand any more. When it's holiday time, any weather report that doesn't fit the bill is unwelcome. The truth is, when we reached the waters of Cape Creus, we encountered a choppy, swirling sea, which made sailing by Cape Begur seem like child's play. What's more, we had a northwesterly head wind that had settled in at implacably gale force. When we went up the Claveguera strait, which is the far end of the horn of the Gulf of Lion (the other end being the Hyères Islands), it was as if a battle against nature was unleashed. Perhaps we should have entered the Claveguera strait. . ." added the Frenchman pensively.

"No, senyor!" said Gibert. "You should have stayed outside. And not because you'd have met better weather outside but because any engine failure could have been fatal while you were so close to land."

"That was precisely the source of all our troubles. . ."

"Of course it was. You were too close to land, your engine gave up the ghost and the sea and wind literally blew you onto the rocks. . . It was inevitable. But forgive me, that was just a passing comment, please do carry on. . ."

"So we entered the Claveguera strait and became locked in a terrible struggle. The sea was choppy and the spray brought tears to our eyes. They were literally streaming. The waters were churning infernally above a huge swell. . .

"The sea and wind were clashing against the current coming from the opposite direction that I mentioned before.

"We could have done three things in that situation: first, retreat and find shelter; second, leave the strait, hoist a jib sail and keep away from the coast; third, continue hugging the coast using our engine. We chose the last option because we thought it would be the easiest, and it turned out disastrously. I'm sure that if the yacht hadn't had an engine, we'd have decided to do what the situation required from a sailor's point of view or turned round to seek out a safe haven or hoisted the jib sail and kept away from the coast. Now, Professor Burgoing's state was on my mind, he was so sick and out of sorts, on his last legs as the result of our day at sea, that I'm sure we'd have decided to retrace our steps. But that engine was our undoing. We sailed on very close to land, an unknown, dangerous coast that seemed inaccessible, sheer, though I have seen that really wasn't the case, because that coast does have its safe havens, if you know it at all well. . ."

"Few and far between. . ." muttered Gibert.

"On the other hand, it was getting dark. We were facing a fearsome sea. The distance to Port-Vendres had shortened, though, in fact, it was farther away than ever. I'd spent the whole day dreaming we'd already arrived. I could see Professor Burgoing lying comfortably in his sleeping car on the Paris express, a light on behind his pillow, reading a book about Tarraco. Suddenly, a huge parcel of water crashed on deck, and our engine spluttered ominously and then just cut out. . ."

"Right, the engine gets doused and packs up. . ." said Gibert, smiling oddly. "I bet if you'd have been sailing in your local sea, you'd have managed things better."

"That's very likely. . ."

"How come you thought the seawater here wouldn't soak it?" asked Gibert, as kindly as he could.

"Our engine's demise was the beginning of the end. As a result, we couldn't steer. We tried to hoist a sail but that proved impossible. We were so close to land that fishermen sheltering in an inlet by the cape told us our yacht was pitching and heeling so much it must have hit an underwater reef to the west of the Claveguera strait. I don't know if we did or didn't graze it. What I do know is that we sprang a leak, the yacht began to lean over and we could think only of abandoning ship. We quickly gathered up what we could, forgetting the money, and lowered the dinghy with difficulty. It was hard work shifting Professor Burgoing's body. He was a deflated, dead weight. I don't know how we reached the coast and landed, particularly with the burden of the professor. It must be what people call a miracle. When we crawled up to the first plateau, I looked back for a moment. The yacht had disappeared. It was almost pitch black. I saw a light to the northwest, far away: it must have been the light at the entrance to the port of Béar. Yes, it was the light at the entrance to Port-Vendres, which is where we wanted to end up. You could see next to nothing of the immediate coast: only hear the growling roar of the sea and whistling gusts of wind."

Gibert said nothing. I lit a cigarette. The Frenchman ordered another absinthe and rested a hand on his shoulder for a while as if he was embarrassed. With that we saw a tall, skinny middle-aged man with a receding hairline standing by our table. He wore spectacles and looked pallid; one arm in a sling and one hand bandaged. There was a plug of cotton wool in each of his ears: he seemed exhausted and on his last legs. We imagined this had to be Professor Burgoing. When the Frenchman registered his presence, he gulped down his aperitif, stood up, paid and said goodbye to us, then warmly took the newcomer's arm and left the terrace with him.

Now we were by ourselves. Gibert gave me a lengthy stare and said not a word. I assumed that after his surprisingly loquacious outburst, his organism was returning to its natural state – namely, to its usual silence. But he hadn't yet finished that chatty streak, because after straightening the peak of his cap, he came out with this rush of words: "This is an amateur's shipwreck. There are people who never know where they're going. The misfortune experienced by these gents only confirms what you may have heard me say previously: the same folk always go down. If they go back out to sea, they go down again."

I felt he was laying it on rather thick and quite inopportunely, but Captain Gibert always inspired great respect in me as a seafarer, so I didn't dare raise the slightest objection. However, I tried to emphasize my lack of response, leading him to understand I really thought he was being too harsh in his judgments.

"Bah. . . !" he finally exclaimed. "I see you don't agree. Senyor Víctor, may God have forgiven him, always said I was too stubborn and independent. That must be why I've ended up in the office at the magistrates' court in Cadaqués. . . not that I'm complaining! Be that as it may, the shipwreck of these French gentlemen reminds of a Basque skipper I met one day, years ago, in the port of Naples, a man with a fantastic reputation, who told me, rather bemused, that he'd spent the worst hours of his career sailing in the Gulf of Lion. I didn't even respond. That captain was as foolish as those Frenchmen who've gone off to eat supper. At sea, a professional in the trade can never meet surprises. If there are any surprises, it's because something has gone wrong, right? Too many people have been shipwrecked by Cape Creus for such disasters to be at all novel. There can be no surprises. The sea is the sea. . ."

I tried to persuade the old captain from the merchant navy to elaborate and make his reasoning more explicit. But that proved futile. His harangue was limited to what I've transcribed. Once he'd said all that, he returned to his impenetrable silence. Seeing we'd reached the end of our exchange, we said goodbye. In later conversations Captain Gibert has never referred back to the events I've just noted.

Valin the jurist relates that in some places in Germany they used to pray in public to God asking for lots of shipwrecks on their coasts. "There was a singular abuse in Protestant churches in the Electorate of Hanover, where public requests were made to Heaven, especially in stormy weather for the cargo and other effects from vessels shipwrecked

*in the German sea to land up on the coast of that electorate, rather
than others, so they could derive full benefit. The Council that was
charged with the Regency of that state had to ban such requests most
rigorously."*

*In 1794, Cambry, in his excellent book on Brittany, wrote in his
descriptions of the Lesneven coast: "Shipwrecks are frequent along
those coasts and their inhabitants display a fondness for pillaging that
nothing has been able to stop, for they regard the objects that storms
or the sea brings to their coasts as gifts from God. In any case, there
are also families that never join in the thieving and feel dishonored if,
when the horde rushes to the beach to share in the spoils from wrecks,
they take steps to be involved in the proceeds."*

Zurcher et Margollé, Naufrages Célebres.

Over the years many people have been shipwrecked off the Cadaqués
coast of Mar d'Amunt, or, if you will, Cape Creus. It's a forsaken,
inhospitable place. In ancient times Cape Creus was called Cape Dia-
ble. It was an appropriate name. During the baroque period, "Devil"
was switched to something hallowed. However, I think it was easier
to hallow the geographical name than the weather thereabouts.

The Mar d'Amunt coast has a geographical incision called the Galera beach (a small affair with the finest sand), which lies opposite a
promontory bearing the same name: the Galera promontory. On 22
March 1654 two large galleons were wrecked in the area, one under
a Dutch flag, and the other under the flag of the masters of Genoa.
No trace of the memory of those wrecks remains in Cadaqués. Our
memory of things is very short. The memory of what's pleasant is
short, of what is unpleasant, even shorter. A couple of generations
and everything fades and is erased.

First of all, you will be struck by the date of the wrecks: 22 March – that is, the day after the spring equinox. A bad time to be sailing, with evident danger, especially in that area. I've already said that it's impossible now to find any trace of these misfortunes. All we know comes from a book printed in Barcelona in 1659 with the title *Legal Defence on Behalf of Doctor Antonio Pastor de Costa*, which Josep Rahola spotted and bought in an antiquarian bookshop in that city. Josep Rahola, a dentist in Barcelona, son of the Cadaqués doctor, is today the man who knows most about his town. If his spirit of curiosity ever finds a structure, one day we'll have his book, a history of Cadaqués full of revelations and surprises. As things stand now, we know almost nothing.

The sinking of the two galleons is the basic subject of the book I have just mentioned, as I was informed by Josep Rahola himself, although the actual shipwrecks are practically hidden in its pages by what followed afterward, which was quite remarkable. The information on the wrecking is sparse, as are details concerning the weather at the time. Naturally the galleons were looted and what wasn't looted was salvaged in strange, equivocal circumstances. These actions make up the bulk of the book.

The galleons were coming from Cádiz and sailing in a convoy. According to the book mentioned, the Dutch galleon was the *Great Pelican* and was carrying a cargo of solid silver, money amounting to one hundred fifty thousand pieces of eight, and other items. The Genoese vessel, named *L'Annunziata* like the Superba's cathedral, was transporting Brazilian tobacco, pepper, cinnamon, precious stones and an unspecified amount of money to support pious work in Jerusalem. The first vessel is a typical example of shipping in the era of the Spanish empire, when the wealth of America entered through the ports legally registered for trade with the other hemisphere and exited by way of frontiers in the north. This process was generally a way to pay back the finance lent to the Habsburgs for their follies, usually by Genoese bankers.* Those bankers were the discoverers of America. It seems that the Genoese boat specialized in dealing in spices.

One day in the Bar Marítim in Cadaqués, equipped with these scraps of information, I talked to Captain Gibert, whom readers have already met, about the wrecks, hoping his comments might cast some light on what happened. He listened to me with that impassive, distant, almost stolid mien he adopted when concentrating, his bluish eyes focusing on the shoulder of the customer seated at the next table. When I'd had my say, he smiled at me wryly.

"You shouldn't surmise that the wrecking of those galleons was much different from the sinking of that French yacht we were arguing about the other day. They all let themselves be caught in a mousetrap. Perhaps they were also in too much of a rush. At sea, boats with no power of their own should never be in a hurry. A mistake of that kind can cost you dearly. . ."

He paused for a moment, then continued: "Those galleys, as if I were seeing them now, were sailing toward Cape Leucate, intending, once they'd arrived there, to head for Cape Corona on the Provence coast, in the Camargue, thus avoiding the Tinyaus, which is at the bottom of the sack of the Gulf of Lion. They could have reached Genoa by keeping close to the coast from Cape Corona. . . What I can't understand is why they sailed so close to the coast at the time of the

---

* The House of Austria frittered away all the riches they plundered from South America and depended on loans from northern European bankers.

equinox. Perhaps it was because that stretch of sea was dangerous, infested as it was by all manner of pirates, corsairs, Moors and other dubious types. If that was the case, then the shipwrecks are understandable, because if they were close to the coast, a sudden northwesterly could have blown them off course onto the rocks, where they'd have broken up. If they went close to land, it was because they were ignorant of this coast. They didn't even know they were making a serious mistake, a tremendously foolhardy act. It's incredible. . . even if you aren't familiar with the ways of the sea, it's easy enough to bungle."

"Perhaps they were scared and in a rush. They were carrying such valuable cargo. . ."

"That's right! Just what I was saying a moment ago. If those people were forced, for whatever reason, to hug the coast and, into the bargain, weren't acquainted with local conditions, I mean were ignorant of the signs warning of a coming mistral, then they were doomed if one did blow up. Gales from the east usually set in during the equinox and solstice. Now, a sudden change in the wind, however slightly pointed up, is always possible. The mistral must have blown them onto La Galera, where they were battered to smithereens in a second. It's a mistake to believe that safety at sea comes from sailing close to rocks. Not at all. Boats need water, the more water the better, so they can move freely. The names Galera and the Galera promontory must be the only remaining memory of those events."

"It's very likely. They are names that have an aura of shipwrecks. . ."

"And you say the galleons were looted?"

"That's what the book says. The general situation favored such a finale. Spain was at war with France and the Ampurdan was in the hands of French troops. Only Cadaqués had yet to be captured. Just imagine the hunger and devastation there must have been in those parts. When news of the shipwrecked galleys reached Cadaqués, a large section of the population went to the scene of the disaster, following their civilian and religious leaders. They must, naturally, have helped those shipwrecked, if anyone was saved, and I'm not sure anyone was. Of course, they took everything else they could lay their hands on. Nobody held back, and according to the book the parish priest led the way. Even if the Ampurdan hadn't been in such a parlous state, things wouldn't have turned out differently. When boats were shipwrecked on more or less uninhabited coasts, they were always ravaged and robbed. It went with the times. There was no real, active ethical sense in the baroque era: there were only grandiloquent sermons and speeches and outward show. When the social history of the baroque era in this country is written, it will attest to an impressive amount of banditry and criminality. There was a lack of natural authority and that was the characteristic outcome. . ."

As he heard my comments, the taciturn, misanthropic Captain Gibert seemed to cheer up.

"Are you suggesting," he said, "that the more fiery and eloquent the sermons, the more nefarious were the acts of the people?"

"I'm not sure. . . In any case, they coincided, were parallel. I should tell you that, as Senyor Rahola, the book's owner, explains, the looting of the galleons in the area we now call La Galera produced a hue and cry far and wide, and despite the remoteness of this area, it reached Barcelona and the ears of the highest authorities in the principality. Don Juan of Austria was viceroy of Catalonia at the time. When he heard the news, this gentleman decided that those wrecks belonged to His Majesty's Royal Patrimony and he appointed Doctor Pastor de Costa to expedite in his name all the necessary steps to recover what had been lost. Part of the hoard being transported by the *Great Pelican* was money that belonged to the state and, apart from what had been looted, a good lot was at the bottom of the sea. The said Pastor de Costa moved to Cadaqués with the usual risks associated with those dangerous times: he probably went by sea. Once he'd arrived and been informed of the circumstances of the wrecks and visited the location, he initiated the salvaging of the silver using iron hooks that were immersed in the sea and then trawled the area where the *Great Pelican* had gone down. Solid silver and coins were in sacks, and if a hook chanced to catch a sack, the inevitable often happened: the hook tore the sack, and the contents were scattered over the floor of the sea, with the inevitable losses. They tore so many sacks that poor Senyor Costa suspended the operation, told Barcelona what had happened and asked them to send some other means to recover what was still underwater. At the time one Andreu Ximénez had invented a timber diving bell to go down to the bottom of the sea (that is, where it was relatively shallow), which allowed the person inside the bell to breathe, just about. Don Juan of Austria ordered one of these bells to be transported to Cadaqués, and that was done, with great difficulty, by sea, given that all roads overland had been cut off by the French occupation."

Gibert listened silently and passively, as if he were at the theater.

"As soon as the bell reached Cadaqués, the crew began preparations to use it (which were long and complicated), until one day, when the weather was very good, the bell was moved to the area of the wrecks. A kind of nautical contingent set out from the port of Cadaqués transporting the bell. The leaders of the exercise were Andreu Ximénez and his colleagues on the expedition, Pere Joan Rams, a state prosecutor, and the friar Bernat Soler, representing the Jerusalem trust. Rams (his presence showed that Antonio Pastor de Costa had already fallen out of grace, probably for thieving) was to look after His Majesty's silver and coins while Friar Bernat Soler was there to salvage the alms heading to the Holy Land. Once the retinue reached the site of the disaster, they probably had a bite to eat, because the sea makes you ravenous, and then got to work. The bell was positioned between two large vessels, both of which had a pulley to lift and lower it. The bell was made of timber, bound tight by iron hoops, and inside were crossbeams, where the divers sat as the bell was immersed in the sea. As it was quite a large size, it had to be given plenty of weight if it was to go down, and that was done with eight hundred pounds' worth of lead pieces. It was a huge bulk. It was sunk four or five feet from the bottom of the sea and suspended there. Seated on the crossbeams, the divers recced the area, and if they spotted anything of value, they dove down and tried to secure it until their air ran out. In that event, they returned to the crossbeams, where there was one or two feet of air between the beams and the bell's ceiling because (says the book) "the water didn't reach that far because the air in the atmosphere kept it out, as experience teaches us according to the rules of Natural Philosophy." So then, when the divers got hold of an item they'd glimpsed on the seabed, they placed it in a sack tied to a rope that passed through a hole in the bell (a rope that was pulled up from above when the sack was full of salvaged items). The book doesn't reveal whether any silver or alms for the Holy Land were salvaged. Everything indicates that very little was reclaimed. What it does describe is the amount of damage wrought by the bell. Nature must be treated with respect; otherwise things can turn nasty. To begin with, the air in the bell wasn't renewed in time, and that led to more than one fatality. Once the breath of the divers had poisoned the air so much, two people suffocated on the artifact's crossbeams. On another occasion, a diver, finding that the air was unbreathable, decided to escape from the bottom and when he hit fresh air, he died. This was quite a natural outcome given the depth at which the bell was anchored: over thirty-two yards down. Those and other mishaps forced them to renew the air more frequently by constantly hauling up the bell, which was very heavy, and so they wasted lots of time. I imagine it made all concerned wiser rather than wealthier, and what with one thing and another, pickings were poor."

"I see that. . ." said Gibert, his eyes flickering over his deadpan features, as if he were watching the climax of the show.

"Those operations lasted all that summer. Summers by Mar d'Amunt are usually short. Bad weather interrupted them at the end of September, as was to be expected. On 1 July of the following year, Cadaqués fell to French troops and everything was washed away. The bell, which must have been abandoned somewhere or other along the harbor front, was then used by the newcomers who tried to harvest what they could (which is rather sad). In the meantime, the trial of Senyor Antonio Pastor de Costa started, and in self-defense, he did what people always do: he tried to dismiss the accusations against him by steering them onto the backs of others. Costa tried to show that the looters were inhabitants of Cadaqués, including, in the front line, the most respected figures in the community. The town of Cadaqués defended itself implacably on every claim. The trial was such a raucous, juicy affair that its documentation forms the bulk of the book I mentioned. After all these years, the legal wrangles can give us some idea of the nature of the wrecked galleons and how they were looted by locals and by the people appointed to avoid thievery. That locals should loot is natural, because this kind of disaster in this kind of place has always ended with looting, ever since the world was the world. However, it's quite amazing that the judges should have followed the example set by the people they were supposed to be stopping (and judging). But there you are. . . We shouldn't be too upset. It's not the first or last time such things have happened. It is an instinctive evil, so deeply rooted that it forms part of our most venerable traditions and ancient heritage. However, Captain Gibert, we have perhaps strayed from the point of our conversation. I'm not particularly interested in what we might call the ethical aspect of these wrecks, even though I'm glad to have any excuse to reinforce my belief that baroque foliage camouflaged an abject, false society. I'm in fact more interested in the meteorological aspect of the wrecks, the cosmic context of the catastrophe."

"As I was saying a moment ago. . ." whispered Captain Gibert, as if he were just emerging from a dream. "Those weighty galleons were caught in a rat trap and battered on the rocks by the sea and the mistral. The causes of the wrecks are unclear. Out at sea you need water. Perhaps they were sailing too close to land. There's no way out of the gulf of La Selva when the mistral is blowing. Wind and sea make a wall that can't be broken down, a phenomenally strong wall. Blink for a moment and you'll find yourself on the rocks, as if the sea and wind had driven you there on purpose. Those places are criminally hard. The rocks stick out like the sharpest of spears. They pierce your timbers; they shatter the wood. The Gulf of Lion is an evil place everywhere. It shuts its doors with the mistral, it becomes impenetrable. If you're inside, it's a horrible place to be. Now that boats have powerful engines, the sea has had to yield to their might. But I can tell you that, in the age of sailing, for hundreds and hundreds of years, one of the places where people have most suffered has been the gulf that begins in Cape Creus and ends with the most eastern of the Hyères Islands. The sea plus the mistral is a horrible combination. You don't really know that until you've had a run in with the mistral and were in a vessel that could resist it. In the era of sailboats, which was mine, people suffered too much."

Gibert spoke of those things with complete indifference – as if he were talking about the harvest from his olive grove. Perhaps he might have emphasized the odd word in a way he didn't usually. He continued: "I've never been the kind to complain. Complaining is a futile activity, generally practiced by good-for-nothings and often by people who are instinctive complainers, when there are no grounds. There's a lot of playacting in this world, much more than we think, though we see plenty. In any case, what good does it do? The world doesn't come ready-made: rather, it's a place that's hard to control, even in its tiniest detail. You must take it as it comes. That's the only way, as I see it. On land, you can hope for a degree of safety; at sea, it's more difficult. Everything is much more fragile, and in my time. . ."

As I'd never heard Captain Gibert make general assertions or say anything in the way of a confession, my surprise must have been obvious from the expression on my face, which led him to interrupt his flow.

"Well, you know!" he said, opening his tobacco pouch, "you know me, so no need to say any more. . . Sailors in my day knew the area and how tough it is, like today's mariners. This gulf has a bad reputation everywhere. That's recognized universally. Anyone who denies it is a freshwater sailor, spouting nonsense. Just talk to northern seamen, genuine mariners, and see what they tell you. I know the waters of the Mediterranean and other seas. I've crossed the Atlantic scores of time in ships that were a joke. Atlantic waves are different from waves in gulfs around here. They are hard, very deep waves, but very long; waves that flee and surface more gently, if I can use that word. Waves here are also very hard, but are less deep, narrower and choppier, and they seem on the slant, because the changing wind constantly alters the direction they are heading, obviously within limits. However, these changes are enough, even if you have a full head-on wind, for the waves to come from one side or the other and shake your boat from prow to poop, from starboard to port, so that it bobs around like a bottle cork in the churning waters. That means your body is subject to real torture, with pressure coming from the four points of the compass. After a few hours, you feel literally twisted, as if your body had been redrawn in a spiral. That's why people who suffer from seasickness feel it more lethally in the Mediterranean than anywhere else. Seasickness that hurts only your flesh, your stomach, is unpleasant; one that penetrates your entrails and reaches your bones brings on a pitiful state beyond words. The twisting and turning are so insidious that the low spirits that follow are painful to witness. I can tell you, even though I've skippered many boats, I too have been sick. All us seamen have been sick at one time or another, and anyone who tells you the contrary is a fool. . . Nowadays, I sometimes read the newspapers in the café. I say in the café because if my wife saw me come home holding a newspaper, she'd throw me out of the house. So I've read most of your articles, though not all, on the horrors wrought by the sea through the ages on people from these shores and coasts. These horrors are a fact. You've quoted eyewitness accounts by ancient Greek and Roman writers. You didn't need to go to so much trouble. Just going from door to door and talking to people locally, you'd have achieved the same results. Now there's a reason for that, as I've just outlined. The Mediterranean can be a real force for evil.

When the mistral is blowing, the Gulf of Lion is one hellish place. It's hellish for people who get seasick and for those who don't. The sea and the mistral are a nasty combination. They bring indescribable disorder, disorder to people by your side, who you have to rely on at every stage. And disorder is the worst thing that can happen on board ship. It signals the breakdown of trust. . ."

Captain Gibert paused and relit the cigarette he was smoking.

"Those galleons that sank in Mar d'Amunt all those years ago," he said, "must have been half demolished when they reached land. The sea itself must have done the demolishing. I was really surprised by one thing you told me about the shipwrecks that you read about in the book owned by Rahola the dentist, son of the old Cadaqués doctor, who was a very fine doctor: that they fished out the sacks of silver using hooks. That probably means the sacks were already scattered over the seabed when the galley transporting them hit the bottom, because it would have been very hard to fish them out if they'd been inside the boat's hull. Blindly trying to fish a sack of whatever from the bilge of a vessel, which one presumes is closed, using hooks that have to be dragged along would have been a fool's game. That, at least, has been the experience of a man who has seen so much merchandise dragged out of the bilges of boats. Before the hooks reached the bottom they'd have caught on the countless obstacles offered by the ship's hull. The ships probably reached the coast already battered and smashed up. When they hit the first rock, they must have literally fallen apart. It's unthinkable that they built ships then as well as they did later, let alone as they do now. Now a vessel can be split in half, but it can't be smashed to smithereens. So then the silver must have been fished out around the sunken hull (the silver that could be salvaged, because I don't think they could have hoisted any coins).

Because all that diving-bell business, you know, must have served to rescue the odd loose coins but not to bring up a single wretched sack. How could a bareheaded, deep-sea diver handle a sack at such a depth? Come on!"

"Be that as it may, all that remains of the shipwrecks is the place-name on the coast – La Galera."

"Who knows?" replied Gibert, with a vague smile, rendered even hazier by the bluish smoke from his cigarette. "There may have been wrecks of other galleys and all kinds of ships by La Galera and Galera Beach. The Gulf of Lion, from Cape Creus to the island of Llevant, is a vessels' graveyard. It's an evil place, where much evil has been wrought, a place that has brought a lot of grief to people who have encountered the mistral."

I'm holding a piece of paper that refers to the shipwreck of *Nostra Senyora de la Concepció*, captained by Antoni Serra, Genoese by birth. The shipwreck took place on 22 March 1730 on the beach in Pals that is described as the beach of Torroella de Montgrí. It's an intriguing date: the day after the spring equinox. One can almost be certain that the shipwreck was caused by the storm from the east that usually coincides with the equinox – as was the case with the 1688 "storm of beans."* When an easterly wind blows, Pals Beach is no place to be. The wind and sea pound it furiously. As a result of the shallows in the area, there is a powerful swell – an undertow that is impossible to defeat if one is too close to land. For whatever reasons, *Nostra Senyora*

---

* One of a series of peasant uprisings against landowners and the Spanish monarchy, the so-called storm of beans took place in Manresa in 1688.

de la Concepció was thrown onto the sandbars by the breaking waters and couldn't resist the sea's might. After being battered against the sandbanks, it must have flapped like a wounded fish on the flat expanse of sand, where, over time, it was dismantled and rotted by corrosive salt water. At the time of the wreck, the area of the disaster – the spot where the River Massot flowed into the sea – was entirely uninhabited.

Antoni Serra and the crew members who had managed to survive the wreck jumped onto dry land, and battling against the natural hardships of being in an unknown land, in virgin territory, they reached Mas Gelabert, where they were welcomed and helped by the steward, Domingo Torres, and other people in the house. After sleeping and eating, they were reinvigorated and went back to their ship and started to salvage what they could from the wreck, carrying lots of items to terra firma and storing them in a hut they'd built in the immediate vicinity. They posted a guard at night to avoid any looting of what they'd salvaged. The fact that Serra took such a precaution showed he was a wily old hand in times of misfortune. The first reaction is usually to think ingenuously that one can leave everything safe and secure in such forsaken spots, as if they *were* completely uninhabited. Now it's very likely there is no such thing as a forsaken spot by the sea: there's always some vagabond waiting behind a shrub for whatever turns up. Those who lurk in solitary places are no fools.

Shortly after, the court in Pals ordered the skipper Antoni Serra and his crew to obey health regulations, and thus they were forced to move from Mas Gelabert and to endure a period of quarantine that was rigorously imposed by the presence of armed men. Serra succeeded – and one can imagine the passion with which he argued – in having a proper guard placed on the hut and the area where they'd stored the salvaged goods. The Pals authorities and health officers appointed completely trustworthy folk to keep those goods safe. Quarantine lasted until 6 April, when they were all set free.

Serra and his men, their papers in order, returned to the hut and found that everything had been looted: boxes and chests had been broken into and a large number of items had disappeared. All the efforts made by the shipwrecked men to save what they could from the wreck had come to naught. If one analyzes the situation, the decision to put the survivors into quarantine was strange and seems quite suspicious. No doubt there was a solid case from a legal perspective. But fulfilling the requirements of the law seems like a facile pretext to facilitate the looting officially, robbery by the hand of the authorities. It's not a rare occurrence in life, and one has seen it happen quite frequently.

Faced by that second catastrophe, Serra must have shouted to high heaven and knocked on every door – to no avail. He thanked the people in Mas Gelabert, who'd been so hospitable, and gave them the ship's bell – a bell that still exists in the grand farmhouse of the Coll family, the present owners of the land and house – which they use to signal the time for the various tasks on the farm. The time came when Serra and his men returned to their country. They reached Genoa absolutely on their uppers, flat broke.

They issued a protest from Genoa and started legal action against the Pals authorities, concretely against Pere Bou i Marès, a local farmer and representative of the navy and deputy of the authorities on the shore where the ship was wrecked. The piece of paper I am looking at now is in fact one sent by Pere Bou to the main minister for the navy, asking for His Majesty's consul in Genoa to give the skipper Antoni and his shipwrecked crew a questionnaire, which they should answer in the presence of a judge. It is a paper that was destined to be forwarded as evidence in the case over looting initiated against the said deputy. It is all frankly curious: shipwrecks inevitably lead to looting, and when this happens, the local powers that be are usually quick to join the fray.

ON THE ROCKS

The oldest known shipwreck on the Cape Creus coast (and here I mean coast in the broadest sense of the word, including the Roses and Mar d'Amunt to Tres Frares stretches, the latter being where Selva de Mar's legal powers begin) is to be found in Galladera. Of course, there must be more ancient wrecks, but they have left no trace in human memory.

At the entrance to the Galladera inlet, at the bottom of the sea, are remnants of the *Boxhill*, an English steamship that went down in 1884 in mysterious circumstances nobody ever clarified.

Galladera is a remote, desolate spot, beyond the plain of Tudela, one of the last inlets of Mar d'Amunt, by the bend in the coast as it traces the gulf of La Selva. It is a purely rocky incision, forged by the sea and reasonably protected from the north wind and mistral. Galladera hasn't the grace or charm of Portaló, the adjacent cove, one of the most elegant coves in this country. Portaló is so beloved it even sports a communal hut where you can lodge and a strand so white, unspoiled, and rarely trod, you feel the pull of pristine nature. It is the jewel of this coast – though it has one small defect: it is so shallow only small boats with little depth can enter.

The dark, elevated islet between Galladera and Portaló goes by the name of Portaló Island. This rock is located in such a way that it protects Portaló from the mistral and Galladera from "*provençades*," as they are known locally. It is a providential presence. The strait it creates with the coast is navigable, if challenging. For a vessel holed up in Galladera, the strait guarantees a feasible escape route – something that's unthinkable in Culip. When it rains in the first and fourth quadrant, Culip is a cathedral of nature, Galladera, a cul-de-sac, but if you must flee those places in a squall, I really hope you are in Galladera and not Culip, though please forgive me for offering this unsolicited advice.

There's been a lot of speculation locally about the sinking of the *Boxhill*, and Senyor Pell, who made paintings for parlors in Cadaqués, turned the catastrophe into a marine drama. I've only ever seen a single copy; Senyor Pell didn't have the popular naïveté of makers of ex-voto images or the interest in blood and gore of those ignorant folk; he knew about line and perspective and endowed his works with the touch of frosty realism that prints had in his day. His shipwreck is a chocolate-box picture.

His little painting gives an idea of what the vessel was like: a tall, thin funnel, a forward mast with two yards, which shows it did use its sails to sail, a practice still common in those times. The engines had little power and sails not only helped in that respect but also gave more stability. The *Boxhill*'s hull was long and thin, like a cigar.

Oral tradition around the shipwreck indicates that the vessel went aground on the island of Portaló, which it hit head on, wham, quite inexplicably. I use the word "inexplicably" because it is the word the last living eyewitnesses of the wreck usually use. The word is meaningless when applied to maritime matters – except for things one has actually witnessed, and even then. . . ! It seems there's always something dark and beyond our grasp in matters of the sea.

What caused the ship to sink? Was it a deliberate, provoked accident? Was it carelessness, a silly trifle, a momentary loss of the notion of reality triggered by an excessive concentration of alcohol in the brains of the captain and his officers? That hypothesis is always feasible particularly when it's a vessel from the north. So many of them navigate with a shot of alcohol in their wing! The weather wasn't poor on the night of the disaster: it was a winter's night like so many.

It must have been a violent crash. The *Boxhill* was left like a grenade about to explode. The next day the mistral began to blow. All efforts to extricate the ship were to no avail. Wind and sea battered her so fiercely that naturally she shattered like a wicker basket and sank to the bottom of the sea.

She has rested there for nigh on seventy years, and now nobody remembers the shipwreck. Senyor Pell's little pictures have disappeared from parlors and tastes have changed. Some three hundred tons of iron were salvaged along with other things of value. The wreck is now in an advanced state of deterioration inflicted by active forces in the sea. Drawn to mineral deposits, a whole botanic and zoological invasion encrusted the ship's hull; deep-sea divers who have recced her speak of a hull in the process of becoming unreal and phantasmagoric.

The *Llanisshen* was a large steamboat – eight or nine thousand tons – registered in Glasgow. What the English call a tramp.

One day in August 1917, the *Llanisshen* set out from the port of Marseille, carrying only ballast, and headed toward the Strait of Gibraltar. It was the most hazardous, dangerous moment of submarine activity in the First World War. She was a magnificent, new vessel, solidly built and of the highest quality. A Clydesider.

When she left Marseille, she sailed within sight of land but followed her own set route; she wasn't in a convoy. Halfway across the Gulf of Lion, she was torpedoed by a submarine. The torpedo sliced through her, from one side to the other, right through the engine room. She was left with a hole in both sides and completely at the mercy of the elements. After a detailed investigation, on captain's orders, it was revealed that the boilers had been totally destroyed. There was very little to ponder: the vessel was declared a complete loss, beyond salvation. The order went up to lower the lifeboats and the whole crew disembarked. These craft landed on the Nouvelle-Aquitaine coast.

The *Llanisshen* drifted without a soul on board, haltingly, dead, dramatically silent – a pathetic listlessness that augured total destruction. I have the impression that when the captain abandoned ship after his crew, he presumed she would sink rapidly, ineluctably. But she continued to float, lurching slightly to one side.

Across a tranquil sea, the sunset that day seemed straight out of paradise, a protracted death agony of light and color, voluptuousness on a cosmic scale. However, in the early hours of the night, the mistral began to blow, and the *Llanisshen* was dragged out to sea in a southeasterly direction, and if the wind had continued in that vein, the vessel would have been blown into the waters of Cape Creus, the southern horn of the Gulf of Lion. I can imagine the spectacle of the abandoned vessel meandering in the gulf's murky waters, in solemn, anguished silence, the wind whining through its masts and defunct rigging.

After drifting for hours like a ghost, the huge wreck was spotted by a small steamer registered in Barcelona (belonging to the Freixas company) that was involved in coastal trade transporting foodstuffs – it was the era for smuggling on the grand scale – to Port-Vendres and Sète. The ship was the *Colón*, an old, shabby, stinking hulk like the *Empordanès*, which belonged to the same company – except that the *Colón* had a funnel in her stern and masts to the fore. She was a cockamamy, undersized clingfish.

The *Colón* approached the torpedoed vessel and lowered a boat into the water. The reconnaissance – carried out in a state of amazed astonishment – concluded that the vessel had been abandoned. It was intact, except for the engine room, which the torpedo had cut through and devastated.

The *Colón*'s captain judged that it was worthwhile taking her in tow, but when he made that decision, he must have thought the English vessel offered few guarantees in terms of safety. He put her on a towrope but left nobody on the tiller, no doubt fearing she would sink and drag down the man steering. If there had been a man in the stern of the wreck, it would have made towing much easier. At any rate, he put her on a towrope and prepared to drag her to one harbor or another.

Sailing at a slow pace they rounded Cape Creus – it was like watching an ox being dragged along by a rat – and skimmed past the ends of Cadaqués Bay. Unfortunately, by Cape Creus they met a southwesterly wind and towing turned into a struggle. With nobody steering, the wreck zigzagged. Now and then the towrope tensed and vibrated dangerously. The *Colón* was a mere empty shell; the *Llanisshen*, despite carrying no cargo, was a terrific weight. The towrope snapped by Figuera Point.

Faced by that unhelpful development, the *Colón*'s captain had, objectively speaking, three options: a challenging path consisted of renewing the tow and dragging the steamship, against wind and sea, to the port of Roses; an easier possibility was to tow her with a tail wind and sea into Cadaqués Bay, which is welcoming in all weathers and has good anchorage; the easiest of all would have been to abandon the hulk.

So, despite the tramp's huge value, even after she had been torpedoed, the *Colón*'s captain decided to abandon her. He was probably worried by the amount of work towing had already involved. It's also possible he thought it was too much bother to go back, that he'd wasted too much time. Once the towrope snapped, the *Colón* continued on her course toward Cape Begur and the solitary wreck was once more left to drift. The mistral had dragged her toward Cape Creus for hours on end and a southwesterly was now pushing it the same way but from the opposite direction.

That was when a few people in Cadaqués spotted a strange vessel beyond the ends of the bay, driven willy-nilly by wind and sea. No sign of life was visible on board; not the slightest whiff of smoke emerged from her funnel; the vessel was huge and unreal. She progressed slowly, drifting with the wind, tending to lean toward the coast, no doubt subject to the strong currents that reign in those waters. She had been abandoned off Figuera Point, under a mile from land. That distance had now shortened.

Encouraged by the apparition, a group of idlers from Cadaqués manned a boat and headed toward her. Senyor Iu Sala, a well-known figure in the town, owner of a fish-salting house, agreed to sponsor them. Once they had drawn near, the spectacle with the *Colón* was repeated: they were astonished by the sight of such a huge, abandoned, empty vessel. It was a vision that sent their heads into a spin, even though they saw things only in the shape of the wealth being sent their way. Something or other had to be done. . . A man by the name of Baîlon, a sturdy, corpulent fellow, who'd been a sailor and then worked transporting the luggage of people who came and went from Cadaqués, climbed on board the vessel. He'd barely begun his spellbound explorations when a deep, dull noise came up from the bilge – as if something had collapsed. In the end he realized that nothing had happened. The vessel had simply lurched more sharply and a load of coal in her hold had been displaced making a loud, lugubrious din. Nevertheless, Baîlon was scared and lowered himself down on a rope. He was so nervous and agitated he almost fell into the water.

The people in the boat looked at each other; they were perplexed and worried. What *was* to be done? At sea, any problem is massive, because nothing can be limited and controlled by human might alone – I mean another source of power is necessary to fight its onslaught.

If at that time – it was 1917 – any relatively powerful motor had existed in Cadaqués (let's say with the power of a small, present-day fishing boat), the *Llanisshen* might have been saved. It would have taken much less time to tow her into Cadaqués Bay, and considerable patience, but there'd have been no insuperable difficulties. However, in Cadaqués at the time, there were no engines of note. Everything was done with sails – if you were lucky. Given the urgency of the situation, there was no time to wait for one to be brought from outside. . . The wreck was drifting visibly and ineluctably toward the coast.

In any case, a decision had to be made; after tedious, specious deliberations – as people could see the vessel wouldn't get past S'Oliguera Point, which is the far, eastern end of the bay – they decided to pluck up courage, climb on board and anchor her before she hit the rocks I just mentioned. They climbed on board scared stiff, though increasingly amazed, and after a lot of hard work, they cast the anchors into the sea. At that moment, the vessel was opposite and just outside the treacherous Caials Bay. The rocks around this bay, like so many on that coast, look worm eaten, but they are strong and razor sharp. They cast out the anchors too late. By the time they hit the bottom, the *Llanisshen* had already hit and been trapped by rocks.

Several strange things ensued. The vessel was anchored and grounded on those rocks on an August afternoon when a south-westerly was blowing. However, the mistral usually blows at night, and this wind produced a miracle, no doubt because the vessel was only superficially grounded on the rocks. The mistral pushed the ship out to sea so hard she came off the rocks. Once released from those obstacles, she swung round on her anchor chains and by next morning was completely freed up and perfectly anchored in deep, manageable waters. By dint of the strength of the mistral, the *Lla-nisshen* had totally changed position: the previous night, with the southwesterly, her prow had pointed seaward, and now, with the mistral, she pointed landward. If she had been able to maintain that position for a reasonable amount of time, it would definitely have been possible to save her. However, in her present state she had become a plaything at the mercy of the weather: possible salvation depended on which weather predominated from one moment to the next. When one thinks of the *Llanisshen*, one is astounded by the many possible ways that she might have been rescued before she finally went down, the powerful resistance she sustained in the course of a protracted death agony.

With that latest development, the news of the vessel's abandoned presence started to spread. When it reached the attention of the Barcelona firm of Tayà, then at the height of its commercial activity, they quickly contacted the vessel's owners. When Tayà purchased the wreck, she was still afloat.

The firm immediately went into action, showing it was really interested in salvaging the vessel. The rumor mill said the company had offered a million pessetes to Captain Ferriol, the company's inspector, if he saved the ship. Be that as it may, while a large, showy rescue operation was being mounted and the paperwork signed, the weather changed radically. After a gusting westerly wind filled the sky with clouds and tinged the air blue, an easterly sea breeze set in. Storms at sea never hit like a round of grapeshot. First, long, tall waves come, ushering in the approaching wind. The waves swell. The wind settles in, unfettered. The waves' swell increases with the wind. The waves reach unheard-of heights, race powerfully, sweep along with the foam, the wind floating on their crests – waves that spread, invading coast, rocks, beaches and cliffs in a fantastic tumult.

The last hours – we would say – of the *Llanisshen*'s life were those when the westerly blew. The storm from the east settled in, and her huge bulk was thrown onto the Caials rocks and began to be shredded down below. She resisted the onslaught of sea and wind like a dying animal. Perhaps the anchors helped her resist – perhaps they broke her. Curiously, for a few days the vessel was abandoned completely. The storm was accompanied by a tremendous downpour: the horrendous squalls of 1 September of that year, which so ravaged Cadaqués and which so many people still remember. As long as the storm lasted and for hours afterward, few in Cadaqués had time to think about the *Llanisshen*. Probably nobody at all. They had other tasks at hand dealing with the water that had descended from the heavens. This is why there are no eyewitness accounts of the boat sinking. When calm was restored and people went back to the Caials rocks, the *Llanisshen* had already sunk to the bottom of the sea.

The divers who later recced her noted that as a result of the storm the iron plates of bilge number two had crashed against the rocks so violently they'd eventually caved in. A gash was opened up and that started the flooding. The two holes made by the torpedo accelerated the process. The vessel went down slowly. As it sunk, rushing waves overwhelmed it and floored it. Nothing more of the vessel was ever seen above water. The *Llanisshen* was sunk more or less twenty-five fathoms deep. Tayà had bought a floating wreck; a few days later they owned an invisible wreck, sunk for good.

However, let's return to the thread of our story.

The new situation didn't seem to discourage Tayà. They first ordered a recce to be carried out by a Greek diver from the island of Symi in the Dodecanese, peremptorily Turkish by nationality, my dear friend Costas Contos. The Costas family had come to the peninsula to fish sponge and coral. When he was given this job, Contos was the head of a company of deep-sea divers in the port of Barcelona.

Younger than he is now, with the looks of an energetic adolescent, he went to Cadaqués and carried out a detailed recce of the vessel. The storm had so thoroughly embedded her on the sharp angles and points of those rocks he judged she was now impossible to refloat. "The vessel will have to be salvaged in bits and pieces," thought

Contos. "She will never be refloated on the surface as a whole." And that was what he told old Tayà.

"Contos, you are too young, you don't have the experience. . ." that fine man told Contos with a snigger. "You rush to conclusions. We, on the other hand, are ready to do whatever it takes to salvage that boat. . ."

Contos wished him a very good day with a dash of that ceremonial courtesy he'd learned from the Turks in the eastern Mediterranean.

The Tayà company immediately went into action. A team of Italian divers arrived to salvage the ship. A diver from the port of Barcelona, Roca, nicknamed Fleshy, joined them. Italian divers are first rate when it comes to salvaging ships. They probably last as long as Greek sponge divers in deep waters. However, objectively speaking, they are highly skilled.

The Italian divers decided the first thing they had to do to refloat the *Llanisshen* was to fill the holes. They asked for a fantastic amount of cement – what they thought was necessary to that end. A large steamer, the *Teresa Tayà*, began to transport goods from Barcelona to Cadaqués: cement, timber, machinery – all kinds of items, tackle and useful gear. At one point, over sixty people from Cadaqués worked on the salvaging of the *Llanisshen*. An aura of prosperity reigned. Activating all the required initiatives cost rivers of gold – and I say gold because at the time our currency was on the gold standard.

The Italian divers poured a colossal quantity of cement into the three holes that the dead weight of the *Llanisshen* was carrying. When they thought the holes were filled, they were ecstatic. A sheath of extremely strong material arrived, with which they more or less enveloped the vessel – I say more or less because there are always unknown factors in underwater work that those not experienced in the area find difficult to evaluate. Once it was sheathed, two pumps from the Port of Barcelona Works Department were attached to the ship to extract water, two powerful pumps that could shift eight hundred tons of water a day. As the sack gradually emptied, the *Llanisshen* should have started to rise spontaneously to the surface. However, the vessel didn't budge. It was dead still down below. That could be explained by two incontrovertible facts: firstly, that it wasn't absolutely true that the sheath totally covered the enormous tramp. And that wasn't because there wasn't enough material – there was material to spare. Something else had happened. The holes in the *Llanisshen* had been filled with vast amounts of cement when the vessel was touching rocks underwater. The cement stuck the vessel's iron plating to the surrounding rocks. A homogeneous, indestructible, unmovable paste was created – huge cement fetters that bound her to the bottom of the sea, which wouldn't let her die in the whole of eternity.

After wasting extraordinary sums of money on their salvage operation, the Tayà company abandoned the vessel for good.

The wreck has subsequently been brought up in bits and pieces, as the diver Costas Contos had foreseen after his first recce. In 1927, in the course of the first campaign, twenty tons of metal and eight hundred tons of wrought iron were hauled up. In 1951 there was a second fruitful campaign with excellent results.

Today the huge vessel no longer has the shape of a tramp. It has been dynamited so many times that all that remains is an unruly pile of iron fragments, which have melded into the dramatic underwater orography of the Caials.

In the winter of 1921, during a storm from the east, a French four-master merchant ship, the *Douamont*, registered as a four thousand tonner, was wrecked on S'Arenella Island off Cadaqués, the one many people still call Rahola Island (after Don Víctor Rahola). Years ago, I was the guest of the owner of this unforgettable island at the far eastern end of Cadaqués Bay. I wrote about that most pleasant experience in a previous story "A Frustrated Voyage."

The *Douamont* was a large timber four-master that had originally sailed under a North American flag and was later transferred to France as a result of the famous 1920s American stock-market crash. She was named after the famous fort from the Battle of Verdun. Equipped as a merchant ship, she possessed two huge five-hundred-horsepower diesel engines. The triangular sails had been removed from her rigging, but she was still spectacular, a magnificent specimen, even if she couldn't rival the great display made by the most recent clippers on the Australian corn race. Four masts will always be four masts.

The final decline of sailing ships began in the wake of the First World War. There was a great crisis in maritime transport and for several years sailing ships that weren't old enough to be scrapped were provided with auxiliary engines. Sailing vessels were stripped of the sails that were difficult to handle, the ones people in the trade called "expensive," and the only sails left were those that could be handled by the smallest of crews, crews that were generally half-hearted, ignorant of the trade and recruited from the rabble in ports. The *Douamont*'s triangular sails fell and only the lower ones were left, as a mere adjunct to the engines. That supposed a great loss of character, because it destroyed the slender, vertical profile of a sailing ship. In this case, it may also have been the reason she sank. Those hybrid sail and engine vessels always looked like birds with grapeshot in one wing. In an abuse of the language, those vessels continued to be described as sailing ships with auxiliary engines. They were exactly the opposite: vessels with engines and auxiliary sails.

In the specific case of the *Douamont*, it would have been difficult to pinpoint what the vessel was. For whatever reasons, her huge engines were in a dreadful state. They had a dubious, if not totally nil, level of efficiency. The *Douamont* was a sailing ship with few sails and clapped-out engines.

She had set out from Marseille laden with floor tiles and roof slates from the huge Provence brickworks and was heading for Havana and New York. She also carried an amazing amount of cargo on deck.

When she entered within view of Cape Creus, the weather was poor: the sky was overcast and low, and easterly squalls were roaring on the rocks along the coast, with intermittent heavy downpours. Perhaps the wind wasn't gusting as much as it sometimes did, but high waves were surging. It was one of those winter days when people gathered by the fireside can't imagine anyone might be out in that weather, let alone out at sea. The sight of the merchant ship in the blue-black light, swathed by curtains of water, in the middle of a wild, empty sea, wasn't a happy one.

The *Douamont* was sailing with sea and wind battering its sides. It was progressing slowly using all available sails: the jib sail and four lower sails. Its speed suggested it wasn't using its engines. Later that became obvious. It was clear to the naked eye that it was drifting toward the coast. From land it would have been difficult to determine whether that movement was voluntary or forced. There was more sea than wind, which meant that the vessel's landward lurches seemed perilous – or at any rate most peculiar.

When she reached what her captain decided was a prudent distance from the coast, the merchant ship attempted to maneuver round and head out in search of deeper water. But the maneuver failed. The rudder didn't respond and the maneuver simply *failed* – there's no other way to describe the precise nature of the captain's defeat. For the relatively small amount of sail the *Douamont* had raised there was too little wind, and the power of the sea meant the rudder hadn't enough pull to make the vessel turn. Soon after, she repeated the maneuver and failed again. The situation suddenly became alarming. Given its tonnage, the vessel hadn't enough sails to achieve the necessary agility of movement. As she couldn't use her engines, the ship's maneuver had been calculated as if she were using all her sails. But as a large number of those had been removed, particularly those that were best in maneuvers when there was little wind, she was left like a bird with broken wings, with insufficient defenses.

She tried to turn for a third time, with the same outcome: nothing doing. The forward boom didn't move. In the meantime, pressure from wind and sea kept forcing her landward.

The moment came when it was quite obvious they would be hard put to miss the rocks to the east of Cadaqués Bay: S'Oliguera Point. To say the ship had entered treacherous waters would have been an understatement: in truth, she had set out on a path to destruction that only a miracle – one must describe certain eventualities one way or another – could change in its favor.

From that point in time things unraveled quickly. The *Douamont* gave out signals that she was in distress. Someone on the coast saw these signals. The information was quickly relayed to Cadaqués. The lifeboat bell was rung. The lifeboat was speedily launched. The sound of the bell stirred the town from its slumbers. It had been years since anything so unusual had shattered the soporific winter haze over

Cadaqués, and people spilled into the street instinctively, sponta-neously. The most cautious – there are always cautious people in that neck of the woods – put on their clogs and grabbed their umbrellas. Most went onto the beach in their fireside attire. They saw the life-boat rowing strongly, against wind and sea, out of the bay. It was clear a shipwreck was on the cards. By the way they were rowing, you could see it was an emergency. Rain was pouring down. The weather was appalling. There were huge pools of water on the Podritxó espla-nade. The turbid sea seethed. Waves boomed against the coast. The whole country seemed immersed in distant church-organ music, produced afar by a surging sea. Reverberations that floated in the air, tangible and dynamic, only immediately to disappear into the immense, indifferent void. It wasn't suitable weather to go and watch a shipwreck – it wasn't weather to go and watch anything. Even so, people headed over to S'Arenella Island, because in the end, among other reasons, the presence of that lifeboat speeding out of the bay was quite unusual. It was impossible to quell the children's curiosity. When they heard the word "shipwreck," they were so intrigued that all but the sick and the meek followed en masse where everyone else was heading.

As the lifeboat left the bay, it encountered more obstacles, down to the poor weather. The floor of Cadaqués Bay is hospitable in all kinds of weather; however, when the storm comes from the east, as you leave the bay, past the Ros beach and reefs, the swell of the sea turns heavy and deep. The lifeboat began to hop over the waves like a nutshell. There have always been good rowers in Cadaqués. More-over, the tiller was in the hands of Senyor Pío Ribas, a merchant navy captain and an intelligent, cold, taciturn gentleman, with lengthy experience at sea. Despite the difficulties, the lifeboat made progress, and when it found the endangered vessel, it redoubled its efforts to move closer. It was not an easy situation to resolve. It's a well-known fact that when big waves hit shallow seas their volume assumes unheard-of proportions. That's why vessels never intentionally come close to land: the deeper the water, the more confidently they can sail. The *Douamont* was fatally, tragically, entering shallow waters. As she did so, the sea swelled, and her position became more passive amid phenomenal squalls of water, and her hulk more resigned and dead, lurching dramatically this way and that. People had reached S'Arenella Beach; some, using whatever means, had crossed the small strait between the mainland and the island and were silently observing the tragedy with anguished hearts. The *Douamont* was three or four rope lengths from the island, and the waves were so tall that, though they were so near, the onlookers often lost sight of the hull and lower part of the masts. It was a depressing spectacle, as might be a beheading of the innocents, because there was no possible defense against the inevitable outcome.

The lifeboat finally reached the side of the merchant ship, and if it had been difficult to establish contact, it became even harder to maintain in those swirling waters. Nevertheless, Captain Ribas, with his hand on the tiller, performed wonderful operations. He was a man who had a real touch out at sea. They found the *Douamont*'s crew, driven crazy, rather than demoralized, and in a state of benumbed stupefaction. Why hadn't they tried to anchor? They did so now, but it was already too late. They should have done that when the water was deeper, not so close to land where the waves surged so turbulently. Part of the crew was involved in the maneuver to anchor; the Senegalese sailors on board didn't move from the corner where they lay cowering, more dead than alive, a black human mass that seemed to grow sallow as their fear heightened.

Nevertheless, it is absolutely true that, despite the terrible situation, the lifeboat was able to establish two lifelines with the *Douamont*. In the course of establishing the second, they managed to throw them a magnificent new hemp rope, more than seventy fathoms long, in case the crew needed to abandon ship. It was a struggle to tie the rope halfway up one mast, with the idea of creating a sloping lifeline with the other end tied to land, down which the crew could slide. In fact, nobody was sure the *Douamont* would remain at anchor as she was being so pounded by the sea. Any such prophecy was worth less than a puff of pipe smoke.

Very quickly reality confirmed that was the case. The anchorage was severed and the vessel was again a huge dead weight at the mercy of the crashing sea. She slowly lurched onto the coast off S'Arenella Island. It was only a matter of time before she hit the first line of rocks – the vessel could hardly float, she was so full of cargo.

It was time to rescue people. When they had managed to establish the sloping hemp lifeline, the crew started to slip down, each man using a sliding loop. The captain enforced perfect discipline during the operation: there was no violence or rushing. The crew reached land one after another. Their bodies exuded the stench of sopping wet animals. There was only one tragic case: a Senegalese crew member couldn't keep his body in the loop and by the time he landed, he'd been strangled by the rope around his neck.

The *Douamont* had kept a small herd of live, tame animals on board: sheep, hens, chickens and a cow. The captain, who was the last to abandon ship, released them before doing so. The animals immediately hurled themselves into the sea and swam to the coast. The cow and sheep struggled to get a footing on land. The odd leg was broken, though they were all rescued. What most impressed the children watching: the frenzied attempts made by the cow to scramble onto the slippery coastal rocks, its anguished look as it emerged from the water.

Meanwhile, the denouement took place. The *Douamont* was thrown up like a feather on the crest of a wave, and as she crashed down, a loud crack was heard that echoed through the air. It was a violent blow, like a sudden discharge of electricity or a huge hammer striking a block of steel, coldly precise. The crash made it lurch, as if it was being decapitated: all the cargo on deck fell into the water. That first, almost metallic collision with the rocks shattered the thousands and thousands of tiles and slates the *Douamont* was carrying. The merchant ship was gripped by a second, hurtling wave, which, in a furious crescendo, hit the ship's lower decks: the eyewitnesses were terrified: they watched the vessel burst like a grenade. Rigging clattered heavily into the sea. The ship rapidly began to sink. The tiles in the salt water created a murky, pinkish color around the wreck. The struggle between the half-submerged ship and the pounding waves lasted for two or three hours. Objects began to float on the surface of the surrounding water. Over subsequent days, those items were collected and sold to rag-and-bone men. After four hours of smashing against the rocks, no trace of the ship was left. All was lost and invisible, and the waves concealed the site of the catastrophe with a show of stunning might.

The strangled Senegalese sailor was buried in the sailors' graveyard. Some sailors were kept in hospital for a few days. Others got drunk that very same night, crawling from tavern to tavern, in silent, elemental fashion. Once the paperwork was completed, they were all repatriated.

A few years later, the ship's anchors and chains were salvaged.

Only a few remnants of that huge four-master are left. The floor of the sea around S'Arenella Island contains an enormous quantity of floor-tile and roof-slate fragments, between which purply-green or reddish-mauve seaweed grows. For many years there were also rusty iron deposits on the small beach nearest the island. These deposits pertained to the *Douamont*. However, the last time I was in those parts, I noticed they had vanished. Today, not a single trace remains of the wreck in the place where the disaster unfolded

"The Ferrera or Montjoi *bau* is right there. Take a look!" the boat's skipper told me, leaning over the side of the boat.

I leaned over next to him.

"Can you see it?"

"I think so. . . Yes, it's as clear as anything!"

Four fathoms down I could see a whitish, vaguely yellow colloidal shape that was bright and luminous. From under the water it pointed toward the surface like an upside-down pyramid of light, white and dazzling.

The sea was becalmed. It was a clear, radiant day. There wasn't a breath of wind. We were on the edge of the outer rim of Ferrera Bay, on a straight line from Falconera to Cape Norfeu.

"Is that the *bau*?" I asked.

"Yes, senyor. That's the Ferrera *bau*. Look how precipitous the rock is, to the south. It looks as if it's been hewn out. The Greek vessel lies at the foot of that precipice. . ."

When the Roses fishermen on board heard mention of the Greek vessel they all laughed loudly. No doubt that shipwreck had brought to mind something amusing.

The day was so clear, the sea so calm, it was hard to imagine a ship sinking there, a Greek one, by the name of *Phaedo*, that's right, like Plato's dialogue in which professors debate dogma.

In Catalan, a *bau* is one thing, a *niell* another and an *escull* yet another. An *escull* is a rock that always juts out from the surface of the sea. A *niell* is rock that is superficially immersed by the sea. When there's a drought, a *niell* may feel the sun; however, generally, it's under quite a lot of water, and that's the reason why a *niell* may also be called a submerged *escull*. A *bau* is a *niell* that is deeper down – that is, a rock several fathoms under the surface. Evidently, when the waves are deep, they hit the *bau* and that collision produces the same swirling waters as an *escull* or *niell*. By virtue of their invisibility, *baus* are a danger to shipping, and that's why they are usually marked on good maritime charts. At any rate, the Ferrera *bau* is marked. And if I'm not mistaken, that's the place where the *Phaedo*, registered in Piraeus, foundered.

I was first told about the existence of that Greek wreck by fishermen who hailed from the port of Roses, when we were returning from some paternoster line fishing. I was later sufficiently intrigued to investigate further.

The *Phaedo* reached the port of Barcelona from a North African port – Algiers, if my memory doesn't deceive me – two or three years late, in terms of its commercial value. It was transporting a cargo of drums of sodium hydrate and a large amount of beans – hundreds of tons.

"You say it was transporting beans?"

"Yes, senyor. Various. Black-eyed peas and white beans. When the

Phaedo reached Barcelona, the big trade in foodstuffs during the First World War was over. The smuggling of previous years had fizzled out. Obviously, if the goods had looked in better shape, they would still have been marketable."

"What was wrong with the goods?"

"The beans were in a bad state; they were damaged. In fact, they were unsellable – only a Greek could have imagined he might still close a deal on them. In any case, although Greeks have a sharp business sense, they sometimes show their cards and go far too far."

"That's an ancient habit."

"Yes, senyor! Very ancient. That's true. But let's not be sidetracked. The *Phaedo*'s captain was a sailor of the most ancient stripe. He didn't just own his vessel, but, except in cases when he was hired (something he hated), he also almost always owned the cargo he was transporting. He was a shipper who doubled as a businessman – as the most recalcitrant coastal skippers were. That man had bought for a rock-bottom price a load of beans in North Africa he intended to sell in Barcelona. Once he reached this side of the Mediterranean, he spared no effort to do so; however, despite his persuasive, wily cunning, a fortnight later, he hadn't managed to off-load his beans."

"I understand."

"And one thing became as bright and clear as the sun shining down on us: the Greek had invested all his wealth in that piece of business. The fact he'd been unable to bring it off meant he was totally bankrupt. Every day that passed, the beans rotted more, making the bilge of that pestilent old hull fouler by the moment. I imagine you realize that vessel with such a Socratic moniker was incredibly old. In any case, apparently it was the last trip she was going to make under the Greek flag, because the captain's plans to sell the boat to Italy were well advanced. Great mariners, the Greeks and Italians, have always specialized in the art of sailing aging vessels retired by English and Scandinavian owners – above all by the English. When, for whatever reason, an English ship owner decided that a boat he owned had come to the end of her working life and that any attempt to keep her on the sea would be dangerous, a Greek or Italian buyer would come along and sail her for another twenty or so years, with total peace of mind. Obviously, it's not clear what that total peace of mind represented; the art of keeping that kind of ramshackle ship afloat is full of hazards and triggers many a headache. Nonetheless, by the shores of the Mediterranean, poverty has always been the source of all possible theoretical and practical knowledge, and in that sense, the art of sailing battered hulls past their halcyon days is one of the mysteries of the culture of that sea – one of its most complex, intriguing and decent aspects. Clearly, after all I've said, these boats are almost inevitably fated to become wrecks. Even so, giving them another twenty or thirty years of life by virtue of continuous patching and mending, performing miracles daily – even earning money! – with everything hanging by a thread, shows a genuinely impressive merit. The case of the *Phaedo* scaled almost sublime heights. To have succeeded in interesting another buyer after the last drop of Greek science had squeezed her dry represented a nigh on ineffable miracle."

"But did that buyer really exist?"

"The captain said he did."

"Do you think that enough proof?"

"How do I know? I've never required total precision when it comes to people's intentions or words. The fact of the matter is, once all possibility of a deal had gone, the captain found himself in a most unpleasant situation. The *Phaedo* had in its hold only a tiny amount of coal, and the possibility of buying more, with real money, was out of the question. The time came when the situation was exposed in all its rawness. The captain had only one route to take – a route that might make us laugh, but it was one he judged to be the only way out: a clear-sighted, full-scale, perfect shipwreck in order to get insurance money. When the boat left the port of Barcelona (very slowly, to save fuel), supposedly heading for Marseille, the captain had already taken every necessary measure to ensure what we might dub a model shipwreck. Naturally, he had to find a quiet place, a place with the best conditions for achieving a wreck. It takes as much effort to do things badly as it takes to do them well; however, there are often considerable financial benefits to doing them one way or another. That Greek captain wanted to do things the best way possible. . . This may seem unlikely at this point in the tale, but events will show that this is unquestionably true.

"And so, one fine day, the idlers of Cadaqués spotted a steamship sailing by very close to land, unusually slowly, going in the direction of Cape Creus. At the time so many steamships passed by they didn't raise an eyebrow. However, their curiosity was aroused when an hour and a half later the vessel turned and retraced the route by which it had come. What was behind this retreat? If the steamship was sailing around Cape Béar – that is, toward Port-Vendres – it was unimaginable that the weather had forced it to drift, because the weather was as placid as a pond. It was a splendid and clear day. Their curiosity was aroused even further when they saw the ship repeat the operation for a second time: in effect, they watched it pass by a second time and return yet again. What did those strange movements mean? For the moment nobody could fathom it. If she had been a familiar ship, they'd no doubt have speculated endlessly, but they'd never seen that hull before, so all was soon forgotten.

"Those unusual comings and goings revealed one thing: the captain's immense professional quality, at that specific juncture at least, in the operation he was trying to execute. Obviously, one can shipwreck anywhere at all – that's within the scope of all brains, even the most elemental. But choosing the most appropriate spot is no spur-of-the-moment act. There are infinite places on Cape Creus where one *could* sink a boat. The Ferrera *bau* offers exceptional conditions and even seems providentially marked on maritime charts to that end. However, the captain wasn't content with what we might call official indications. He wanted to conduct a detailed recce himself to see if there might be an even more suitable spot. That was the reason for his to-and-froing opposite Cadaqués.

"I am so sure of this that I will add that if the *Phaedo*'s captain had had more coal, he'd have recced much farther, to the gulf of La Selva and the Roussillon coast. But his coal was running out and he had to reach a decision. All things considered, he felt that the *bau* we've mentioned offered the best conditions, and without more ado, he steered toward it, perfectly clear minded and displaying a high level of professional expertise.

"The captain had a crew that was very fond of him: he wouldn't have hurt his people, and his sailors bore him no ill feeling; moreover, they were aware of his present difficulties and sympathized. They hardly needed to speak a word to understand each other. When the crew saw that the *Phaedo* was returning to the Roses coast, they realized the operation was reaching a climax, that the hull had entered its pre-demise state. The sailors accepted this philosophically, with perfect calm. Almost all the old crew members had been involved in repeated shipwrecks. They had been victims of Greek ship owners' commercial acumen, of their ability to postpone shipwrecking and fight off the inevitable fate of their fleet. Some had shipwrecked in infinitely more dramatic circumstances. In any case, there was this difference: that operation faced benign, harmless conditions, with scant danger: everything was so patently placid. Such an operation always entails an element of unexpected, random danger, a moment of genuine peril. A shipwreck close to the coast is always more feasible that one six hundred miles from land in an overcast, stormy Atlantic. The weather was good: it was weather, one might say, for a fail-safe shipwreck: the sky was clear and the sea soporific, and there wasn't a breath of air. Who could have asked for anything more?

"That was how the situation appeared on the surface. The psychological state of the less-experienced crew members wasn't poor either. Tragic possibilities, tricky decisions, arouse a crew's spirit of adventure and hankering for change. They are men who are always restless, who like to be transported by their imagination (however modest and low grade they might be), so anything is welcome provided it is distinct and challenging. The inventive minds of these men are so marked by blood-and-guts brio, they can be satisfied only by situations where there is no way out, scenarios of absurdity and gritty, out-of-this-world fun. Misadventures of all sorts appeal to their elemental vanity – the vanity that fills taverns in the Mediterranean and everywhere else, especially those visited by mariners. So when the *Phaedo*'s crew faced the possibility of a change of climes, with subsequent repatriation to Marseille and a return to Greece in a magnificent, clean, white, spick-and-span Messageries Maritimes vessel, not having to do a thing, not having to move an inch, with food, drink and comfort guaranteed, they reckoned the world had suddenly become a much kinder place.

"Meanwhile, their captain had discovered the bay of Montjoi and the Ferrera *bau* on his charts. He decided the place was interesting enough to warrant a recce. Like the inhabitants of Cadaqués, the Roses fishermen were rather surprised to see that unknown vessel sail to and fro past the bay so slowly. What did those movements mean? Nevertheless, they felt it was all quite relative, because in that area, in those years, too many curious things had happened at sea for people to get easily worked up. In truth, we cultivated – or inherited – all our thick skin from those times.

"Finally, the captain seemed content. It was all about finding a convincing enough alibi and he felt he'd found it. His idea went like this: the *Phaedo* had sprung a leak. Every necessary measure was taken to keep the water out after this disaster occurred; all these measures showed it was hopeless; given the amount of water flooding into the bilge, he'd been forced to give the order for the vessel to be run aground in the most practical, favorable spot; he'd thus had to give the order to head toward the beach in Montjoi Bay, which the captain felt was relatively sheltered from winds; he ordered the engines to be turned full on and it was in the course of carrying out that order that the *Phaedo* hit an unknown (and unmarked) rock and sank there and then. . .

"The signs indicated that was the captain's idea, but things had turned out differently.

"As the *Phaedo* slowly approached the site of the 'indescribable catastrophe' (the words in the captain's report), the crew, in a most disciplined fashion, perhaps with a grin or two, headed to their berths in the prow to spruce themselves up. They shaved, combed their hair, put on the best clothes from their suitcases and proceeded to organize all their belongings in the best way they knew. The vessel was on course to destruction, but the crew was preparing itself as if she had anchored in the best port and it was time to jump on land. As they were completing their gaudy toilettes, they gathered on the bridge by the ladder to disembark. Lifeboats were ready; everything was perfectly in order; they only had to be lowered into the sea; every measure had been taken to avoid accidents.

"The group was a sight for sore eyes. Greeks like to be flashy – they are somewhat oriental in that sense – and when they are in all their finest regalia, they seem particularly happy. If they are lucky enough to have curly hair, they feel highly important. If they have that kind of special hair, they put theirs caps on carefully, so as not to flatten it. Unless they are the kind who wear nothing on their head so people can stare in wonder at their fabulous hair. That group of men, so well attired, so straight and stiff in their party outfits, with hairdos out of pictures taken in a studio, looked like people going to a wedding or christening: in the context of that vessel, it was hugely comic.

"From what one could see, the captain had calculated remarkably well. He arrived near the Ferrera *bau* – hardly half a mile outside the bay – in the midafternoon. His vessel proceeded very slowly. The weather remained excellent. The captain swung the *Phaedo*'s prow toward the *bau* – slowing down her engines as much as he could. The whole crew gathered in front of the ladder that had been lowered over the side. Longboats from Roses were passing by to go fishing off Cape Creus. Those on board the *Phaedo* signaled to one, which made an approach. Speaking in a strange language, of which the longboat skipper grasped only the odd, Italian-sounding word, they conveyed to him that he should pick up the crew. The skipper, who really understood nothing, shrugged his shoulders and steadied himself passively to do everything those strange men were asking. 'Pessetes, pessetes!' the Greek repeated now and then, to back his opaque declarations with a weighty argument. The crew clambered down the ladder with their bundles and battered suitcases and settled down in the sides of the longboat. They silently descended one after another, saying nothing, and slotted themselves in stiffly, politely, on their best behavior. In the meantime, the *Phaedo* drew closer to the *bau*, extremely slowly. Its captain was still on the upper bridge, with the rode in front. The longboat kept up with the steamship, next to the ladder. The fishermen were so astonished, were so surprised to see the vessel heading onto the rock, that perhaps seeing it all so clearly rendered them speechless. It was so unconceivable and odd they could only gawp. Then the moment came when they could no longer hear the engines. The *Phaedo* was some forty yards from the rock. It continued forward, impelled by its previous speed. The collision took place and was perceptible, though not at all dramatic: a dull, muffled sound. After the collision, the ship naturally jolted backward. A moment later, they heard the muted noise of an explosion, as if a depth charge had exploded inside the wreck. The Greek crew looked down. The captain rapidly abandoned the bridge and appeared at the top of the ladder. He was embarked on the longboat in a second. The *Phaedo* lurched significantly and slowly and gently began to slip down – like a wafer dunked into a glass of water that's slowly coming apart. Three quarters of an hour after the explosion that created the leak, she was on the bottom of the sea.

"Once the captain had observed his boat was going down slowly but surely, he didn't think it worth wasting another moment. He asked the skipper to take them to the port of Roses, where they disembarked and were repatriated a few days later, after the routine paperwork had been completed. Five months after these curious happenings an English gentleman arrived in Roses who said he was an agent for Lloyds of London. He contacted Senyor Llorens, a highly esteemed man in the locality and the famous insurance company's representative in Roses. The agent's job was to investigate the circumstances of the *Phaedo*'s wrecking on the Montjoi *bau*.

"Senyor Llorens suggested that Costas Contos, the Greek deepsea diver living in Cadaqués, should recce the wreck. His idea was immediately accepted. The Lloyd's agent gave Contos two precise instructions: first he asked him to examine minutely the impact on the rock of the collision with the ship's prow, then the nature of the leak caused by the explosion.

"Contos went down and scrutinized the *Phaedo*, and in particular the two issues raised by the agent. The diver's statement was a model affair. The vessel's collision with the rock wasn't powerful enough to have caused it to go down: it had left only a scrape, not a deep incision, on the rock. The artifact that caused the explosion had produced a hole some two square yards in size on the port side – a hole produced from the inside outward, because the iron plating was bent in that direction. Contos's statement was confirmed by the fisherman on the longboat who had witnessed the shipwreck. The economic outcome of the operation was negative. Blinded by his bad losses in the business of the rotten beans, the Greek had planned and executed a shipwreck that was too perfect, that had nothing untoward. He had showed his hand and lost his every drachma."

I once conversed with Contos about the Montjoi shipwreck.

"'When I went down the first time,' he told me, 'the vessel was intact. She had barely been in the water six months. I recced her every inch. She was a vessel with certain pretensions. Before being a cargo boat, she had been a mail boat. You could see the radiators, she still retained some of her passenger cabins; the dining room had those typical rotating chairs fixed to the floor. The steamship, which was absolutely flat some thirty fathoms down, still seemed alive; her funnel, mast and rigging were in place; everything seemed normal; naturally, the doors had swelled, and I had to force them open, but inside the dining room nothing seemed amiss. She sank so slowly and gently, without any undue violence that some items were still on the tables. I brought up a coffee cup and saucer from my first recce. When I showed them to that English gentleman, he asked me very politely to restore those items to their rightful place, because Lloyds of London didn't want anything that wasn't rightfully its property. I thought that was taking things too far, you know? The hole where the leak was had filled with beans. The *Phaedo* was carrying beans loose in the bilge. The mouth of the hole was one amazing fish breeding ground. I've never seen such a shoal of white sea bream as I saw there. The fish ate the beans the sea had swollen. Some beans were twice their normal size on land. The fish ate everything and their greed was literally indescribable. There were deep-sea mussels hanging in clusters from the boat's rigging – they are much bigger than those from farmed mussel beds. I brought up some thirty kilos of mussels and tried to sell them in Roses but with no success, though they were extremely tasty. People thought they were too big and weren't interested.'"

Later on there were several campaigns to bring some of these articles up from the wreck, and many tons of items have been salvaged including excellent, though rusty, iron, as you'd expect of things manufactured during the much-vaunted reign of "glorious" Queen Victoria.

The downpours that usually accompany squalls from the east are never preceded by electric storms, by the crackle of thunder and lightning. The huge rainfalls brought on by autumnal and wintry southwesterly gales, on monotonous, depressing afternoons, do, on the other hand, generally provide spectacular electric fireworks. Downpours from the east are a dirty yellow, seem passive and resigned; southwesterly squalls are porous and bluey-white, and they create strikingly active haze. Downpours from the east move, pass by and flee; those from the southwest are static and fall by virtue of their mathematical verticality. On land and sea, they hurl down large bluish bubbles that bounce off roofs, hop over stones, in an intense, cosmic, stupefied, momentary show of strength.

On the night of the sinking of the *Tregastel*, a French steamship that lies off Bona Cove in Mar d'Avall, a malign southwesterly was blowing – it was raining cats and dogs and was frightening and foul, with nil visibility.

The first news of the sinking of the *Tregastel* reached Cadaqués when a life jacket that bore the ship's name was found in the sea. Later, news came of survivors from the wreck reaching the Cape Creus lighthouse and even remoter spots on the peninsula. The appearance of hirsute, desolate, bedraggled men caused more fear than joy. A lifeboat was also discovered in Guillola Bay and another in an unlikely place at La Pelosa on the Roses coast. The two boats were clearly part of the *Tregastel*'s life-saving equipment.

Only the vaguest of conjectures exist as to why the shipwreck happened. Only one thing is really certain: on the night of the catastrophe, the lights were out, because the country was engaged in a civil war, and as a result of the likelihood of aerial bombing raids, use of the lights had been suspended. Today that might seem incredible, but the lights *were* switched off. The Cape Creus lighthouse had been hit by a bomb, and so it too was in darkness.

The vessel, registered with a tonnage of 1,800, was coming from North Africa and was empty, carrying only ballast. She was heading – or so the circumstances of her sinking would indicate – somewhere on the western coast of the Gulf of Lion, most probably to Port-Vendres. If she had been intending to go to a port farther into the body of the gulf, she wouldn't have come so close to land. Even though visibility was extremely poor, because the lighthouses weren't up and running, we can ascertain this much. In a word, the *Tregastel* at some point in time turned toward Cape Béar, thinking she had negotiated Cape Creus; in reality, however, when she began that turn, she hadn't yet rounded the cape. That error inevitably guided her onto the rocks. She got it wrong by only two or three miles – nothing more. The rudder turned a quarter of an hour too soon.

According to the stories, the *Tregastel's* first collision with rocks was on the island of Messina, which is outside and to the east of Cadaqués Bay. It must have been a hellish, lightning crash. She was brought aground by the collision, but she must have been left in such a precarious, listless state that she no longer had the strength to head back out into deeper water. As the rain poured down, one imagines the boat shuddered tragically.

Apart from that first disastrous incident everything else is conjecture that can't be clarified. The small island of Messina is rocky but has no *esculls*, *niells* or *baus*. The wind and sea must have pushed the steamship off the rocks, and rudderless, damaged by the collision and leaking, the *Tregastel* must have been dragged toward the coast by the sirocco.

On that path to perdition, those on board must have had a sure, if imprecise, sense of the approaching coast – no doubt because of the roiling sea. It is a fact, revealed by later underwater reconnaissance, that the *Tregastel* at some point cast out her anchors. The steamship lies outside Bona Cove, her prow upturned and her stern seated on the sea's sloping underwater plain. The *Tregastel*'s strange position, incongruous with the regular gusts of the sirocco in Bona Cove, can partially be explained by the decision to cast the anchors once the vessel was already on the rocks. But that's another ex post facto explanation, and such conjectures are but empty blather when it comes to the sea. There are at least two extenuating circumstances explaining why the *Tregastel* anchored too late: the anchor ropes may have snapped, or the steamship might have reached the coast so submerged in the sea, with so much water in her bilge, that anchoring her was seen as a lesser evil, aimed at stabilizing the wreck rather than helping to save the vessel.

At this point, people must have begun to scatter. The two lifeboats were lowered into the sea, and the crew swarmed into them. Neither of the boats tried to reach the coast that was right in front of their noses, a few yards away. The sound of the sea on the rocks must have led them to think it was a rough, dangerous coast. But in that kind of boat, a more feasible spot for them to reach would have been Bona Cove or – even more feasible, given the weather – Jugadora Cove, which they could have quickly reached. Not knowing the lay of the land, unable to see a thing, they fled far from their safest options.

Those wretched folk started to row against wind and sea. Given the implacable blasts of the sirocco – it was a proper sea storm – it is easy to imagine the efforts they had to make. Life, however, feels much more valuable when its loss is imminent. One of the boats had less nerve than the other. Those aboard this boat no doubt reached Guillola Bay. It seems likely that when they found themselves sheltered from the sea's onslaught, they decided it was a suitable place to disembark. They landed and, stripped of everything that could have satisfied their most elemental needs, they decided to divide into search parties. One group groped its way across terrain difficult even for people who know the area and reached the Cape Creus lighthouse many hours later. Some were lost in the mountains and finally found remote farmhouses in the hinterland.

The other lifeboat showed remarkable prowess, given the weather and the effort required to win out. They rowed against a relentless sea and gusting wind and covered over four miles to reach La Pelosa, a beach on the Roses coast, between Norfeu and Montjoi. The boat foundered on the beach, and the crew abandoned it and scattered inland.

After a few days and countless difficulties – it being the middle of the civil war – the crew members gathered together in Roses and were finally repatriated.

Ever since the winter of 1937, the *Tregastel* has lain at the bottom of the sea in Bona Cove. So far it has not been touched by a soul, although the wreck has been recced. Its sacking has been delayed time and again because the hulk sparked a degree of diplomatic activity between Spain and France. The French owners believe themselves still in possession of rights to the contents of the wreck and wish to participate in the salvaging of the submerged scrap iron. As a result, the wreck is subject to litigation.

Even though her location is relatively shallow – the prow is thirty or so yards under water and the stern twenty or so – there is no danger that the sea will break her up. She's in deep enough that the waves and sea swells can't reach her. Over time, mineral chemical reactions, the activity of maritime flora and fauna, could devour the vessel. Destruction by some mechanical means, on the other hand, is unlikely.

Two or three yards beneath the sea's surface movements, immense tranquility reigns; it is a static, motionless place. As depth increases, the chill grows and the light dims. There is only one phenomenon that can disrupt this stasis: underwater currents, which are stronger or weaker depending on location. The depths of the sea become more or less murky depending on the direction of these currents. The *Tregastel* is too close to the coastline for sea currents to affect the area where she is submerged. It would be another matter if she were in the area of the currents from Cape Creus, which are, as pointed out in *Nautical Instructions* and demonstrated in daily reality, very strong. The hulk is but a shadow – there are only shadows at the bottom of the sea – located in still waters, enjoying a silent, deathly peace.

THE SINKING
OF THE *CALA GALIOTA*:
Conversations with Dalí
The Painter's Father

⁓

The motor-powered schooner *Cala Galiota*, registered in Palma, Majorca, and owned by La Naviera Mallorquina SA, weighing one hundred twenty tons, with a crew of seven, went down on 3 December 1946, when it was making the crossing – without cargo, but with proper ballast – from Barcelona to Palma. When the news reached Cadaqués quite a few days later, people were shocked because its boatswain, Ferran Ribera Dalmau, hailed from there. As I was living in Cadaqués at the time, I experienced this sense of shock firsthand. There was a similar emotional reaction in Palafrugell, where the Ribera family had lived and was well liked. The sinking of the schooner made me personally very depressed, not only because it affected the two towns to which I was most attached at the time – Cadaqués, where I was living, and Palafrugell, my birthplace – but also because her sinking was dramatic and strange in the extreme. Everything was lost when she went down: the whole crew and the whole boat. Not a single trace of the *Cala Galiota* has ever been found: not a piece of timber, a remnant of sail, rope or tiniest item. Nothing at all. Everything went down to the bottom of the sea and left not the slightest trace. That means – as I see it – that people haven't a clue about why she was wrecked: not the causes, not the mechanics, not a single detail. We haven't a scrap of information, and that has led to a huge amount of conjecture. People like to imagine, which is very easy! The event was blown up out of proportion, because the schooner was following a route where there was a lot of traffic, night and day: Barcelona to Palma via Sa Dragonera.

After living in L'Escala for a few years, I decided I ought go to live in Cadaqués. I was intending to finish my *Guidebook to the Costa Brava* there. This was a commission from a publishing house, like most of what I've written. I described the central part of the coast in the house I rented in Fornells de Begur. Then I went to Tossa to write the southern section. Only the north remained to describe and I decided that Cadaqués would be the most suitable base. Senyor Tianet Rahola, the chemist in the El Poal neighborhood, rented me a house on La Riba, a wonderful house that had a balcony overlooking the bay, with views over the Pitxot establishment, El Llaner, El Baluard and the church, which were a constant source of fascination. I spent several days on that balcony in a state of deep contemplation. By dint of so much contemplation, I realized I was becoming wiser rather than richer by the day, and much to my regret, I had to relent. Life was good in Cadaqués. There were a few local tourists in summer. In other months, there was just the presence of the town and a wonderful sense of solitude and remoteness. The fish was delicious, the olive oil, anchovies, bread, wine, crustaceans and mussels, unrivaled. The northern gales blew, sometimes you couldn't even walk out in them; the climate was dry and seemed to have been made expressly for my metabolism. The geology was dark, Pyrenean and mysterious, and the wind made the olive groves glitter with silvery foam. It was a delightful place to live off your investments, to do nothing but contemplate land and sea. On the other hand, I myself had to do something to make ends meet. So I had to reduce my hours of contemplation, or at least change them. Living off investments was far out of my reach. A real shame.

At the time Senyor Rahola, a fine gentleman, helped me enormously. He lent me books, introduced me to his friends and relatives, invited me into the Casino, which had few members, but possessed a solitary corner, a library I found very useful. I located there the speech made by Frederic Rahola i Trémols on his entry into the Academy of Fine Literature in Barcelona, a document that is little known but unsurpassed in its account of medieval and eighteenth-century Cadaqués. I also found a few histories of Sant Pere de Roda and the land that was controlled by the great Benedictine monastery, material on the past of Roses, whose fascinating history has yet to be written, on the Treaty of the Pyrenees, etc. There was a lot to enable me to start on the last part of my *Guidebook to the Costa Brava*, scattered over a landscape that has been so devastated. I had secured the means to live in Cadaqués for a long stretch of time. I didn't regret my decision. Cadaqués was a pure delight at the time. Today there is a constant hullabaloo that is intolerable: when so many artists and their respective spouses gather in a town, with the confusion inherent in the species and the music that comes in tow, the results come straight out of the most overbearing literary fiction.

One winter's day in 1947, when the north wind was blowing and there was a clear sky and a diamond-bright sun, I went for an after-lunch stroll along La Riba, which is a very sheltered promenade. I had the pleasure of bumping into the rector of Cadaqués, a gentleman who was beginning to age and who, at that time of day, used to walk to the Oliveres beach, following the sheltered path around the bay.

"Are you doing anything in particular?" he asked immediately.

"No, nothing at all, senyor."

"Come with me for a while and I'll tell you something I've been charged to tell you. This will save me having to knock on your door and waste your time. Three or four days ago Senyor Dalí begged me to tell you to go see him at home because he has something he wants to tell you. Senyor Dalí lives on the other side of town, in El Llaner, and it's probably easier for you to go to his place than for him to come to yours. Senyor Dalí is getting on in years and doesn't usually budge from his home in winter."

I must have looked astonished. The rector reacted with a laugh: "Naturally you must think it odd I refer to Senyor Dalí the notary in these terms. You must think it odd that a priest like myself is speaking to you about Senyor Dalí. . ."

"Indeed I am."

"Well, it's not odd at all. Senyor Dalí nowadays is a very different man from the man he was years ago with that reputation he enjoyed in so many quarters. The revolution and war we suffered have quite subdued him. Senyor Dalí is no longer the anticleric he once was and is probably not even a republican. Today he is one of the most practicing Catholics in this parish, an exemplary Catholic."

"Now I understand! You must forgive my total ignorance of these matters."

"That's all right, senyor. Times have been trying and individuals have taken strange paths. Do you know Senyor Dalí?"

"Not very well, but obviously everyone knows everyone to an extent in the Ampurdan. He's a well-known, popular figure. He's made an intellectual and political impact well beyond notary circles."

"Absolutely. Senyor Dalí is a formidable character. He's retired from the notary world now. He has come to live in Cadaqués, after being the most senior notary in the regional college. He is a remarkable man and held in high regard. I often see him. I drop by. We talk, often at length. He's an impulsive, edgy individual and hates to be inactive. There are few like him in our country."

"The Dalís from the Figueres branch of the family are very unusual."

"It's a family that comes from Llers. . ." the rector says, smiling pleasantly.

"They might also be Irish. The surname Dalí makes one think of the Irish Ó Dálaigh. There have been many people with Gaelic, Scottish or Irish names in Spain. These adventurers have made little impact with the exception of General O'Donnell, whom Senyor Mañé i Flaquer held in such high esteem. When General O'Donnell led the Liberal Union Party, they built lots of roads and lighthouses – in the reign of Donya Isabel II."

We'd reached the corner of the street to go onto the Oliveres beach. The churchman stopped and said: "The north wind is really gusting. It seems to have ratcheted up. At my age. . . If you don't mind, we'll retrace our steps."

"Whatever you'd like. . ."

While we walked back, I asked the rector if he knew why exactly Senyor Dalí wanted to me to pay him a visit.

"Senyor Dalí right now is very much preoccupied by the sinking of the *Cala Galiota*. He has taken it to heart and wants to get the business resolved. He says it's taking too long. One of the victims is from Cadaqués, Ferran Ribera. He wants to clear up some doubts he has. I think he wants to ask you about something related to the press and the ship going down."

"If you see him before I do, please tell him that I will do anything he asks if I can, although I can't guarantee any outcome. Over three months have passed since the *Cala Galiota* was lost and nothing has been decided in relation to the men who went down. I can understand why Senyor Dalí is up in arms. Everybody is."

We said our goodbyes when we reached El Poal.

Two days later I want to Senyor Dalí's house in El Llaner. The north wind was still blasting. It's a long walk. I didn't meet a soul the whole way. Cadaqués seemed deserted. The only thing that was moving was the smoke from house chimneys, which the wind was blowing away.

Dalí the painter's father – which was how he always referred to himself throughout our long conversations, rather strangely in my view – gave me a very warm welcome in his magnificent gravelly baritone voice and his vaguely monstrous features lit up. I imagined he'd start by telling me about the sinking of the *Cala Galiota* immediately, but that wasn't the case. He spoke about himself, very specifically, in terms of the revolution and civil war we'd just experienced.

"You and I," he began, "met for the first time in the house and bookshop of our friend the herbalist Canet on La Rambla – he's a real saint. You know my brother Rafel, Doctor Dalí, who went to the gatherings in Barcelona's Athenaeum. When the revolution started, my brother weighed well over two hundred sixy pounds. You saw him when the storm was over in Plaça de Catalunya, with Camps Margarit. That fellow who was a fine, pleasant man, who'd never hurt anyone, can't have been seventy. I must confess I have always disliked ideas that act only to enfeeble people and transform them into wild animals: I find them repellent, they drive me crazy. The same happened to Camps Margarit, who was such a lively mind, a super-civilized humanist and generous to a fault. And even then they were lucky to escape with their lives. I spent the whole revolution in Figueres and still don't know how I survived. The notary office went bust. The office was then run by the Committee, which was a collection of resentful, demented, ignorant characters, at once incredibly dangerous and hair-raisingly frivolous. I do think that in the Ampurdan, we federal republicans and those who didn't think like us created a most pleasant level of coexistence,which had eliminated all forms of brutality. We had reached a *modus vivendi* that was courteous and viable. I don't think you could have hoped for anything better in the history of humanity. We'd rage at each other, but there was mutual respect. All that was destroyed thanks to theories about human progress and happiness."

Dalí the painter's father paused and then continued: "You've also met my brother-in-law Domènec, the bookseller on La Rambla in Barcelona. The Domènec bookshop was a good one, wasn't it?"

"Of course! It was the best in Barcelona even when I was a student. It stocked genuine books, the sort that sell few copies but that in the long run always keep selling. Books one wants to own and keep. All the others were stores that sold huge amounts of pulp fiction. Now, pulp fiction is important, just for a second. But what can we do? The world's like that, and there is no other. I liked Verdaguer the bookseller because he combined extreme politeness with disenchanted skepticism. And despite this, he never crumbled, and that's noteworthy, if I'm not mistaken."

Dalí the painter's father spoke up again and, after telling me he'd wanted to get in contact with me via the rector, he added that after spending half his life as a clergy basher, he now reckoned the town priest was the best friend he had.

"There are all kinds of priests. There are the hallowed sort who defend themselves with their claws when they think they need to. I do likewise when my own interests are threatened. Absolutely. The Church has this in its favor: it is a gigantic field of law in which every issue ends in agreement or a sentence. And that is my conception of the world: legality. Against violence, or the rule of might or depredation, legality. You know, the rector of Cadaqués is a wonderful, understanding man, a saint. He's my best friend. He's a real pleasure to talk to."

He paused, took a sip of coffee and continued: "We've had a very rough time. In those three years I spent in Figueres, I saw such a lot of bestial, brutal and ruthless acts that I was broken. I'd never have thought human beings were capable of such savagery. I'd always been an enlightened person, a supporter of progress, a supporter of strictly ethical behavior, a federal republican in good faith and over and beyond the pettiness of traditional politics here. All my beliefs were confounded. A time came when I was so downcast, I was so disillusioned, my state of mind was so low, that I sought out a friend and told him: 'If I'm not dead by then, please tell me when the doors of Figueres parish church are open for worship, and you'll find me there in the front pew opposite the priest and the altar.' The party is over. I feel that I've spent my entire life mouthing a few lunatic slogans, literally copied from France – copied, that is, mindlessly. In this country, I mean the Ampurdan, all these commonplaces are fake to the core. Just imagine the degree of fakery they represent on the peninsula, which has been so ravaged in human terms. Our mutual friend Joaquim Bech de Careda has popularized this view. It's absolutely right."

As I see this tirade has livened him up, I dare ask: "Now you've mentioned our friend Joaquim Bech, I'd like to tell you what he said about your attitude as a notary. According to him, you've been a very idiosyncratic notary. Notaries represent the wishes of their clients and that's the point of all their paperwork. Now, it seems that the wishes of your clients have more often been your own. . ."

"Perhaps, sometimes. . . A notary has to advise. In truth, that's a thorny. . ."

It was only after this long preamble that Senyor Dalí began to tell me about the sinking of the *Cala Galiota*.

"Did the *Cala Galiota* go down? Did she sink? From the very first I've always believed she was lost on the crossing from the port of Barcelona to Palma de Majorca, via Sa Dragonera. She was carrying no cargo. Apparently she'd been in dry dock in Barcelona and undergone a number of repairs that had restored her to a decent state. While they carried out these repairs, they replaced the usual engine-room man. She was a small schooner, a tonnage of one hundred twenty. She had a crew of seven: Antoni Ramon Marí, skipper; Antoni Perelló, engine-room man; Ferran Ribera Dalmau, boatswain; Josep Seva Javaloges, cook; Bartomeu Jofre, Vicenç Mayans, Vicenç Marí, seamen. Everything seems to indicate they encountered a fierce storm from the west on their crossing. After Cape Tossa, our coastline bends inward, which is why the wind we call a *garbí* on the north coast, or southwesterly in Barcelona, is called a westerly farther south. News reports suggest it was a gale-force storm, and the press also noted that several vessels that were due to go to Ibiza and Valencia never left the port of Palma. The truth is that nothing more was heard of the *Cala Galiota* after she left the port of Barcelona! Not a dicky bird had been heard of the schooner's plight in the course of its crossing. The *Cala Galiota* disappeared. The first question asked by the owners – La Naviera Mallorquina – after they registered her disappearance was, 'Did she go down?' If not, where did she end up? Given the storm and the direction of the wind that had set in, it is unthinkable they'd have tried to get back to the coast of the peninsula. It's much more feasible to imagine the vessel made its escape from the storm by trying to head south (North Africa) or eastward (Italy).

"The *Cala Galiota* left the port of Barcelona on 3 December 1946. Over the next few months, different investigations were set in motion to establish what had happened. The Ministry of State for Foreign Affairs asked various consulates in North Africa and Italy to report back any information they might cull. They didn't send any because there was none. There was a moment when the sea cast up a number of objects in the port of Pollença: timber, ropes, etc. It was all collected up and taken to Palma, where the most savvy people from La Naviera Mallorquina scrutinized it. They found no connection whatsoever to the *Cala Galiota*. Navy Command posts along the coast were also asked for any information they had. As they had none, they could say nothing. Naturally the crew's families were questioned: those of the Majorcan crew members by the company management and the others by their consignee in Barcelona. Their questioning brought nothing to light, so that after the first month when all possible investigations had been pursued, it was concluded that the schooner had simply gone down, without leaving the slightest trace, without the tiniest object being located that would allow the formulation of the flimsiest of hypotheses.

"So where did the *Cala Galiota* go down? What caused her to sink? Obviously, there was the storm from the west, fierce gales that it met head on. It's also true the schooner had been in other equally violent storms and had survived. On the other hand, when she disappeared, she was on a route she knew well. She had often plied that route, and in all weathers. It was a very busy route. Was the vessel in a fit state to sail? She was carrying no cargo, did she have sufficient ballast? Everyone agreed the crew knew what it was doing: it was excellent, experienced and efficient. What then *had* happened? Where, when and how? The investigations revealed nothing; people were totally stumped.

"After that first month of intense inquiries that produced no results – inquiries mainly carried out by the company – its managing director, Senyor Ramis Mut, sent a request to the Balearic Islands Navy Command audit committee to produce their final report. The investigating judge was the corvette captain Senyor Joan Serra Bonet, assisted by Senyor Francesc Baralduch. These two gentlemen signed off the file.

"The owners of the *Cala Galiota*, La Naviera Mallorquina SA, acted with all due caution as regards her disappearance. The whole business shocked seafaring folk in Palma and Barcelona, where the schooner was very well-known. People's opinions carry a lot of weight in these matters and things can't be dealt with lightly. The lives of seven men were involved, and that made a considerable impact, aggravated by lack of news. A lack of news always intensifies sadness and pessimism."

At this point, Dalí the painter's father, as Senyor Salvador preferred to be called at the time, paused, took another sip of coffee and continued: "I am convinced that right from the start La Naviera Mallorquina SA thought that it was purely and simply a case of the ship sinking. I did too. The crew's families were also unanimously of the same opinion. The schooner's company wanted to clear up some fake news in the press, to the effect that the boat might have tried to escape the storm and was now somewhere or other, what the English call 'whereabouts unknown.' The schooner was apparently off the coast of Corsica – that, at least, as we shall see, is what they were saying. The boat's owners wanted to clarify these claims and didn't want to pour oil on the fire of what people were generally already feeling, and so when none of the investigations bore fruit, they asked the naval committee of inquiry in the Balearic Islands to have the last word. Which is what it did.

"Now, this investigation is proving a very drawn out affair. I hardly need add that their report will officially declare that the vessel went down with all her crew and appurtenances. It's the only thing it can possibly say. In the meantime it's ongoing. I'm pretty sure that when we have it in our hands, it will be a paltry document. All that bureaucratic red tape drives me crazy, puts me at my wits' end. While the report is ongoing, the families of those drowned haven't been paid a cent and are absolutely poverty-stricken. The case will be closed, because there is no reason why it shouldn't be. But meanwhile, the families, who aren't being paid the drowned men's wages, are in sorry state."

"Were they insured?" I ventured.

"I think they were and I don't think that La Naviera Mallorquina SA is raising any objections on that front. You can't imagine the colossal amount of information that's needed to make an official declaration of a shipwreck. That's the stage we're at now. Nonetheless, I can tell you that all that paperwork makes my head spin. I can't understand it. As far as I'm concerned, it's a cruel shambles. In the meantime those poor families are starving to death. What can be done? I'm told you know high ups in La Naviera Mallorquina."

"Yes, senyor, I do. I've met them at some point. I don't know if those gentlemen will remember me. I can assure you I'm just one of many who have shaken their hands. . . and that's all. In today's world, people have met a fabulous number of individuals. . . who are then consigned to oblivion. Everything is oblivion."

"You could write to them explaining the state of play."

"Senyor Dalí, I'll do whatever you ask. You know that only too well."

"Who *are* these people who own La Naviera Mallorquina?"

"La Naviera Mallorquina is a company that owns a number of schooners that take cargo from the peninsular coast to the Balearic Islands. The company also has interests in salt production centers it owns in Ibiza and Torrevella, or Torrevieja in Spanish. I could almost say for sure that they're the biggest supplier of salt to Barcelona and the whole of Catalonia. The *Cala Galiota* transported salt to Barcelona for years. The company chair is Senyor Salas, a fine gentleman, key in the economy of Majorca, an open-minded, pleasant, cultured, extremely affable, stout fellow. I met him in the port of Andratx one day when I was there with Senyor Ventosa i Calvell, and Senyor Salas invited us to supper on his three-master, which he'd had converted into a large, luxurious yacht. At the time Senyor Ventosa was a minister, and consequently, Senyor Salas offered us a dinner that was unforgettable, above all because it was Majorcan, on his boat, the *Cala Encantada*. I've always liked this kind of thing, the little bonuses life brings. I will also add that I've always been the suspicious, wary kind, I've never believed in anything, I'm a hundred percent pessimistic, and I have always tried to be polite and undemanding, and that's as far as I've taken it. I've never asked anybody for anything and nobody has ever given me anything. There are no bones of contention. So, Senyor Dalí, if you want me to write to Senyor Salas about these poor drowned sailors, I will do so immediately. If there is no reply or if the reply is purely formal, the usual rhetoric, I'll be happy enough. How do you expect Senyor Salas to remember me, despite that magnificent supper he served up to Senyor Ventosa and myself on the *Cala Encantada*? I've never been an optimist. When it relates to men and women, I've never believed in anything. Now, you've always been a progressive, republican and priest gobbler, and look what a pay off you've got! Cannibalizing priests has brought you no profit at all. Poor Senyor Dalí!"

"Fine, agreed. You're right. These are the facts. But you and I were quite different in temperament."

"What do you mean by 'different in temperament'? You're a man shaped by the newspapers you've read and by the silly, nonsensical books you've studied. I've read few books, simple, straightforward ones, if at all possible, ones based on life, on the terrible realities of life. Temperaments are necessarily different."

"Then there is also the era. My era was very different from yours."

"Only yokels understand the difference between eras."

"What do you mean by 'yokels'?"

"I mean fools, right?. . . And now, if you don't mind, let's go back to La Naviera Mallorquina. Another person I knew from this firm is the present managing director, Senyor Ramis, with whom I had dealings in Madrid when he was a member of parliament after some election or other. Senyor Ramis was a short, wiry, alert man and was like lots of Majorcans. Sometimes they are very Spanish and talk as if they're issuing orders; sometimes they are themselves, pleasant, conscientious and attentive. Senyor Ramis was in the latter camp. If you like, we can write to him. Now, if he doesn't reply or replies only with a polite formula, it will be all the same to me. Oblivion takes all, right?"

"Yes, we should write to him," replied Senyor Dalí. "Whatever it takes, we should attempt to sort out the situation the families of the drowned men find themselves in. I've made a commitment to the Ribera family. I will do all I can to that end. Now you could also give the sinking of the *Cala Galiota* an airing in the Barcelona press, couldn't you?"

"Forgive me, Senyor Dalí, how can I write in the press about a shipwreck we know nothing about? What newspaper will want to print a story on a shipwreck about which you, I and everyone else have nil information? Writing an article on a ship going down implies you know something, however minimal. You must agree?"

"Possibly. At any rate, an article in the press on the *Cala Galiota* would create a stir."

"Agreed. But what's also damn well true about even this press of ours is that you need something real and objective to report if you're going to write an article. And we don't have a scrap of information about this shipwreck, not a single bit. . . There might perhaps be another angle. That angle could be to report on what you've told me about the situation of the families. What do you reckon?"

"Yes, that might be the most feasible angle. I'm so distressed by the situation I'm thinking of going to Barcelona any moment now to see if we can solve their plight."

"In the meantime, I can get your thoughts on the matter into print."

"Agreed. Come back tomorrow and we'll resolve this. I'll be expecting you. And I can show you some paperwork."

So that was how our long conversation on the *Cala Galiota* and her disappearance ended, after the old Figueres notary Senyor Salvador Dalí i Cusí had told me all his ideas on life.

I returned to Senyor Dalí's house in El Llaner two days later. He gave me a warm welcome. He had coffee served. The north wind was still blasting. Nature's excesses have created humanity's idea of limits. "Everything has a limit!" we often say. There are no limits in nature. If it rains, sometimes it rains too much and sometimes hardly at all. If the north wind blows, sometimes it blows too hard and sometimes hardly at all.

There was a dossier on the table in front of Senyor Dalí. It was the dossier on the sinking of the *Cala Galiota*. He opened it and gave me some press cuttings to read. I read them. They were organized chronologically and were mostly from the Palma de Majorca press. After the schooner disappeared they stated they were categorically sure she had sunk. They said that as if it were dogma concerning the Holy Spirit, without giving the slightest detail, not even the weather on the day of the shipwreck. From a newspaper perspective, the reports had been dashed off so quickly and light-headedly that the display of ignorance took your breath away. A few days later, and probably influenced by popular opinion – after all, seven men had embarked on the *Cala Galiota* – there was a change of criterion, and they reported that the sailing freighter had fled the storm from the west and was by the island of Corsica, without providing further detail. This affirmation, made without any basis in fact, was false but was presented as if it were gospel. A few days passed and the press cuttings returned to the original idea – namely, that the *Cala Galiota* had purely and simply gone down. I should note that none of these news stories mentioned any of the features of the motor sailer or of the presence on its decks of seven genuine, real-life men. I read those cuttings as carefully as I could and told Senyor Salvador Dalí: "I've been a journalist for many years and these reports show yet again that it's quite impossible to know what's going on in this world. This is something that happened practically the day before yesterday, yet you see the confusion that still reigns. You people in Cadaqués never know what's happening in Roses or Port de la Selva, even though they're only just up the road. We people in Llofriu never know what's happening in Palafrugell, and those in Palafrugell, what's happening in Llofriu. It's sad to say, but when someone has seen something with his own eyes, when he passes on the news, he embellishes, unravels, fakes it, invents things. Just imagine what it's like when personal interest is involved. I don't know whether man is a rational animal – I've always had my doubts. Man is a lying animal. Lying is a normal reaction in the lives of men and women. Now, you project news like this on a vaster scale, on a national situation, and the reporting is entirely false. And if by chance it isn't, then it's even more difficult to accept, because humans can agree only to see lies as the norm.

Now, project this human condition onto the past, onto history, and then legends assume astonishing proportions. Things that we know, that we have more or less heard about, assume a legendary status. The others that we don't know about, which are probably the most important, pass us by and land in the densest, most impenetrable darkness."

Dalí the notary listened to my excruciating tirade and became increasingly nervous. When I finished – and now I'm sorry I ever came out with it – he said I was exaggerating, that I just liked to stir. "Now you seem to want to dispute the distinguished profession of notaries," he said, laughing sarcastically. After he'd said that, he seemed to calm down.

"We must do something. This investigation by Navy Command in the Balearic Islands is progressing very slowly. The interminable bureaucracy drives me crazy. Weeks go by and the families of the drowned are poverty-stricken and desperate. That is terribly depressing. My feeling is that whether the *Cala Galiota* went down and bodies and goods were lost or she's in some unknown place (something I've never believed), these wretched folk, the descendants of the drowned, must be paid something. I'd never have thought it would be so difficult in this country to declare a shipwreck a shipwreck."

"Just a moment. You did say that La Naviera Mallorquina SA had insured the *Cala Galiota*'s crew."

"That's right, completely insured, and it was public knowledge."

"So why doesn't it pay up?"

"It won't pay because the *Cala Galiota*'s legal situation is unclear. We still don't know whether or not she went down. We'll know only when the naval committee publishes its findings."

"So what must we do, Senyor Dalí?"

"We must activate this inquiry they're so slowly conducting. It's never ending. We must start out from the position that nobody can deny the ship sank. And ensure that the families of the drowned are paid by one means or another. That's why I want to go to Barcelona. Don't think the idea of going appeals to me. One is comfortable here in Cadaqués, especially in the winter, when nobody is around! But I must go."

"La Naviera Mallorquina will have a lawyer or two in Barcelona who deal with these matters," I tried to suggest.

"Yes, indeed. I'm in touch by letter with one who is very intelligent and helpful. A most pleasant individual."

"Very good. It all seems set up. Now I'd just like to ask you what my role might be in the strange, mysterious saga of the *Cala Galiota*?"

"As I see it, it's very straightforward. We must begin with the undeniable fact that she sank. Don't doubt for one minute that that will be the conclusion of the Palma inquiry. No other outcome is possible, unless something incredible and literally extraordinary comes to light. Now as we are in the position where the inquiry is still ongoing, despite the time that's gone by since the boat went down, we've no choice but to argue that, whether the *Cala Galiota* went down or not, the crew or the family members of the crew must be paid what they are legally due. That's what we must press for urgently. Those poor people *must* be paid."

"Your stance is admirable. But. . ."

"What do you mean 'but'?"

"I just mean that when the inquiry is closed, it will be easy for them to be paid and it will all be sorted. I don't think it will be so easy before that happens. In terms of our bureaucratic system, your idea is like trying to put a square peg in a round hole. I don't think it's at all practical or easy."

"I've always been in favor of square pegs in round holes. What do you expect? It's my temperament."

"All right then, I must say in the press what you want me to say. Let's get on with it. Speak your mind."

"In principle, we can't preempt the official inquiry. This investigation is still ongoing. We still don't know whether the *Cala Galiota* went down or is in 'whereabouts unknown.' Meanwhile, there are seven men – or seven families – that have become seven ghosts, or seven entelechies. It's laughable. . . but I don't think it's necessary. This is what the lawyer Senyor Gispert, a friend of mine and a man who does things by the book, tells me: 'On the advice of its insurers, La Compañía Naviera is sticking to the position that nothing can be paid out, because there is no evidence that the sailing freighter went down. All recent legal dispositions related to accidents at sea favor the damaged parties, not only because they are evaluated on a level with other workplace accidents but also because civil procedures for declaring the drowned presumed dead have been simplified and rendered more precise.' I've left that in Spanish legalese, so it has more impact. The fact is, three months after the *Cala Galiota* went down, we still don't know if she really did. The inquiry is slow and isn't concluded. I said this a minute ago, and will repeat myself now: it's a dreadful situation. The positions of La Naviera and the insurance company are perfectly legal. They won't pay out until there is an official declaration that the boat sank and everything is crystal clear: namely, that nobody could question that the crew is dead. I must confess I find this very depressing. I've taken it very much to heart. And

I've done so not only because poor Ribera Dalmau from Cadaqués was drowned and his family is in a parlous state but because six other families are in a similar situation and they're all equal in my view.

"I've discussed this whole wretched issue with many distinguished folk. Some were most pessimistic. They think it will be a long time before any of the families receive help. They say that workplace insurance has only just started up and nothing's tried and tested. Others are less so."

"I'll do my utmost to speed things up. As I said, driving a square peg into a round hole is sometimes vital. How can there be any argument about the need to give those families something, if only the day wage of the seamen? When the inquiry is over and the insurance company pays up, that money can be taken from the compensation awarded. I'm not asking for anything exorbitant or outlandish. I simply want a humanitarian gesture."

Senyor Dalí paused, took his usual sip of coffee and resumed: "I will now go to Barcelona. I must go because friends from my graduation year are putting on a supper and I would like to see them. However, I suspect that on this occasion the supper will be a secondary matter. It's the *Cala Galiota* that's uppermost in my mind. I will do all I can to move this business on. From my humble point of view, the situation of the ship's crew poses a dilemma: they are either dead or alive. If they are alive, they should be receiving their usual wage. If they are dead – as I believe – the insurance company must pay out what is laid down in the relevant social legislation. Thus, this compensation is fated and cannot be denied. And if that's the case, how is it possible the families of the drowned haven't received a penny, which could then be paid back out of the eventual compensation awarded? All this nonsense about 'whereabouts unknown' is what they call in the Roussillon a load of cobblers. There are no 'whereabouts unknown' in the Mediterranean. It's impossible to allege the boat may have ended up on a deserted island, because there are no deserted islands in this sea and no area that isn't charted and sailed. The Mediterranean isn't like the Pacific, where there are countless unknown, uncharted places, as one reads in popular travel books and novels. To imagine that the *Cala Galiota* will turn up one of these days from 'whereabouts unknown' in the Mediterranean is plainly absurd and demented. It is inhuman to delay the payment of the small amounts necessary to rescue the families of the drowned from their poverty-stricken state until the deaths of the crew members are legally established. That's how I at least see it and that's what you should write in a newspaper. As you see, nothing I've said is earth shattering, it's blindingly obvious, a Columbus's egg. Columbus's eggs are simply dashes of reality that occur in a world like this, full of fantasies, absurd pretensions and permanent deceit. You know, Columbus's eggs are usually very useful and highly effective.

"Now I'll tell you my inspiration for the dilemma over the *Cala Galiota* that I've just explained. When I was a student in Barcelona, I got to know Senyor Aleu, who was renowned for his sense of humor and was thought by some to be an outright cynic. He was a friend of the Altadills and all the picturesque bohemians who lived around La Rambla – a world that's vanished for good. You must have heard about Senyor Aleu from the protagonist of your book *Un senyor de Barcelona*, Senyor Rafael Puget, whose intellect and sense of observation are extraordinary. So one day Senyor Aleu asked a friend of his – a man not known for his generosity – to lend him fifteen hundred pessetes. This gentleman replied that he would agree to give him the money, but on one condition: that it was a fixed-term loan. The comedian concurred and they signed the necessary papers, crossing all the *t*s. Naturally, Senyor Aleu didn't repay the money and a few days later received a legal demand because he'd broken the terms of the agreement. He defended himself in the subsequent court case. He was a qualified lawyer and had been a judge in Cuba. Senyor Aleu said the following: 'Absolutely, that gentleman gave me, in effect, fifteen hundred pessetes. When he handed them over, one of two things was certain: either he knew me or he didn't. If he knew me, he must have been totally aware of my lighthearted attitude toward money and my regrettable tendency to forget to return money according to the terms agreed. If he didn't know me, how on earth can one understand him giving me such a huge amount as a fixed-term loan? No. The operation was driven by something else. . . ' Naturally, Senyor Aleu won his point. The judicial authorities recognized it hadn't been a fixed-term loan but a loan between friends, and consequently, those involved had to resolve the issue as such."

Senyor Dalí made his customary pause and then added: "Obviously, the comedian Aleu's dilemma was nothing like the one I detailed to you as regards the *Cala Galiota*, but it is my contention that such dilemmas, legally speaking, are always important, often have a depth to them and may enable things to be sorted out because they remove all confusion."

Dalí the painter's father went to Barcelona and spoke to lots of people about the situation of the families of those who went down with the *Cala Galiota*; he was a busy beaver. Meanwhile, I published in the *Destino* magazine a long report on Senyor Dalí's dilemma and the facts; it appeared in issue 512.

When he got back, he sent for me.

"It now seems that things have perked up," he said. "I'm under the impression that very little had been done. They knew where they had to start but never started. Now perhaps they have. I'm also under the impression that nobody had ever really worried about anyone drowned in a wreck, and now that's changed. Just consider the case of the *Cala Galiota*. Where would we be if the families of the drowned hadn't exerted pressure? It would be an unpleasant situation. Better not to even think about it."

The fact that the inquiry led by the naval base in the Balearics had been spurred on gave the families involved some hope. From that moment on it became clear that perhaps for the first time the schooner's drowned would enjoy a legal status different from the one that had been obtained over the centuries: the drowned would cease to be mere lost items, like timber, sails or any item from any shipwreck. The families would receive compensation. In the first place – at least everything pointed that way – they'd succeeded in getting the inquiry to endorse that the ship had sunk and thus ended the doubts over whether the *Cala Galiota* had gone down or was in "whereabouts unknown." Recognition that the ship had sunk implied that her crew had died, and consequently, their deaths were official and their families could have access to their due legal compensation. The shipping company had stopped paying wages in December, when the vessel disappeared, and refused, under pressure from the insurance company, to make any advances on account, from the compensation that they would have to pay one day or another, by law.

The resolution of the inquiry took much longer than Senyor Dalí had imagined. Bureaucratic red tape, then and today, goes at a scandalously slow pace. My visits to Senyor Dalí's house in El Llaner in Cadaqués and his trip to Barcelona took place in February 1947. Now, the inquiry was concluded by the commission in May of that same year, six months after the ship went down. The delay could be explained only by the cumbersome procedures. At any rate, there were considerable gains. The commission would declare that the ship had sunk. The owners of the *Cala Galiota* had always been understanding, but they had never acted decisively. (At the time, because of the civil war, people were convinced that the organs of state were always right, unequivocally and dogmatically so.) Later the name of the insurance company was finally revealed, something that hitherto had been kept hidden. In the end, Senyor Dalí's visit to Barcelona led to an excellent outcome.

"You played a decisive role in the business of the *Cala Galiota*," Senyor Dalí told me one day. "The articles you wrote were quite influential."

"You're wrong. Please leave me out of this. I merely did what you told me, because I believed from the very first that you were right and it was worth championing a just outcome."

Senyor Dalí accepted my absurd declarations and looked self-satisfied and preening. I immediately saw that Senyor Dalí was more susceptible to flattery than I'd thought. People around here are that way inclined.

The Palma report was finished 26 May 1947. Once it was ready, it was sent to the corresponding office in the naval headquarters in Cartagena, and everything points to the fact that no objections were raised there. It declared, loud and clear, that the *Cala Galiota* had sunk with all her goods and able-bodied crew. Death certificates were issued and the families received their compensation after all the misery they had experienced.

Ferran Ribera Dalmau, the *Cala Galiota*'s boatswain, was a Cadaqués man, a registered seaman – that is, a true mariner. Like so many from this area, he was a man with many skills; he was a fisherman and a sailor, and was prepared to turn his hand to any trade, depending on his needs. He was married with two daughters. His wife was the sister of an acquaintance of mine in Cadaqués, Senyor Albert, an extremely intelligent individual who was very knowledgeable about the locality and managed probably the biggest olive-oil press in the area, which belonged to the Pont family. Senyor Albert's sister Caterina married Ferran Ribera and they had two daughters, Josefa and Maria, who at the time of the shipwreck were – according to the report – twenty-three and eighteen.

Cadaqués experienced hard times between the two Great Wars. Lots of people emigrated during that period from the Ampurdan and from the towns along the coast. The Ribera-Albert family immigrated to Palafrugell, where they worked in the big factory that we usually call Can Mario – initially Miquel, Winke and Meyer, and later Armstrong Cork Co. They lived on the side street that leads into the center of town; the municipal magistrates' court stood on the left on the corner (today, it's all been demolished with no remaining trace). Following the Palafrugell custom that names newcomers after the town where they come from, Ribera was dubbed "en Cadaqués" and nothing more, just as there are en Vidreres, en Blanes, etc. Well, Ribera was fascinated by the sea, and when the weather was good, he left his job in Palafrugell and went to Llafranc, where he worked as a fisherman or boatman for holidaymakers who owned a boat and spent a while by that beach. If I remember correctly, Ribera, alias en Cadaqués, worked as a fisherman and mariner for a gentleman, Senyor Gich, who, despite being from Palafrugell, was a military health commander, an excellent doctor and a big roulette player in the clubs of Barcelona. He was also Senyor Pancho's brother – that is, Senyor Panchito, who comes from the Gich pharmacy on Carrer Cavallers in the town of my birth: a liberal family and, consequently, great friends of the Vergès-Barrises. The commander was small, thin and inflexible, rather blustery and fond of giving orders; at times he was rich, and at others not so flush. It depended on his gambling forays, which people said were considerable. He was a close friend of Ribera – a friendship that lasted through to the Gich heirs. Indeed the Ribera family left a lot of friends and acquaintances in Palafrugell and Llafranc. Ribera did quite well in Llafranc as a fisherman and sailor for rich holidaymakers: little work, good food and pleasant, pretty surroundings. In fact, families that had their own mariner were thought to be well off. Ribera had a good life, and even today his family feels nostalgic for those happy days.

I asked Senyor Dalí why Ribera had left the job he had in that cove and moved with his family to Cadaqués and then taken up another maritime job on La Naviera Mallorquina's tin-pot schooner.

"I'll tell you why," he replied. "In this neck of the woods there have always been a number of people who can't sit still. They're soon bored and are always on the go. That was probably the case with our much-lamented friend Ribera."

"Are you suggesting that our mariner was a little, shall we say, bohemian, a tad unhinged? People in our country can be hard to understand, downright peculiar."

"Yes, it's most likely. But don't go overboard. I don't think he was at all bohemian or unhinged. He did everything in good faith, thinking it was all for the good of his family, his household and himself. You know how that is, when someone does the most ridiculous things in good faith, people are always ready to be understanding and charitable."

"Agreed. But even so he embarked. . ."

"Yes, unfortunately, he did. But you're familiar with this terrain, you know that mariners here who sail the world want only to live on land, and those who live on land move heaven and earth to get on board a ship. If we're like that, what can be done? It's an inbred disease and that's one way of going about it."

"That's all very well, but it's difficult to believe such a discerning fellow as our friend Ribera would sail as boatswain on a down-at-heel, precarious hulk like the *Cala Galiota*. Her disappearance. . ."

"Please don't say any more. It's a shipwreck that has really upset me. It's one of the most incredible, extraordinary shipwrecks along this coast. Not a trace was left, not a whisker. Total loss of crew and goods. The *Cala Galiota* sank to the bottom of the sea and left no signs of life. It's impossible to explain what happened, because we know absolutely nothing. Our friend Riba lost his life there, at its peak, with so much experience and knowledge, just like the others. It was a good, knowledgeable crew. What happened? Nobody knows and nobody ever will. It's the most technically perfect shipwreck there's ever been along this coast."

At some point, the daughters from the Ribera-Albert marriage moved to France. They'd had a wretched, unpleasant time as a result of the sinking of the *Cala Galiota*. The drawn-out business of the Palma commission of inquiry, which made it impossible to certify the crew was dead when that was obvious all along, was inexplicable. When they crossed the frontier, they encountered a different atmosphere and thought they were now protected from everything they'd suffered. When they left for France, the tourist boomtown Cadaqués has become hadn't yet started. Its inhabitants lived a totally gray life. In the post-civil-war period, existence in Cadaqués was hand to mouth, though it was ideal for moneyed people.

In France the Ribera-Albert girls worked mainly in restaurants and learned to cook; they were intelligent and remarkably quick on the uptake. Eventually they decided to return. Cadaqués was changing and there was quite a tourist trade. They must have missed the town, because, as is well known, Catalans are wont to be nostalgic. Once established, they set up a restaurant they called La Galiota, in memory of the schooner that sank. It is a small restaurant, that's what such places must be – cozy and pleasant, with a cuisine that is often quite interesting. It is undoubtedly the best restaurant in Cadaqués. As it is a small space and they often can't fit everyone in, they don't serve coffee after dessert, to avoid customers engaging in too much table talk. Personally, I think that's a mistake, because I believe you should be able to drink coffee at the same table where you have eaten. If it wasn't for that, I would say La Galiota is one of the very few proper restaurants along this coast.

So there you are: all these words I have just written on the sinking of the *Cala Galiota* show that the lives of men and women suffer many twists and turns, which are always unexpected and extraordinary, and that everything that happens in life – whether good or bad – is beyond reasoning.

TRANSLATOR'S NOTE

Dictatorship and civil war, confinement and exile – as well as the need to earn a living as a journalist – had a profound impact on the work of Josep Pla. He began writing the first version of *The Gray Notebook* in 1918 when the "Spanish" flu led to the closure of Barcelona University and his return to the family house in Llofriu close to the fishing port of Calella de Palafrugell. When he eventually graduated, he landed a post as a foreign correspondent for a Catalan newspaper in Paris. Pla incurred the wrath of dictator Primo de Rivera for articles criticising Spanish military interventions in Morocco and continued his foreign journalism that included a year of weekly dispatches from Germany, 1923-24, a series of articles on the rise of Mussolini in Italy and the state of Russia in 1925 that became a best-selling book. After the Spanish civil war his passport was withdrawn because of critical comments on the Franco regime (he was horrified, among other things, by the criminalization of the use of the Catalan language) and he embarked on writing as an internal exile. He lived on the Costa Brava, in the tiny fishing hamlet of Fornells, near Begur, and then for longer spells in the fishing ports of L'Escala and Cadaqués. Although in his preface, Pla states that the maritime stories and chronicles are writings from his youth, they were, in fact, mainly written in the 1940s, where he incorporates and refashions earlier pieces about the sea from earlier publications. Why would he make such a statement? Perhaps to wrongfoot potential censors? In the 1940s Pla was a prolific journalist writing in Spanish for the weekly *Destino* magazine, and his articles containing veiled critiques of the dictatorship made him the most censored journalist in Spain. Whether he was detailing the struggle of fishing communities to survive or wryly commenting on the enthusiastic participation of local clergy and worthies in the looting of shipwrecked vessels in the distant past, contemporary readers, adept at detecting critical subtexts, would have recognized that even at his most quietistic, Pla remained a writer who spoke to their daily experience of fascism which he also challenged by simply returning to write in public in Catalan.

Most of *Salt Water* was published for the first time by Biblioteca Selecta in the early 1950s when the regime began to allow literary work to be published in Catalan. I have based this translation on *Aigua de mar*, the second volume of Josep Pla's *Obra completa* that he prepared for *Destino* and was published in 1966. Only one other essay has been added to complement the others that deal with shipwrecks, Cadaqués and the post-war situation: his conversations with Dalí, the painter's father.

archipelago books
is a not-for-profit literary press devoted to
promoting cross-cultural exchange through innovative
classic and contemporary international literature
www.archipelagobooks.org